Annual Editions: Social Problems, 41/e

Kurt Finsterbusch

http://create.mheducation.com

ISBN-10: 1259667553   ISBN-13: 9781259667558

Contents

Detailed Table of Contents

less and shipped jobs abroad. Workers lost power and the owners gained power which resulted in shockingly high inequality and the shrinking of opportunity for lower groups. Something must be done to reverse some of these trends and Obama offers his plans.

The Wages of Global Capitalism, Richard D. Wolff, *Truthout*, 2014
Capitalists in Europe, Japan, and the United States have the power over their governments to prevent them from stopping their relocation to developing countries. This greatly increases corporate profits while preventing income gains for the working class.

Nice Places Finish First: **The Economic Returns of Civic Virtue**, John M. Bridgeland and Alan Khazei, *Washington Monthly*, 2013
The authors are concerned about the substantial loss of upward social mobility in America. In the past, America lead the world in social mobility but now trails several countries. High levels of social mobility are associated with high levels of civic virtue which is working with others for the public good. Civic virtue greatly benefits society and is related to economic prosperity.

To Make Immigration More Fair and More Just, Barack Obama, *Vital Speeches of the Day*, 2015
Obama appeals to the historic American value of welcoming immigrants to push for an immigration policy that would deal with the important immigration issues of today. He advocates stronger efforts to prevent illegal immigration and just and compassionate policies to deal with the millions of undocumented workers in this country.

Unit: Problems of Poverty and Inequality

Overwhelming Evidence that Half of America Is In or Near Poverty, Paul Buchheit, *AlterNet*, 2014
How widespread is poverty in America? Analysts disagree on the definition and extent of poverty. There are many different ways to define poverty. Some would say that America's poor are rich compared to the developing world. Others say that the official poverty rate is too low because the basket of goods on which it is based is not suited to today. Paul Buchheit argues that almost half of Americans should be considered poor. Almost half have no savings. He also observes that the safety net is a big help in lowering poverty rates.

Slow Growth and Inequality Are Political Choices. We Can Choose Otherwise, Joseph E. Stiglitz, *Washington Monthly*, 2014
Stiglitz observes the slow growth and high inequality in America and denies that these are dictated by unalterable conditions but are the outcomes of political choices and America can have higher growth and less inequality if we make the right choices. We can choose to redistribute downward instead of upward and still have a vibrant economy.

America's Misguided Approach to Social Welfare, Kimberly J. Morgan, *Foreign Affairs*, 2013
America's social welfare system accomplishes much less than European welfare systems and costs almost as much when all relevant moneys are taken into account. A main reason is the much higher percentage of all welfare that goes to the non-poor.

Are You Racist?, Chris Mooney, *Mother Jones*, 2015
Almost everyone is an unconscious racist. Research shows that everyone is biased favorably toward their own group and unfavorably to other groups despite desires to be otherwise. Bias even has evolutionary value. Mooney suggests some subtle ways to reduce these unconscious prejudices.

Black Pathology and the Closing of the Progressive Mind, Ta-Nehisi Coates, *The Atlantic*, 2014
Ta-Nehisi Coates acknowledges that the cultural argument against Blacks is still prevalent. The conservative version leaves out the role of white supremacy and is theoretically weak. The liberal version notes that structural conditions shape the Black culture which then is responsible for Black shortcomings. The structural conditions can be labeled white supremacy. Coates examines the facts and finds a strong Black culture that highly regarded family life and education when possible. Conditions have changed but white supremacy is still strong.

When Slavery Won't Die: The Oppressive Biblical Mentality America Can't Shake, Valerie Tarico, *AlterNet*, 2015
Tarico traces current racism and injustice toward blacks to "the ancient strands of brutality and inequality that are woven into the fabric of our society." She focuses on police behavior toward blacks and explains how police behavior can be improved.

Back to the Real World: Why Feminism Should Focus Less on Culture, Katha Pollitt, *The Progressive*, 2015
Pollitt appreciates the feminist actions of young women but suggests that for the best results they should work harder on gaining

economic equality and less on cultural issues though those issues are also important. Businesses control the most crucial rewards and many programs that facilitate work-family accords are greatly needed.

Sex Slaves on the Farm, Max Kutner, *Newsweek*, 2015
This is a painful article to read. The exploitation of women for brutal sex trafficking attacks our values and feelings. Mercifully, Kutner also discusses the many programs which are trying to stop the trafficking and to save the exploited women.

Joe Biden Takes a Marriage Equality Victory Lap, Jay Michaelson, *Daily Beast*, 2015
Though Biden came late to the side of LGBT he became a strong supporter of their equal rights. In this article he makes a good case for legalizing LGBT marriage.

Do Boys Face More Sexism Than Girls?, Christina Hoff Sommers, *Huffington Post*, 2013
Christina Hoff Sommers focuses on how boys and girls are treated in school. She shows the many ways that the school experience is more unsuitable for boys than girls. It involves unsuitable structure, treatment, attitudes, incentives, judgments, and culture. It is time to improve the treatment of schoolboys without mistreating schoolgirls.

Unit: Institutional Problems

It's the Parents, Reihan Salam, *National Review*, 2015
The main reason for the great inequality in America and the decline of equality of opportunity is the parents. Nurturing parents work hard to train up their children to have the education, skills, attitudes, and character that will get them ahead in life. Middle and upper class parents do a better job of this than lower class parents. Other factors play a role but none are as important as the parents.

Modest Workplace Reforms Will Strengthen Families and the Economy, Judith Warner, *Washington Monthly*, 2014
Work-family conflict has been linked to mental and physical health problems and to wider economic problems. The country would benefit by changes in the workplace which would benefit families. Inflexible job demands are both a personal problem and a social problem.

From Parent to Parenting: Children, Grandchildren, and Cultural Imperatives, Joseph Epstein, *Commentary*, 2015
A major social change in the last half century has been in the way parents raise their children as explained by Joseph Epstein based on his own experience. His parents left him alone much of the time to learn and work out things by himself or through his friends. Now parents over manage their children.

Myths and Reality About Student Debt and the Cost of Higher Education, Richard Ekman, *Vital Speeches of the Day*, 2013
Some myths that Richard Ekman refutes are that college costs too much and is a bad investment, student debt has increased greatly, private colleges are way too expensive, most financial aid does not go to the neediest students, and liberal arts majors do not get jobs. Some of the trends that support these myths have greatly expanded community colleges, so average college costs have not risen that much in constant dollars. Many other adaptations to new economic conditions lead to surprising overall outcomes.

Fighting Back Through Resistance: Challenging the Defunding and Privatization of Public Education, Curry Malott, *Truthout*, 2015
According to Malott the movement to privatize the public schools and to reduce their funding should be resisted. He advocates less emphasis on high stakes testing as in No Child Left Behind and more emphasis on critical thinking and creativity.

A Thousand Years Young, Aubrey de Grey, *The Futurist*, 2012
How would you like to live a thousand years? Aubrey de Grey says that advances in medical and biochemical treatments can overcome the aging process and keep us young for many centuries.

Why Is Health Care So Expensive? *Consumer Reports*, 2014
Health care in the United States costs about twice as much as it does in the rest of the developed world and is not as good as the European systems. There is a lot that health insurance does not cover in America and drugs and doctor fees are very high.

Unit: Crime, Violence, and Law Enforcement

The Criminality of Wall Street, William K. Tabb, *Monthly Review*, 2014
The great change on Wall Street is the immense growth of financial capital which went from eleven times the value of foreign

exchange trading in 2005 to seventy-three times in 2009. Financial capital contributes almost nothing to the world economy but takes the majority of the profits. It is very hard to regulate and it is very exploitive.

This Man Was Sentenced to Die in Prison for Shoplifting a $159 Jacket, Ed Pilkington, *Alternet,* 2013
Timothy Jackson was caught shoplifting a jacket and sentenced to life in prison without the possibility of parole. He has already served 16 years. He is used by the author to prove that the criminal justice system in many parts of the United States is too punitive. There are 3,281 people incarcerated for life in America for non-violent crimes. One was sentenced to die in prison for siphoning gas from a truck. The point of the article is that some laws and some judicial judgments are crazy but "the law is the law" so petty criminals die in prison. Change is needed.

South Carolina's Police State, Kevin Alexander Gray, *The Progressive,* 2015
Gray reports that South Carolina has a police state by presenting a lot of statistics and by telling the story of the killing of Walter Scott who was unarmed and running away from patrolman Slager. Slager would have gotten away with the murder except his action was caught on video. Gray offers ten suggestions "for ending the scourge of police violence."

Public Safety, Public Justice, Daniel Rose, *Harlem Times,* 2015
Rose argues that we must change our criminal justice philosophy and our punitive laws. Imprisonment rates are too high and unfair to Blacks who are imprisoned six times as much as whites. Rose advocates rehabilitation and many other reforms.

It's Not Just about Race, It's about Power, Matt Welch, *Reason,* 2015
Welch discusses the racial biases of the police that result in their unequal treatments of Blacks. His larger point, however, is the way the criminal justice system protects the police, thus giving the police the power.

"Broken Windows," Broken Lives, and the Ruse of "Public Order" Policing, Nancy A. Heitzeg, *Truthout,* 2015
The theory that justifies overzealous policing and the oppression of Blacks is the "Broken Window" theory. It asserts that if the police come down hard on minor infractions then the more major crimes will decline substantially. There is some truth to it but it does not justify the brutal treatment of Blacks.

Wrongful Convictions, Radley Balko, *Reason,* 2011
Radley Balko shows that there are many wrongful convictions. DNA testing has cleared 268 convicted persons, but few cases can be tested by DNA. Balko makes a valiant effort to estimate the number of wrongful convictions and ends up with a 3–5 percent number for felony crimes, but in the end one can only guess. His careful explication of the criminal justice system shows the many ways that injustice can be committed and demonstrates the need for reforms.

Statement for the Record: Worldwide Threat Assessment of the US Intelligence Community, James R. Clapper, *Office of the Director of National Intelligence,* 2015
Clapper presents the official assessment of worldwide terrorist threats. This report covers cyber-attacks, potential use of weapons of mass destruction, and other terrorist attacks. We must remain on the alert but this report does not suggest that the American mainland has a lot to be afraid of.

A Problem from Heaven: Why the United States Should Back Islam's Reformation, Ayaan Hirsi Ali, *Foreign Affairs,* 2015
America has largely misunderstood the Islamic threat. We look at it in war terms but it is a problem of ideas and our military might is not the answer. The problem is radical or fundamentalist Islam and the answer is moderate Islam. Islam needs a reformation like Christianity had and the reformation is in process. It may take time but eventually the Islamic reformation will take care of radical Islam.

Low-Tech Terrorism, Bruce Hoffman, *The National Interest,* March/April 2014
This article is a rather extensive assessment of all (despite the title) current terrorist threats to America. Fortunately, terrorists have not yet acquired and successfully set off a weapon of mass destruction, though they have tried. The article extensively reviews Al Qaeda's and other terrorist groups' considerable efforts to acquire such weapons and their failure. As a result, most terrorism involves guns and bombs.

Unit: Problems of Population, Environment, Resources, and the Future

Happy Planet, Robert Adler, *New Scientist,* 2014
The current state of the planet is very good and very bad. The current economic systems have lifted billions out of poverty and created great affluence and economic growth. They have also created too much CO_2, cleared too much land, overfished the oceans, and reduced biodiversity. Robert Adler points out that continuing on our current path has considerable risks. We must live within nature's limits. He reviews many proposals and predictions and presents his vision of a sustainable world which he thinks could be a happy planet.

Preface

The reason we study social problems is so that we can do something about them. Corrective action, however, is not taken until the situation is seen as a problem and the fire of concern is kindled in a number of citizens. A democratic country gives those citizens means for legally trying to change things, and this freedom and opportunity is a great pride for our country. In fact, most college students have already given time or money to some cause in which they believe. This is necessary because each generation will face struggles for rights and justice. Daily forces operate to corrupt, distort, bias, exploit, and defraud as individuals and groups seek their own advantage at the expense of others and the public interest. Those dedicated to a good society, therefore, constantly struggle against these forces. Furthermore, the struggle is often complex and confusing. Not always are the defenders of the status quo wrong and the champions of change right. *Important values will be championed by both sides.*

Today there is much debate about the best way to improve education. Opposing spokespersons think that they are serving the good of the children and of the United States. In a similar manner, conscientious students in the same college class and reading the same material will hotly disagree. Therefore, solving problems is usually not a peaceful process. First, it requires information and an understanding of the problem, and we can expect disagreements on both the facts and the interpretations. Second, it requires discussion, compromise, and a plan with majority support, or at least the support of the powerful groups. Third, it requires action. In a democratic society, this process should involve tolerance and even goodwill toward one's opponents as long as they act honestly, fairly, and democratically. Class discussions should involve respect for each other's opinions.

In some ways, the study of social problems is easy and in some ways it is hard. The easy aspect is that most people know quite a lot about the problems that this book addresses; the hard part is that solving those problems is very difficult. If the solutions were easy, the problems would have been solved by now, and we would not be studying these particular issues. It may be easy to plan solutions, but it is hard to implement them. In general, however, Americans are optimistic and believe in progress; we learn from our mistakes and keep trying until conditions are acceptable. For instance, the members of Common Cause, including myself, have worked for campaign finance reform since 1970. Our efforts failed until Watergate created a huge public demand for it, and both campaign finance reform and public-right-to-know laws were passed. The reform, however, led to the formation of PACs (Political Action Committees) to get around the law and buy influence legally.

In 2002 a new campaign finance reform law, the McCain–Feingold Act, was passed. Nevertheless, the role of big money in campaign finances is today larger than it has been for many decades. This will eventually precipitate yet another major reform effort. It could be that at the end of the twenty-first century, Americans will still be struggling with many of the same problems as today. But it is reasonable to believe that things will be somewhat better at that point because throughout this century people will mobilize again and again to improve our society; some will even do this at considerable cost to themselves.

The articles presented here were selected for three reasons: (1) their attention to important issues, (2) the value of the information and ideas they present, and/or (3) their ability to move the reader to concern and possibly even action toward correcting social problems. This edition of *Annual Editions: Social Problems* begins by broadly describing the United States and recent changes in forces that affect our lifestyles. It then examines some big issues in the political and economic systems that have society-wide impacts, as well as issues of inequality and injustice that challenge basic American values. The next section considers how well the various institutions of society work. Most institutions are being heavily criticized—these articles help to explain why. The following section studies the traditional problem of crime and law enforcement. Fortunately, there is some good news here. Finally, the last section focuses on the future and problems of population, environment, technology, globalization, community, and long-term change.

Editor

Kurt Finsterbusch received a bachelor's degree in history from Princeton University in 1957 and a bachelor of divinity degree from Grace Theological Seminary in 1960. His PhD in sociology, from Columbia University, was conferred in 1969. Dr. Finsterbusch is the author of several books, including *Understanding Social Impacts* (Sage Publications, 1980), *Social Research for Policy Decisions* (Wadsworth Publishing, 1980, with Annabelle Bender Motz), and *Organizational Change as a Development Strategy* (Lynne Rienner Publishers, 1987, with Jerald Hage). He is currently teaching at the University of Maryland, College Park, and, in addition to serving as editor for Annual Editions: Social Problems, he is also editor of Annual Editions: Sociology, McGraw-Hill's Taking Sides: Clashing Views on Social Issues, and Sources: Notable Selections in Sociology.

Dedication

Dedicated to the many heroes and heroines who are trying to fix the various social problems addressed here.

Academic Advisory Board

Members of the Academic Advisory Board are instrumental in the final selection of articles for each edition of ANNUAL EDITIONS.

Their review of articles for content, level, and appropriateness provides critical direction to the editors and staff. We think that you will find their careful consideration well reflected in this volume.

Pamela Altman
Georgia Southern University

Thomas E. Arcaro
Elon University

Sylven Beck
The George Washington University

Heather Boone
Atlantic Cape Community College

Mamie Bridgeforth
Essex County College

M. Jennifer Brougham
Arizona State University

Shakira Cain-Bell
Jackson State University

Judy Chiasson
California State University

Elizabeth F. Cohen
Syracuse University

Lynn Connolly
Chestnut Hill College

Maria Cuevas
Yakima Valley Community College

Roger G. Dunham
University of Miami

Kathy Edwards
KCTCS—Ashland Community & Technical College

Leslie Elrod
University of Cincinnati—Raymond Walters College

Nancy Federman
San Diego State University

Sylvia Haith
Forsyth Technical Community College

Gary Heath
Ashford University

Elizabeth Hegeman
John Jay College—CUNY

David Hunt
Augusta State University

Mark Killian
University of Cincinnati

Rosalind Kopfstein
Western Connecticut State University

Timothy LaFountaine
Quinsigamond Community College

Diane Lindley
University of Mississippi

Celia Lo
University of Alabama

John P. Lynxwiler
University of Central Florida, Orlando

James F. MacNair
Atlantic Cape Community College

Karith Meyers
Moorpark College

Christopher P. Morley
SUNY Upstate Medical University

Kathryn S. Mueller
Baylor University

Robert G. Newby
Central Michigan University

Wendy Parker
Albany College of Pharmacy

Dean G. Rojek
University of Georgia

Larry Rosenberg
Millersville University

Goldie Satt-Arrow
Empire State College

Karl Smith
University of Maryland Eastern Shore

Leretta Smith
North Dakota State University

Casey Welch
Flagler College

Signe Whitson
The LSCI Institute

Unit 1

UNIT

Prepared by: Kurt Finsterbusch, *University of Maryland, College Park*

Introduction: Clashing Values and Problematic Transformations of Social Life

This unit offers an introduction to the study of American social problems. It looks at American culture that provides the value system by which we decide what are the significant social problems. Immediately we recognize that people have different values. Some of these value differences are related to different positions in the social structure and different experiences. Racial, religious, gender, income, occupational, and age differences lead to different experiences, and therefore, different perspectives. For example, all races in America will share a common culture but also have different subcultures. Same with each generation. Some of these differences will be explored in this unit.

We propose a perspective that should be helpful as we observe value differences. We suggest that most people share roughly the same set of values. They differ however, on how these values should be ranked. For example, almost all Americans are both materialists and environmentalists. Even the business person who pollutes the environment while producing products for sale and profits wants to live in a clean and healthy environment. Even an environmentalist drives a car to work and uses air conditioning in warm weather. Both have the same values but rank them differently and therefore act differently. In this unit, we try to get a general picture of American culture and then select specific areas for closer examination. Some of the areas examined are civic virtue, Facebook impacts, and generational differences.

Article

Prepared by: Kurt Finsterbusch, *University of Maryland, College Park*

The American Narrative: Is There One & What Is It?

Wℕ︎ℙ︎ℓℓ︎ᴍ H. Cℏᴀꜰᴇ

WILLIAM H. CHAFE

Learning Outcomes

After reading this article, you will be able to:

- Trace the role of the culture of serving the public good and the role of the culture of individual freedom in American history.

- Analyze how these two value systems are opposing each other today.

- Discuss the importance of balance between these sets of values and the danger of destroying that balance today.

Who are we? Where have we been? Where are we going? Can we even agree on who "we" includes? At no time in our history have these questions been more relevant. The American political system seems dysfunctional, if not permanently fractured. A generational gap in technological expertise and familiarity with the social network divides the country to an even greater extent than the culture wars of the 1960s and 1970s. Soon, more "Americans" will speak Spanish as their first language than English. For some, access to health care is a universal right, for others, a privilege that must be earned. Rarely—and certainly not since the Civil War—have we been so divided on which direction we should be heading as a country. How can there be an American narrative when it is not clear what it means to talk about an American people or nation? Two overriding paradigms have long competed in defining who we are. The first imagines America as a community that places the good of the whole first; the second envisions the country as a gathering of individuals who prize individual freedom and value more than anything else each person's ability to determine his own fate.

When the Puritans arrived in the Massachusetts Bay Colony in 1630, their leader, John Winthrop, told his shipmates aboard the *Arabella* that their mission was to create a "city upon a hill," a blessed society that would embody values so noble that the entire world would admire and emulate the new colony. Entitled "A Modell of Christian Charity," Winthrop's sermon described what it would take to create that beloved community: "We must love one another. We must bear one another's burdens . . . make others' conditions our own. We must rejoice together, mourn together, labor, and suffer together, always having before our eyes a community [where we are all] members of the same body."

Consistent with Winthrop's vision, Massachusetts was governed in its early decades by a sense of communal well-being. While the colony tolerated differences of status and power, the ruling norm was that the common good took precedence. Thus, "just prices" were prescribed for goods for sale, and punishment was imposed on businesses that sought excess profits. Parents who mistreated their children were shamed; people who committed adultery were exposed and humiliated.

Soon enough, a surge of individualism challenged the reigning norms. Entrepreneurs viewed communal rules as shackles to be broken so that they could pursue individual aspirations—and profits. The ideal of a "just price" was discarded. While religion remained a powerful presence, secularism ruled everyday business life, and Christianity was restricted to a once-a-week ritual. Class distinctions proliferated, economic inequality increased, and the values of *laissez-faire individualism* displaced the once-enshrined "common wealth." Aid to the poor became an act of individual charity rather than a communal responsibility.

Not surprisingly, the tensions between those who put the good of the community first and those who value individual freedom foremost have reverberated throughout our history. Thomas Jefferson sought to resolve the conflict in the Declaration of Independence by embracing the idea of "equal opportunity" for all. Note that he championed not equality of results, but equality of opportunity. Every citizen might have an "inalienable" right to "life, liberty, and the pursuit of happiness," but what happened to each person's "equal opportunity" depended on the performance of that particular individual. Success was not guaranteed.

Throughout American history, the tensions between the value of the common good and the right to unbridled individual freedom have resurfaced. The federal government sought to build roads and canals across state lines to serve the general good. The nation fought a Civil War because slavery contradicted the belief in the right of equal citizenship. In the aftermath of the war, the Constitution guaranteed all males the right to vote, and its Fourteenth Amendment promised each citizen "equal protection" under the law.

But by the end of the nineteenth century, rampant economic growth had created myriad enterprises that threatened the common good. In *The Jungle,* Upton Sinclair highlighted the danger of workers falling into vats of boiling liquid at meat-packing plants. The influx of millions of immigrants brought new dangers of infectious disease. As sweatshops, germ-filled tenements, and unsafe factories blighted American cities, more and more Americans insisted on legislation that fostered the general welfare. Led by women reformers such as Jane Addams and Florence Kelley, social activists succeeded in getting laws passed that ended child labor, protected workers from injury from dangerous factory machines, and created standards for safe meat and food. The Progressive Era still left most people free to pursue their own destiny, but under President Theodore Roosevelt, the government became the ultimate arbiter of minimal standards for industry, railroads, and consumer safety.

The tensions between the two narratives continued to grow as the nation entered the Great Depression. Nearly a million mortgages were foreclosed, the stock market crashed, 25 percent of all American workers were chronically unemployed, and banks failed. When Franklin Roosevelt was elected president, he promised to use "bold, persistent experimentation" to find answers to people's suffering. The legislation of the first 100 days of his presidency encompassed unprecedented federal intervention in the regulation of industry, agriculture, and the provision of welfare payments to the unemployed. The good of the whole reemerged as a dominant concern. By 1935, however, the American Liberty League, a political group formed by conservative Democrats to oppose New Deal legislation, was

indicting **fdr** as a socialist and demanding a return to laissez-faire individualism. But the New Deal rolled on. In 1935, Congress enacted Social Security, the single greatest collective investment America had ever made, for *all* people over 65, and the Wagner Labor Relations Act gave unions the right to organize. Roosevelt ran his 1936 reelection campaign on a platform emphasizing that "one third of [our] nation is ill-housed, ill-clothed, and ill-fed."

This focus on the good of the whole culminated during World War II, a time when everyone was reminded of being part of a larger battle to preserve the values that "equal opportunity" represented: the dignity of every citizen, as well as the right to freedom of religion, freedom from want, and freedom of political expression. For the first time since Reconstruction, the government acted to prohibit discrimination against African-Americans, issuing an executive order to allow blacks as well as whites to be hired in the war industries. Similarly, it supported policies of equal pay to women workers while leading a massive effort to recruit more women into the labor force to meet wartime demands. From wage and price controls to the universal draft, government action on behalf of the good of the whole reached a new height.

After the war ended, the tension between the competing value systems returned, but, significantly, even most Republicans accepted as a given the fundamental reforms achieved under the New Deal. Anyone who suggested repeal of Social Security, President Dwight Eisenhower wrote to his brother Milton midway through his term in office, was "out of his mind." Eisenhower even created a new Cabinet department to oversee health and welfare.

The stage was set for the revolutions of the 1960s: that is, the civil rights movement, the women's movement, the student movement, and the War on Poverty. Blacks had no intention of accepting the status quo of prewar Jim Crow segregation when they returned from serving in World War II. Building on the community institutions they had created during the era of Jim Crow, they mobilized to confront racism. When a black woman was raped by six white policemen in Montgomery, Alabama, in the late 1940s, the Women's Political Council, organized by local black women, and the Brotherhood of Sleeping Car Porters, an all-black union, took on the police and forced a trial. That same network of black activists sought improvements in the treatment of blacks at downtown department stores and on public transport. Thus, when one of their members, Rosa Parks, was arrested in 1955 for refusing to give up her seat on a city bus to a white person, both groups took action. By initiating a phone tree and printing 4,000 leaflets, they organized a mass rally overnight. Held at a local

Baptist church to consider a bus boycott, the rally featured an address by Martin Luther King, Jr., who later became the embodiment of the movement (though it should be noted that the movement created King and not vice versa). After that night, Montgomery's black community refused to ride the city buses for 381 consecutive days, until the buses were desegregated.

A few years later, four first-year students at the all-black North Carolina Agricultural and Technical College in Greensboro, North Carolina, carried the movement a step further. Although they had come of age after the Supreme Court outlawed school segregation, little had changed. Now that their generation was reaching maturity, they asked what they could do. The young men had gone to an all-black high school where their teachers had asked them to address voter registration envelopes to community residents and encouraged them to think of themselves as first-class citizens. They had participated in an **naacp** youth group in which weekly discussions had centered on events such as the Montgomery Bus Boycott. They attended a Baptist church where the pastor preached the social gospel and asked for "justice now." Embittered by how little the status of black Americans had improved, they sought new ways of carrying forward what they had learned.

Their solution was simple: highlight the absurdity of segregation by going to a downtown department store and acting like regular customers. At the Woolworth's in Greensboro, they bought notebooks at one counter, purchased toothpaste at another, then sat down at the lunch counter and ordered a cup of coffee. "We don't serve colored people here," they were told. "But you served us over there," they responded, showing their receipts. Opening their school books, they sat for three hours until the store closed. The next day, they returned to the lunch counter with 23 of their classmates. The day after there were 66, the next day 100. On the fifth day, 1000 black students and adults crowded the streets of downtown Greensboro.

The direct-action civil rights movement had begun. Within two months, sit-ins occurred in 54 cities in nine states. By April 1960, the Student Nonviolent Co-ordinating Committee (sncc) had been founded. Soon, *The New York Times* was devoting a special section each day to civil rights demonstrations in the South. On August 28, 1963, a quarter-million people came together for the March on Washington. There, Martin Luther King, Jr., gave his "I Have a Dream" speech, a contemporary version of what John Winthrop had said 238 years earlier that celebrated the same idea of a "beloved community" where "neither Jew nor Gentile, black man, or white man" could be separated from each other.

At long last, the government responded. The Civil Rights Act of 1964 ended Jim Crow. The Voting Rights Act of 1965 restored the franchise to black Americans. The War on Poverty gave hope to millions who had been left out of the American dream. Medicare offered health care to all senior citizens, and Medicaid offered it to those who could not otherwise afford to go to the doctor. Federal Aid to Education created new and better schools. The Model Cities Program offered a way for blighted neighborhoods to be revitalized.

The narrative of progress toward the common good reached a new crescendo. With the civil rights movement as an inspiration, women started their own movement for social equality. Access to previously closed careers opened up under pressure. By 1990, half of all medical, law, and business students were women. Young girls grew up with the same aspirations as young boys. Latinos, gay Americans, and other minorities soon joined the march demanding greater equality. It seemed as though a permanent turning point had occurred.

But the counternarrative eventually rediscovered its voice. Millions of white Americans who might have supported the right of blacks to vote or eat at a lunch counter were appalled by affirmative action and demands for Black Power. When the war in Vietnam caused well-off students to take to the streets in protest against their country's military actions, thousands of ordinary workers were angered by the rebellion of the young against authority. Traditional families were outraged when feminists questioned monogamy and dared to challenge male authority.

By 1968, the nation was divided once more, and the events of that election year crystallized the issues. Incumbent Lyndon Johnson withdrew from the presidential race at the end of March. Martin Luther King, Jr., was assassinated in April, with riots spreading like wildfire across the country in response. Student protestors took over Columbia University in May, making a mockery of the idea of civil discourse and respect for authority. Robert F. Kennedy was assassinated in June, just as he seemed ready to move decisively toward the Democratic presidential nomination. And when the Democratic party met for its convention in Chicago, thousands of protestors were pummeled by police as they demonstrated against conventional politics.

At the same time, Richard Nixon was nominated by the Republican party on a platform of "law and order" and respect for authority. Adopting a "Southern strategy," he appealed for white Southern votes by opposing forced desegregation of schools. Lambasting students who protested the war, he pleaded for a return to respect for traditional institutions. Nixon claimed to speak on behalf of "the silent majority" who remained proud to be American citizens, who celebrated the flag rather than mocked it, and who affirmed the rights of individuals to do as they wished.

Richard Nixon's election in Fall 1968 launched the resurgence of a conservative consensus in American politics. Though on issues such as the environment Nixon pursued many policies consistent with the "good of the whole" framework, on most issues he moved in the opposite direction. He opposed busing as a tool to create greater school desegregation, started to dismantle War on Poverty programs, based his 1972 reelection campaign on attacking the "collectivism" of the Democratic party, and insisted on defending the values of "traditional" Americans against attacks by the young, minorities, and women.

As social issues provided a rallying point for those set against further social change, the conservative narrative gained new proponents. Those opposed to gay rights mobilized to curtail further efforts to make sexuality a civil rights issue. Evangelical Christians joined groups such as Jerry Falwell's Moral Majority or Pat Robertson's "Praise the Lord" clubs to lobby against advances for minority rights. Direct mail campaigns and the use of cable television helped the Right galvanize new audiences of potential supporters.

Presidential politics also continued on a conservative path. Even though Richard Nixon was compelled to resign in shame over his illegal activities in the Watergate scandal, each of his successors—even Democrats—advanced the conservative agenda he initiated. Gerald Ford vetoed more legislation in two years than most presidents veto in eight. Jimmy Carter, though a liberal on gender equality and black civil rights, proved conservative on most economic issues. Ronald Reagan personified the conservative revival. He not only celebrated patriotism, but also revived the viewpoint that the best America was one without government intervention in the economy, and one that venerated the ideal of individualism.

Even Democrat Bill Clinton, excoriated by the Right as a demonic embodiment of counterculture values, was in practice more a Dwight Eisenhower Republican than a Lyndon Johnson Democrat. Dedicated to cultivating the political mainstream, he achieved legislative victories primarily on traditionally Republican issues: deficit reduction; the North American Free Trade Agreement; an increased police presence on the streets; welfare reform that took people off the public dole after two years; and the use of V-chips to allow parents to control their children's television viewing habits. Only his failed health care proposal acted in tune with the ideology of fdr and lbj.

George W. Bush simply extended the conservative tradition. With massive tax cuts, he created lower rates for the wealthy than had been seen in more than a half-century. His consistent support of deregulation freed up countless companies and investment capital firms to pursue profits without restriction. He made nationalism a cherished part of his political legacy, including the pursuit of a doctrine that emphasized unilateral initiatives defined as in the best interests of the United States, and downplayed multilateral cooperation that would subject America to constraint by the wishes of its partners and allies.

From 1968 to 2008, the American political and ideological trajectory hewed to a conservative narrative that celebrates individualism over collective action and criticizes government activity on behalf of the common good.

In recent years, the tension between the two narratives has escalated to an alarming degree. Barack Obama's 2008 election appeared to revitalize a focus on the common good. More people voted, embracing the idea of change, and elected a black American who seemed to embody those values. The fact that Obama became the first president in 100 years to successfully pass national health care reform—albeit without the provision of a public alternative to private insurance companies—appeared to validate that presumption.

But with the midterm elections of 2010, the rejection of Democratic politics—especially state intervention on behalf of the common good—resulted in the most dramatic electoral turnaround since 1946, when President Harry Truman's Democrats lost 81 seats in the House of Representatives. "Tea Party" Republicans not only stood for conservative positions on most social issues, but most dramatically, they insisted that all taxes should be cut, that federal expenditures for Medicare, Social Security, and other social programs must be slashed, and that it is preferable for the government to default on its financial responsibilities than to raise the national debt ceiling.

A backward glance through United States history would reveal no clearer example of the tension between the two competing American narratives, existing side by side, seemingly irreconcilable. The moment is historic, particularly at a time when climate change, stalled immigration reform, and a depressed global economy cry out for action. Thus, the conflict between the good of the whole and the ascendancy of individualist freedom has reached new heights. The choice that voters make in the 2012 presidential election will define our country's political future. Which narrative will we pursue? Are health care and quality education universal rights or privileges reserved for only those with the means to pay? Do we wish to bear "one another's burdens . . . make others' conditions our own . . . mourn together [and] labor and suffer together?" Or do we wish to make each individual responsible for his or her own fate? These questions are not new. But now, more than ever, they challenge us to find an answer: Who are we? In which direction do we wish to go?

Despite the trend over the past three-and-a-half centuries toward legislation that creates a safety net to protect the larger community, millions of Americans appear committed to dismantling government, slashing federal spending, and walking away from previous commitments to the good of the whole. A number of candidates running for the

Republican presidential nomination in 2012 wish to curtail federal responsibility for Social Security for senior citizens. Every Republican candidate seeks to repeal Obama's national health insurance program. Cutting taxes has become a holy mantra. While it is true that in the coming decades demographic change will dramatically increase the number of Latino voters, who historically have favored legislation on behalf of the common good, it is not inconceivable that a reversal of social welfare legislation will happen first.

The tension between these two narratives is as old as the country itself. More often than not, it has been a healthy tension, with one set of values checking and balancing the other. But the polarization of today is unparalleled. The decisions the electorate makes in 2012 are of historic importance in determining which direction the country will take.

Critical Thinking

1. How does the value system focused on the public good benefit American society and how might it hurt American society?

2. How does the value system focused on individual freedom benefit American society and how might it hurt American society?

3. How can balance between these two value systems be maintained?

Create Central

www.mhhe.com/createcentral

Internet References

New American Studies Web
   www.georgetown.edu/crossroads/asw
Social Science Information Gateway
   http://www.sosig.esrc.bris.ac.uk
Sociosite
   http://www.topsite.com/goto/sociosite.net
Socioweb
   http://www.topsite.com/goto/socioweb.com
Sociology—Study Sociology Online
   http://edu.learnsoc.org
Sociology Web Resources
   http://www.mhhe.com/socscience/sociology/resources/index.htm

WILLIAM H. CHAFE, a Fellow of the American Academy since 2001, is the Alice Mary Baldwin Professor of History at Duke University. His publications include *Private Lives/Public Consequences: Personality and Politics in Modern America* (2005) and *The Rise and Fall of the American Century: The United States from 1890 to 2008* (2008). His current project is titled *Behind the Veil: African American Life During the Age of Segregation.*

Article　　　Prepared by: Kurt Finsterbusch, *University of Maryland, College Park*

Is Facebook Making Us Lonely?

Social media—from Facebook to Twitter—have made us more densely networked than ever. Yet for all this connectivity, new research suggests that we have never been lonelier (or more narcissistic)—and that this loneliness is making us mentally and physically ill. A report on what the epidemic of loneliness is doing to our souls and our society.

STEPHEN MARCHE

Learning Outcomes

After reading this article, you will be able to:

- Know the trends in loneliness over the past several decades.
- Understand the role of Facebook in present-day loneliness.
- Understand the effects of loneliness on the mental and physical health of individuals and on society.

Yvette Vickers, a former *Playboy* playmate and B-movie star, best known for her role in *Attack of the 50 Foot Woman,* would have been 83 last August, but nobody knows exactly how old she was when she died. According to the Los Angeles coroner's report, she lay dead for the better part of a year before a neighbor and fellow actress, a woman named Susan Savage, noticed cobwebs and yellowing letters in her mailbox, reached through a broken window to unlock the door, and pushed her way through the piles of junk mail and mounds of clothing that barricaded the house. Upstairs, she found Vickers's body, mummified, near a heater that was still running. Her computer was on too, its glow permeating the empty space.

The *Los Angeles Times* posted a story headlined "Mummified Body of Former Playboy Playmate Yvette Vickers Found in Her Benedict Canyon Home," which quickly went viral. Within two weeks, by Technorati's count, Vickers's lonesome death was already the subject of 16,057 Facebook posts and 881 tweets. She had long been a horror-movie icon, a symbol of Hollywood's capacity to exploit our most basic fears in the silliest ways; now she was an icon of a new and different kind of horror: our growing fear of loneliness. Certainly, she received much more attention in death than she did in the final years of her life. With no children, no religious group, and no immediate social circle of any kind, she had begun, as an elderly woman, to look elsewhere for companionship. Savage later told *Los Angeles* magazine that she had searched Vickers's phone bills for clues about the life that led to such an end. In the months before her grotesque death, Vickers had made calls not to friends or family but to distant fans who had found her through fan conventions and Internet sites.

Vickers's web of connections had grown broader but shallower, as has happened for many of us. We are living in an isolation that would have been unimaginable to our ancestors, and yet we have never been more accessible. Over the past three decades, technology has delivered to us a world in which we need not be out of contact for a fraction of a moment. In 2010, at a cost of $300 million, 800 miles of fiber-optic cable was laid between the Chicago Mercantile Exchange and the New York Stock Exchange to shave three milliseconds off trading times. Yet within this world of instant and absolute communication, unbounded by limits of time or space, we suffer from unprecedented alienation. We have never been more detached from one another, or lonelier. In a world consumed by ever more novel modes of socializing, we have less and less actual society. We live in an accelerating contradiction: the more connected we become, the lonelier we are. We were promised a global village; instead we inhabit the drab cul-de-sacs and endless freeways of a vast suburb of information.

At the forefront of all this unexpectedly lonely interactivity is Facebook, with 845 million users and $3.7 billion in revenue last year. The company hopes to raise $5 billion in an initial public offering later this spring, which will make it by far the largest Internet IPO in history. Some recent estimates put the company's potential value at $100 billion, which would make it larger than the global coffee industry—one addiction preparing to surpass the other. Facebook's scale and reach are hard to comprehend: last summer, Facebook became, by some counts, the first website to receive one trillion page views in a month. In the last three months of 2011, users generated an average of 2.7 billion "likes" and comments every day. On whatever scale you care to judge Facebook—as a company, as a culture, and as a country—it is vast beyond imagination.

Despite its immense popularity, or more likely because of it, Facebook has, from the beginning, been under something of a cloud of suspicion. The depiction of Mark Zuckerberg, in *The Social Network,* as a bastard with symptoms of Asperger's syndrome, was nonsense. But it felt true. It felt true to Facebook, if not to Zuckerberg. The film's most indelible scene, the one that may well have earned it an Oscar, was the final, silent shot of an anomic Zuckerberg sending out a friend request to his ex-girlfriend, then waiting and clicking and waiting and clicking—a moment of superconnected loneliness preserved in amber. We have all been in that scene: transfixed by the glare of a screen, hungering for response.

When you sign up for Google+ and set up your Friends circle, the program specifies that you should include only "your real friends, the ones you feel comfortable sharing private details with." That one little phrase, *Your real friends*— so quaint, so charmingly mothering—perfectly encapsulates the anxieties that social media have produced: the fears that Facebook is interfering with our real friendships, distancing us from each other, making us lonelier; and that social networking might be spreading the very isolation it seemed designed to conquer.

Facebook arrived in the middle of a dramatic increase in the quantity and intensity of human loneliness, a rise that initially made the site's promise of greater connection seem deeply attractive. Americans are more solitary than ever before. In 1950, less than 10 percent of American households contained only one person. By 2010, nearly 27 percent of households had just one person. Solitary living does not guarantee a life of unhappiness, of course. In his recent book about the trend toward living alone, Eric Klinenberg, a sociologist at NYU, writes: "Reams of published research show that it's the quality, not the quantity, of social interaction, that best predicts loneliness." True. But before we begin the fantasies of happily eccentric singledom, of divorcées dropping by their knitting circles after work for glasses of Drew Barrymore pinot grigio, or recent college graduates with perfectly articulated, Steampunk-themed, 300-square-foot apartments organizing croquet matches with their book clubs, we should recognize that it is not just isolation that is rising sharply. It's loneliness, too. And loneliness makes us miserable.

We know intuitively that loneliness and being alone are not the same thing. Solitude can be lovely. Crowded parties can be agony. We also know, thanks to a growing body of research on the topic, that loneliness is not a matter of external conditions; it is a psychological state. A 2005 analysis of data from a longitudinal study of Dutch twins showed that the tendency toward loneliness has roughly the same genetic component as other psychological problems such as neuroticism or anxiety.

Still, loneliness is slippery, a difficult state to define or diagnose. The best tool yet developed for measuring the condition is the UCLA Loneliness Scale, a series of 20 questions that all begin with this formulation: "How often do you feel . . . ?" As in: "How often do you feel that you are 'in tune' with the people around you?" And. "How often do you feel that you lack companionship?" Measuring the condition in these terms, various studies have shown loneliness rising drastically over a very short period of recent history. A 2010 AARP survey found that 35 percent of adults older than 45 were chronically lonely, as opposed to 20 percent of a similar group only a decade earlier. According to a major study by a leading scholar of the subject, roughly 20 percent of Americans—about 60 million people— are unhappy with their lives because of loneliness. Across the Western world, physicians and nurses have begun to speak openly of an epidemic of loneliness.

The new studies on loneliness are beginning to yield some surprising preliminary findings about its mechanisms. Almost every factor that one might assume affects loneliness does so only some of the time, and only under certain circumstances. People who are married are less lonely than single people, one journal article suggests, but only if their spouses are confidants. If one's spouse is not a confidant, marriage may not decrease loneliness. A belief in God might help, or it might not, as a 1990 German study comparing levels of religious feeling and levels of loneliness discovered. Active believers who saw God as abstract and helpful rather than as a wrathful, immediate presence were less lonely. "The mere belief in God," the researchers concluded, "was relatively independent of loneliness."

But it is clear that social interaction matters. Loneliness and being alone are not the same thing, but both are on the rise. We meet fewer people. We gather less. And when we gather, our bonds are less meaningful and less easy. The decrease in confidants—that is, in quality social connections—has been dramatic over the past 25 years. In one survey, the mean size of networks of personal confidants decreased from 2.94 people in 1985 to 2.08 in 2004. Similarly, in 1985, only 10 percent of Americans said they had no one with whom to discuss important matters, and 15 percent said they had only one such good friend. By 2004, 25 percent had nobody to talk to and 20 percent had only one confidant.

In the face of this social disintegration, we have essentially hired an army of replacement confidants, an entire class of professional carers. As Ronald Dworkin pointed out in a 2010 paper for the Hoover Institution, in the late 40s, the United States was home to 2,500 clinical psychologists, 30,000 social workers, and fewer than 500 marriage and family therapists. As of 2010, the country had 77,000 clinical psychologists, 192,000 clinical social workers, 400,000 nonclinical social workers, 50,000 marriage and family therapists, 105,000 mental-health counselors, 220,000 substance-abuse counselors, 17,000 nurse psychotherapists, and 30,000 life coaches. The majority of patients in therapy do not warrant a psychiatric diagnosis. This raft of psychic servants is helping us through what used to be called regular problems. We have outsourced the work of everyday caring.

We need professional careers more and more, because the threat of societal breakdown, once principally a matter of nostalgic lament, has morphed into an issue of public health. Being lonely is extremely bad for your health. If you're lonely, you're more likely to be put in a geriatric home at an earlier age than a similar person who isn't lonely. You're less likely to exercise. You're more likely to be obese. You're less likely to survive a serious operation and more likely to have hormonal imbalances. You are at greater risk of inflammation. Your memory may be worse. You are more likely to be depressed, to sleep badly, and to suffer dementia and general cognitive decline. Loneliness may not have killed Yvette Vickers, but it has been linked to a greater probability of having the kind of heart condition that did kill her.

And yet, despite its deleterious effect on health, loneliness is one of the first things ordinary Americans spend their money achieving. With money, you flee the cramped city to a house in the suburbs or, if you can afford it, a McMansion in the exurbs, inevitably spending more time in your car. Loneliness is at the American core, a by-product of a long-standing national appetite for independence: The Pilgrims who left Europe willingly abandoned the bonds and strictures of a society that could not accept their right to be different. They did not seek out loneliness, but they accepted it as the price of their autonomy. The cowboys who set off to explore a seemingly endless frontier likewise traded away personal ties in favor of pride and self-respect. The ultimate American icon is the astronaut: Who is more heroic, or more alone? The price of self-determination and self-reliance has often been loneliness. But Americans have always been willing to pay that price.

Today, the one common feature in American secular culture is its celebration of the self that breaks away from the constrictions of the family and the state, and, in its greatest expressions, from all limits entirely. The great American poem is Whitman's "Song of Myself." The great American essay is Emerson's "Self-Reliance." The great American novel is Melville's *Moby-Dick*, the tale of a man on a quest so lonely that it is incomprehensible to those around him. American culture, high and low, is about self-expression and personal authenticity. Franklin Delano Roosevelt called individualism "the great watchword of American life."

Self-invention is only half of the American story, however. The drive for isolation has always been in tension with the impulse to cluster in communities that cling and suffocate. The Pilgrims, while fomenting spiritual rebellion, also enforced ferocious cohesion. The Salem witch trials, in hindsight, read like attempts to impose solidarity—as do the McCarthy hearings. The history of the United States is like the famous parable of the porcupines in the cold, from Schopenhauer's *Studies in Pessimism*—the ones who huddle together for warmth and shuffle away in pain, always separating and congregating.

We are now in the middle of a long period of shuffling away. In his 2000 book *Bowling Alone,* Robert D. Putnam attributed the dramatic postwar decline of social capital—the strength and value of interpersonal networks—to numerous interconnected trends in American life: suburban sprawl, television's dominance over culture, the self-absorption of the Baby Boomers, and the disintegration of the traditional family. The trends he observed continued through the prosperity of the aughts, and have only become more pronounced with time: the rate of union membership declined in 2011, again; screen time rose; the Masons and the Elks continued their slide into irrelevance. We are lonely because we want to be lonely. We have made ourselves lonely.

The question of the future is this: Is Facebook part of the separating or part of the congregating; is it a huddling-together for warmth or a shuffling-away in pain?

Well before facebook, digital technology was enabling our tendency for isolation, to an unprecedented degree. Back in the 1990s, scholars started calling the contradiction between an increased opportunity to connect and a lack of human contact the "Internet paradox." A prominent 1998 article on the phenomenon by a team of researchers at Carnegie Mellon showed that increased Internet usage was already coinciding with increased loneliness. Critics of the study pointed out that the two groups that participated in the study—high-school journalism students who were heading to university and socially active members of community-development boards—were statistically likely to become lonelier over time. Which brings us to a more fundamental question: Does the Internet make people lonely, or are lonely people more attracted to the Internet?

The question has intensified in the Facebook era. A recent study out of Australia (where close to half the population is active on Facebook), titled "Who Uses Facebook?," found a complex and sometimes confounding relationship between loneliness and social networking. Facebook users had slightly lower levels of "social loneliness"—the sense of not feeling bonded with friends—but "significantly higher levels of family loneliness"—the sense of not feeling bonded with family. It may be that Facebook encourages more contact with people outside of our household, at the expense of our family relationships—or it may be that people who have unhappy family relationships in the first place seek companionship through other means, including Facebook. The researchers also found that lonely people are inclined to spend more time on Facebook: "One of the most noteworthy findings," they wrote, "was the tendency for neurotic and lonely individuals to spend greater amounts of time on Facebook per day than nonlonely individuals." And they found that neurotics are more likely to prefer to use the wall, while extroverts tend to use chat features in addition to the wall.

Moira Burke, until recently a graduate student at the Human-Computer Institute at Carnegie Mellon, used to run a longitudinal study of 1,200 Facebook users. That study, which is ongoing, is one of the first to step outside the realm of self-selected college students and examine the effects of Facebook on a broader population, over time. She concludes that the effect of Facebook depends on what you bring to it. Just as your mother said: you get out only what you put in. If you use Facebook to communicate directly with other individuals—by using the "like" button, commenting on friends' posts, and so on—it can increase your social capital. Personalized messages, or what Burke calls "composed communication," are more satisfying than "one-click communication"—the lazy click of a like. "People who received composed communication became less lonely, while people who received one-click communication experienced no change in loneliness," Burke tells me. So, you should inform your friend in writing how charming her son looks with Harry Potter cake smeared all over his face, and how interesting her sepia-toned photograph of that tree-framed bit of skyline is, and how cool it is that she's at whatever concert she happens to be at. That's what we all want to hear. Even better than sending a private Facebook message is the semi-public conversation, the kind of back-and-forth in which you half ignore the other people who may be listening in. "People whose friends write to them semi-publicly on Facebook experience decreases in loneliness," Burke says.

On the other hand, nonpersonalized use of Facebook—scanning your friends' status updates and updating the world on your own activities via your wall, or what Burke calls "passive consumption" and "broadcasting"—correlates to feelings of disconnectedness. It's a lonely business, wandering the labyrinths of our friends' and pseudo-friends' projected identities,

trying to figure out what part of ourselves we ought to project, who will listen, and what they will hear. According to Burke, passive consumption of Facebook also correlates to a marginal increase in depression. "If two women each talk to their friends the same amount of time, but one of them spends more time reading about friends on Facebook as well, the one reading tends to grow slightly more depressed," Burke says. Her conclusion suggests that my sometimes unhappy reactions to Facebook may be more universal than I had realized. When I scroll through page after page of my friends' descriptions of how accidentally eloquent their kids are, and how their husbands are endearingly bumbling, and how they're all about to eat a home-cooked meal prepared with fresh local organic produce bought at the farmers' market and then go for a jog and maybe check in at the office because they're so busy getting ready to hop on a plane for a week of luxury dogsledding in Lapland, I do grow slightly more miserable. A lot of other people doing the same thing feel a little bit worse, too.

Still, Burke's research does not support the assertion that Facebook creates loneliness. The people who experience loneliness on Facebook are lonely away from Facebook, too, she points out; on Facebook, as everywhere else, correlation is not causation. The popular kids are popular, and the lonely skulkers skulk alone. Perhaps, it says something about me that I think Facebook is primarily a platform for lonely skulking. I mention to Burke the widely reported study, conducted by a Stanford graduate student, that showed how believing that others have strong social networks can lead to feelings of depression. What does Facebook communicate, if not the impression of social bounty? Everybody else looks so happy on Facebook, with so many friends, that our own social networks feel emptier than ever in comparison. Doesn't that *make* people feel lonely? "If people are reading about lives that are much better than theirs, two things can happen," Burke tells me. "They can feel worse about themselves, or they can feel motivated."

Burke will start working at Facebook as a data scientist this year.

John Cacioppo, the director of the Center for Cognitive and Social Neuroscience at the University of Chicago, is the world's leading expert on loneliness. In his landmark book, *Loneliness,* released in 2008, he revealed just how profoundly the epidemic of loneliness is affecting the basic functions of human physiology. He found higher levels of epinephrine, the stress hormone, in the morning urine of lonely people. Loneliness burrows deep: "When we drew blood from our older adults and analyzed their white cells," he writes, "we found that loneliness somehow penetrated the deepest recesses of the cell to alter the way genes were being expressed." Loneliness affects not only the brain, then, but the basic process of DNA transcription. When you are lonely, your whole body is lonely.

To Cacioppo, Internet communication allows only ersatz intimacy. "Forming connections with pets or online friends or even God is a noble attempt by an obligatorily gregarious creature to satisfy a compelling need," he writes. "But surrogates can never make up completely for the absence of the real thing." The "real thing" being actual people, in the flesh. When I speak to Cacioppo, he is refreshingly clear on what he sees as Facebook's effect on society. Yes, he allows, some research has suggested that the greater the number of Facebook friends a person has, the less lonely she is. But he argues that the impression this creates can be misleading. "For the most part," he says, "people are bringing their old friends, and feelings of loneliness or connectedness, to Facebook." The idea that a website could deliver a more friendly, interconnected world is bogus. The depth of one's social network outside Facebook is what determines the depth of one's social network within Facebook, not the other way around. Using social media doesn't create new social networks; it just transfers established networks from one platform to another. For the most part, Facebook doesn't destroy friendships—but it doesn't create them, either.

In one experiment, Cacioppo looked for a connection between the loneliness of subjects and the relative frequency of their interactions via Facebook, chat rooms, online games, dating sites, and face-to-face contact. The results were unequivocal. "The greater the proportion of face-to-face interactions, the less lonely you are," he says. "The greater the proportion of online interactions, the lonelier you are." Surely, I suggest to Cacioppo, this means that Facebook and the like inevitably make people lonelier. He disagrees. Facebook is merely a tool, he says, and like any tool, its effectiveness will depend on its user. "If you use Facebook to increase face-to-face contact," he says, "it increases social capital." So if social media let you organize a game of football among your friends, that's healthy. If you turn to social media instead of playing football, however, that's unhealthy.

"Facebook can be terrific, if we use it properly," Cacioppo continues. "It's like a car. You can drive it to pick up your friends. Or you can drive alone." But hasn't the car increased loneliness? If cars created the suburbs, surely they also created isolation. "That's because of how we use cars," Cacioppo replies. "How we use these technologies can lead to more integration, rather than more isolation."

The problem, then, is that we invite loneliness, even though it makes us miserable. The history of our use of technology is a history of isolation desired and achieved. When the Great Atlantic and Pacific Tea Company opened its A&P stores, giving Americans self-service access to groceries, customers stopped having relationships with their grocers. When the telephone arrived, people stopped knocking on their neighbors' doors. Social media bring this process to a much wider set of relationships. Researchers at the HP Social Computing Lab who studied the nature of people's connections on Twitter came to a depressing, if not surprising, conclusion: "Most of the links declared within Twitter were meaningless from an interaction point of view." I have to wonder: What other point of view is meaningful?

Loneliness is certainly not something that Facebook or Twitter or any of the lesser forms of social media is doing to us. We are doing it to ourselves. Casting technology as some vague, impersonal spirit of history forcing our actions is a weak excuse. We make decisions about how we use our machines, not the other way around. Every time I shop at my local grocery store, I am faced with a choice. I can buy my groceries from a human being or from a machine. I always, without exception, choose the machine. It's faster and more efficient, I tell myself, but the truth is that I prefer not having to wait with the other customers who are lined up alongside the conveyor belt: the hipster mom who disapproves of my high-carbon-footprint pineapple; the lady who tenses to the point of tears while she waits to see if the gods of the credit-card machine will accept or decline; the old man whose clumsy feebleness requires a patience that I don't possess. Much better to bypass the whole circus and just ring up the groceries myself.

Our omnipresent new technologies lure us toward increasingly superficial connections at exactly the same moment that they make avoiding the mess of human interaction easy. The beauty of Facebook, the source of its power, is that it enables us to be social while sparing us the embarrassing reality of society—the accidental revelations we make at parties, the awkward pauses, the farting and the spilled drinks, and the general gaucherie of face-to-face contact. Instead, we have the lovely smoothness of a seemingly social machine. Everything's so simple: status updates, pictures, your wall.

But the price of this smooth sociability is a constant compulsion to assert one's own happiness, one's own fulfillment. Not only must we contend with the social bounty of others; we must foster the appearance of our own social bounty. Being happy all the time, pretending to be happy, actually attempting to be happy—it's exhausting. Last year a team of researchers led by Iris Mauss at the University of Denver published a study looking into "the paradoxical effects of valuing happiness." Most goals in life show a direct correlation between valuation and achievement. Studies have found, for example, that students who value good grades tend to have higher grades than those who don't value them. Happiness is an exception. The study came to a disturbing conclusion:

Valuing happiness is not necessarily linked to greater happiness. In fact, under certain conditions, the opposite is true. Under conditions of low (but not high) life stress, the more people valued happiness, the lower were their hedonic balance, psychological well-being, and life satisfaction, and the higher their depression symptoms.

The more you try to be happy, the less happy you are. Sophocles made roughly the same point.

Facebook, of course, puts the pursuit of happiness front and center in our digital life. Its capacity to redefine our very concepts of identity and personal fulfillment is much more worrisome than the data mining and privacy practices that have aroused anxieties about the company. Two of the most compelling critics of Facebook—neither of them a Luddite—concentrate on exactly this point. Jaron Lanier, the author of *You Are Not a Gadget,* was one of the inventors of virtual-reality technology. His view of where social media are taking us reads like dystopian science fiction: "I fear that we are beginning to design ourselves to suit digital models of us, and I worry about a leaching of empathy and humanity in that process." Lanier argues that Facebook imprisons us in the business of self-presenting, and this, to his mind, is the site's crucial and fatally unacceptable downside.

Sherry Turkle, a professor of computer culture at MIT who in 1995 published the digital-positive analysis *Life on the Screen,* is much more skeptical about the effects of online society in her 2011 book, *Alone Together:* "These days, insecure in our relationships and anxious about intimacy, we look to technology for ways to be in relationships and protect ourselves from them at the same time." The problem with digital intimacy is that it is ultimately incomplete: "The ties we form through the Internet are not, in the end, the ties that bind. But they are the ties that preoccupy," she writes. "We don't want to intrude on each other, so instead we constantly intrude on each other, but not in 'real time.'"

Lanier and Turkle are right, at least in their diagnoses. Self-presentation on Facebook is continuous, intensely mediated, and possessed of a phony nonchalance that eliminates even the potential for spontaneity. (Look how casually I threw up these three photos from the party at which I took 300 photos!) Curating the exhibition of the self has become a 24/7 occupation. Perhaps not surprisingly, then, the Australian study "Who Uses Facebook?" found a significant correlation between Facebook use and narcissism: "Facebook users have higher levels of total narcissism, exhibitionism, and leadership than Facebook non-users," the study's authors wrote. "In fact, it could be argued that Facebook specifically gratifies the narcissistic individual's need to engage in self-promoting and superficial behavior."

Rising narcissism isn't so much a trend as the trend behind all other trends. In preparation for the 2013 edition of its diagnostic manual, the psychiatric profession is currently struggling to update its definition of narcissistic personality disorder. Still, generally speaking, practitioners agree that narcissism manifests in patterns of fantastic grandiosity, craving for attention, and lack of empathy. In a 2008 survey, 35,000 American respondents were asked if they had ever had certain symptoms of narcissistic personality disorder. Among people older than 65, 3 percent reported symptoms. Among people in their 20s, the proportion was nearly 10 percent. Across all age groups, one in 16 Americans has experienced some symptoms of NPD. And loneliness and narcissism are intimately connected: a longitudinal study of Swedish women demonstrated a strong link between levels of narcissism in youth and levels of loneliness in old age. The connection is fundamental. Narcissism is the flip side of loneliness, and either condition is a fighting retreat from the messy reality of other people.

A considerable part of Facebook's appeal stems from its miraculous fusion of distance with intimacy, or the illusion of distance with the illusion of intimacy. Our online communities become engines of self-image, and self-image becomes the engine of community. The real danger with Facebook is not that it allows us to isolate ourselves, but that by mixing our appetite for isolation with our vanity, it threatens to alter the very nature of solitude. The new isolation is not of the kind that Americans once idealized, the lonesomeness of the proudly nonconformist, independent-minded, solitary stoic, or that of the astronaut who blasts into new worlds. Facebook's isolation is a grind. What's truly staggering about Facebook usage is not its volume—750 million photographs uploaded over a single weekend—but the constancy of the performance it demands. More than half its users—and one of every 13 people on Earth is a Facebook user—log on every day. Among 18 to 34-year-olds, nearly half check Facebook minutes after waking up, and 28 percent do so before getting out of bed. The relentlessness is what is so new, so potentially transformative. Facebook never takes a break. We never take a break. Human beings have always created elaborate acts of self-presentation. But not all the time, not every morning, before we even pour a cup of coffee. Yvette Vickers's computer was on when she died.

Nostalgia for the good old days of disconnection would not just be pointless, it would be hypocritical and ungrateful. But the very magic of the new machines, the efficiency and elegance with which they serve us, obscures what isn't being served: everything that matters. What Facebook has revealed about human nature—and this is not a minor revelation—is that a connection is not the same thing as a bond, and that instant and total connection is no salvation, no ticket to a happier, better world or a more liberated version of humanity. Solitude used to be good for self-reflection and self-reinvention. But now we are left thinking about who we are all the time, without ever really thinking about who we are. Facebook denies us a pleasure whose profundity we had underestimated: the chance to forget about ourselves for a while, the chance to disconnect.

Critical Thinking

1. What are the advantages of social media for mental health?
2. What are the tradeoffs for time using social media?
3. What in your opinion are the best ways to use social media?

Create Central

www.mhhe.com/createcentral

Internet References

Global X Social Media Index ETF
 http://www.globalxfunds.com/SOCL

Social Science Information Gateway
 http://sosig.esrc.bris.ac.uk

Sociology Web Resources
 http://www.mhhe.com/socscience/sociology/resources/index.htm

Sociology—Study Sociology Online
 http://edu.learnsoc.org

Sociosite
 http://www.topsite.com/goto/sociosite.net

Socioweb
 http://www.topsite.com/goto/socioweb.com

The American Studies Web
 http://lamp.georgetown.edu/asw

Article Prepared by: Kurt Finsterbusch, *University of Maryland, College Park*

Re-evaluating the "Culture of Poverty"

STEPHEN SUH AND KIA HEISE

Learning Outcomes

After reading this article, you will be able to:

- Explain the culture of poverty thesis.

- Present the arguments against the culture of poverty thesis.

- Be able to explain poverty or at least present the major theories that try to explain the causes of poverty.

Despite its great wealth, the United States has long struggled with poverty. One popular theory for the paradox suggests that a "culture of poverty" prevents the poor from economic betterment despite social programs designed to assist them. The phrase was originally coined by *Oscar Lewis,* who believed that children growing up in poor families would learn to adapt to the values and norms that perpetuated poverty. The children would replicate these in their own lives, creating a cycle of intergenerational poverty. It wasn't until Daniel Patrick Moynihan's infamous 1965 study on the black American family (often dubbed *"The Moynihan Report"*) that the "culture of poverty" idea set off a firestorm. Moynihan described the problems of inner-city black families as stemming from a "tangle of pathology," characterized by single-mother families and unemployment. His claims were harshly criticized by many black and civil rights leaders, among others, for explaining black poverty as a product of black culture rather than deeper structural inequalities. Because of this criticism, social scientists have since generally avoided discussing cultural factors when studying poverty, though the "culture of poverty" rhetoric has remained a popular topic in public and political spheres. The debate about its relevance has re-emerged with controversial comments by politician Paul Ryan, as well as numerous editorials in the *Atlantic, The New York Times,* and elsewhere.

In this roundtable, we asked three renowned scholars to discuss the lasting significance of the "culture of poverty" rhetoric, and what social scientists could do to contribute to (or end) this debate.

How has the culture of poverty debate evolved over the years?

Mario Luis Small: There has been some evolution, but it has probably been less in the political sphere than among social scientists. Political commentators seem to think of culture as the sum of people's norms and values and of "the culture of poverty" as the norms and values that cause people to enter or remain in poverty. This model is much more common among commentators on the right than among those on the left, for whom this kind of explanation merely "blames the victims" for their problems. Both positions are quite old, dating at least to the 1960s.

Few social scientists use the term "culture of poverty" in a scientific sense. Those who study poverty rarely think about cultural questions in this way, instead tending to focus on basic structural factors, such as the quality of schools or the availability of jobs, as explanations for poverty. Those who study culture—and these are largely a different group of scholars altogether—tend to think of culture in far more sophisticated and diverse ways than as the "norms and values" of a group. Few social scientists have attempted to understand poverty through these alternative conceptions. Many of those who do focus on questions such as the impact of poverty on culture or cultural practices, rather than the impact of culture on poverty.

Kaaryn Gustafson: Early writings on the culture of poverty, for example those by Oscar Lewis and Michael Harrington, suggested that the culture of poverty was an *effect,* namely an effect of economic and social exclusion. Those writings suggested that people who faced few economic opportunities in society grew hopeless. In many ways, the early discussions of the culture of poverty were a call for action, a demand that the United States, a country that prides itself in economic opportunity, take notice of the many who could not realize those opportunities.

In the mid-1960s, the culture of poverty became associated with African Americans living in concentrated pockets of poverty in urban areas. Daniel Patrick Moynihan's report, *The Negro Family: The Case for National Action* (1965), noted high rates of divorce, non-marital childbearing, and welfare use among black families in urban centers and described these families as exhibiting a "tangle of pathology." During a radio address in 1986, then-President Ronald Reagan quipped that while a War on Poverty had been famously declared in 1964, "you could say that poverty won the war." His reason for reaching this conclusion? He noted that a lot of families were using federal anti-poverty programs, or, in his terms, were "dependent" upon federal programs—a not-so-subtle reference to the culture of poverty.

Since then, the idea that social and economic well-being ought to be measured by how few people are using government programs and not by the well-being of American families themselves has come to guide government programs. For example, the success of the federal welfare reforms passed under President Bill Clinton has been measured by the dramatic decline in the number of families receiving cash benefits. What is forgotten is that the number of American families living in poverty has risen since the welfare reforms.

Why have culture of poverty arguments been so persistent?

Small: The notion of a "culture of poverty" remains part of the conversation for a number of reasons. Some are political. For some people, the idea that people's poverty results from their own choices and values seems to explain a lot, regardless of whether that particular idea is actually consistent with the available evidence. The term itself, "culture of poverty," is also broad enough that it can be taken by different people to mean different things. The term is easy to reinvent from year to year.

Mark Gould: Since the Civil Rights Movement, almost everyone in the USA has come to believe that all citizens deserve equal opportunity and most have come to believe that all *have* equal opportunity. Most of us believe that our values are actually implemented.

If most Americans believe that African Americans should be treated as if they are the same as whites, given equal opportunities, and if most Americans believe that poor African Americans have equal opportunities, the disproportionate failure of African Americans to "succeed" can only be attributed to traits internal to them and their communities. Logically, it does not matter on what traits we focus, but often it is a "culture of poverty" that is seen as inhibiting success, as inhibiting the inability of poor blacks to take advantage of the opportunities open to them. (I limit myself here to a discussion of African Americans.)

"Culture of poverty" arguments persist given our dominant values and our dominant social science, when they are coupled with the conviction that those values are implemented effectively—that equal opportunity exists. In consequence, it is no surprise that "culture of poverty" arguments recur over and over again; nor is it a surprise that they tend to be manifest in multiple variations, focusing on one or another "cultural" attribute.

In addition, there is apparently empirical support for "culture of poverty" arguments. African Americans do less well than otherwise comparable whites on many measures of performance; poor people do less well, by definition, economically, but they also do less well educationally and are incarcerated at higher rates (whatever their actual criminal activity). Recognizing this and thinking within the dominant values in our society, many Americans think that they are "facing facts" when invoking "culture of poverty" arguments. [T]he same thing is true of many social scientists who study poverty. Social scientists are, however, less likely to believe that equal opportunity is in place, which immunizes many of them from falling into this trap.

Gustafson: The appeal of the "culture of poverty" is that it offers a clear explanation for poverty, an explanation that removes both individual agency and collective responsibility from the equation. This simplistic account of poverty—one that suggests that certain populations have developed settled social and economic sub-cultures outside the mainstream—blinds us from the historical contingencies and the political decisions that have led to a high rate of poverty relative to most wealthy nations. The current understanding of the culture of poverty suggests that poverty is intractable and dismisses that idea that policy changes can lower the rate of poverty in the United States or address the concentration of poverty in certain populations such as African Americans, Latinos, Native Americans, and recent Asian immigrants; the disabled; and the parents of young children.

How has the idea of a culture of poverty affected politics and society?

Gould: The consequences of "culture of poverty" arguments have been disastrous. These arguments result in policies that seek to change blacks. If there is equal opportunity, their "culture of poverty," in its various guises, means that African Americans are unable to take advantage of that opportunity.

Such arguments miss the nature and consequences of contemporary discrimination. While there is plenty of overt discrimination, disparate treatment, the more important form of discrimination in the USA today, is disparate impact. This is where ostensibly neutral structures and organizations, organizations that treat blacks and whites as if they were the same, generate adverse consequences for blacks.

The consequences of "culture of poverty" arguments have been disastrous. They result in policies that seek to change blacks rather than change organizational constraints and persistent discrimination.

Think about the discussions of "acting white." If African Americans who act black are expected to perform poorly, this becomes a self-fulfilling prophecy, and (almost) only those blacks who "act white" perform well. When blacks and whites perform different cultures, act out different cultural identities, there is no reason to think that the differences are intrinsically relevant to educational performance; however, they may well affect performance when taken in conjunction with how students who perform these cultural differences are regarded and dealt with in organizations. African Americans may have a different subculture than whites, but if they perform less well than whites, it is not because of that subculture, but because of how they are processed in organizations because of it.

This discussion is, of course, too simple. It ignores the structurally-different positions blacks and whites occupy in American society, but perhaps it suggests that just because black culture correlates with "deficient performance" does not mean that black culture is deficient. We have learned to see black culture as deficient, as something we ought not to value, because of "culture of poverty" arguments, because our commonsense understanding precludes our comprehending that the problem is not intrinsic to the culture, but to the way bearers of that culture are constrained organizationally.

Gustafson: The pathologizing of the poor, the popular belief that poverty is a result of individuals' failings to exercise personal responsibility, and the belief that government programs are by nature wasteful and breed dependency remain widespread and influential today. This perpetuates the illusion that *those people*—the poor people who lack a real work ethic—are poor for a reason, but that others, particularly hardworking members of the middle class, are invulnerable to economic risk so long as they are working hard enough. The persistence of the culture of poverty theory also distracts the public and lawmakers from celebrating the policy decisions that have been successful in ameliorating poverty. As a result, popular and governmental commitments to fighting poverty are slight.

Does talk about the US as a post-racial society influence the rhetoric around the culture of poverty?

Gould: Before the Civil Rights Movement, when discrimination against African Americans was overt, liberal-minded people could explain differential performance between blacks and whites as due to overt discrimination.

In post-Civil Rights Movement America, which some erroneously see as a post-racial society, the logic of this argument changes fundamentally. In the absence of overt discrimination . . . liberals either have to think social structurally about the nature of discrimination, or they fall into "culture of poverty" arguments. Likewise, social scientists, even when claiming to eschew "culture of poverty" arguments, fall into them.

There is a paradox here. Participants in the Civil Rights Movement fought for the inclusion of African Americans, and derivatively others (within the American Creed), for their inclusion as full citizens. The success of the Movement, the inclusion of African Americans, including the poor, within the egalitarian values dominant in American society, and given the reality of African Americans performing less well than whites in many areas, has resulted in the construction of a New Racism. This New Racism does not result primarily in invidious biological distinctions between African Americans and whites as explanations for the "facts," but instead in the characterization of African Americans as performing less well than whites (including in their concentrated poverty) because of their "cultural attributes."

What is missing from the current public discourse about the culture of poverty? What can sociologists contribute to the discussion of poverty policies?

Gustafson: Social scientists concerned about social inequality should turn their attention to poverty, especially child poverty. Scholars can play a role in informing students and the public of the very fact that child poverty is widespread, can take opportunities to study the long-term effects of child poverty on families and society, and can use their skills to study the effectiveness of particular policies in reducing child poverty. More work needs to be done in tracing and examining the successes of government led-anti-poverty efforts, from the drop in poverty among elderly Americans to the documented, long-term effects of Head Start programs.

We tend to focus on failures and ignore successes. Sociologists keen on historical and comparative work might promote awareness that the United States is an outlier and that policies common in other countries—universal health care, paid family leave for workers with young children, and universal child allowances—are effective in reducing poverty there.

We tend to focus on failures and ignore successes. Sociologists might promote awareness that the United States is an outlier, that policies common in other countries—universal health care, paid family leave for workers with young children, and universal child allowances—are effective in reducing poverty.

Finally, qualitative sociologists can serve an important function in carefully and critically documenting the experiences of the poor, particularly because there is little in the popular media about the experiences of the poor and poor people have little political access in a country where money is speech. While most Americans are overexposed to the lifestyles of the rich and famous, we rarely hear about how poverty affects daily lives and how it limits choices and life chances.

Small: I think three things are missing:

First, a broader understanding of the many ways that anthropologists and others who study culture (but not poverty) have conceptualized culture, its impact on behavior, its response to intervention, and its limitations as an explanatory factor.

Second, better data.

Third, more dispassionate analysis.

The one advantage of the new generation of scholars working on these questions is that they were not part of the highly acrimonious debate over culture during the 1960s and 1970s. The debate was so contentious and the rhetoric so heated that it has been difficult to address even basic empirical questions from a scientific perspective. [Now] there is space for a new round of clear, disinterested research that can illuminate much more than the old models have found.

For example, a lot of people assume that social scientists who examine the relationship between culture and poverty must have a particular political agenda. Some even believe that studying *culture* necessarily implies a particular political posture. Yet notice that entire academic disciplines—most notably, anthropology—are fundamentally devoted to the study of culture. The fact that anyone believes that studying culture means rehashing that old idea shows how far we need to go.

A lot of people assume that social scientists who examine the relationship between culture and poverty must have a particular political agenda. This shows how far we need to go.

Gould: There are a number of conceptual distinctions we need to make before we can formulate effective policies. So far, I have been using the term "culture" as if we knew what it meant. In reality, "culture of poverty" arguments are a hodgepodge that confuse much more than they illuminate.

Implicit in many "culture of poverty" discussions is a notion of social values. Social values regulate what is desirable; they constitute obligations. There is a lot of evidence that inner-city blacks share the dominant values of hard work and a commitment to education.

Implicit in many "culture of poverty" discussions is a notion of social values. Social values regulate what is desirable; they constitute obligations. If folks do not find a good job desirable, if they do not feel the obligation to work, they will not seek out jobs when the opportunity to do so arises. If students do not value education, do not feel an obligation to do well in school, they will not orient themselves to educational opportunities. In contrast to these contentions, there is a lot of evidence that inner-city blacks share the dominant values of USA society, including the positive evaluation of hard work and a commitment to education. If this is correct, we would expect them, for example, to seek work when it is available, and they do so.

The notion of an "oppositional culture" is important here. Often, an oppositional culture is understood to inhibit intrinsically educational or occupational success; it may be seen, for example, as devaluing educational success. It is treated as a "culture of poverty." If, instead, black culture inhibits success not because of its inherent traits (it is *not* the case that poor blacks devalue educational success), but because of the way a black man wearing baggy jeans is treated, the question becomes why many African Americans, unlike some immigrant groups, are unwilling to give up their culture and their cultural performances, unwilling to "act white." The answer, I think, is because for African Americans, this cultural identity and the performances that actualize it (in dress, music, language, speech act, and style) are crucial; they represent, if in a form more fractured than previously, the collective solidarity that has enabled African Americans to endure and to excel culturally. This is an oppositional culture, but only in the sense that African Americans do not want to sacrifice it. As an oppositional culture, it is fully compatible with the values dominant in United States society.

Thus, while the black subculture is *not* a "culture of poverty"—it does not inhibit success due to its inherent attributes—it may inhibit success, due to how people who share it are considered in the larger society. This distinction, between a "culture" that inhibits success because of qualities inherent to it (for example, not valuing hard work), and a culture that inhibits success, not because of its inherent qualities, but because of the (racist) orientation of a dominant (and sometimes others in the subordinate) group towards people within that culture, is crucial, but too often missing from discussions of culture and poverty.

If this analysis makes sense, our concern should be to construct opportunities for the inner-city poor to succeed, ladders of achievement that facilitate their success in school, that make it possible for them to find jobs that will support their families in dignity, and to reconstruct organizations in a way that makes it possible for African Americans to share in organizational governance so that African American cultural identities might be actualized to the benefit of all Americans.

Critical Thinking

1. Identify cultural norms that make it difficult for teenagers to get ahead.

2. Identify the structural conditions that make it difficult for teenagers to get ahead.

3. How can norms and conditions be changed to give poor teenagers a better chance to get ahead?

Internet References

New American Studies Web
   https://blogs.commons.georgetown.edu/vkp/
Social Science Information Gateway
   http://www.ariadne.ac.uk/issue2/sosig
Sociology—Study Sociology Online
   http://edu.learnsoc.org/
Sociology Web Resources
   http://www.mhhe.com/socscience/sociology/resources/index.htm
Sociosite
   http://www.topsite.com/goto/sociosite.net
Socioweb
   http://www.topsite.com/goto/socioweb.com

MARK GOULD is in the sociology department at Haverford College. A social theorist, one of his areas of interest is the nature of contemporary racism, culture, opportunity structures, and poverty in the inner-city US. **KAARYN GUSTAFSON** is at the University of California–Irvine's School of Law, where she is also the co-director of the Center on Law, Equality, and Race. She is the author of *Cheating Welfare: Public Assistance and the Criminalization of Poverty*. **MARIO LUIS SMALL** is a sociologist at Harvard University. He studies urban neighborhoods, social networks, inequality, organizational capacity, and the sociology of knowledge.

Article

Prepared by: Kurt Finsterbusch, *University of Maryland, College Park*

Free and Equal in Dignity and LGBT Rights

"Be on the right side of history."

Hillary Rodham Clinton

Learning Outcomes

After reading this article, you will be able to:

- Evaluate the significance of the Universal Declaration of Human Rights passed by the United Nations in 1948 without a negative vote.

- Understand the progress on human rights that has occurred since the declaration.

- Identify the critical issues that are involved in extending the declaration to LGBT equality.

Good evening, and let me express my deep honor and pleasure at being here. I want to thank Director General Tokayev and Ms. Wyden along with other ministers, ambassadors, excellencies, and UN partners. This weekend, we will celebrate Human Rights Day, the anniversary of one of the great accomplishments of the last century.

Beginning in 1947, delegates from six continents devoted themselves to drafting a declaration that would enshrine the fundamental rights and freedoms of people everywhere. In the aftermath of World War II, many nations pressed for a statement of this kind to help ensure that we would prevent future atrocities and protect the inherent humanity and dignity of all people. And so the delegates went to work. They discussed, they wrote, they revisited, revised, rewrote, for thousands of hours. And they incorporated suggestions and revisions from governments, organizations and individuals around the world.

At three o'clock in the morning on December 10th, 1948, after nearly two years of drafting and one last long night of debate, the president of the UN General Assembly called for a vote on the final text. Forty-eight nations voted in favor; eight abstained; none dissented. And the Universal Declaration of Human Rights was adopted. It proclaims a simple, powerful idea: All human beings are born free and equal in dignity and rights. And with the declaration, it was made clear that rights are not conferred by government; they are the birthright of all people. It doe not matter what country we live in, who our leaders are, or even who we are. Because we are human, we therefore have rights. And because we have rights, governments are bound to protect them.

In the 63 years since the declaration was adopted, many nations have made great progress in making human rights a human reality. Step by step, barriers that once prevented people from enjoying the full measure of liberty, the full experience of dignity, and the full benefits of humanity have fallen away. In many places, racist laws have been repealed legal and social practices that relegated women to second-class status have been abolished, the ability of religious minorities to practice their faith freely has been secured.

In most cases, this progress was not easily won. People fought and organized and campaigned in public squares and private spaces to change not only laws, but hearts and minds. And thanks to that work of generations, for millions of individuals whose lives were once narrowed by injustice, they are now able to live more freely and to participate more fully in the political, economic, and social lives of their communities.

Now, there is still, as you all know, much more to be done to secure that commitment, that reality, and progress for all people. Today, I want to talk about the work we have left to do to protect one group of people whose human rights are still denied in too many parts of the world today. In many ways, they are an invisible minority. They are arrested, beaten, terrorized, even executed. Many are treated with contempt and violence by their fellow citizens while authorities empowered to protect them look the other way or, too often, even join in the abuse. They are denied opportunities to work and learn, driven from their homes and countries, and forced to suppress or deny who they are to protect themselves from harm.

I am talking about gay, lesbian, bisexual, and transgender people, human beings born free and given bestowed equality and dignity, who have a right to claim that, which is now one of the remaining human rights challenges of our time. I speak about this subject knowing that my own country's record on human rights for gay people is far from perfect. Until 2003, it was still a crime in parts of our country. Many LGBT Americans have endured violence and harassment in their own lives, and for some, including many young people, bullying, and exclusion are daily experiences. So we, like all nations, have more work to do to protect human rights at home.

Now, raising this issue, I know, is sensitive for many people and that the obstacles standing in the way of protecting the human rights of LGBT people rest on deeply held personal, political, cultural, and religious beliefs. So I come here before you with respect, understanding, and humility. Even though progress on this front is not easy, we cannot delay acting. So in that spirit, I want to talk about the difficult and important issues we must address together to reach a global consensus that recognizes the human rights of LGBT citizens everywhere.

The first issue goes to the heart of the matter. Some have suggested that gay rights and human rights are separate and distinct; but, in fact, they are one and the same. Now, of course, 60 years ago, the governments that drafted and passed the Universal Declaration of Human Rights were not thinking about how it applied to the LGBT community. They also weren't thinking about how it applied to indigenous people or children or people with disabilities or other marginalized groups. Yet in the past 60 years, we have come to recognize that members of these groups are entitled to the full measure of dignity and rights, because, like all people, they share a common humanity.

This recognition did not occur all at once. It evolved over time. And as it did, we understood that we were honoring rights that people always had, rather than creating new or special rights for them. Like being a woman, like being a racial, religious, tribal, or ethnic minority, being LGBT does not make you less human. And that is why gay rights are human rights, and human rights are gay rights.

It is violation of human rights when people are beaten or killed because of their sexual orientation, or because they do not conform to cultural norms about how men and women should look or behave. It is a violation of human rights when governments declare it illegal to be gay, or allow those who harm gay people to go unpunished. It is a violation of human rights when lesbian or transgendered women are subjected to so-called corrective rape, or forcibly subjected to hormone treatments, or when people are murdered after public calls for violence toward gays, or when they are forced to flee their nations and seek asylum in other lands to save their lives. And it is a violation of human rights when life-saving care is withheld from people because they are gay, or equal access to justice is denied to people because they are gay, or public spaces are out of bounds to people because they are gay. No matter what we look like, where we come from, or who we are, we are all equally entitled to our human rights and dignity.

The second issue is a question of whether homosexuality arises from a particular part of the world. Some seem to believe it is a Western phenomenon, and therefore people outside the West have grounds to reject it. Well, in reality, gay people are born into and belong to every society in the world. They are all ages, all races, all faiths; they are doctors and teachers, farmers and bankers, soldiers and athletes; and whether we know it, or whether we acknowledge it, they are our family, our friends, and our neighbors.

Being gay is not a Western invention; it is a human reality. And protecting the human rights of all people, gay or straight, is not something that only Western governments do. South Africa's constitution, written in the aftermath of Apartheid, protects the equality of all citizens, including gay people. In Colombia and Argentina, the rights of gays are also legally protected. In Nepal, the supreme court has ruled that equal rights apply to LGBT citizens. The Government of Mongolia has committed to pursue new legislation that will tackle antigay discrimination.

Now, some worry that protecting the human rights of the LGBT community is a luxury that only wealthy nations can afford. But in fact, in all countries, there are costs to not protecting these rights, in both gay and straight lives lost to disease and violence, and the silencing of voices and views that would strengthen communities, in ideas never pursued by entrepreneurs who happen to be gay. Costs are incurred whenever any group is treated as lesser than the other, whether they are women, racial, or religious minorities, or the LGBT. Former President Mogae of Botswana pointed out recently that for as long as LGBT people are kept in the shadows, there cannot be an effective public health program to tackle HIV and AIDS. Well, that holds true for other challenges as well.

The third, and perhaps most challenging, issue arises when people cite religious or cultural values as a reason to violate or not to protect the human rights of LGBT citizens. This is not unlike the justification offered for violent practices towards women like honor killings, widow burning, or female genital mutilation. Some people still defend those practices as part of a cultural tradition. But violence toward women isn't cultural; it's criminal. Likewise with slavery, what was once justified as sanctioned by God is now properly reviled as an unconscionable violation of human rights.

In each of these cases, we came to learn that no practice or tradition trumps the human rights that belong to all of us. And this holds true for inflicting violence on LGBT people, criminalizing their status or behavior, expelling them from their families and communities, or tacitly or explicitly accepting their killing.

Of course, it bears noting that rarely are cultural and religious traditions and teachings actually in conflict with the protection of human rights. Indeed, our religion and our culture are sources of compassion and inspiration toward our fellow human beings. It was not only those who've justified slavery who leaned on religion, it was also those who sought to abolish it. And let us keep in mind that our commitments to protect the freedom of religion and to defend the dignity of LGBT people emanate from a common source. For many of us, religious belief and practice is a vital source of meaning and identity, and fundamental to who we are as people. And likewise, for most of us, the bonds of love and family that we forge are also vital sources of meaning and identity. And caring for others is an expression of what it means to be fully human. It is because the human experience is universal that human rights are universal and cut across all religions and cultures.

The fourth issue is what history teaches us about how we make progress towards rights for all. Progress starts with honest discussion. Now, there are some who say and believe that all gay people are pedophiles, that homosexuality is a disease that can be caught or cured, or that gays recruit others to become gay. Well, these notions are simply not true. They are also unlikely to disappear if those who promote or accept them are dismissed out of hand rather than invited to share their fears and concerns. No one has ever abandoned a belief because he was forced to do so.

Universal human rights include freedom of expression and freedom of belief, even if our words or beliefs denigrate the humanity of others. Yet, while we are each free to believe whatever we choose, we cannot do whatever we choose, not in a world where we protect the human rights of all.

Reaching understanding of these issues takes more than speech. It does take a conversation. In fact, it takes a constellation of conversations in places big and small. And it takes a willingness to see stark differences in belief as a reason to begin the conversation, not to avoid it.

But progress comes from changes in laws. In many places, including my own country, legal protections have preceded, not followed, broader recognition of rights. Law have a teaching effect. Laws that discriminate validate other kinds of discrimination. Laws that require equal protections reinforce the moral imperative of equality. And practically speaking, it is often the case that laws must change before fears about change dissipate.

Many in my country thought that President Truman was making a grave error when he ordered the racial desegregation of our military. They argued that it would undermine unit cohesion. And it wasn't until he went ahead and did it that we saw how it strengthened our social fabric in ways even the supporters of the policy could not foresee. Likewise, some worried in my country that the repeal of "Don't Ask, Don't Tell" would have a negative effect on our armed forces. Now, the Marine Corps Commandant, who was one of the strongest voices against the repeal, says that his concerns were unfounded and that the Marines have embraced the change.

Finally, progress comes from being willing to walk a mile in someone else's shoes. We need to ask ourselves, "How would it feel if it were a crime to love the person I love? How would it feel to be discriminated against for something about myself that I cannot change?" This challenge applies to all of us as we reflect upon deeply held beliefs, as we work to embrace tolerance and respect for the dignity of all persons, and as we engage humbly with those with whom we disagree in the hope of creating greater understanding.

A fifth and final question is how we do our part to bring the world to embrace human rights for all people including LGBT people. Yes, LGBT people must help lead this effort, as so many of you are. Their knowledge and experiences are invaluable and their courage inspirational. We know the names of brave LGBT activists who have literally given their lives for this cause, and there are many more whose names we will never know. But often those who are denied rights are least empowered to bring about the changes they seek. Acting alone, minorities can never achieve the majorities necessary for political change.

So when any part of humanity is sidelined, the rest of us cannot sit on the sidelines. Every time a barrier to progress has fallen, it has taken a cooperative effort from those on both sides of the barrier. In the fight for women's rights, the support of men remains crucial. The fight for racial equality has relied on contributions from people of all races. Combating Islamaphobia or anti-Semitism is a task for people of all faiths. And the same is true with this struggle for equality.

Conversely, when we see denials and abuses of human rights and fail to act, that sends the message to those deniers and abusers that they won't suffer any consequences for their actions, and so they carry on. But when we do act we send a powerful moral message. Right here in Geneva, the international community acted this year to strengthen a global consensus around the human rights of LGBT people. At the Human

Rights Council in March, 85 countries from all regions supported a statement calling for an end to criminalization and violence against people because of their sexual orientation and gender identity.

At the following session of the Council in June, South Africa took the lead on a resolution about violence against LGBT people. The delegation from South Africa spoke eloquently about their own experience and struggle for human equality and its indivisibility. When the measure passed, it became the firstever UN resolution recognizing the human rights of gay people worldwide. In the Organization of American States this year, the Inter-American Commission on Human Rights created a unit on the rights of LGBT people, a step toward what we hope will be the creation of a special rapporteur.

Now, we must go further and work here and in every region of the world to galvanize more support for the human rights of the LGBT community. To the leaders of those countries where people are jailed, beaten, or executed for being gay, I ask you to consider this: Leadership, by definition, means being out in front of your people when it is called for. It means standing up for the dignity of all your citizens and persuading your people to do the same. It also means ensuring that all citizens are treated as equals under your laws, because let me be clear—I am not saying that gay people can't or don't commit crimes. They can and they do, just like straight people. And when they do, they should be held accountable, but it should never be a crime to be gay.

And to people of all nations, I say supporting human rights is your responsibility too. The lives of gay people are shaped not only by laws, but by the treatment they receive every day from their families, from their neighbors. Eleanor Roosevelt, who did so much to advance human rights worldwide, said that these rights begin in the small places close to home—the streets where people live, the schools they attend, the factories, farms, and offices where they work. These places are your domain. The actions you take, the ideals that you advocate, can determine whether human rights flourish where you are.

And finally, to LGBT men and women worldwide, let me say this: Wherever you live and whatever the circumstances of your life, whether you are connected to a network of support or feel isolated and vulnerable, please know that you are not alone. People around the globe are working hard to support you and to bring an end to the injustices and dangers you face. That is certainly true for my country. And you have an ally in the United States of America and you have millions of friends among the American people.

The Obama Administration defends the human rights of LGBT people as part of our comprehensive human rights policy and as a priority of our foreign policy. In our embassies, our diplomats are raising concerns about specific cases and laws, and working with a range of partners to strengthen human rights protections for all. In Washington, we have created a task force at the State Department to support and coordinate this work. And in the coming months, we will provide every embassy with a toolkit to help improve their efforts. And we have created a program that offers emergency support to defenders of human rights for LGBT people.

This morning, back in Washington, President Obama put into place the first U.S. Government strategy dedicated to combating human rights abuses against LGBT persons abroad. Building on efforts already underway at the State Department and across the government, the President has directed all U.S. Government agencies engaged overseas to combat the criminalization of LGBT status and conduct, to enhance efforts to protect vulnerable LGBT refugees and asylum seekers, to ensure that our foreign assistance promotes the protection of LGBT rights, to enlist international organizations in the fight against discrimination, and to respond swiftly to abuses against LGBT persons.

I am also pleased to announce that we are launching a new Global Equality Fund that will support the work of civil society organizations working on these issues around the world. This fund will help them record facts so they can target their advocacy, learn how to use the law as a tool, manage their budgets, train their staffs, and forge partnerships with women's organizations and other human rights groups. We have committed more than $3 million to start this fund, and we have hope that others will join us in supporting it.

The women and men who advocate for human rights for the LGBT community in hostile places, some of whom are here today with us, are brave and dedicated, and deserve all the help we can give them. We know the road ahead will not be easy. A great deal of work lies before us. But many of us have seen firsthand how quickly change can come. In our lifetimes, attitudes toward gay people in many places have been transformed. Many people, including myself, have experienced a deepening of our own convictions on this topic over the years, as we have devoted more thought to it, engaged in dialogues and debates, and established personal and professional relationships with people who are gay.

This evolution is evident in many places. To highlight one example, the Delhi High Court decriminalized homosexuality in India two years ago, writing, and I quote, "If there is one tenet that can be said to be an underlying theme of the Indian constitution, it is inclusiveness." There is little doubt in my mind that support for LGBT human rights will continue to climb. Because for many young people, this is simple: All people deserve to be treated with dignity and have their human rights respected, no matter who they are or whom they love.

There is a phrase that people in the United States invoke when urging others to support human rights: "Be on the right side of history." The story of the United States is the story of a nation that has repeatedly grappled with intolerance and inequality. We fought a brutal civil war over slavery. People from coast to coast joined in campaigns to recognize the rights of women, indigenous peoples, racial minorities, children, people with disabilities, immigrants, workers, and on and on. And the march toward equality and justice has continued. Those who advocate for expanding the circle of human rights were and are on the right side of history, and history honors them. Those who tried to constrict human rights were wrong, and history reflects that as well.

I know that the thoughts I've shared today involve questions on which opinions are still evolving. As it has happened so many times before, opinion will converge once again with the truth, the immutable truth, that all persons are created free and equal in dignity and rights. We are called once more to make real the words of the Universal Declaration. Let us answer that call. Let us be on the right side of history, for our people, our nations, and future generations, whose lives will be shaped by the work we do today. I come before you with great hope and confidence that no matter how long the road ahead, we will travel it successfully together. Thank you very much.

Critical Thinking

1. Do you agree with Hillary Clinton that the Universal Declaration of Human Rights should apply to LGBT people?
2. What actions does Clinton advocate at this time?
3. Where is the Obama Administration on this issue?

Create Central

www.mhhe.com/createcentral

Internet References

Human Rights and Humanitarian Assistance
www.etown.edu/vl/humrts.html

Human Rights Watch
http://www.hrw.org

Sociology—Study Sociology Online
http://edu.learnsoc.org

Sociology Web Resources
http://www.mhhe.com/socscience/sociology/resources/index.htm

Sociosite
http://www.topsite.com/goto/sociosite.net

Socioweb
http://www.topsite.com/goto/socioweb.com

Clinton, Hillary Rodham, "Free and Equal in Dignity and LGBT Rights," Speech or Remarks, December 6, 2011.

Unit 2

UNIT

Prepared by: Kurt Finsterbusch, *University of Maryland, College Park*

Problems of the Political Economy

Since the political system and the economy interpenetrate each other to a high degree, it is now common to study them together under the label political economy. The political economy is the most basic aspect of society, and it should be studied first. The way it functions affects how problems in other areas can or cannot be addressed. Here, we encounter issues of power, control, and influence. It is in this arena that society acts corporately to address the problems that are of public concern. It is important, therefore, to ascertain the degree to which the economic elite control the political system. The answer determines how democratic America is. Next, we want to know how effective the American political economy is. Can government agencies be effective? Can government regulations be effective? Can the economy be

effective? Can the economy make everyone, and not just the owners and top administrators, prosper and be happy?

The first section of this unit covers the political system. The most basic issue is the extent that the economic elite and major corporations control the government. If their control is tight, then democracy is a sham. The following section includes topics such as the degree that the governing institutions can provide for the common good, the question of whether American organizations and institutions have gotten so big that they have become unaccountable, and what should be done about the welfare system. The next section deals with the type of capitalism that is dominate today, the devolution of the relations between capitalism and labor, and the general conditions of the working class. The final section covers urbanism and immigration policy.

Article   Prepared by: Kurt Finsterbusch, *University of Maryland, College Park*

Those Nutty Nullifiers

Formerly fringe ideas are going mainstream in some states.

NINA BURLEIGH

Learning Outcomes

After reading this article, you will be able to:

- Describe the attitudes toward government that are common to many militia groups and espoused by many republican office holders.

- Analyze the thesis that extreme right wing fringe ideas have gone mainstream.

- Explain why the political culture has evolved to its present state.

Republican presidential candidates gathered last month at the Oklahoma City Cox Conference Center, just a few blocks from the site of what was the Alfred R. Murrah Federal Building. Two decades ago, anti-government militia sympathizer Timothy McVeigh blew it up in what he called an act of war against the U.S. government. It was the worst crime of domestically bred terrorism in American history. McVeigh was executed in 2001, but since then, some of his militia ideals have gone mainstream and even been introduced as laws in many states, including Oklahoma.

Legislators in dozens of states have submitted proposals to nullify or block federal laws—a longtime goal of militias. These have included exempting states from federal gun laws and educational standards, as well as, of course, Obamacare. That doesn't make these anti-federal statutes part of McVeigh's madness, but Republican politicians now often echo conspiracy theories once relegated to troglodyte pamphlets. And several states have passed laws making gold a currency—a step toward returning to the gold standard—even though currency is a federal responsibility.

When Cliven Bundy engaged in an armed standoff with Bureau of Land Management agents in 2014, after a federal court order demanded he get his cattle off federal land, as he hadn't paid grazing fees for 20 years, several of the current Republican presidential candidates sided with the outlaw. As armed militia members converged in Nevada to protect Bundy, Senator Ted Cruz of Texas called the events "the unfortunate and tragic culmination of the path President Obama has set the federal government on." Rick Perry, then the governor of Texas, said: "I have a problem with the federal government putting citizens in the position of having to feel like they have to use force to deal with their own government." Mike Huckabee opined: "There is something incredibly wrong when a government believes that some blades of grass that a cow is eating is [such] an egregious affront to the government of the United States that we would literally put a gun in a citizen's face and threaten to shoot him over it."

Tarso Ramos, executive director of Political Research Associates, which tracks right-wing extremism, says these and other formerly fringe ideas mainstreamed after McVeigh's assault—just not right away. "The Oklahoma City bombing had a sobering effect for a while," he says. "Then, with the election of Obama, you get a whole new wave of Patriot [militia] activity and a new variant of conspiracy-ism, including the birther stuff and the idea that Obama is an agent of powerful elites."

The surge in fringe activism was so dramatic after Obama's election that the Department of Homeland Security issued a warning in 2009 predicting that right-wing extremists would multiply and "the consequences of their violence [could be] more severe." The report was withdrawn after an outcry by conservatives.

Militia sympathizers today have the ears of many Republican politicians. Texas Governor Greg Abbott vowed to keep watch on the U.S. military this spring as it runs a series of war games called Jade Helm 15. Some Texans sensed an armed federal takeover of the Lone Star State and demanded action. Cruz said of their fears, "I understand the reason for concern and uncertainty, because when the federal government has not demonstrated itself to be trustworthy in this administration, the natural consequence is that many citizens don't trust what it is saying."

The nullifiers fear Washington and the United Nations. Anti-U.N. anxiety dates back to the John Birch Society, but today some of those doing the raving are lawmakers. State legislators and local officials have passed dozens of laws barring implementation of Agenda 21, a nonbinding 1992 U.N. white paper about environmental sustainability. President George H.W. Bush and the leaders of 177 other nations signed it.

Twenty years later, the Republican National Committee in 2012 denounced Agenda 21 in a resolution as a "destructive and insidious scheme" that would impose "socialist/communist redistribution of wealth." Cruz, a presidential candidate, claims Agenda 21 would "abolish" golf courses and paved roads. Last year, Oklahoma lawmakers passed an Agenda 21 nullification law.

Conservatives are also using the 10th Amendment—which reserves powers for the states not mentioned in the rest of the Bill of Rights and the Constitution—to audaciously challenge federal authority. In 2004, a Montana gun enthusiast named Gary Marbut found another use for the 10th Amendment: pushing a bill exempting guns manufactured and retained in Montana from federal regulation. The bill in 2009 became a law called the Firearms Freedom Act, which declared that federal gun laws did not apply. A half-dozen other states soon followed suit. A survey by ProPublica in 2012 found that 37 states have since passed laws circumventing federal gun laws and 12 states are considering so-called Second Amendment Preservation Acts, which would nullify federal gun laws altogether. In some cases, the state laws have criminalized federal agents who try to enforce the federal laws. Versions of that twist passed in Kansas, Alaska and Idaho.

Besides freeing guns from Washington's control, there are bills nullifying Obamacare, the National Security Agency, and Common Core State Standards, as well as federal laws on environmental standards, marijuana, and tracking license plates. The federal government is "diving off into areas unchecked that they're not supposed to be involved in," said Montana state Representative Krayton Kerns, who introduced a bill in 2013 to limit the ability of local police to help enforce federal laws. "Not only is it our right in state legislatures to do this, it's our obligation to do it," Kerns told NBC News. "Somebody's got to put a 'whoa' on it." Oklahoma Attorney General Scott Pruitt is such a nullification enthusiast that he created a separate "Federalism Unit" devoted to fighting federal government "abuses of power."

Oklahoma joined Utah and Arizona last summer in giving a glimmer of hope to fans of another goal of the militia world—returning America to the gold standard. In 2014, Oklahoma made it law that "gold and silver coins issued by the United States government are legal tender in the State of Oklahoma." Similar proposals are being pushed in at least a dozen states.

When I asked Oklahoma Governor Mary Fallin about the gold currency law she signed, she deferred to her press secretary, Alex Weintz. He later emailed to say the governor's counsel reads the law as one that would help gold investors—not necessarily promote the use of gold as money. But Michael Boldin, founder of the libertarian Tenth Amendment Center, writes that by passing the law, Oklahoma "took the first step towards following the tender requirements of the Constitution and nullifying the Federal Reserve's near-monopoly on money."

There are some intriguing similarities between the current political climate and that of the mid-'90s, when McVeigh gathered up the fertilizer for his Ryder truck bomb. Back then, as now, a Democratic president presided over an improving American economy, and his popularity provoked the fear and loathing of an edge of the right-wing political spectrum contemplating—and occasionally engaging in—armed resistance.

Then, as now, the number of anti-government armed resistance groups was at a watermark high. According to the Southern Poverty Law Center (SPLC), the amount of "Patriot" militias peaked at 858 in 1996, just after McVeigh killed 168 people, including children, in the heart of Oklahoma City. The militia tally fell almost immediately—a consequence, analysts say, of shame over the horrific act, followed by new fears of Islamic terrorism, which in the minds of some militia members made the American government look like the lesser of two evils.

Then came Obama. Since his election in 2008, the number of anti-government extremist groups tracked by the SPLC has risen to another record high, 874.

Ramos says he and his colleagues believe the difference now is that fringe rage is being channeled into a larger right-wing populist movement. "The Tea Party represents this coalition between those working in the formal system and those focused outside—white nationalists who depict Obama with a Hitler mustache," Ramos says. "What's happening now is a little hard to say, but there are strong indicators that the forces that redirected a lot of that energy into the formal arena of politics do not hold the sway that they once did. The ability of formal politics to deliver sufficiently to appease the most hardline elements at the base almost never succeeds in the long run."

To suggest that today's tyranny rhetoric bears any link to McVeigh-style violence provokes outrage among conservatives, and Wichita State University political scientist Neal Allen, who has studied nullification laws past and present, says the politically active new-model nullifiers do differ from their anti-government precursors. "There is a lot of distance between Timothy McVeigh and attempts by state government to block or limit federal power, not least because Timothy McVeigh was coming from a clearly racist position," he says.

Allen says the most tangible problem with the GOP's absorption of all this extremist rhetoric and goals is not that it encourages more violence but that it obstructs the normal ebb and flow of politics. When politicians court a base that believes the federal government is the enemy, it becomes nearly impossible to negotiate. Judging by the gridlocked committee rooms of the Capitol, that metaphorical truck bomb has already detonated in the heart of the American political process.

Critical Thinking

1. Analyze the impact that the nullifiers are having on the American political process.
2. Analyze why the Federal government is seen by many Americans as the enemy.

Internet References

New American Studies Web
https://blogs.commons.georgetown.edu/vkp/
Social Science Information Gateway
http://www.ariadne.ac.uk/issue2/sosig
Sociology—Study Sociology Online
http://edu.learnsoc.org/
Sociology Web Resources
http://www.mhhe.com/socscience/sociology/resources/index.htm
Sociosite
http://www.topsite.com/goto/sociosite.net
Socioweb
http://www.topsite.com/goto/socioweb.com

Article

Prepared by: Kurt Finsterbusch, *University of Maryland, College Park*

Finding the Common Good in an Era of Dysfunctional Governance

THOMAS E. MANN AND NORMAN J. ORNSTEIN

Learning Outcomes

After reading this article, you will be able to:

- Understand the role of the government according to the Constitution.

- Be able to compare what the Constitution says about the role of government and the present state of affairs.

From Federalist No. 1 on, the framers of the American political system showed a deep concern about the role of government as a trustee of the people, grappling with questions about the power, structural stability, and credibility of government. In that first Federalist paper, Alexander Hamilton defended a vigorous role for government: "[It] will be equally forgotten that the vigor of government is essential to the security of liberty; that, in the contemplation of a sound and well-informed judgment, their interests can never be separated; and that a dangerous ambition more often lurks behind the specious mask of zeal for the rights of the people than under the forbidding appearance of zeal for the firmness and efficiency of government."[1]

In Federalist No. 46, James Madison wrote, "The federal and state governments are in fact but different agents and trustees of the people, constituted with different powers and designed for different purposes."[2] And in Federalist No. 62, Madison, outlining and defending the special role of the Senate, reflected at length on the need for stable government and the danger of mutable policy: "[G]reat injury results from an unstable government. The want of confidence in the public councils damps every useful undertaking, the success and profit of which may depend on a continuance of existing arrangements."[3]

Stable government, to Madison, included an underlying and enduring legitimacy in the legislative process. This meant both a disciplined government that did not spew out a plethora of unnecessary and careless laws, and a government that did not produce contradictory laws or reversals of laws so frequently that citizens questioned the content and legitimacy of the standing policies affecting their lives. Madison wrote in Federalist No. 62 of mutable policy: "It will be of little avail to the people, that the laws are made by men of their own choice, if the laws be so voluminous that they cannot be read, or so incoherent that they cannot be understood; if they be repealed or revised before they are promulgated, or undergo such incessant changes that no man, who knows what the law is today, can guess what it will be tomorrow."[4]

Madison ended Federalist No. 62 with a warning that resonates today: "But the most deplorable effect of all is that diminution of attachment and reverence which steals into the hearts of the people, toward a political system which betrays so many marks of infirmity, and disappoints so many of their flattering hopes. No government, any more than an individual, will long be respected without being truly respectable; nor be truly respectable without possessing a certain portion of order and stability."[5]

The actions and functions of government, a vibrant political process and system, were thus essential for the common good of a society. The framers saw several challenges peculiar to the new American country. It was, as they wrote, an "extended republic," a huge geographic expanse and a society containing dramatically diverse populations, including people living in rural areas so remote that they literally might not see other human beings for months, and others living in urban areas far more densely packed than today's Manhattan. How could the new government build consensus and legitimacy around policies that would affect all citizens, in light of their different interests, lifestyles, and backgrounds? The demands of the American political system differed from those in Britain, a much smaller and far more homogeneous culture and society. Instead of a parliamentary system, the framers carefully constructed a system that would be practicable and desirable for their nation, built around the following elements:

Debate and deliberation. The legislative branch was called Congress—not parliament. This was not simply a different word, but reflective of a different approach to governance. The word *congress* comes from the Latin word *congredi,* meaning to come together; *parliament* comes from the French word *parler,* meaning to talk. In a parliament, the legislators vote on a program devised by the government; the majority members reflexively vote for it, the minority members reflexively vote against. Citizens accept the legitimacy of the actions, even if they do not like them, because within four or five years, they have the opportunity to hold the government accountable at the polls. The minority expresses its power by publicly questioning government actions and intentions during regular periods of "Question Time."

In contrast, the American framers wanted a system in which representatives of citizens from disparate regions would come together and meet face to face, going through extended periods of debate and deliberation across factional and partisan lines. This model would enable the representatives to understand each other's viewpoints and ultimately reach some form of consensus in policy-making. Those who lost out in the deliberative process would be satisfied that they had been given ample time to make their case, adding to the likelihood that they would accept the legitimacy of the decisions made, and communicate that acceptance back to their constituents. Of course, in contrast to a parliament, it was a process that made swift action extremely difficult. But the trade-off was that government power would be constrained and that Americans would be more likely to accept the decisions and implement them fairly and smoothly.

Debate and deliberation could not be limited to governmental actors. For the system to work and be perceived as legitimate, there had to be debate and deliberation among citizens, via local and national "public squares," and in campaigns, where candidates and their partisans could press their cases and voters could weigh the viewpoints and preferences of their alternatives for representation.

Divided powers competing with one another. America's unusual system of the separation of powers did not offer a clean and pure division between the executive, legislative, and judicial branches, nor between the House of Representatives and Senate. Instead, as constitutional scholar Edward Corwin put it, it was an "invitation to struggle" among the branches and chambers. But that invitation to struggle, which anticipated vibrant,

assertive, and proud branches, also was infused with *the spirit of compromise,* as eloquently analyzed by Amy Gutmann and Dennis Thompson in this volume and in their recent book on the subject.[6] A political system with separation of powers and separate elections for House, Senate, and president could easily have institutions at loggerheads. The system, and the culture supporting it, required safeguards to enable the government to act when necessary and desirable, without getting caught in stalemate or gridlock.

Regular order. To make the processes work and to foster legitimacy, legislative, and executive procedures had to be regularized and followed. This would in turn enable real debate by all lawmakers, opportunity for amendments, openness and reasonable transparency, and some measure of timeliness. Executive actions, including crafting and implementing regulations to carry out policy, would also require elements of transparency, responsiveness to public concerns, and articulated purpose. Similarly, judicial actions would have to allow for fairness, access to legal representation, opportunities for appeal, and a parallel lack of arbitrariness.

Avenues to limit and punish corruption. Public confidence in the actions of government—a sense that the processes and decisions reflect fairness and enhance the common good—demands that the cancer of corruption be avoided or at least constrained. If small groups of special interests or wealthy individuals can skew decisions in their favor, it will breed cynicism and destroy governmental legitimacy. Thus, it is necessary to find ways to constrain the role of money in campaigns, to build transparency around campaign finance and lobbying, to discourage "old boy networks" and revolving doors, to investigate and prosecute bribery, and to impeach and remove government officials who commit high crimes and misdemeanors, which include corrupt behavior.

On all these fronts, there is ample reason to be concerned about the health and function of America's current political institutions. Of course, no political system operates exactly as intended. Politics and policy-making are inherently messy, occurring at the intersection of power, money, and ambition, and leading to temptations and imperfections. We have been immersed in these processes in Washington for more than 43 years, and we have observed frequent governmental failures, deep tensions, and challenges to the political system—from profound societal divisions over wars like Vietnam to the impeachment proceedings against two presidents. But those challenges were modest compared to what we see today: a level of political dysfunction clearly greater than at any point in our lifetimes.

Fundamentally, the problem stems from a mismatch between America's political parties and its constitutional system. For a variety of reasons, all recounted in our book *It's Even Worse Than It Looks: How the American Constitutional System Collided With the New Politics of Extremism*, the two major political parties in recent decades have become increasingly homogeneous and have moved toward ideological poles.[7] Combined with the phenomenon of the permanent campaign, whereby political actors focus relentlessly on election concerns and not on problem-solving, the parties now behave more like parliamentary parties than traditional, big-tent, and pragmatic American parties.

Parliamentary parties are oppositional and vehemently adversarial, a formula that cannot easily work in the American political system. The parliamentary mindset has been particularly striking in recent years with the Republican Party, which has become, in its legislative incarnation especially, a radical insurgent, dismissive of the legitimacy of its political opposition. Of course, substantial majorities in the House and Senate, along with the presidency, can give a majority party the opportunity to behave like a parliamentary majority. But that phenomenon, which occurred for Democrats in the first two years of the Obama administration, resulted in major policy enactments but not a smoothly functioning political system. It featured neither a widespread sense of legitimacy nor deep public satisfaction.

Why? The processes of debate and deliberation were disrupted first by the Republicans' unprecedented use of the filibuster and the threat of filibuster as purely obstructionist tools. This deluge was designed to use precious floor time without any serious discussion of the reasons behind the filibusters, or any real debate on differences in philosophy or policy. Second, when Democrats were able to pass legislation, it was against the united and acrimonious opposition of the minority. America's political culture does not easily accept the legitimacy of policies enacted by one party over the opposition of the other— much less the continued, bitter unwillingness of the minority party to accept the need to implement the policies after lawful enactment. But this dynamic, which accompanied the economic stimulus package in 2009, the health care reform law of 2010, and the financial regulation bill in 2010, among others, resulted in greater divisions and public cynicism, not less.

The approach of the minority party for the first two years of the Obama administration was antithetical to the ethos of compromise to solve pressing national problems. The American Recovery and Reinvestment Act of 2009, a plan which included $288 billion in tax relief, garnered not one vote from Republicans in the House. The Affordable Care Act, essentially a carbon copy of the Republican alternative to the Clinton administration's health reform plan in 1994, was uniformly opposed by Republican partisans in both houses. A bipartisan plan to create a meaningful, congressionally mandated commission to deal with the nation's debt problem, the Gregg/Conrad plan, was killed on a filibuster in the Senate; once President Obama endorsed the plan, seven original Republican co-sponsors, along with Senate Republican Leader Mitch McConnell, joined the filibuster to kill it. McConnell's widely reported comment that his primary goal was to make Barack Obama a one-term president—a classic case of the permanent campaign trumping problem-solving—typified the political dynamic.

The succeeding midterm election brought a backlash against the status quo—which meant divided government once Republicans captured a majority in the House of Representatives. As a result, the 112th Congress had the least productive set of sessions in our lifetimes, enacting fewer than 250 laws, more than 40 of which were concerned with naming post offices or other commemoratives.[8] The major "accomplishment" of the 112th Congress was the debt limit debacle, which marked the first time the debt limit had been used as a hostage to make other political demands. The result was not just the first ever downgrade in America's credit, but another blow to the public's assessment of its government's capacity to act on behalf of the common good.

The 2012 elections were in most respects a clear expression of public will. President Obama earned reelection with a majority of popular votes, as did Democrats in elections for the House and in the 33 contests for the Senate. But in the House, a concentration of Democratic voters in high-density urban areas, contributing to a more efficient allocation of Republican voters across congressional districts, and a successful partisan gerrymander in the redistricting process left Republicans with a majority of seats, and hence control. Despite the election, the dysfunction in the policy process continued in the succeeding lame duck session of Congress, as efforts to resolve America's fiscal problems before a January 1, 2013, deadline were thwarted until after the deadline had passed. House Speaker John Boehner was himself undermined by members of his own party when he tried to devise an alternative to the president's plan. In this case, a substantial share of safe House Republican seats were immune to broader public opinion and to their own Speaker, but were more sensitive to threats from well-financed challenges in their next primaries—from the Club for Growth and other ideological organizations—and to incendiary comments from radio talk show hosts and cable television commentators popular among Republican voters in their districts.

Tribal politics and vehement adversarialism has also led to deterioration of the regular order. In recent years, there have been more and more closed rules in the House, denying opportunities for amendments from the minority, and more uses of a majority tactic in the Senate called "filling the amendment tree," in which the majority leader precludes amendments, usually as a way to forestall or limit the impact of filibusters.

There have been more omnibus bills, pooling action across areas because of the increased difficulty in getting legislation enacted; and fewer real conference committees to iron out differences between bills passed by each house of Congress. There have been fewer budget resolutions adopted and appropriations bills passed; fewer authorizations of programs and agencies; and less oversight of executive action. Fewer treaties have gained the two-thirds vote needed for ratification in the Senate, leading to more executive actions. There have been more holds and delays in the Senate in executive nominations. All of these pathologies lead to more acrimony inside Congress and between Congress and the executive, and a diminished sense of confidence by Americans in their political and policy institutions.

At the same time, the administration of elections has been politicized. Partisan legislatures have passed stringent voter ID laws to narrow the vote; several of these laws have been thrown out by courts for targeting or unfairly affecting minorities. In other cases, shortened voting hours and restrictions on early voting, in states such as Florida and Ohio, were also aimed at constraining minority voters. Fortunately, the 2012 election was not close; had it been more like the 2000 election, it is very likely that it would have further reduced public trust in the fundamentals of democratic elections.

The world of money and politics has also taken an alarming turn toward at least the appearance of corruption, of democracy driven by big money and large interests. A combination of factors—the Supreme Court's *Citizens United* decision, an appeals court decision called *SpeechNow,* a Federal Election Commission that is unable or unwilling to enforce campaign finance laws, and an Internal Revenue Service that allows the operation of faux social-welfare organizations set up to influence elections but not required to disclose donors—has given wealthy individuals, corporations, and other entities an overweening influence on elections and on the policy process. If super PACs did not determine the outcome of the presidential election, their impact did expand as one moved down through Senate and House elections and on to state, local, and judicial elections. In states like Kansas, North Carolina, and Arkansas, large donations from a handful of individuals and groups targeted moderate Republicans and replaced them with reactionary conservatives, creating more division and polarization, not to mention politicians beholden to those whose money put them in power.

Organizations such as the American Legislative Exchange Council (ALEC) have used large and often anonymous contributions from corporations and individuals to write laws, including the voter ID laws and laws favoring the corporate sector, that many state legislatures have simply enacted as written, obviating their independent role. And inside Congress, many

lawmakers have told us about the intimidating effect that occurs when a lobbyist tells them that if they do not support a bill or amendment, they might face a multimillion dollar independent attack days or weeks before the election, which they will be unable to counter due to a lack of time or fundraising limitations. Such threats can result in the passage of bills or amendments without any money even being spent. By any reasonable standard, this is corruption.

All of this exhibits a level of dysfunction in American political institutions and processes that is dangerous to the fundamental legitimacy of decisions made by policy-makers, not to mention the ability of those policy-makers to act at all. Tribal politics at the national level has metastasized to many states and localities, and has affected the broader public as well. The glue that binds Americans together is in danger of eroding. What can be done about these problems?

There is no easy answer, no panacea. The problems are as much cultural as structural. But if structural change inside and outside Washington cannot solve the problems, it can ameliorate them, and perhaps also begin to change the culture.

One strategy for structural change is to accept the emergence of parliamentary-style polarized parties and try to adapt our political institutions to operate more effectively in that context. This is easier said than done. Eliminating or constraining the Senate filibuster would give unified party governments a better shot at putting their campaign promises into law.[9] But separate elections for the presidency and Congress, as well as the midterm congressional elections, often conspire to produce divided party government, which has become more a basis of parliamentary opposition and obstruction than consensus-building and compromise. Shifting more power to the presidency, which is already under way, may produce more timely and coherent policies but at a considerable cost to deliberation, representation, and democratic accountability. A president is, of course, elected by the entire nation. Especially on national security issues, Americans are willing to tolerate and even embrace many unilateral presidential actions; think Grenada and Abbottabad. But America's political culture has ingrained in the public a sense that legitimate policies more often call for some form of broad leadership consensus and institutional buy-in. A series of unilateral actions by the president would not necessarily result in public acceptance of the decisions as being made for the common good. The same can be said for other forms of delegation, from Congress to fed-like independent agencies, or boards that encourage more expert and evidence-based decision-making that is at least somewhat removed from the clash of polarized parties. Each of these ideas has some limited promise, but none can be the basis of constructively reconciling a fundamental mismatch between parliamentary-like political parties and the American constitutional system.

Another approach emphasizes trying to bring the warring parties together: by reaching for consensus through increased social interaction (the House experiment with civility retreats); encouragement of or pressure on politicians to come together to make a deal (Fix the Debt); the mobilization of centrists in the citizenry to create political space for more collegial and collaborative policy-making (No Labels); the use of outside bipartisan groups to map policy solutions that split the differences between the polarized parties (Committee for a Responsible Federal Budget); and the support of independent presidential candidates or third parties to lay claim to the allegedly abandoned political "center" (Americans Elect). These efforts by and large seek to create a spirit of compromise, an atmosphere of civility and mutual respect, and a focus on problem-solving— outcomes which are indeed commendable.

But we believe that these well-intentioned efforts are limited by the strength and reach of party polarization, which is buttressed not only by genuine ideological differences among elected officials, but also by like-minded citizens clustered in safe districts, committed activists, a partisan media, a tribal culture, interest groups increasingly segregated by party, a party-based campaign funding system that now encompasses allegedly independent groups, and a degree of parity in party strength that turns legislating into strategic political campaigning. Most of these efforts also suffer from an unwillingness to acknowledge the striking asymmetry between today's political parties, which in the process gives a pass to obstructionist and dysfunctional behavior.

A more promising strategy of reform is to bring the Republican Party back into the mainstream of American politics and policy as the conservative, not radical, force. Ultimately, this is the responsibility of the citizenry. Nothing is as persuasive to a wayward party as a clear message from the voters. The 2012 election results and the widespread speculation of the diminishing prospects of the Republican coalition in presidential elections may be the start of that process. But it can be boosted and accelerated by the groups discussed above speaking clearly and forthrightly about the damage caused to constructive public policy by tax pledges, debt limit hostage-taking, the abuse of the filibuster, climate change denial, the demonization of government, and ideological zealotry. The mainstream press could also do its part by shedding its convention of balancing the conflicting arguments between the two parties at the cost of obscuring the reality. Voters cannot do their job holding parties and representatives accountable if they do not have the necessary information. Some in the media think it is biased or unprofessional to discuss the many manifestations of our asymmetric polarization. We think it is simply a matter of collecting the evidence and telling the truth.

More significant, for both parties, would be to enlarge the electorate to dilute the overweening influence of narrow, ideologically driven partisan bases that dominate party primaries. As a result, these bases have an outsized role in choosing candidates, who often do not reflect the views of their broader constituencies; and as a means of heading off primary challenges, the bases can intimidate lawmakers searching for compromise or a common good into moving away from solutions. Meanwhile, the enlarged influence of party bases pushes campaign operatives and candidates away from broader appeals and toward strategies to turn out one's own base (often by scaring them to death), and to suppress the other side's base. The politics of division trump the politics of unity.

To counter this set of problems, we propose adoption of the Australian system of mandatory attendance at the polls, where voters who do not show up (they do not have to vote for specific candidates, but can cast unmarked ballots) and do not have a written excuse are subject to modest fines, the equivalent of a parking ticket. This system moved Australian turnout from around 55 percent, similar to the United States, to over 90 percent.[10] Most important, it changed Australian campaign discourse. Politicians of all stripes have told us that when they know that their own base will turn out en masse, and will be balanced by the other party's base, they shift their efforts to persuading voters in the middle. That means talking less about wedge issues, like abortion or guns, and more about larger issues like education and jobs; and it means using less of the fiery or divisive rhetoric that excites base voters but turns off those in the middle.

Another option is to expand the use of open primaries and combine them with preference voting. Several states, including California, now use open primaries, in which all candidates from all sides run together; the top two finishers go on the ballot for the general election. Add in preference voting, whereby voters rank their choices in order of preference (something also done in Australia), and it reduces the chances of an extreme candidate winning a top-two finish because multiple nonextreme candidates divide the votes of the more populous, moderate electorate. Another advantage of an open primary is that lawmakers who cast contentious votes would be less intimidated by threats of a primary challenge funded by ideological organizations if they knew the primary electorate would be expanded beyond a small fringe base. If we could combine these changes with redistricting reform, using impartial citizen commissions to draw district lines as we have seen operate in states like Iowa and California, we might get somewhere.

Of course, the enhanced leverage that smaller groups possess over the sentiments of the larger populace has other roots, including especially the post—*Citizens United* campaign finance world. When groups like the Club for Growth, wealthy individuals, or "social welfare" organizations funded by anonymous sources threaten lawmakers with massive negative campaigns sprung in the final weeks of the election season, or threaten to finance primary opponents against them, it gives immense leverage to the well-heeled few against the viewpoints of the many. Absent a new Supreme Court, a multiple public match for contributions from small donors would give additional leverage to the broader population.

The pull toward tribal politics and away from a focus on the common good has also been shaped by the emergence of tribal media, via cable television and talk radio. The tribal media have established lucrative business models built on apocalyptic rhetoric and divisive messages that guarantee regular audiences within select demographics. These business models have emerged in large part because of the dramatic technological changes that have created hundreds or thousands of alternative information outlets, which are amplified by the emergence of social media. All of this has devastated the concept of a public square, where most Americans could get their information, share a common set of facts, and debate vigorously what to do about common problems. Having real debate and deliberation at the public level, much less the governmental level, depends on sharing a common set of facts and assumptions.

Recreating a public square is a Herculean task given the contemporary media and technology landscape. But it must be attempted. Public media would be the best venue; finding a way to fund a public/private foundation that would focus on innovative ways to use public media for straightforward analysis and discourse, including vigorous debate based on common understanding of the facts, should be a priority here. One way to do so would be to apply a rental fee to broadcasters and others for their use of the public airwaves, in return for erasure of the public-interest requirements that now have little impact.[11]

Most of these changes will be hard to implement in the short run. The best we can hope for is a more tempered Republican Party willing to do business (that is, deliberate, negotiate, and compromise without hostage-taking or brinksmanship) with their Democratic counterparts. Over the long haul, both political parties in the United States need to depolarize to some degree. The parties may maintain clear differences in philosophy and policy, to be sure, but they must also cultivate enough agreement on major issues to permit the government to work as designed. The parties must also serve an electorate that shares a common vision and common facts, even with sharp differences in philosophy, lifestyles, and backgrounds. Despite the obstacles, we must think big about changing the structures and the culture of our partisan government and populace; the stakes are high.

Notes

1. Alexander Hamilton, "Federalist No. 1," *The Federalist Papers,* http://thomas.loc.gov/home/histdox/fed_01.html.

2. James Madison, "Federalist No. 46," *The Federalist Papers,* http://thomas.loc.gov/home/histdox/fed_46.html.

3. James Madison, "Federalist No. 62," *The Federalist Papers,* http://thomas.loc.gov/home/histdox/fed_62.html.

4. Ibid.

5. Ibid.

6. See Amy Gutmann and Dennis Thompson, *The Spirit of Compromise: Why Governing Demands It and Campaigning Undermines It* (Princeton, N.J.: Princeton University Press, 2012).

7. See Thomas E. Mann and Norman J. Ornstein, *It's Even Worse Than It Looks: How the American Constitutional System Collided With the New Politics of Extremism* (New York: Basic Books, 2012).

8. Amanda Terkel, "112th Congress Set To Become Most Unproductive Since 1940s," *The Huffington Post,* December 28, 2012, http://www.huffingtonpost.com/2012/12/28/congress-unproductive_n_2371387.html.

9. For more on this topic, see Norman J. Ornstein, "A Filibuster Fix," *The New York Times,* August 27, 2010, http://www.aei.org/article/politics-and-public-opinion/legislative/afilibuster-fix/.

10. Australian Electoral Commission, "Who Voted in Previous Referendums and Elections," October 26, 2012, http://www.aec.gov.au/Elections/Australian_Electoral_History/Voter_Turnout.htm. Compulsory voting was implemented in Australia in 1924.

11. For in-depth discussion of the recreation of a public square, see Norman J. Ornstein with John C. Fortier and Jennifer Marsico, "Creating a Public Square in a Challenging Media Age: A White Paper on the Knight Commission Report on *Informing Communities: Sustaining Democracy in the Digital Age,*" American Enterprise Institute White Paper, June 23, 2011, http://www.knightcomm.org/wp-content/uploads/2011/06/CreatingaPublicSquare.pdf.

Critical Thinking

1. Why is the US government currently dysfunctional according to the authors?

2. What does the common good mean and why is the government not providing it very well today?

3. What should the United States do to fix this problem?

Create Central

www.mhhe.com/createcentral

Internet References

National Center for Policy Analysis
www.ncpa.org

New American Studies Web
www.georgetown.edu/crossroads/asw

Sociology—Study Sociology Online
http://edu.learnsoc.org

Sociology Web Resources
http://www.mhhe.com/socscience/sociology/resources/index.htm

Sociosite
http://www.topsite.com/goto/sociosite.net

Socioweb
http://www.topsite.com/goto/socioweb.com

THOMAS E. MANN, a Fellow of the American Academy since 1993, is the W. Averell Harriman Chair and Senior Fellow in Governance Studies at the Brookings Institution. He previously served as the Director of Governmental Studies at Brookings and as the Executive Director of the American Political Science Association. His publications include *It's Even Worse Than It Looks: How the American Constitutional System Collided With the New Politics of Extremism* (with Norman J. Ornstein, 2012), *The Broken Branch: How Congress is Failing America and How to Get It Back on Track* (with Norman J. Ornstein, 2006), and *Party Lines: Competition, Partisanship and Congressional Redistricting* (2005).

NORMAN J. ORNSTEIN, a Fellow of the American Academy since 2004, is Resident Scholar at the American Enterprise Institute for Public Policy Research. He also writes the weekly column "Congress Inside Out" for *Roll Call*. His publications include *It's Even Worse Than It Looks: How the American Constitutional System Collided With the New Politics of Extremism* (with Thomas E. Mann, 2012), *The Broken Branch: How Congress is Failing America and How to Get It Back on Track* (with Thomas E. Mann, 2006), and *The Permanent Campaign and Its Future* (edited with Thomas E. Mann, 2000). He is chair of the Academy's Stewarding America project.

Article

Prepared by: Kurt Finsterbusch, *University of Maryland, College Park*

Kludgeocracy in America

STEVEN M. TELES

Learning Outcomes

After reading this article, you will be able to:

- Explain the complexity and incoherence of our government.

- Analyze the problems of compliance costs.

- Discuss the problems of kludgeocracy in the areas of education and health care.

I n recent decades, American politics has been dominated, at least rhetorically, by a battle over the size of government. But that is not what the next few decades of our politics will be about. With the frontiers of the state roughly fixed, the issues that will define our major debates will concern the complexity of government, rather than its sheer scope.

With that complexity has also come incoherence. Conservatives over the last few years have increasingly worried that America is, in Friedrich Hayek's ominous terms, on the road to serfdom. But this concern ascribes vastly greater purpose and design to our approach to public policy than is truly warranted. If anything, we have arrived at a form of government with no ideological justification whatsoever.

The complexity and incoherence of our government often make it difficult for us to understand just what that government is doing, and among the practices it most frequently hides from view is the growing tendency of public policy to redistribute resources upward to the wealthy and the organized at the expense of the poorer and less organized. As we increasingly notice the consequences of that regressive redistribution, we will inevitably also come to pay greater attention to the daunting and self-defeating complexity of public policy across multiple, seemingly unrelated areas of American life, and so will need to start thinking differently about government.

Understanding, describing, and addressing this problem of complexity and incoherence is the next great American political challenge. But you cannot come to terms with such a problem until you can properly name it. While we can name the major questions that divide our politics—liberalism or conservatism, big government or small—we have no name for the dispute between complexity and simplicity in government, which cuts across those more familiar ideological divisions. For lack of a better alternative, the problem of complexity might best be termed the challenge of "kludgeocracy."

A "kludge" is defined by the Oxford English Dictionary as "an ill-assorted collection of parts assembled to fulfill a particular purpose . . . a clumsy but temporarily effective solution to a particular fault or problem." The term comes out of the world of computer programming, where a kludge is an inelegant patch put in place to solve an unexpected problem and designed to be backward-compatible with the rest of an existing system. When you add up enough kludges, you get a very complicated program that has no clear organizing principle, is exceedingly difficult to understand, and is subject to crashes. Any user of Microsoft Windows will immediately grasp the concept.

"Clumsy but temporarily effective" also describes much of American public policy today. To see policy kludges in action, one need look no further than the mind-numbing complexity of the health care system (which even Obamacare's champions must admit has only grown more complicated under the new law, even if in their view the system is now also more just), or our byzantine system of funding higher education, or our bewildering federal–state system of governing everything from welfare to education to environmental regulation. America has chosen to govern itself through more indirect and incoherent policy mechanisms than can be found in any comparable country.

The effects of this approach to public policy are widespread and profound. But to understand how to treat our government's ailment, we first need to understand the symptoms, the character, and the causes of that ailment.

The Costs of Complexity

The most insidious feature of kludgeocracy is the hidden, indirect, and frequently corrupt distribution of its costs. Those costs can be put into three categories—costs borne by individual citizens, costs borne by the government that must implement the complex policies, and costs to the character of our democracy.

The price paid by ordinary citizens to comply with governmental complexity is the most obvious downside of kludgeocracy. For example, one of the often overlooked benefits of the Social Security program—which represents an earlier era's approach to public policy—is that recipients automatically have taxes taken out of their paychecks, and, then without much effort on their part, checks begin to appear upon retirement. It's simple and direct. By contrast, 401(k) retirement accounts, IRAs, state-run 529 plans to save for college costs, and the rest of our intricate maze of incentivized-savings programs require enormous investments of time, effort, and stress to manage responsibly. But behavioral economics—not to mention common sense—makes clear that few investors are willing to make these investments, and those who do are hampered by basic flaws in decision-making.

Health insurance, too, is made nearly impossible to understand by the interplay of federal and state rules that only insurance companies fully understand. In fact, a recent study by George Loewenstein found that only 14% of people with health insurance could correctly answer basic questions about the definitions of deductibles and co-pays. Understanding the rules and the options involved requires an enormous amount of time (and often money); failing to understand them can be even more costly. Straightforward social insurance would dramatically reduce the transaction costs in the system—not to mention the rents paid to asset managers and health insurers—while depending far less on the free time and capacity for calculation of ordinary citizens.

The transaction costs of the tax code are just as impressive and disturbing. The American tax code is almost certainly the most complicated in the Western world. The Internal Revenue Service's taxpayer advocate estimates that in 2008 the direct and indirect costs of complying with that complexity amount to $163 billion each year. Included in that cost are the remarkable 6.1 billion hours a year that American individuals and businesses spend complying with the filing requirements of the tax code.

The web of deductions and credits also pushes up marginal tax rates for everyone: The National Commission on Fiscal Responsibility and Reform (more commonly known as the Simpson-Bowles commission) estimated that eliminating all tax deductions other than the Earned Income Tax Credit, the child tax credit, and a few others would allow marginal rates on middle-income taxpayers to be cut in half and those on the top earners to be cut by about a third, without reducing government revenue. It's highly unlikely we could achieve anything like that level of tax simplicity, but it is a striking illustration of just how much we are paying in higher marginal tax rates to preserve our kludgey tax system.

The compliance costs that kludgeocracy imposes on governments are just as impressive as those that confront private citizens. The complexity of our grant-in-aid system makes the actual business of governing difficult and wasteful, sometimes with tragic results. As Melissa Junge and Sheara Krvaric argue in a recent report published by the American Enterprise Institute, the multiplicity of overlapping and bewildering federal programs for K-12 education creates a compliance mentality among school leaders, making them wary of new ideas and pushing them to focus on staying on the right side of the rules rather than on improving their schools.

Similarly, in a 2007 paper published in *Public Administration Review,* Martha Derthick showed that the tangled joint administration of the flood-protection system in New Orleans played a key role in the system's failure during Hurricane Katrina. Derthick quotes Maine senator Susan Collins as having found that there was "confusion about the basic question of who is in charge of the levees"—the type of problem that is common as a consequence of our pervasive, kludgey interweaving of federal and state responsibilities. Because administering programs through inter-governmental cooperation introduces pervasive coordination problems into even rather simple governmental functions, the odds are high that programs involving shared responsibility will suffer from sluggish administration, blame-shifting, and unintended consequences.

Kludgeocracy is also a significant threat to the quality of our democracy. The complexity that makes so much of American public policy vexing and wasteful for ordinary citizens and governments is also what makes it so easy for organized interests to profit from the state's largesse. The power of such interests varies in direct proportion to the visibility of the issue in question. As Mark Smith argues in his book *American Business and Political Power,* corporations are most likely to get their way when political issues are out of the public gaze. It is when the "scope of conflict" expands that the power of organized interests is easiest to challenge. That is why business invests so much money in politics—to keep issues *off* the agenda.

Policy complexity is valuable for those seeking to extract rents from government because it makes it hard to see just who is benefitting and how; complexity so thoroughly obscures the actual mechanism of political action that it is difficult to mobilize against. That is why businesses prefer to receive benefits through the tax code or through obscure regulatory advantages rather than in straightforward handouts from the state. Politicians may posture against "corporate welfare," but kludgeocracy makes it hard for voters to see how much business profits from government, which makes it difficult to effectively target their anger. As a consequence, that anger diffuses onto our system of government as a whole, leading to a loss of trust and to skepticism of the possibility that the public sector could ever be an effective instrument of the public good.

Policy complexity also benefits interests other than business. For example, the federal government has become increasingly involved in funding K-12 education over the last 50 years. But instead of just handing over big checks to school districts on the basis of need, the federal government showers the states with dozens of small programs. There is not much evidence that federal funding has improved the quality of schooling, and yet the morass of federal grant programs in primary and secondary schooling survives and grows. It persists because the system's sheer complexity makes it easier to organize a supportive coalition for federal education funding. When that funding is divided into individual grants targeted to specific constituencies, those recipients will act to secure their particular aid. The complicated structure of federal education policy has thus created an army of Lilliputians who lock in the multitude of grants even though the work of keeping those grants coming often makes it harder to actually run school districts. Kludgeocracy ensures that what William Bennett and Chester Finn have called the "blob" of education interests wins, while the capacity of the federal government to actually improve educational opportunity diminishes.

Neither party is immune to the costs of kludgeocracy—the interests of both liberals and conservatives are ill-served by policy complexity. It hurts conservatives by concealing the true size of government. As Suzanne Mettler argues in her important recent book *The Submerged State,* our complex, hidden welfare state obscures government action, leading citizens to mistake as "private" programs that are in fact pervasively shaped by government. Mettler's research shows, for instance, that Americans who benefit from education-savings programs run through the tax code (like 529 plans) do not experience them as government at all, despite the fact that they redistribute huge sums of money. The same is true for the deduction for employer-provided health care and a variety of other pieces of the welfare state hidden in the tax and regulatory codes. This perpetuates the national myth of radical individualism and independence while creating the impression that only other, less deserving people draw upon government largesse. Pursuing public goals through regulation and litigation does not eliminate the costs of government, but it does make it hard for citizens to see the costs of public action, which appear in the prices of goods and services rather than on the government's books. Perversely, pushing inevitable government action into these lower-profile mechanisms results in trading a type of government institution that is well understood and relatively easy to control for one that conservatives have always found difficult to rein in. We know, for instance, what the government spends down to the dollar and have a reasonably centralized means of allocating it, but serious estimates of the costs of litigation (like that encouraged by laws such as the Americans with Disabilities Act) vary by orders of magnitude, and

the individuals imposing the costs are often hundreds of very imperfectly coordinated judges and juries.

Kludgeocracy also harms liberalism, by creating both the image and the reality that government is incompetent and corrupt. The complexity of the tax code, for instance, facilitates tax cheating and creative accounting, and along with it the impression that tax compliance is lower than it actually is. Much of the legitimacy of the law and the willingness of citizens to contribute to public goods rests on the perception that others are doing their share. Complexity eats away at this perception, which is crucial for maintaining public support for the expansion of the kinds of state activity that liberals favor.

Because the current political environment nurtures suspicion of government action, liberal politicians have developed the sneaky habit of finding back doors through which to advance their goals. This habit has had a corrosive effect on liberalism. In searching for ways to promote public activism in spite of institutional and cultural resistance, liberals have developed a pattern of dishonesty and evasiveness instead of openly making the argument for a muscular role for government. This is why, despite liberalism's legislative victories, very few recent liberal policies have successfully provided platforms from which to launch new rounds of policy innovation.

So while liberals are harmed by the opacity of kludgeocracy's successes, conservatives are hurt by the inscrutability of its failures. In both cases, the complexity of government is not good for our politics. And the fact that so much of our welfare state is jointly administered—either inter-governmentally or through contracting with private agents—makes it hard for Americans to attribute responsibility when things go wrong, thus leading to blame being spread over the government in general, rather than targeted precisely where it could do some good. Complexity thereby leads to diffuse cynicism, an attitude certain to undermine good citizenship—of either the conservative or liberal form—in our republic.

The Causes of Kludgeocracy

The costs of kludgeocracy, therefore, are considerable. Addressing the problem, however, requires that we understand why American politics turns to kludgey solutions so regularly. A condition as chronic as kludgeocracy inevitably results from many causes at once, but the key interlocking causes in this instance are the structure of American government institutions, the public's ambivalent and contradictory expectations of government, and the emergence of a "kludge industry" that supplies a constant stream of complicated, roundabout policy solutions.

We were all taught in school that American institutions were designed to constrain the growth of government. This is, of course, why some on the right tend to defend our founding institutional heritage, while many liberals as far back as the Progressive era have voiced considerable skepticism about the Constitution's architecture. But there are reasons to question the idea that federalism and the separation of powers limit the growth of government: A great deal of political-science scholarship shows that when we look beyond spending and taxation and focus on the policy tools that the United States has historically relied on more heavily—such as regulation, litigation, and tax expenditures—the activity of the American state is not significantly more limited than those of other industrialized countries.

American institutions do, in fact, serve to constrain the most direct forms of government taxing and spending. But having done so, they do not dry up popular or special-interest demands for government action, nor do they eliminate the desire of politicians to claim credit for new government activity. When public demand cannot be addressed directly, it is met instead in complicated, unpredictable ways that lead to far more complex legislative solutions.

The most obvious reason why American institutions generate policy complexity is our system's numerous veto points. The separation of powers means that any proposal must generate agreement at three different stages—each house of Congress and the president. But opportunities for vetoes turn out to be more extensive than the simple text of the Constitution would imply. Most legislation has to pass through separate subcommittee and committee stages, each of which presents opportunities for legislators to stymie action. Many ambitious proposals are considered by Congress under "multiple referrals," in which more than one single committee is given jurisdiction. This multiplies the number of veto points, as we saw with the Affordable Care Act, which had to pass through five separate committees in Congress. Finally, the super-majority requirement for breaking a filibuster in the Senate, combined with the intense partisanship that accompanies most major policy reforms, means that any single member can stall the progress of a piece of legislation, and a cohesive minority can kill it.

A superficial analysis would predict that this proliferation of veto points would lead to inaction, generating a systematic libertarian bias. In practice, however, every veto point functions more like a toll booth, with the toll-taker able to extract a price in exchange for his willingness to allow legislation to keep moving. Most obviously, the toll-taker gets to add pork-barrel projects for his district or state in exchange for letting legislation move onto the next step. This increases the cost of legislation, even if, as John Ellwood and Eric Patashnik have argued, it might be a reasonable price to pay for greasing the wheels of a very complicated legislative machine.

But the price of multiple veto points is much larger than an accounting of pork-barrel projects would suggest. First, many of our legislative toll-takers have a vested interest in the status quo. In exchange for their willingness to allow a bill to proceed,

therefore, they often require that legislation leave their favored programs safe from substantive changes. Consequently, new ideas have to be layered over old programs rather than replace them—the textbook definition of a policy kludge. Second, the need to gain consent from so many actors makes attaining any degree of policy coherence difficult at best. Finally, the enormous number of veto points that legislation must now pass through gives legislative strategists a strong incentive to pour everything they can into giant omnibus legislation. The multiplication of veto points, therefore, does not necessarily stop legislation from passing, but it does considerably raise its cost and, more importantly, its complexity.

America's federal system of government also does its part to add to policy complexity. In a purely federal system, in which governmental functions were clearly differentiated between the national and state governments, federalism would not translate directly into complexity. But that is not American federalism as it is currently practiced.

Many of our major social programs were created when the South, and to a lesser degree urban political machines, exercised a veto over expansions of federal spending that failed to leave the details of administration to local officials. The decline of these regional power centers did not, however, lead to a more streamlined national pattern of policy development. Even as the government expanded in the 1960s and '70s in areas ranging from the environment to education to health care, the federal government and the states continued to share the duties of governing in a complex web of responsibilities. While states and localities actually administer essentially all programs in these domains, the federal government is deeply involved as a funder, regulator, standard-setter, and evaluator. The result is the complicated "marble-cake federalism" structure that characterizes almost all domestic policy in the United States, making clear lines of responsibility hard to establish.

American political culture and ideology have also, in sometimes obscure ways, contributed to kludgeocracy. One of the clearest findings in the study of American public opinion is that Americans are ideological conservatives and operational liberals. That is, they want to believe in the myth of small government while demanding that government address public needs and wants regarding everything from poverty and retirement security to environmental protection and social mobility.

This ambivalence in expectations creates a durable bias in the actual outputs of American government. The easiest way to satisfy both halves of the American political mind is to create programs that hide the hand of government, whether it is through tax preferences, regulation, or litigation, rather than operating through the more transparent means of direct taxing and spending.

Housing is perhaps the most striking and perverse example of this pattern of government growth through seemingly non-governmental means. The 30-year, fixed interest-rate mortgage exists on a mass scale only in the United States, and only because of massive distortions of the free market by government-sponsored entities like Fannie Mae. Added on top of that are the deduction of mortgage interest from taxable income—the third-largest exclusion in the tax code—and the delay in capital-gains taxation on home sales when another home is purchased. Taken together, the tax code and government-sponsored enterprises amount to a massive housing-welfare state. And although it delivers benefits to many citizens, this set of programs is fundamentally regressive—vastly favoring people in the highest tax brackets and artificially increasing the prices of homes, thus increasing barriers for first-time home buyers.

A similar pattern can be found in government subsidies of retirement savings (for example, through IRAs and 401(k) plans), employer-provided health insurance, and student loans. All of these aspects of what Christopher Howard has called our "hidden welfare state" fail to serve their putative goals while also redistributing upward. IRAs and 401(k)s, for example, do not appear to actually increase personal savings; instead, their main effect is to cause wealthier investors to shift their savings from taxable to untaxed accounts (from which, again, the wealthy gain the greatest savings since their tax rates are highest). But these programs are not generally thought of as "big government" because they operate primarily by channeling resources to mutual-fund companies, health insurers, and the housing market through the tax code.

Where our government does spend, it increasingly does so indirectly. The myth of what George Mason University's Michael Greve calls "our federalism" creates a bias toward sending money to the states, even though the cash always comes with a laundry list of regulations and requirements attached.

The strategic decisions of conservatives over the last 50 years have abetted the growth of such public misunderstanding of government. A half-century ago, conservatives found they were unable to stop the growth of the federal government's role in education, but, as Patrick McGuinn has shown, what they were able to do was force that funding to come in the form of multiple small programs, on the theory that these would be less likely to grow than a simple, clean handover of cash to poor districts. They turned out to be wrong—this division of funding helped facilitate the growth of small, powerful interest groups that have made it virtually impossible to untangle our ineffective web of federal education programs.

More recently, Republicans have faced similar questions regarding how to deal with an irrepressible public demand for government action, and in many cases they have decided to concede on the condition that the growth of government cut their allies in on the action. During the George W. Bush administration, Republicans sued for peace over the popular cry for a prescription-drug benefit for the elderly, but had enough power to ensure that the program would not be administered through the existing Medicare system. Instead, as Kimberly Morgan and Andrea Campbell show in *The Delegated Welfare State*, conservatives insisted as a condition of their cooperation that the program be administered through privately run plans.

This was more than just a payoff to business interests. Republicans hoped that by sidestepping the Medicare bureaucracy, they could make the system more cost-efficient and encourage better consumer and provider decisions. Just as important, however, it would also cut the chains connecting citizens and government, leading the elderly to associate the improvement in their standard of living with private providers instead of the state. If they couldn't stop the program entirely, then programmatic complexity would make it difficult for Democrats to take credit for it, and make it less likely that the program would increase citizens' support for government overall.

Similar stories could be told in a variety of other policy areas, where liberals got bigger government but conservatives funneled benefits to business, keeping liberals from taking political credit. The result of the last three decades of ideological trench warfare is that the American public got a more active, but also incoherent, ineffective, and politically intractable state.

Finally, kludgeocracy is now self-generating, as its growth has created a "kludge industry" that feeds off the system's appetite for complexity. In the name of markets and innovation, and driven by increasingly strict (and often arbitrary) limits on government personnel, the United States has created what public administrators call a "hollow state," in which core functions of government have been hired out to private contractors, operating under the oversight of increasingly overwhelmed civil servants. Christopher McKenna, in his book *The World's Newest Profession*, shows that, for over half a century, management consultants brought in to advise governments (at great expense) have—not surprisingly—recommended a greater role for consultants and contractors.

This army of consultants and contractors then became a lobby for even greater transfer of governmental functions to outsiders—including, as Janine Wedel shows in *Shadow Elite*, the transfer of such core roles as formulating policy recommendations and overseeing contractors. This kludge industry, having pulled the fundamental knowledge needed for government out of the state and into the private sector, has thus made itself nearly indispensable. And with its large, generally non-competitive profits, the kludge industry has significant resources to invest in ensuring that government continues to layer on complex policies, and hence continues to need to purchase more services. As vital as the material interests of consultants and contractors have been in encouraging policy complexity, an important role has also been played by the army of think-tank analysts on all sides of our politics. As the institutional and cultural incentives reinforcing kludgeocracy have gotten ever more intense, the suppliers of policy ideas have generally adapted to kludgeocracy rather than resisting it.

For example, instead of repeatedly making the case for fairly simple and direct mechanisms of social insurance, writers in liberal think tanks have pushed for often bewilderingly complicated policies to increase savings under the banner of "asset-building" strategies. Conservative policy scholars, meanwhile, have seen in the privatization of government's administrative functions a way to reduce the power of the bureaucracy.

Much of the preference for complexity comes from trying, against the background of permanent austerity, to get the equivalent of two dollars in social benefit out of one dollar (or less) in governmental effort. But some of it comes from a preference for clever or innovative policy mechanisms; relatively simple, direct uses of governmental brute force are just not as interesting. Whatever the cause, policy intellectuals are very much a part of the kludge-industry problem.

The Cure for Kludgeocracy

Kludgeocracy is not an accident—it is a predictable consequence of deeply rooted features of the American regime. It would be facile, therefore, to pretend that its baleful effects can be reduced without major (and extremely unlikely) changes in our larger system of government and political values. But institutions can be changed at the margins, values can shift incrementally, and, in any case, knowing what one would do to reverse the problem is helpful if only to think about how to keep the problem from getting any worse.

The deepest cause of kludgeocracy is the structure of American governing institutions, and the incentives that they provide for individual politicians. Any attempt to chip away at policy complexity must involve reducing the number of extra-constitutional veto points in our system. These are not features of the original design of our system of government but are more like barnacles that have built up over time. If anything, removing them would lead to institutions that function in ways that are truer to the founding design.

The first reform that would tend to reduce kludgeocracy would be to eliminate or radically reduce the filibuster in the Senate, which increases the number of members who can demand changes in legislation as the price of their vote. Second, we should reduce multiple referrals to congressional committees, which create extra opportunities for rent seeking and produce policies with fundamentally divergent logics that need to be reconciled with one another (before they even reach a House–Senate conference). Both of these changes would increase the power of the congressional majority, and reduce the power of individual members to demand adjustments that add to policy complexity. A more majoritarian Congress—regardless of which party had the majority—would also be more likely to effectuate wholesale changes in policy, be it to the right or left.

These sorts of institutional changes are hardly unimaginable. In fact, in the last few years the filibuster has faced greater criticism than at any time over the last four decades. And at least in the House, the trend since the Gingrich years has been in the direction of greater power for the majority leadership and less for committees. If the Senate were to become as majoritarian as the House, the institutional hooks that facilitate complexity would be reduced considerably.

Public policies would also become less kludgey if Congress shifted the power over the "micro-design" of policies away from Capitol Hill and toward the agencies that will actually have to administer them once they are passed. This is not a plea for greater delegation of congressional power to the executive. In some ways, it is the opposite. Congress often avoids actually producing a piece of legislation that is worthy of the name—a general, abstract statement of authoritative lawmaking and basic policy design—and instead passes a wave of specific measures unconnected by any general logic. It does too much of what the executive is best equipped to do, and too little of what it actually has the authority to command. Giving the people who will actually have to administer policies greater power over the design of those policies would likely increase their simplicity.

We should also thoroughly reconsider our system of federal grants to the states. Michael Greve recently suggested that we adopt a norm of "one problem, one sovereign." In other words, in policy areas like education or health care, give the problem either to the federal government or to the states to deal with, but don't give it to both. If the federal government wants to expand access to health care, it should pay the bill and administer the program itself. In education, either we should considerably nationalize education (by, for example, creating a national voucher paid for out of tax funds that would go directly to individuals and pre-empt local funding through property taxes) or cut out the complicated web of federal education funding and regulation altogether. A realignment of responsibility for both of these problems is conceivable; we could relieve states of the costs of Medicaid entirely and send education—lock, stock, and barrel—back to the states. This was, in fact, what President Reagan proposed back in the 1980s, and it is still a sound idea.

This is an area where the conservative majority on the Supreme Court could actually generate greater pure nationalism, forcing federal programs to be fully and openly run by the federal government, by establishing rules that make it harder for Democrats to expand federally supported, state-administered social-welfare programs (like Medicaid). Democrats would vociferously object in the short term, but over the long term, constitutional standards like these might actually serve the interests of liberalism as well as conservatism better than the law of anything goes. Democrats would be prevented from proposing policies that, as Suzanne Mettler has shown, actually fail to serve their political interests over the long term by hiding the hand of government when it delivers benefits. And they would be forced to rediscover their capacity to argue transparently for social action in the interest of social justice, rather than trying to come up with ever more complicated kludges.

Another potentially valuable reform would be to change institutional rules in Congress to increase the visibility of policy complexity's costs. Shining a light on the costs of kludgeocracy would encourage more publicly-spirited politicians to seek to minimize them, while their more electorally minded colleagues would be made to worry about being held responsible for them. As the late senator Daniel Patrick Moynihan argued, what counts is what's counted. While Congressional Budget Office deficit scoring powerfully influences politicians as they consider policy options, the large compliance costs associated with our kludgeocracy are uncounted, and thus invisible. Requiring that CBO issue an estimate of governmental and private compliance costs along with its deficit scores may reduce somewhat the incentives to lower deficit estimates by substituting more complicated alternatives for straightforward programs. Moreover, the addition of an extra "distributive score" to CBO estimates would reveal that kludgey policies typically redistribute upward rather than downward. Mettler has shown in experimental work that tax expenditures are considerably less popular when the fact that they disproportionately benefit the wealthy is made clear.

While institutional change is likely to come incrementally, if at all, a more direct, near-term strategy is an attack on the kludge industry, given that it both lives off of and helps create demand for policy complexity. The best place to start could be the Department of Defense: The growth of the private military over the last few decades has been explosive, and congressional efforts at deficit reduction have put the Pentagon's budget on the chopping block. Increasing the salaries of high-level federal workers throughout the government and reducing caps on their numbers could also go hand in hand with drastically cutting the amounts that agencies can spend on consultants and contractors.

Much of the kludge industry has benefitted from the ideological support it has garnered from Republicans, who have seen the army of consultants and contractors as an attractive alternative to government bureaucrats. But the increasingly populist spirit of the Republican Party may be a signal that this cozy relationship with the kludge industry is coming to an end. Republicans are starting to recognize that companies that receive the vast majority of their business from the government are not really in the private sector at all. Private profits and public risk is hardly a conservative combination, and it is not hard to see how the spirit that has lately led conservatives to question government support for the big banks could be turned against the rest of modern government's corporate dependents.

Going further than just attacking the crony capitalism inherent in kludgeocracy, however, will require deeper reconsiderations of the orthodoxies of both conservatives and liberals. While it is hard to imagine in an era of tax pledges, Republicans convinced that kludgeocracy is a problem will need to rethink their exclusive emphasis on controlling direct federal taxation and spending. Resistance to carbon taxation, for example, has not eliminated pressure for action on global warming; instead it has deflected it into highly inefficient and incomprehensible regulations and subsidies. Limiting growth in federal taxation has redirected pressure for social protection into the hidden welfare state, rather than encouraging greater self-reliance. Trying to stop the growth of nationally administered social and regulatory programs has not led to freer markets; it has only encouraged the spread of complex inter-governmental kludges.

Conservatives might do better to insist that if we are going to have a government of a certain size, it should be national, transparent, and tax funded. There is no way in a democratic polity for the public to get less government than it wants—demand for state action will always yield a supply. But conservatives should insist that voters get only the government they are willing to pay for directly and out in the open, and liberals should not be able to expand government beyond that point through complicated mechanisms that hide the hand of the state. Insisting on constraints that force state action into the open would lead to a government with higher levels of outright taxing and spending, but one that was less sprawling, less intrusive, more democratically accountable, and more transparent than today's kludgeocracy.

Liberals, too, will need to change their thinking in order to claw back kludgeocracy. Perhaps above all, they will need to accept constitutional constraints that they currently identify with conservatism. Two areas in particular come to mind. First, liberals should look more favorably on constitutional interpretations that make joint federal–state programs more difficult to establish and administer. Such interpretations include Chief Justice Roberts's ruling in the 2012 Obamacare cases limiting the penalty on states that fail to join the law's Medicaid expansion.

Second, liberals should also come to accept various quasi-constitutional rules (like those Congress sometimes imposes on itself) establishing super-majority requirements for the creation of any new deductions or credits in the tax code. While these rules make it harder to engage in forms of shadowy government activism, liberals should insist that, in exchange, majoritarian rules govern all other lawmaking. So long as a 60-vote majority is required for any meaningful action in the Senate, the inclination to buy votes with complex kludges to piece together a super-majority is irrepressible. A Congress that operated under rules that restricted *hidden* taxing and spending but enabled more *transparent* forms of both would probably be one that passed fewer, but larger and more effective pieces of major legislation. In the long run, this would be in the interests of both liberals and conservatives, even if they found it frustrating in the short term.

Few of the reforms sketched out above have much of a chance of being enacted at the moment, since the institutions and practices they propose to alter are too deeply entrenched to remove quickly. But there are levers for change short of major institutional reform, the most important of which is a shift in problem definition. Grand "problems" do not naturally appear in politics—it is only through research, discussion, deliberation, and argument that we patch together smaller, individual problems into a complex whole that comes to be defined as a critical "issue." For example, air and water quality, public lands, and toxic waste were all thought of as discrete problems until writers and a nascent movement made "the environment" a problem that politicians were able to discuss as one issue.

Only when Americans give a name to what ails their government, therefore, will we be able to achieve a system that is simpler, more effective, and better for democracy. Introducing kludgeocracy into the public vocabulary as a recognized problem will be an uphill battle. First, ordinary citizens will need help seeing the problem and recognizing its manifestations in their daily lives. When they get frustrated trying to navigate federal education-aid programs, or flustered trying to understand their taxes, or perplexed at the complications of our civil-litigation system, they need to recognize their problem as a part of a larger set of issues that links to other, seemingly unconnected grievances and frustrations. Clarifying such links is the quintessential work of public intellectuals, writers, bloggers, researchers, and entrepreneurial politicians.

Self-Government Worthy of the Name

While it might seem like an uphill climb, a simpler, less kludgey government is an immensely attractive goal, and should appeal to Americans of all parties and ideologies.

Imagine a world in which the tax code was scrubbed clean of byzantine savings incentives and Social Security payments were increased instead; in which tax deductions for health insurance were eliminated and either Medicare was expanded or subsidies for catastrophic insurance in a competitive market were established; in which taxes on pollution were imposed but complicated regulatory and subsidy schemes were thrown out; in which government contractors and consultants were purged and a sharper division was established between federal and state responsibilities; and in which a maze of loans, grants, and subsidies was replaced with vastly more straightforward programs to help Americans pay for college tuition and housing. Imagine a world in which constitutional norms forced government to act directly and transparently or forgo action altogether. Americans would have a government that did fewer, simpler, bigger things, and they would be able to more effectively reward politicians for policy successes and to hold them accountable for failures.

The politics of that world would be neither more "liberal" nor more "conservative" in any simple sense. Government would be bigger and more energetic where it clearly chose to act (and so received public sanction for doing so), but smaller and less intrusive outside of that sphere. Unlike the kludgey mess that neither party seems willing to take on today, that would be a vision of American government worth fighting for.

Critical Thinking

1. What is kludgeocracy, and how do you explain it?
2. Does complexity explain why America makes so many policy mistakes or has so many shortcomings?
3. What steps could be taken to reduce kludgeocracy?

Internet References

New American Studies Web
https://blogs.commons.georgetown.edu/vkp/

Social Science Information Gateway
http://www.ariadne.ac.uk/issue2/sosig

Sociology—Study Sociology Online
http://edu.learnsoc.org/

Sociology Web Resources
http://www.mhhe.com/socscience/sociology/resources/index.htm

Sociosite
http://www.topsite.com/goto/sociosite.net

Socioweb
http://www.topsite.com/goto/socioweb.com

STEVEN M. TELES is an associate professor of political science at Johns Hopkins University. An earlier version of this article was published as a working paper by the New America Foundation's Next Social Contract Initiative and Economic Growth Program.

Article   Prepared by: Kurt Finsterbusch, *University of Maryland, College Park*

Predatory Capitalism: Old Trends and New Realities

C.J. POLYCHRONIOU

Learning Outcomes

After reading this article, you will be able to:

- Understand the evolution of capitalism into its present system of predatory capitalism.

- Be able to explain how globalization has affected the evolution of capitalism.

- Understand the past and present relation of capitalism and labor to each other.

I n seeking to understand the nature of contemporary capitalism, it is important to realize that the whole is indeed greater than the sum of its parts. It is also pertinent that we recognize the importance of structural causality in making sense of contemporary capitalist developments while avoiding methodological reductionism.

Thus, in trying to come to terms with the nature of the beast at hand, a capitalist system running amok, we need to look at the overall structure of the system; that is, we need to comprehend the different constitutive parts of the system that keep it together and running in ways which are harmful to the interests of the great majority of the population, dangerous to democracy and public values, and detrimental to the environment and earth's ecosystem. Focusing on one element of the system while ignoring other things (perhaps because we think that they constitute incidental outcomes or processes of secondary nature) may limit our understanding by creating a flawed perspective about the dynamics and the contradictions of contemporary capitalism and thereby undermine our ability to propose sound and realistic solutions.

Capitalism as a socioeconomic system is neither egalitarian nor democratic

In considering the central question, why contemporary capitalism pursues goals which benefit almost exclusively big capital and the rich (this is the underlying issue behind virtually all recent studies dealing with inequality), it should be clear from the outset that capitalism as a socioeconomic system is neither egalitarian nor democratic. Capitalism is not an economic system designed to cater to the needs of the common folk, and, left to its own devices—especially the financial component—it can wreak havoc on societies. As for the so-called trickle-down theory, or the horse-and-sparrow theory, as John Kenneth Galbraith referred to it[1], it is nothing more than a propaganda tool used by those who seek to justify policies favoring the rich.

Some Notes on the Dynamics and Contradictions of Capitalism

Capitalism represents a specific, historically determined mode of production. It is a ruthless economic system, representing the most advanced form of commodity production. In this system, the extraction of profit is the driving force of capitalist commodity production, with exploitation and inequality representing structural necessities. Capital itself is nothing but a sort of self-expanding value, that is, value that generates surplus value.

The production of surplus value is the fundamental law of capitalism. Capitalist production has as its objective aim and goal not the production of use-values as such, but rather that of surplus value. Under capitalism, it is of course the workers themselves who create new value, which is greater than the value of their labor power. This is the essence of surplus value.

Capital accumulation is an anarchic and contradictory process. The logic of the accumulation of capital leads to enormous wealth (there is no other known economic system which can match capitalism's inherent capacity to generate wealth), on the one hand, and to the relative impoverishment of the working population on the other. Unemployment is a structural element of capitalism. The manifold activities of capitalist accumulation also tend to accelerate the process of the concentration and centralization of capital, eventually giving rise to the dominance of finance capital and to the emergence of financialization as a possible new stage in the evolution of capitalism.[2]

Capitalism is an expansionist socioeconomic system. Capitalist expansion has taken place in the course of history via different venues, ranging from plunder and exploitation, through trade, to investment in industry and the financialization of assets. There is no point in going into details here about the history of global capitalism, but suffice to say that capitalism has a long and brutal history of expansion, exploitation, and injustice, dating back to the 15th century and to the subsequent rise of imperial powers across Europe and North America, with the subjugation and the exploitation of people and resources from the periphery providing the growth engine for the economies of the imperial centers.[3]

It is only in the postwar era that the most destructive tendencies of capitalism are contained (at least inside the advanced capitalist economies), thanks to the spread of progressive economic thinking, the influence of socialism and the power exerted by trade unions. However, since the late 1970s, capitalism is seeking to return with a vengeance to its cruel, brutal, and barbaric past by breaking the social contract and intensifying the rate of exploitation in order to shift increasingly greater amounts of wealth from the bottom to the top.[4] A study released in early 2014 by the British humanitarian group Oxfam International shows that the richest one percent had 65 times the total wealth of the bottom half of the population. Stating the case of inequality in more dramatic terms, the report reveals that the richest 85 individuals on the planet share a combined wealth that is equal to that owned by the bottom half of the world's population.[5]

Along with increasing inequality, mass unemployment is once again displaying itself as an intrinsic feature of capitalism and poverty rates are sharply on the rise. There is a consensus that today's young people in the Western world will be worse off than their parents' generation.[6]

Why is capitalism fouling things up again by returning to the more ugly practices of the past? Is it because today's capitalists are greedier than those of the past? Even if we assume that this rather silly suggestion is true, greed alone can hardly explain away why capitalism is running amok in our own time.

For a convincing answer to the question of why capitalism has embarked on a journey back toward the future (and perhaps in the process is making the money class even greedier), we need to come to terms with the structural changes in the operation of the capitalist economy.

Resurrecting Anarcho-Capitalism

Contemporary capitalism is characterized by a political economy which revolves around finance capital, is based on a savage form of free market fundamentalism and thrives on a wave of globalizing processes and global financial networks that have produced global economic oligarchies with the capacity to influence the shaping of policymaking across nations.[7] As such, the landscape of contemporary capitalism is shaped by three interrelated forces: financialization, neoliberalism and globalization. All three of these elements constitute part of a coherent whole which has given rise to an entity called predatory capitalism.[8] Under this system, as Henry A. Giroux has consistently pointed out, democracy and the social state are under constant attack and "citizens are now reduced to data, consumers and commodities."[9]

In this regard, Pope Francis hit the nail on the head when he described today's capitalism as "a new tyranny."[10] Today's brand of capitalism is particularly antidemocratic and simply incapable of functioning in a way conducive to maintaining sustainable and balanced growth. By waging the most vicious class warfare in the entire postwar period, the economic elite and their allies have managed to roll back progress on the economic and social fronts by resurrecting the predatory, free-market capitalism that immiserated millions in the early twentieth century while a handful of obscenely wealthy individuals controlled the bulk of the wealth.

As indicated in the report on inequality by Oxfam International cited earlier, evidence in support of this dramatic state of affairs has been growing for a number of years, and the latest work to underscore this point, Thomas Piketty's publishing sensation, *Capital in the Twenty-First Century,* does it with such powerful impact that, as Paul Krugman said, writing in *The New York Review of Books,* it may very well "change both the way we think about society and the way we do economics."[11]

But let's take things from the start. The capitalist order we have in place today has its roots in the structural changes that took place in the accumulation process back in the mid-to-late 1970s. The 1970s was a decade of economic slowdown and inflationary pressures in the advanced capitalist world. The crisis, brought about by new technological innovations, declining rates of profit, and the dissolution of the social structures of accumulation that had emerged after World War II, led to sluggish growth rates, high inflation and even higher rates of unemployment, bringing about a phenomenon that came to be known as "stagflation." From a policy point of view, "stagflation" signaled the end of an era in which there was a trade-off between inflation and unemployment (shown by the Phillips curve) and, by extension, the end of the dominance of the Keynesian school of thought.

As with all other capitalist crises in the past, the crisis of the 1970s compelled capital, and the economic elite to restructure the way the capitalist economy had functioned up to that time. The restructuring process unfolded in several ways, which included, among other things, increasing the pace of market liberalization, attacking the traditional welfare state, and the interests of unionized workers in an attempt to eliminate social programs and suppress wages and create greater flexibility in the labor market, respectively, and initiating a new wave of globalization under the aegis of both industrial and financial capital.

The new economic orthodoxy (which came to be known as the "Washington Consensus") called for open markets, deregulation, privatization, labor flexibility, short-term optimization as a more attractive way to ensure competition and growth, low taxation for corporations and the rich, and a minimum welfare state. The desire was to return to an era in which capitalism functioned unfettered by government and social constraints, in other words, back to the age when capital grew by running roughshod over labor.

Indeed, a counterrevolution was under way, and it seemed to be global in nature and scope. The radical paradigm shift in economics was taking place in highly diverse economic environments, ranging from Chile under Augusto Pinochet's reign of terror to liberal democracies in the Anglo-Saxon world (in the UK under Margaret Thatcher and in the United States under Ronald Reagan) and to communist China under Deng Xiaoping. By the mid-1980s, most capitalist nations around the world, including many Western European countries with long traditions with social democratic policies, had shifted from Keynesianism to neoliberalism.

The march to "economic freedom," which is how the neoliberal counterrevolution was celebrated by arch-conservative thinkers (such as Thomas Sowell, for example) captivated by the nonsense of Austrian economics, did not take place on the basis of some abstract entity known as the "free market." On the contrary, it required active intervention by the capitalist state across society and the economy. Indeed, how else was the welfare state going to be reduced and the power of the labor unions weakened? How else could policies be introduced that increased the upward flows of income, created new investment sites, promoted a new wave of privatization and permitted banks and other financial institutions to practice financial chicanery? How else could failed financial institutions be bailed out with public funds if governments and elected officials had not been turned into the minions of the money class?

The capitalist state everywhere resorted to the use of both hard (i.e., repression) and soft (propaganda) power in order to secure the transition to the new economic and social order commanded by finance capital and big business interests. International organizations such as the International Monetary Fund and the World Bank, but also countless nongovernmental organizations throughout the world, were mobilized for the promotion of this goal. The corporate-owned mainstream media and the overwhelming majority of academics and intellectuals also joined the show as cheerleaders of the neoliberal vision.

In sum, the return to predatory capitalism was prompted by a crisis in the workings of the postwar capitalist regime and realized through active political intervention, i.e., class politics, by the capitalist state and international organizations, and the support provided by the intellectual elite and mass media.[12]

On the Links Between Financialization, Neoliberalism, and Globalization

The three pillars on which contemporary capitalism is structured around—financialization, neoliberalism, and globalization—need to be understood on the basis of a structural connectivity model, although it is rather incorrect to reduce one from the other. Let me explain.

The surge of financial capital long predates the current neoliberal era, and the financialization of the economy takes place independently of neoliberalism, although it is greatly enhanced by the weakening of regulatory regimes and the collusion between finance capital and political officials that prevails under the neoliberal order. Neoliberalism, with its emphasis on corporate power, deregulation, the marketization of society, the glorification of profit and the contempt for public goods and values, provides the ideological and political support needed for the financialization of the economy, and the undermining of the real economy. Thus, challenging neoliberalism—a task of herculean proportions given than virtually every aspect of the economy and of the world as a whole, from schools to the workplace and from post offices to the IMF, functions today on the basis of neoliberal premises—does not necessarily imply a break on the financialization processes under way in contemporary capitalist economies. Financialization needs to be tackled on its own terms, possibly with alternative finance systems and highly interventionist policies, which include the nationalization of banks, rather than through regulation alone. In any case, what is definitely needed in order to constrain the destructive aspects of financial capitalism is what the late American heterodox economist Hyman Minsky referred to as "big government." We shall return to Minsky later in the analysis.

The surge of finance capital can be traced at least since the beginning of the twentieth century. In a major study addressing "the economic characteristics of the latest phase of capitalist development,"[13] published in 1910, Rudolf Hilferding, an Austrian-born Marxist economist and main theoretician for the Social Democratic Party of Germany during the Weimar Republic, devoted special attention to the processes of the concentration and centralization of capital, and outlined a theory of imperialism as a necessary development in the evolution of capitalism.[14] In the course of this process he also made it clear that systematic investigation of the role of money and credit, the expansion of capitalist enterprises into corporations and their conversion into corporations was of the outmost importance for the understanding of the evolution of capitalism.

Hilferding demonstrated that the rise of the industrial corporation reflects an objective "change in the function of the industrial enterprise."[15] The industrial corporation, or the joint-stock company, allows anyone in possession of money to become a money capitalist. In effect, what Hilferding was observing was the phenomenon of the separation of ownership of capital from control in the joint-stock company. According to him, this process not only accelerated the concentration of capital, but also provided the joint-stock company with the ability to expand far more rapidly than the individually owned enterprise, thereby leading to the centralization of capital.

For Hilferding, however, it was the emergence of financial institutions and banks, in particular, that truly intensified the processes toward concentration. He stressed that in the mature stage of capitalism, banks, which were quite necessary to the growth of industry, had become fully dominant and directly controlled the economic life of the system. Through its vast resources of liquid capital, banks were able to obtain control of major trusts in industry, since the latter needed idle capital in order to increase and expand the production process. Viewed from this perspective, industrial capital was inextricably intertwined with banking capital and wholly dependent on money capital.

The merging process between industrial and banking capital gives rise to a new form of capital: finance capital. Moreover, the establishment of an intimate relationship between banking capital and industrial capital results in an increased tendency toward the export of capital. The concentration of capital, which leads to monopolization, encourages the export of capital by virtue of the fact that the over-accumulation of capital can no longer find profitable investment opportunities at home.

While it is true that Hilferding mistakenly considered the dependence of industrial capital on banking capital as a permanent state of affairs (the great monopolistic corporations became independent of banking capital and today's large corporations use their own retained profits to finance investment), there can be no mistake that the transition "from the domination

of capital in general to the domination of finance capital"[16] emerged as a key feature of "modern" capitalism even before the outbreak of World War I. Indeed, the Great Depression of the 1930s revealed in unmistaken terms the extent to which finance and financial capitalism had taken central stage, reshaping in a profound way the United States' economy and affecting dramatically developments across the world.

While Hilferding, Lenin, and many other Marxist thinkers provided important insights regarding the evolution of capitalism, the significance of financial arrangements in "modern" capitalism was scrutinized and analyzed most insightfully and more thoroughly perhaps than anyone else in the postwar period by the American heterodox economist Hyman Minsky. Although he focused purely on the domestic economy, Minsky based his analysis on the claim that financial capitalism is inherently unstable, leading inevitably to financial crises as those produced by the stock market crash of 1929.

Relying on both empirical observations and theoretical analysis, Minsky underscored the point that the financial component of capitalism was the single most important aspect behind capitalism's inherent tendencies toward crises. Building upon Keynes' *General Theory,* Minsky wrote:

The capital development of a capitalist economy is accompanied by exchanges of present money for future money. The present money pays for resources that go into the production of investment output, whereas the future money is the "profits" which will accrue to the capital asset owning firms (as the capital assets are used in production). As a result of the process by which investment is financed, the control over items in the capital stock by producing units is financed by liabilities—these are commitments to pay money at dates specified or as conditions arise. For each economic unit, the liabilities on its balance sheet determine a time series of prior payment commitments, even as the assets generate a time series of conjectured cash receipts.[17]

In this manner,

" . . . in a capitalist economy the past, the present, and the future are linked not only by capital assets and labor force characteristics but also by financial relations. The key financial relationships link the creation and the ownership of capital assets to the structure of financial relations and changes in this structure. Institutional complexity may result in several layers of intermediation between the ultimate owners of the communities' wealth and the units that control and operate the communities' wealth."[18]

Minsky's analysis of financial capitalism clearly points the way to the development of the financialization of the economy:

In the modern world, analyses of financial relations and their implications for system behavior cannot be restricted to the liability structure of businesses and the cash flows they entail.

Households (by the way of their ability to borrow on credit cards for big ticket consumer goods such as automobiles, house purchases, and to carry financial assets), governments (with their large floating and funded debts), and international units (as a result of the internationalization of finance) have liability structures which the current performance of the economy either validates or invalidates.[19]

Consistent with both Marx's and Keynes' analysis, and "in spite of the greater complexity of financial relations," Minsky treats profits as a "key determinant of system behavior"[20], with aggregate demand determining profits.

In Minsky's analysis, the role of banks as profit-seeking institutions is granted special attention. Noting that banks realize the importance of innovation in the pursuit of profits (he calls bankers "merchants of debt who strive to innovate in the assets they acquire and the liabilities they market"[21]), thus rejecting the orthodox quantity theory in which the circulation of money is treated as constant, Minsky identified three distinct financing positions: hedge, speculative, and Ponzi.

Hedge financing units are those that can fulfill all of their contractual payment obligations by their cash flows: the greater the weight of equity financing in the liability structure, the greater the likelihood that the unit is a hedge financing unit. Speculative finance units are units that can meet their payment commitments on "income account" on their liabilities, even as they cannot repay the principle out of income cash flows. Such units need to "roll over" their liabilities: (e.g., issue new debt to meet commitments on maturing debt. Governments with floating debts, corporations with floating issues of commercial paper, and banks are typically hedge units.

For Ponzi units, the cash flows from operations are not sufficient to fulfill either the repayment of principle or the interest due on outstanding debts by their cash flows from operations. Such units can sell assets or borrow. Borrowing to pay interest or selling assets to pay interest (and even dividends) on common stock lowers the equity of a unit, even as it increases liabilities and the prior commitment of future incomes. A unit that Ponzi finances lowers the margin of safety that it offers the holders of its debts.[22]

This description of lending is closer to the real world of finance that leads to crises than anything available in the existing literature. For Minsky, it is the stability in the system that breeds instability as investors, banks, and financial institutions become complacent and begin to embark on a riskier approach, which results in rising asset prices and eventually financial crashes when people begin to sell en-masse upon the realization that the accumulated debt cannot be paid off. This development is known as a "Minsky moment."

Minsky's "financial instability hypothesis" provides a useful explanation of financial crises, but also carries practical consequences. Essentially, Minsky felt that the internal contradictions of financial capitalism could be constrained by the establishment of strong institutions. He argued that the reason there had been no financial crises in the first few decades of the postwar era was because of the presence of "big government."[23]

The task of stabilizing financial capitalism's inherent tendency towards instability has clearly been severely undermined since the onset of the neoliberal era, with the global financial crisis of 2008 to 2009 representing just the latest act in a long series of financial crises since 1966[24], and with each new crisis getting bigger and becoming more severe than the previous one. Yet, it is equally clear that financial crises have occurred prior to the installation of a neoliberal regime. Moritz Schularick of the Free University of Berlin identified more than 70 "systemic banking crises" that took place in the past 140 years prior to the global financial crisis of 2008 to 2009.[25] Moreover, because of globalization, "big government" action is restrained and the challenges posed to central banking from globalized finance are quite severe, with financial globalization leading "to growing frequency and severity of systemic financial crises."[26] Thus, globalization is in itself a contributing factor to the spread of financial crises while also providing a greater impetus for the deepening of neoliberalism.

Although finance is at the forefront of globalization, there is hardly an aspect of contemporary life that is not affected by globalization, making it a very elusive concept indeed, while adding new levels of complexity to the task of forming appropriate economic and political responses to a system bent on instability and prone to large-scale crises. Globalization creates new systemic risks[27] which we are simply uncertain how to address given the existing power structure in the global political economy where a plutocracy reigns supreme as national governments have capitulated to the whims of the corporate and financial elite and the formal global governance structure needed is missing. Yet, this is precisely the environment that makes predatory capitalism thrive, and one can be certain that its insatiable appetite for more and more profits will only intensify problems in the years ahead if it is not stopped.

Where to Go from Here

Unsurprisingly, given how dysfunctional and dangerous the neoliberal order has proven to be, proposed solutions for the problems stemming from unfettered capitalism are not in short supply. They extend from short-range (proposals for tax reform in order to close the gap between rich and poor) and medium-range goals (reregulation and even nationalization) to some rather long-range structural reforms (redesigning the architecture of the global financial system). *The Stiglitz Report* is a prime example of the latter set of proposals.[28] Controlling climate change also represents a long-range goal, in fact of vital importance for the stability of any future social and economic order.[29]

Nevertheless, proposals for major reforms that fail to incorporate a vision of alternative social orders must be treated with skepticism. The same goes for approaches that rely purely on reforms undertaken by the elite without citizen involvement and participation. By the same token, progressive forces bent on social change must re-embrace fundamental political principles and courses of social action. Building and sustaining a mass movement remains the best route to challenging the practices of predatory capitalism. However, progressive forces need to stop being constantly on the defensive in order to protect basic and fundamental values from neoliberal jackals and vultures and seek, instead, to sharpen strategic abilities in order to go on the offensive. Narrow ideological blinders must be dropped and joining forces with kindred groups is an absolute necessity in today's world.

Theoretically, we need an eclectic political economy approach which relies on Marxian, Keynesian and post-Keynesian traditions in order to understand contemporary capitalist developments. There are no intellectual giants in the neoliberal tradition. We still need to look to Marx, Keynes, and Minsky for great insights into the true workings of capitalism.

On the political front, the task of recapturing the state would seem to be a necessary first step in the drive of any progressive movement or political party seeking to reestablish balance in the relationship between labor and capital, resurrect democracy, redress social injustice, and reorient the economy toward sustainable and balanced growth. Still, such undertakings are likely to fail if they are pursued in the absence of a solid understanding of the nature of the current system and without having captured the public imagination, with ignorance of political and social developments and activist practices in other advanced capitalist countries and elsewhere around the world, and without a vision towards a new global order. A long-term vision should not stand in the way of pursuing immediate reforms that alleviate human pain and suffering, and short-term goals should not block the imagination from opening up a world of new possibilities for human relations.

As this article may have made clear, a major advantage that predatory capitalism has over alternative social orders, especially in the direction of a truly democratic future where the economic system produces wealth for the benefit of society as a whole is that it has managed to (a) break free from national government control, (b) shift the balance of power between labor and capital overwhelmingly towards the latter, (c) establish ideological hegemony, and (d) globalize the environment in which it operates. The future of a progressive social order probably requires nothing short of the reversal these trends.

Notes

1. "If you feed the horse enough oats, some will pass through to the road for the sparrows," Galbraith quipped in response to Ronald Reagan's supply-side economics. See John Kenneth Galbraith, "Recession Economics." *The New York Review of Books* (February 4, 1982) at http://www.nybooks.com/articles/archives/1982/feb/04/recession-economics/

2. See Costas Lapavitsas, *Profiting Without Producing: How Finance Exploits Us All.* New York: Verso Books, 2013.

3. A classic work on this topic, unrivalled in its scope, narration and clarity, is L. S. Stavrianos's *Global Rift: The Third World Comes of Age.* New York: William Morrow and Co., 1981.

4. See C. J. Polychroniou, "Actually Existing Capitalism: Wrecking Societies for the Benefit of Big Capital and the Super-Rich." *Truthout* (December 12, 2013) at http://truth-out.org/opinion/item/20558-actually-existing-capitalism-wrecking-societies-for-the-benefit-of-big-capital-and-the-super-rich

5. Graeme Wearden, "Oxfam: 85 richest people as wealthy as poorest half of the world." *The Guardian* (January 20, 2014) at http://www.theguardian.com/business/2014/jan/20/oxfam-85-richest-people-half-of-the-world

6. See Daniel Boffey, "Middle-class young 'will fare worse than their parents.'" *The Guardian* (October 12, 2013) at http://www.theguardian.com/society/2013/oct/12/middle-class-young-people-future-worse-parents; also Eugene Steuerle, Signe-Mary McKernan, Caroline Ratcliffe, and Sisi Zhang, "Lost Generations? Wealth Building among Young Americans." Urban Institute (March 2013) at http://www.urban.org/publications/412766.html

7. While the existence of a global capitalist class and its power in influencing government policies across the world is undeniable, the analysis advanced here does not subscribe to the instrumentalist and conspiratorial view of a global elite running the world. What it suggests, instead, is that the links that have been created in the global economy have produced a global plutocracy whose vast wealth and control of major corporations and organizations impact heavily on the shaping of domestic economic and social policies. The way national governments bend over backwards in order to accommodate the needs and wants of big corporations and the global rich via low taxation is but one example of the way this influence is carried out. So is the demand placed on national governments by global financial markets for the adoption of austerity measures when deficits and debt ratios are seen as running out of control. The much revered notion of "competitiveness"— national economies undergoing structural reforms in their labor markets in order to reduce unit labor costs—is yet another example of how the global environment shapes domestic policymaking.

8. See C. J. Polychroniou, "The Political Economy of Predatory Capitalism." *Truthout* (January 12, 2014) at http://truth-out.org/opinion/item/21138-the-political-economy-of-predatory-capitalism

9. Henry Giroux, "Neoliberalism and the Machinery of Disposability." *Truthout* (April 8, 2014) at http://truth-out.org/opinion/item/22958-neoliberalism-and-the-machinery-of-disposability

10. Heather Saul, "'A new tyranny': Pope Francis attacks unfettered capitalism and says rich should share wealth." *The Independent* (November 26, 2013) at http://www.independent.co.uk/news/uk/home-news/pope-francis-unfettered-capitalism-is-a-new-tyranny-and-rich-should-share-wealth-8965045.html

11. Paul Krugman, "Why We're in a New Gilded Age." *The New York Review of Books* (May 8, 2014) at http://www.nybooks.com/articles/archives/2014/may/08/thomas-piketty-new-gilded-age/

12. For an interesting and insightful analysis of the ideological factors leading to the making and consolidation of the neoliberal counterrevolution, see Daniel Stedman Jones, *Masters of the Universe: Hayek, Friedman, and the Birth of Neoliberal Politics.* Princeton, NJ: Princeton University Press, 2012.

13. Rudolf Hilferding, *Finance Capital: A Study of the Latest Phase of Capitalist Development,* edited with an Introduction by Tom Bottomore. London: Routledge & Kegan Paul, 1981), p. 21.

14. The discussion on Hilferding draws freely here from the author's own work titled *Marxist Perspectives on Imperialism: A Theoretical Analysis.* New York: Praeger, 1991, pp. 53–58.

15. Rudolf Hilferding, *Finance Capital,* p. 107.

16. V. I. Lenin, *Imperialism: The Highest Stage of Capitalism,* in *Selected Works* in one volume (New York: International Publishers, 1976), p. 200.

17. Hyman P. Minsky, "The Financial Instability Hypothesis." Working Paper No. 74. Annandale-on-Hudson, New York: Levy Economics Institute (May 1992), pp. 2–3 at http://www.levyinstitute.org/pubs/wp74.pdf

18. Ibid., p. 4.

19. Ibid., pp. 4–5.

20. Ibid., p. 5.

21. Ibid., p. 6.

22. Ibid., p. 7.

23. See Dimitri B. Papadimitriou and L. Randall Wray, "Minsky's Analysis of Financial Capitalism. Working Paper No. 275. Annandale-on-Hudson, New York: Levy Economics Institute (July 1999) at http://www.levyinstitute.org/pubs/wp/275.pdf

24. L. Randall Wray, "The 1966 Financial Crisis: A Case of Minskian Instability?" Working Paper No. 262. Annandale-on-Hudson, New York: Levy Economics Institute, January 1999. Available at SSRN: http://dx.doi.org/10.2139/ssrn.150728.

25. Moritz Schularick, "140 Years of Financial Crises: Old Dog, New Tricks." Freie Universität Berlin (August 2010) at http://www.jfki.fu-berlin.de/faculty/economics/team/Ehemalige_Mitarbeiter_innen/schularick/Old_Dog_New_Tricks_Schularick.pdf?1376087682

26. Piero C. Ugolini, Andrea Schaechter, and Mark R. Stone, "Introduction." In Piero C. Ugolini, Andrea Schaechter, and Mark R. Stone (eds.), *Challenges to Central Banking from Globalized Financial Systems.* Washington, DC.: International Monetary Fund, March 2004.

27. See Ian Goldin and Mike Mariathasan, *The Butterfly Defect: How Globalization Creates Systemic Risks and What to Do About It.* Princeton, NJ.: Princeton University Press, 2014.

28. See Joseph E. Stiglitz, *The Stiglitz Report: Reforming the International Monetary and Financial Systems in the Wake of the Global Crisis.* New York: New Press, 2010.

29. See, for example, Bert Metz, *Controlling Climate Change.* Cambridge: Cambridge University Press, 2012.

Critical Thinking

1. How does current capitalism impact on government?
2. What role does ideology have in current institutional arrangements?
3. Is the current form of capitalism harmful to the economy?

Create Central

www.mhhe.com/createcentral

Internet References

National Center for Policy Analysis
www.ncpa.org
New American Studies Web
www.georgetown.edu/crossroads/asw
Social Science Information Gateway
http://sosig.esrc.bris.ac.uk
Sociology—Study Sociology Online
http://edu.learnsoc.org
Sociology Web Resources
http://www.mhhe.com/socscience/sociology/resources/index.htm
Sociosite
http://www.topsite.com/goto/sociosite.net
Socioweb
http://www.topsite.com/goto/socioweb.com

C.J. Polychroniou is a research associate and policy fellow at the Levy Economics Institute of Bard College and a columnist for a Greek daily national newspaper. His main research interests are in European economic integration, globalization, the political economy of the United States, and the deconstruction of neoliberalism's politico-economic project. He has taught for many years at universities in the United States and Europe and is a regular contributor to *Truthout* as well as a member of *Truthout*'s Public Intellectual Project. He has published several books and his articles have appeared in a variety of journals and magazines. Many of his publications have been translated into several foreign languages, including Greek, Spanish, Portuguese, and Italian. The views expressed in this article do not necessarily represent those of the Levy Economics Institute or those of its board members.

Article

Prepared by: Kurt Finsterbusch, *University of Maryland, College Park*

The Bargain at the Heart of Our Economy Has Frayed

The trend toward growing inequality is not unique to America's market economy. But this increasing equality is most pronounced in our country, and it challenges the very essence of who we are as a people.

BARACK OBAMA

Learning Outcomes

After reading this article, you will be able to:

- Understand how social programs helped build the middle class.

- Understand the complexity of the functioning of society in terms of the many interacting factors that are involved in the evolution of society.

- Begin to consider how the identified economic problems could be addressed.

Well, thank you, Neera, for the wonderful introduction and sharing a story that resonated with me. There were a lot of parallels in my life, and probably resonated with some of you.

You know, over the past 10 years, the Center for American Progress has done incredible work to shape the debate over expanding opportunity for all Americans. And I could not be more grateful to CAP not only for giving me a lot of good policy ideas but also giving me a lot of staff. My friend John Podesta ran my transition. My chief of staff, Denis McDonough, did a stint at CAP. So you guys are obviously doing a good job training folks.

I also want to thank all of the members of Congress and my administration who are here today for the wonderful work that they do. I want to thank Mayor Gray and everyone here at THEARC for having me.

This center, which I've been to quite a bit and have had a chance to see some of the great work that's done here, and all the nonprofits that—that call THEARC home offer access to everything from education to health care to a safe shelter from the streets, which means that you're—you're harnessing the power of community to expand opportunity for folks here in DC. And your work reflects a tradition that runs through our history, the belief that we're greater together than we are on our own. And—and that's what I've come here to talk about today.

Now, over the last two months, Washington's been dominated by some pretty contentious debates, I think that's fair to say. And between a reckless shutdown by congressional Republicans in an effort to repeal the Affordable Care Act and, admittedly, poor execution on my administration's part in implementing the latest stage of the new law, nobody has acquitted themselves very well these past few months. So it's not surprising that the American people's frustrations with Washington are at an all-time high.

But we know that people's frustrations run deeper than these most recent political battles. Their frustration is rooted in their own daily battles, to make ends meet, to pay for college, buy a home, save for retirement. It's rooted in the nagging sense that no matter how hard they work, the deck is stacked against them. And it's rooted in the fear that their kids won't be better off than they were.

They may not follow the constant back-and-forth in Washington or all the policy details, but they experience, in a very personal way, the relentless decades long trend that I want to spend some time talking about today, and that is a dangerous and growing inequality and lack of upward mobility that has jeopardized middle-class America's basic bargain that if you work hard, you have a chance to get ahead. I believe this is the defining challenge of our time: making sure our economy works for every working American. That's why I ran for president. It was the center of last year's campaign. It drives everything I do in this office.

And I know I've raised this issue before, and some will ask why I raise the issue again right now. I do it because the outcomes of the debates we're having right now, whether it's health care or the budget or reforming our housing and financial systems—all these things will have real practical implications for every American. And I am convinced that the decisions we make on these issues over the next few years will determine whether or not our children will grow up in an America where opportunity is real.

Now, the premise that we're all created equal is the opening line in the American story. And while we don't promise equal outcomes, we've strived to deliver equal opportunity—the idea that success doesn't depend on being born into wealth or privilege, it depends on effort and merit. And with every chapter we've added to that story, we've worked hard to put those words into practice.

It was Abraham Lincoln, a self-described poor-man's son who started a system of land-grant colleges all over this country so that any poorman's son could go learn something new. When farms gave way to factories, a rich-man's son named Teddy Roosevelt fought for an eight-hour work day, protections for workers and busted monopolies that kept prices high and wages low.

When millions lived in poverty, FDR fought for Social Security and insurance for the unemployment and a minimum wage. When millions died without health insurance, LBJ fought for Medicare and Medicaid. Together we forged a new deal, declared a war on poverty and a great society, we built a ladder of opportunity to climb and stretched out a safety net beneath so that if we fell, it wouldn't be too far and we could bounce back.

And as a result, America built the largest middle class the world has ever known. And for the three decades after World War II, it was the engine of our prosperity. Now, we can't look at the past through rose-colored glasses. The economy didn't always work for everyone.

Racial discrimination locked millions out of opportunity. Women were too often confined to a handful of often poorly paid professions. And it was only through painstaking struggle that more women and minorities and Americans with disabilities began to win the right to more fairly and fully participate in the economy.

Nevertheless, during the post-World War II years, the economic ground felt stable and secure for most Americans. And the future looked brighter than the past. And for some, that meant following in your old man's footsteps at the local plant. And you knew that a blue-collar job would let you buy a home and a car, maybe a vacation once in a while, health care, a reliable pension.

For others it meant going to college, in some cases maybe the first in your family to go to college. And it meant graduating without taking on loads of debt, and being able to count on advancement through a vibrant job market.

Now, it's true that those at the top, even in those years, claimed a much larger share of income than the rest. The top 10 percent consistently took home about one-third of our national income. But that kind of inequality took place in a dynamic market economy where everyone's wages and incomes were growing. And because of upward mobility, the guy on the factory floor could picture his kid running the company someday.

But starting in the late '70s, this social compact began to unravel. Technology made it easier for companies to do more with less, eliminating certain job occupations.

A more competitive world led companies ship jobs anyway. And as good manufacturing jobs automated or headed offshore, workers lost their leverage; jobs paid less and offered fewer benefits.

As values of community broke down and competitive pressure increased, businesses lobbied Washington to weaken unions and the value of the minimum wage. As the trickle-down ideology became more prominent, taxes were slashes for the wealthiest while investments in things that make us all richer, like schools and infrastructure, were allowed to wither.

And for a certain period of time we could ignore this weakening economic foundation, in part because more families were relying on two earners, as women entered the workforce. We took on more debt financed by juiced-up housing market. But when the music stopped and the crisis hit, millions of families were stripped of whatever cushion they had left.

And the result is an economy that's become profoundly unequal and families that are more insecure. Just to give you a few statistics: Since 1979, when I graduated from high school, our productivity is up by more than 90 percent, but the income of the typical family has increased by less than 8 percent. Since 1979 our economy has more than doubled in size, but most of the growth has flowed to a fortunate few. The top 10 percent no longer takes in one-third of our income; it now takes half. Whereas in the past, the average CEO made about 20 to 30 times the income of the average worker, today's CEO now makes 273 times more.

And meanwhile, a family in the top 1 percent has a net worth 288 times higher than the typical family, which is a record for this country.

So the basic bargain at the heart of our economy has frayed. In fact, this trend towards growing inequality is not unique to America's market economy; across the developed world, inequality has increased. Some—some of you may have seen just last week, the pope himself spoke about this at eloquent length. How could it be, he wrote, that it's not a news item when an elderly homeless person dies of exposure, but it is news when the stock market loses two points?

But this increasing inequality is most pronounced in our country, and it challenges the very essence of who we are as a people. Understand, we've never begrudged success in America; we aspire to it, we admire folks who start new businesses, create jobs and invent the products that enrich our lives, and we expect them to be rewarded handsomely for it. In fact, we've often accepted more income inequality than many other nations for one big reason, because we were convinced that America is a place where, even if you're born with nothing, with a little hard work, you can improve your own situation over time and build something better to leave your kids.

As Lincoln once said: "While we do not propose any war upon capital, we do wish to allow the humblest man an equal chance to get rich with everybody else."

The problem is that alongside increased inequality, we've seen diminished levels of upward mobility in recent years. A child born in the top 20 percent has about a 2-in-3 chance of staying at or near the top. A child born into the bottom 20 percent has a less than 1-in-20 shot at making it to the top. He's 10 times likelier to stay where he is. In fact, statistics show not only that our levels of income inequality rank near countries like Jamaica and Argentina, but that it is harder today for a child born here in America to improve her station in life than it is for children in most of our wealthy allies, countries like Canada or Germany or France. They have greater mobility than we do, not less.

You know, the idea that so many children are born into poverty in the wealthiest nation on Earth is heart-breaking enough. But the idea that a child may never be able to escape that poverty because she lacks a decent education or health care or a community that views her future as their own—that should offend all of us. And it should compel us to action. We are a better country than this.

So let me repeat: The combined trends of increased inequality and decreasing mobility pose a fundamental threat to the American dream, our way of life and what we stand for around the globe. And it is not simply a moral claim that I'm making here. There are practical consequences to rising inequality and reduced mobility.

For one thing, these trends are bad for our economy.

One study finds that growth is more fragile and recessions are more frequent in countries with greater inequality.

And that makes sense. You know, when families have less to spend that means businesses have fewer customers and households rack up greater mortgage and credit card debt. Meanwhile, concentrated wealth at the top is less likely to result in the kind of broadly based consumer spending that drives our economy and, together with lax regulation, may contribute to risky, speculative bubbles.

And rising inequality and declining mobility are also bad for our families and social cohesion, not just because we tend to trust our institutions less but studies show we actually tend to trust each other less when there's greater inequality. And greater inequality is associated with less mobility between generations. That means it's not just temporary. The effects last. It creates a vicious cycle.

For example, by the time she turns three-years old, a child born into a low-income home hears 30 million fewer words than a child from a well-off family, which means by the time she starts school, she's already behind. And that deficit can compound itself over time.

And finally, rising inequality and declining mobility are bad for our democracy. Ordinary folks can't write massive campaign checks or hire high-priced lobbyists and lawyers to secure policies that tilt the playing field in their favor at everyone else's expense. And so people get the bad taste that the system's rigged. And that increases cynicism and polarization and it decreases the political participation that is a requisite part of our system of self-government.

So this is an issue that we have to tackle head-on.

And if, in fact, the majority of Americans agree that our number one priority is to restore opportunity and broad-based growth for all Americans, the question is, why has Washington consistently failed to act? And I think a big reason is the myths that have developed around the issue of inequality.

First, there is the myth that this is a problem restricted to a small share of predominantly minority poor. This isn't a broad-based problem; this is a black problem or Hispanic problem or a Native American problem.

Now, it's true that the painful legacy of discrimination means that African-Americans, Latinos, Native Americans are far more likely to suffer from a lack of opportunity—higher unemployment, higher poverty rates. It's also true that women still make 77 cents on the dollar compared to men.

So we're going to need strong application of anti-discrimination laws. We're going to need immigration reform that grows the economy and takes people out of the shadows. We're going to need targeted initiatives to close those gaps.

But—but here is an important point. The—the decades-long shifts in the economy have hurt all groups, poor and middle class, inner city and rural folks, men and women, and Americans of all races.

And as a consequence, some of the social patterns that contribute to declining mobility, that were once attributed to the urban poor—you know, that's a—that's a particular problem for the inner city, you know, single-parent households, or drug abuse or—it turns out now we're seeing that pop up everywhere.

A new study shows that disparities in education, mental health, obesity, absent fathers, isolation from church, and isolation from community groups—these gaps are now as much about growing up rich or poor as they are about anything else. The gap in test scores between poor kids and wealthy kids is now nearly twice what it is between white kids and black kids. Kids with working-class parents are 10 times likelier than kids with middle-or upper-class parents to go through a time when their parents have no income.

So the fact is this: The opportunity gap in America is now as much about class as it is about race. And that gap is growing. So if we're going to take on growing inequality and try to improve upward mobility for all people, we've got to move beyond the false notion that this is an issue exclusively of minority concern. And we have to reject a politics that suggests any effort to address it in a meaningful way somehow pits the interests of a deserving middle class against those of an undeserving poor in search of handouts.

Second, we need to dispel the myth that the goals of growing the economy and reducing inequality are necessarily in conflict when they should actually work in concert.

We know from our history that our economy grows best from the middle out when growth is more widely shared. And we know that beyond a certain level of inequality growth actually slows altogether.

Third, we need to set aside the belief that government cannot do anything about reducing inequality. It's true that government cannot prevent all the downsides of the technological change and global competition that are out there right now—and some of those forces are also some of the things that are helping us grow. And it's also true that some programs in the past, like welfare before it was reformed, were sometimes poorly designed, created disincentives to work, but we've also seen how government action time and again can make an enormous difference in increasing opportunity and bolstering ladders into the middle class. Investments in education, laws establishing collective bargaining and a minimum wage these all contributed to rising standards of living for massive numbers of Americans.

Likewise, when previous generations declared that every citizen of this country deserved a basic measure of security, a floor through which they could not fall, we helped millions of Americans live in dignity and gave millions more the confidence to aspire to something better by taking a risk on a great idea. Without Social Security nearly half of seniors would be living in poverty—half. Today fewer than 1 in 10 do. Before Medicare, only half of all seniors had some form of health insurance. Today virtually all do. And because we've strengthened that

safety net and expanded pro-work and pro-family tax credits like the Earned Income Tax Credit, a recent study found that the poverty rate has fallen by 40 percent since the 1960s.

And these endeavors didn't just make us a better country; they reaffirmed that we are a great country.

So we can make a difference on this. In fact, that's our generation's task, to rebuild America's economic and civic foundation to continue the expansion of opportunity for this generation and the next generation. And like and like Neera, I take this personally. I'm only here because this country educated my grandfather on the GI Bill. When my father left and my mom hit hard times trying to raise my sister and me while she was going to school, this country helped make sure we didn't go hungry. When Michelle, the daughter of a shift worker at a water plant and a secretary, wanted to go to college, just like me this country helped us afford it until we could pay it back.

So what drives me, as a grandson, a son, a father, as an American, is to make sure that every striving, hardworking, optimistic kid in America has the same incredible chance that this country gave me. It has been the driving force between everything we've done these past five years. And over the course of the next year and for the rest of my presidency, that's where you should expect my administration to focus all our efforts.

Now, you'll be pleased to know this is not a State of the Union address.

And many of the ideas that can make the biggest difference in expanding opportunity, I've presented before. But let me offer a few key principles, just a road map that I believe should guide us in both our legislative agenda and our administrative efforts.

To begin with, we have to continue to relentlessly push a growth agenda. And it may be true that in today's economy, growth alone does not guarantee higher wages and incomes. We've seen that. But what's also true is we can't tackle inequality if the economic pie is shrinking or stagnant. The fact is if you're a progressive and you want to help the middle class and the working poor, you've still got to be concerned about competitiveness and productivity and business confidence that spurs private sector investment.

And that's why from day one, we've worked to get the economy growing and help our businesses hire. And thanks to their resilience and innovation, they've created nearly 8 million new jobs over the past 44 months. And now we've got to grow the economy even faster, and we got to keep working to make America a magnet for good middle-class jobs to replace the ones that we've lost in recent decades, jobs in manufacturing and energy and infrastructure and technology.

And that means simplifying our corporate tax code in a way that closes wasteful loopholes and ends incentives to ship jobs overseas. We can—by broadening the base, we can actually lower rates to encourage more companies to hire here and use some of the money we save to create good jobs rebuilding our roads and our bridges and our airports and all the infrastructure our businesses need.

It means a trade agenda that grows exports and works for the middle class.

It means streamlining regulations that are outdated or unnecessary or too costly. And it means coming together around a responsible budget, one that grows our economy faster right now and shrinks our long-term deficits, one that unwinds the harmful sequester cuts that haven't made a lot of sense—and then frees—frees up resources to invest in things like the scientific research that's always unleashed new innovation and new industries.

When it comes to our budget, we should not be stuck in a stale debate from two years ago or three years ago. A relentlessly growing deficit of opportunity is a bigger threat to our future than our rapidly shrinking fiscal deficit. So that's step one towards restoring mobility, making sure our economy is growing faster.

Step two is making sure we empower more Americans with the skills and education they need to compete in a highly competitive global economy. We know that education is the most important predictor of income today, so we launched a Race to the Top in our schools, we're supporting states that have raised standards in teaching and learning, we're pushing for redesigned high schools that graduate more kids with the technical training and apprenticeships, the in-demand high-tech skills that can lead directly to a good job and a middle-class life.

We know it's harder to find a job today without some higher education, so we've helped more students go to college with grants and loans that go farther than before, we've made it more practical to repay those loans and today, more students are graduating from college than ever before.

We're also pursuing an aggressive strategy to promote innovation that reins in tuition costs.

We've got to lower costs so that young people are not burdened by enormous debt when they make the right decision to get higher education. And next week, Michelle and I will bring together college presidents and nonprofits to lead a campaign to help more low-income students attend and succeed in college.

But while higher education may be the surest path to the middle class, it's not the only one. We should offer our people the best technical education in the world. That's why we've worked to connect local businesses with community colleges, so that workers, young and old, can earn the new skills that earn them more money.

And I've also embraced an idea that I know all of you at the Center for American Progress has championed, and by the way, Republican governors in a couple of states have championed, and that's making high-quality pre-school available to every child in America. We know that kids in these programs grow up are likelier to get more education, earn higher wages, form more stable families of their own. It starts a virtuous cycle, not a vicious one. And we should invest in that. We should give all of our children that chance.

And as we empower our young people for future success, the third part of this middle-class economics is empowering our workers. It's time to ensure our collective bargaining laws function as they're supposed to so unions have a level playing field to organize—to organize for a better deal for workers and better wages for the middle class.

It's time to pass the Paycheck Fairness Act so that women will have more tools to fight pay discrimination. It's time to pass the non-Employment non-Discrimination Act so workers can't be fired for who they are or who they love.

And even though we're bringing manufacturing jobs back to America, we're creating more good-paying jobs in education and health care and business services, we know that we're going to have a greater and greater portion of our people in the service sector. And we know that there are airport workers and fast-food workers and nurse assistance and retail salespeople who work their tails off and are still living at or barely above poverty. And that's why it's well past the time to raise a minimum wage that, in real terms right now, is below where it was when Harry Truman was in office.

This shouldn't be an ideological question. You know, it was Adam Smith, the father of free-market economics, who once said, "They who feed, clothe, and lodge the whole body of the people should have such a share of the produce of their own labor as to be themselves tolerably well-fed, clothed and lodged." And for those of you who don't speak old English let me translate. It means if you work hard, you should make a decent living. If you work hard, you should be able to support a family.

Now, we all know the arguments that have been used against the higher minimum wage. Some say it actually hurts low-wage workers; business will be less likely to hire them. There's no solid evidence that a higher minimum wage costs jobs, and research shows it raises incomes for low-wage workers and boosts short-term economic growth.

Others argue that if we raise the minimum wage, companies will just pass those costs on to consumers, but a growing chorus of businesses small and large argue differently and already there are an extraordinary companies in America that provide decent wages, salaries and benefits, and training for their workers, and deliver a great product to consumers.

SAS in North Carolina offers child care and sick leave. REI, a company my secretary of interior used to run, offers retirement plans and strives to cultivate a good work balance. There are companies out there that do right by their workers. They recognize that paying a decent wage actually helps their bottom line, reduces turnover. It means workers have more money to spend, to save, maybe eventually start a business of their own.

A broad majority of Americans agree we should raise the minimum wage. That's why last month voters in New Jersey decided to become the 20th state to raise theirs even higher. That's why yesterday the DC Council voted to do it too. I agree with those voters. I agree with those voters and I'm going to keep pushing until we get a higher minimum wage for hardworking Americans across the entire country. It will be good for our economy. It will be good for our families.

Number four, as I alluded to earlier, we still need targeted programs for the communities and workers that have been hit hardest by economic change in the Great Recession. These communities are no longer limited to the inner city. They're found in neighborhoods hammered by the housing crisis, manufacturing towns hit hard by years of plants packing up, land-locked rural areas where young folks oftentimes feel like they've got to leave just to find a job. There are communities that just aren't generating enough jobs anymore.

So we've put new forward new plans to help these communities and their residents because we've watched cities like Pittsburgh or my hometown of Chicago revamp themselves, and if we give more cities the tools to do it—not handouts, but a hand up—cities like Detroit can do it too.

So in a few weeks we'll announce the first of these Promise Zones, urban and rural communities where we're going to support local efforts focused on a national goal, and that is a child's course in life should not be determined by the ZIP code he's born in but by the strength of his work ethic and the scope of his dreams.

And we're also going to have to do more for the long-term unemployed. You know, for people who've been out of work for more than six months, often through no fault of their own, life is a Catch-22. Companies won't give their resume an honest look because they've been laid off so long, but they've been laid off so long because companies won't give their resume an honest look. And that's why earlier this year I challenged CEOs from some of America's best companies to give these Americans a fair shot. And next month, many of them will join us at the White House for an announcement about this.

Fifth, we've got to revamp retirement to protect Americans in their golden years, to make sure another housing collapse doesn't steal the savings in their homes.

We've also got to strengthen our safety net for a new age so it doesn't just protect people who hit a run of bad luck from falling into poverty, but also propels them back out of poverty.

Today nearly half of full-time workers and 80 percent of part-time workers don't have a pension or a retirement account at their job. About half of all households don't have any retirement savings. So we're going to have to do more to encourage private savings and shore up the promise of Social Security for future generations. And remember, these are promises we make to one another. We—we don't do it to replace the free market, but we do it reduce risk in our society by giving people the ability to take a chance and catch them if they fall.

One study shows that more than half of Americans will experience poverty at some point during their adult lives. Think about that. This is not an isolated situation. More than half of Americans at some point in their lives will experience poverty. That's why we have nutrition assistance, or the program known as SNAP, because it makes a difference for a mother who's working but is just having a hard time putting food on the table for her kids.

That's why we have unemployment insurance, because it makes a difference for a father who lost his job and is out there looking for a new one that he can keep a roof over his kids' heads. By the way, Christmas time is no time for Congress to tell more than 1 million of these Americans that they have lost their unemployment insurance, which is what will happen if Congress does not act before they leave on their holiday vacation.

The point is, these programs are not typically hammocks for people to just lie back and relax.

These programs are almost always temporary means for hardworking people to stay afloat while they try to find a new job, or going to school to retrain themselves for the jobs that are out there, or sometimes just to cope with a bout of bad luck.

Now, progressives should be open to reforms that's actually strengthen these programs and make them more responsive to a 21st-century economy. For example, we should be willing to look at fresh ideas to revamp unemployment disability programs, to encourage faster and higher rates of reemployment without cutting benefits. We shouldn't weaken fundamental protections built over generations because given the constant churn in today's economy, and the disabilities that many of our friends and neighbors live with, they're needed more than ever. We should strengthen and adapt them to new circumstances so they work even better. But understand that these programs of social insurance benefit all of us, because we don't know when we might have a run of bad luck. We don't know when we might lose a job.

Of course, for decades there was one yawning gap in the safety net that did more than anything else to expose working families to the insecurities of today's economy, namely, our broken health care system. That's why we fought for the Affordable Care Act, because 14,000 Americans lost their health insurance every single day, and even more died each year because they didn't have health insurance at all. We did it because millions of families who thought they had coverage were driven into bankruptcy by out-of-pocket costs that they didn't realize would be there.

Tens of millions of our fellow citizens couldn't get any coverage at all.

You know, Dr. King once said, "Of all the forms of inequality, injustice in health care is the most shocking and inhumane." Well, not anymore, because in the three years since we passed this law, the share of Americans with insurance is up, the growth of health care costs are down to their slowest rate in 50 years, more people have insurance, and more have new benefits and protections, a 100 million Americans who've gained the right for free preventive care like mammograms and contraception, the more than 7 million Americans who've saved an average of $1,200 on their prescription medicine, every American who won't go broke when they get sick because their insurance can't limit their care anymore. More people without insurance have gained insurance, more than 3 million young Americans who've been able to stay on their parents' plan, the more than half a million Americans and counting who are poised to get coverage starting on January 1st, some for the very first time.

And it is these numbers, not the ones in any poll, that will ultimately determine the fate of this law. It's the measurable outcomes and reduced bankruptcies and reduced hours that have been lost because somebody couldn't make it to work and healthier kids with better performance in schools and young entrepreneurs who have the freedom to go out there and try a new idea. Those are the things that will ultimately reduce a major source of inequality and help ensure more Americans get the start that they need to succeed in the future.

I've acknowledged more than once that we didn't roll out parts of this law as well as we should have. But the law's already working in major ways that benefit millions of Americans right now, even as we've begun to slow the rise in health care costs, which is good for family budgets, good for federal and state budgets and good for the budgets of businesses, small and large.

So this law's going to work. And for the sake of our economic security, it needs to work. And as people in states as different as California and Kentucky sign up every single day for health insurance, signing up in droves, they're proving they want that economic security. You know, if the Senate Republican leader still thinks he's going to be able to repeal this someday, he might want to check with the more than 60,000 people in his home state who are already set to finally have coverage that frees them from the fear of financial ruin and lets them afford to take their kids to see a doctor.

So let me end by addressing the elephant in the room here, which is the seeming inability to get anything done in Washington these days. I realize we are not going to resolve all of our political debates over the best ways to reduce inequality

and increase upward mobility this year or next year or in the next five years.

But it is important that we have a serious debate about these issues, for the longer that current trends are allowed to continue, the more it will feed the cynicism and fear that many Americans are feeling right now that they'll never be able to repay the debt they took on to go to college, they'll never be able to save enough to retire, they'll never see their own children land a good job that supports a family.

And that's why, even as I will keep on offering my own ideas for expanding opportunity, I'll also keep challenging and welcoming those who oppose my ideas to offer their own. If Republicans have concrete plans that will actually reduce inequality, build the middle class, provide moral ladders of opportunity to the poor, let's hear them. I want to know what they are. If you don't think we should raise the minimum wage, let's hear your idea to increase people's earnings. If you don't think every child should have access to preschool, tell us what you'd do differently to give them a better shot.

If you still don't like "Obamacare"—and I know you don't—even though it's built on market-based ideas of choice and competition and the private sector, then you should explain how exactly you'd cut costs and cover more people and make insurance more secure. You owe it to the American people to tell us what you are for, not just what you're against. That way, we can have a vigorous and meaningful debate. That's what the American people deserve. That's what the times demand. It's not enough anymore to just say we should get our government out of the way and let the unfettered market take care of it, for our experience tells is that's just not true.

Look, I've never believed that government can solve every problem, or should, and neither have you. We know that ultimately, our strength is grounded in our people, individuals out there striving, working, making things happen.

It depends on community, a rich and generous sense of community. That's at the core of what happens at the THEARC here every day. You understand that turning back rising inequality and expanding opportunity requires parents taking responsibility for their kids, kids taking responsibility to work hard. It requires religious leaders who mobilize their congregations to rebuild neighborhoods block by block, requires civic organizations that can help train the unemployed, link them with businesses for the jobs of the future. It requires companies and CEOs to set an example by providing decent wages and salaries and benefits for their workers and a shot for somebody who's down on his or her luck. We know that's our strength: our people, our communities, and our businesses.

But government can't stand on the sidelines in our efforts, because government is us. It can and should reflect our deepest values and commitments. And if we refocus our energies on building an economy that grows for everybody and gives every child in this country a fair chance at success, then I remain confident that the future still looks brighter than the past and that the best days for this country we love are still ahead.

Thank you, everybody.

Critical Thinking

1. Do you agree with Obama's analysis of the current economy?
2. According to Obama, what has caused the middle class to decline?
3. Do you agree that our economy is coming apart?

Create Central

www.mhhe.com/createcentral

Internet References

National Center for Policy Analysis
www.ncpa.org

New American Studies Web
www.georgetown.edu/crossroads/asw

Social Science Information Gateway
http://sosig.esrc.bris.ac.uk

Sociology—Study Sociology Online
http://edu.learnsoc.org

Sociology Web Resources
http://www.mhhe.com/socscience/sociology/resources/index.htm

Sociosite
http://www.topsite.com/goto/sociosite.net

Socioweb
http://www.topsite.com/goto/socioweb.com

Obama, Barack, "The Bargain at the Heart of Our Economy has Frayed," *Vital Speeches of the Day*, vol. 80, 2, February 2014 pp. 54–61.

Article   Prepared by: Kurt Finsterbusch, *University of Maryland, College Park*

The Wages of Global Capitalism

RICHARD D. WOLFF

Learning Outcomes

After reading this article, you will be able to:

- Analyze the basis for wage stagnation in developed countries in recent decades.

- Understand better how capitalists create great wealth for themselves while stagnating the wages for workers.

Wage growth in the world slowed to an average of 2 percent in 2013. That was less than in 2012 and far less than the pre-crisis rate of 3 percent. Starker still were the differences between wage growth in the "developed world" (chiefly Western Europe, North America, and Japan) and wage growth in the major "emerging growth" countries, chiefly China.

In the "developed world" wage growth in 2012 was 0.1 percent, and in 2013 it was 0.2 percent. Far from portending any economic "recovery," that level of wage "growth" is rather called "wage stagnation." In stunning contrast, wage growth in the major emerging growth economies was much better: 6.7 percent in 2012 and 5.9 percent in 2013.

These remarkable statistics come from the Global Wage Report 2014/15 released on December 5, 2014, by its author, the International Labor Organization (ILO). This report clearly exposes the immense costs of a globalizing capitalism for the wage-earning majorities in Western Europe, North America, and Japan. Allowing their leading capitalists to maximize profits by relocating production out of those regions is deeply and increasingly destructive to them.

The ILO report's chart below summarizes the key wage results of the last decade's capitalism. Economic growth, rising real wages and rising standards of living are economic realities in China and other emerging growth countries. Economic crisis, stagnant wages, and declining working and living standards are the economic realities for Western Europe, the United States, and Japan.

Capitalist enterprises keep moving their operations (first manufacturing, now also many services) from high to low-wage regions of the world to raise their profits. Departing capitalists leave their former host communities with unemployment and all its social costs. Such conditions force desperate competition for jobs that drives down wages and guts job benefits. Public services decline as government budgets suffer. Capitalism no longer delivers a rising standard of living in the regions where it began and developed first: Western Europe, North America, and Japan. Instead of goods, capitalism delivers the bads.

A second key insight emerges from another chart (below) in the ILO report. In the developed countries, while real wages stagnated throughout the crisis since 2007, the productivity of workers continued to rise. That explains the deepening inequalities of income and wealth in those countries.

Productivity measures the quantity of goods and services that workers' labor provides to their bosses. The chart shows how labor productivity has kept rising (because of computers,

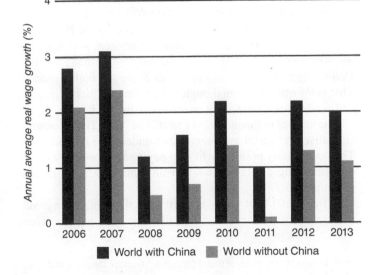

Annual average global real wage growth, 2006–2013

■ World with China   ■ World without China

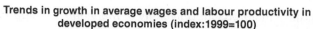

Trends in growth in average wages and labour productivity in developed economies (index:1999=100)

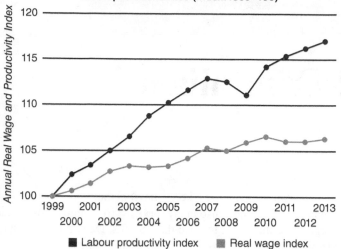

■ Labour productivity index   ■ Real wage index

more equipment, better training, speed-up of work etc.). The chart also shows how much less wages have risen. Wages are what capitalists pay workers for their labor.

There is thus a growing gap between what workers give capitalists (productivity) and what capitalists give workers (wages). That gap measures profits. They have grown the fastest of all. Major capitalist corporations gather those exploding profits into their hands. They pay their top executives huge salaries and bonuses, pay rich dividends, and deliver huge capital gains to their shareholders. Those top executives and major shareholders are most of the super-rich who have taken so much of the nation's wealth.

European, U.S., and Japanese politicians, controlled by their major capitalists, do little to stop the relocation of production that generates the results seen in the charts above. Labor and anti-capitalist movements are still too weak, too divided, or too poorly informed to stop the long-term decline underway.

The real question of the day underscored by the ILO report is this: *Will Western European, North American, and Japanese working people consent to the further undermining of their well-being that follows as capitalists leave for higher profits?* That is *the* question even though mainstream politicians, media, and academics cannot see it or refuse to discuss it.

The answer to that question can still be "no." The labor, anti-capitalist, and social movements can understand this situation. They could rally politically to stop paying the horrendous costs of globalizing capitalism while a tiny minority grabs its ballooning profits.

A final note: Real wages are still three times higher in developed countries than in economically emerging regions. Thus,

capitalists keep getting the higher profits that motivate their relocation out of Western Europe, North America and Japan. They share some of those higher profits (via mergers, acquisitions, bribes etc.) with major local capitalist corporations inside the regions to which they relocate. Relocating capitalists offer such payoffs to facilitate their success in these new centers of capitalism's growth.

Those payoffs help explain the gross inequalities of income and wealth deepening in the emerging economies, too. Globalizing capitalism thus imposes on most countries the worsening inequalities that bring ever closer the validity of that old slogan (premature when first articulated): "Workers of the world unite; you have nothing to lose but your chains."

Critical Thinking

1. What are some of the major problems of global capitalism?
2. Why has the productivity index for developed countries increased so much more than the wage index from 1999 to 2013?
3. How does Wolff think this growing inequality could be changed?

Internet References

New American Studies Web
https://blogs.commons.georgetown.edu/vkp/

Social Science Information Gateway
http://www.ariadne.ac.uk/issue2/sosig

Sociology—Study Sociology Online
http://edu.learnsoc.org/

Sociology Web Resources
http://www.mhhe.com/socscience/sociology/resources/index.htm

Sociosite
http://www.topsite.com/goto/sociosite.net

Socioweb
http://www.topsite.com/goto/socioweb.com

RICHARD D. WOLFF is Professor of Economics Emeritus, University of Massachusetts, Amherst where he taught economics from 1973 to 2008. He is currently a Visiting Professor in the Graduate Program in International Affairs of the New School University, New York City. He also teaches classes regularly at the Brecht Forum in Manhattan. Earlier he taught economics at Yale University (1967–1969) and at the City College of the City University of New York (1969–1973). In 1994, he was a Visiting Professor of Economics at the University of Paris (France), I (Sorbonne). His work is available at rdwolff.com and at democracyatwork.info.

Article Prepared by: Kurt Finsterbusch, *University of Maryland, College Park*

Nice Places Finish First

The economic returns of civic virtue.

JOHN M. BRIDGELAND AND ALAN KHAZEI

Learning Outcomes

After reading this article, you will be able to:

- Understand the importance of civic virtue.

- Understand the reduction of social mobility in the United States and be able to explain it.

- Understand the relationship between civic virtue and social mobility.

T he American Dream is a core part of our national ethos. It is the idea that anyone can advance up the economic ladder with hard work and determination, regardless of where they come from or what zip code they're born into.

Over the last few years, however, the American Dream has taken a beating, and not just because of the Great Recession. A number of careful studies have found that there is less upward mobility in America than in other wealthy countries, such as Germany, Demark, Sweden, and the UK. In fact, only 8 percent of Americans born in the lowest fifth of the income scale ever make it to the top fifth in our so-called classless society, while the percentage is 11 to 14 percent in these "Old European" countries.

These new revelations would have shocked Alexis de Tocqueville, the French aristocrat who traveled through the United States in the 1830s and was among the first to write about the restive, egalitarian scramble for material success that then characterized America, so different from the class-bound Europe of his day.

Fortunately, America may be able to get back in the upward mobility game by paying greater attention to another phenomenon that struck Tocqueville about Americans in the 1830s: our propensity to join groups and volunteer our time for the public good.

"Americans of all ages, all conditions, and all dispositions, constantly form associations," the Frenchman observed in his famous book *Democracy in America*. Americans, he continued, banded together not only to advance their political and commercial interests but also "to found establishments for education, to build inns, to construct churches, to diffuse books . . . and in this manner they found hospitals, prisons, and schools." Whereas in Europe such civic endeavors were typically controlled by wealthy individuals or the state, in the US average citizens worked together to drive these organizations.

Today, Tocqueville would be writing about our nonprofit sector, or civil society. It is comprised of a vast array of different kinds of groups—local sports leagues and PTAs, church-based charities, labor unions, business and professional societies, fraternal organizations like the Elks and the NAACP, and national cause-oriented membership groups like the Humane Society—that operate in the space between the individual and the government.

This sector gained renewed attention in 1995, when Harvard's Robert Putnam published an article (later a book) called "Bowling Alone," in which he posited that the tradition of voluntary association was in steep decline in America. Citizens, he argued, were increasingly apt to spend their time watching TV rather than attending Rotary Club meetings. Many academics questioned Putnam's thesis—old-line fraternal organizations might be losing members, they observed, but youth soccer leagues are burgeoning and social media like Facebook provide alternative ways to connect.

Still, Putnam's work galvanized academic interest in "social capital"—the phrase sociologists use for the benefits that complex networks of friendships and connections bring to individuals and societies. Further studies showed, for instance, that levels of social capital varied greatly across the country. In some regions (the Northeast and the Upper Midwest), citizens are far more engaged in civic activities and connected with each other than in other areas (the Deep South and Nevada). Other studies found that communities with higher levels of social capital suffer less unemployment during recessions. As evidence of a link between civic engagement and economic health accumulated, the group Opportunity Nation included indicators of social capital among the 16 indicators of local economic health in its Opportunity Index (see page 43).

Then, this summer, a much-discussed study from a team of economists from Harvard and the University of California at Berkeley showed, for the first time, how rates of upward mobility vary geographically across the United States. The study from the Equality of Opportunity Project found that children born in the bottom quarter of the income scale in, for instance, the Denver metro area were twice as likely to rise to the top quarter as those born in Charlotte, and those born in the San Francisco Bay Area were three times as likely. Even in areas with similar average incomes, the rates of upward mobility dramatically differ. On average, lower-income children in metro Seattle who grew up in the bottom 25th percentile of income do similarly well as middle-class children in metro Atlanta.

Though the researchers couldn't prove what causes these geographic disparities in social mobility, they showed correlations. Among the strongest correlations—higher even than the quality of local high schools or the availability and affordability of local colleges—turned out to be social capital. Literally, the more bowling leagues, nonprofits, and similar groups per 10,000 residents, the more likely the area's young people were to rise economically. And this was true not just for those whose parents were involved in these groups, but for all young people in the community.

What might account for the connection between a place's social capital and the economic success of its children? No one can say for sure, but Putnam, who is writing a book on the subject, puts it this way: "Upward mobility is aided when everyone in a community thinks of other people's kids as 'their' kids." In other words, in civic-minded communities with thick webs of interpersonal connections, individuals help not only their friends but also others in the community whom they might not know—with a basket of food, or a summer job offer, or inside information on who are the best teachers and counselors at the local high school.

Social capital, in other words, expands our notion of "we."

If social capital is a critical component of social mobility, what can be done to increase its stock? Part of the answer is to be found in two other attributes that correlate with upward mobility: middle-class wages, and families with involved parents. Places with lots of both also tend to have high rates of social capital, which makes sense: two-parent households with sufficient incomes are more likely to be able to be involved in civic affairs. So anything that generally allows families to enter or stay in the middle class, and specifically policies that help them cope with the stresses of modern life—like more-flexible work schedules that free parents to invest more time in their families and communities—will likely strengthen social capital.

Another way to grow social capital is to expand programs of national and community service. These programs strengthen civil society in three ways.

First, they act as a force multiplier of people and resources. Take AmeriCorps, the federal domestic national service program that provides a modest living stipend and education award to those who give a year of full-time service to their country. AmeriCorps members are mostly detailed to nonprofit organizations like Habitat for Humanity, where, instead of swinging hammers themselves, they typically organize armies of unpaid part-time volunteers. They make sure hammers and drywall are at the housing site, that volunteers get the right training, and that food and water are at the ready. In other words, they build the capacity of nonprofits to engage with the broader community. The federal agency that runs AmeriCorps, the Corporation for National and Community Service (CNCS), also smartly ensures that government resources to the nonprofit leverage a private-sector commitment.

The second way service programs build social capital is by opening up opportunities for lower-income young people who are disconnected from school and work. YouthBuild, for instance, a nonprofit service initiative partially funded by federal grants, employs disadvantaged young people in community construction projects while helping them complete their education and get jobs. In 2010, 78 percent of YouthBuild enrollees completed the program, 63 percent obtained their GEDs or high school diplomas, and 60 percent went on to postsecondary education or decent-paying jobs.

A third way national and community service builds social capital is by expanding our notion of "we." Programs like AmeriCorps typically bring individuals from different geographies, races, ethnicities, party affiliations, and income levels together in common national purpose. It's no accident that one of the greatest periods of both civic involvement and upward mobility in America came in the years after World War II. A generation of Americans had grown up having witnessed the Civilian Conservation Corps, which put three million young unemployed men to work on our public lands over a decade. That generation went on to serve in the war, when the universal draft and the experience of fighting beside soldiers from widely different geographic, ethnic, and income backgrounds broadened the nation's sense of collective identity. Not surprisingly, the "Greatest Generation" volunteered more, joined organizations more, gave more in charitable contributions, attended church, school, and community activities more, and were active neighbors, helping those in need more than the generations before or after it. Interestingly, during the same period when our civic stocks rose, Americans also voted more, entered public service in greater numbers, and had much lower levels of political polarization than we see today. Even the gap between rich and poor was smaller.

That willingness to give something back isn't unique to the Greatest Generation. Millennials, who grew up during a time of war and economic stress, are showing such strong civic inclinations that the demand for service opportunities far outstrips supply. Applications to AmeriCorps soared from 359,000 in 2009 to more than 580,000 in 2011 (the latest year for which numbers are available) for only about 80,000 slots, half of which are full-time. There were 150,000 requests for applications to the Peace Corps for the 4,000 annual openings in 2011. Other service programs are similarly oversubscribed, like Teach for America (48,000 applications for 5,800 positions). This gap represents wasted democratic energy and social capital that could be put to work at very low cost to improve our country.

Recognizing this growing demand, a strong bipartisan majority in Congress passed, and Barack Obama signed, the Edward M. Kennedy Serve America Act in 2009, which authorized a tripling of AmeriCorps from 75,000 to 250,000 members. But with the budget wars that commenced after the 2010 midterms, little of those extra funds materialized. The House even voted to eliminate all funding for the CNCS and the programs it administers, like AmeriCorps (thankfully, those cuts didn't become law, although Senior Corps was cut dramatically).

In response to congressional paralysis, Obama in July issued a presidential memorandum instructing federal departments and agencies to use existing recourses to create their own service programs to support their missions. These agency-specific service initiatives will be modeled after programs like FEMA Corps, a new partnership between the Federal Emergency Management Agency and the CNCS that trains and deploys teams for 10 months to aid in disaster relief.

The outside momentum for national service is also building. Groups like Voices for National Service, which leads the effort to boost funding for AmeriCorps, and ServiceNation, which championed the passage of the Serve America Act, are keeping the service field together right at a time when the country needs their advocacy and creativity most. And this summer, the Aspen Institute established the Franklin Project, led by retired General Stanley McChrystal, to help realize the goal of engaging more than one million young Americans between the ages of 18 and 28 in a year of civilian national service, on par with the more than one million Americans on active duty in our military.

To help reach that goal, the Franklin Project will challenge private-sector institutions, be they universities or nonprofits, to create, fund, and manage new opportunities for national service. These new positions will be certified by a new entity and advertised on a digital site listing all national service programs and positions. The site will effectively serve as a combination of Monster.com and Kickstarter—that is, it will make it easy for young people to apply for a wide variety of national service positions, while also enabling corporate and other sources of support for such service opportunities. The system will take advantage of technology, social networks, and civil society to democratize and modernize national service.

The challenges and opportunities facing this country are big. And we need bold solutions to deal with them. For more than 80 years, national service programs have shown that they can strengthen communities, transform service participants, and build the social capital we need to make the American Dream a reality for all. Millennials are clamoring to serve their country, and such service could boost their economic mobility in a tough economy. We should give them that chance.

Critical Thinking

1. What role should the federal government have in helping to create more civic virtue?
2. What forces hinder the development of civic virtue?
3. Why has social mobility decreased and inequality increased in the United States in the past few decades?

Create Central

www.mhhe.com/createcentral

Internet References

Social Science Information Gateway
  http://sosig.esrc.bris.ac.uk
Sociology—Study Sociology Online
  http://edu.learnsoc.org
Sociology Web Resources
  http://www.mhhe.com/socscience/sociology/resources/index.htm

Sociosite

http://www.topsite.com/goto/sociosite.net

Socioweb

http://www.topsite.com/goto/socioweb.com

The American Studies Web

http://lamp.georgetown.edu/asw

JOHN M. BRIDGELAND is CEO of Civic Enterprises, former director of the White House Domestic Policy Council under President George W. Bush, and a member of the White House Council for Community Solutions under President Barack Obama. **ALAN KHAZEI** is CEO of the Action Tank and cofounder of City Year. They are cochairs of the Franklin Project at the Aspen Institute.

Article   Prepared by: Kurt Finsterbusch, *University of Maryland, College Park*

To Make Immigration More Fair and More Just

My fellow Americans, we are and always will be a nation of immigrants. We were strangers once, too. And whether our forebears were strangers who crossed the Atlantic, or the Pacific, or the Rio Grande, we are here only because this country welcomed them in.

BARACK OBAMA

Learning Outcomes

After reading this article, you will be able to:

- Describe the various components of the immigration issue.

- Describe the immigration bill that the Senate passed but the House did not vote on and Obama's current immigration policy.

- Present the arguments for and against a path to citizenship for undocumented immigrants.

My fellow Americans, tonight, I'd like to talk with you about immigration.

For more than 200 years, our tradition of welcoming immigrants from around the world has given us a tremendous advantage over other nations. It's kept us youthful, dynamic, and entrepreneurial. It has shaped our character as a people with limitless possibilities—people not trapped by our past, but able to remake ourselves as we choose.

But today, our immigration system is broken—and everybody knows it.

Families who enter our country the right way and play by the rules watch others flout the rules. Business owners who offer their workers good wages and benefits see the competition exploit undocumented immigrants by paying them far less. All of us take offense to anyone who reaps the rewards of living in America without taking on the responsibilities of living in America. And undocumented immigrants who desperately want to embrace those responsibilities see little option but to remain in the shadows, or risk their families being torn apart.

It's been this way for decades. And for decades, we haven't done much about it.

When I took office, I committed to fixing this broken immigration system. And I began by doing what I could to secure our borders. Today, we have more agents and technology deployed to secure our southern border than at any time in our history. And over the past six years, illegal border crossings have been cut by more than half. Although this summer, there was a brief spike in unaccompanied children being apprehended at our border, the number of such children is now actually lower than it's been in nearly two years. Overall, the number of people trying to cross our border illegally is at its lowest level since the 1970s. Those are the facts.

Meanwhile, I worked with Congress on a comprehensive fix, and last year, 68 Democrats, Republicans, and independents came together to pass a bipartisan bill in the Senate. It wasn't perfect. It was a compromise. But it reflected common sense. It would have doubled the number of border patrol agents while giving undocumented immigrants a pathway to citizenship if they paid a fine, started paying their taxes, and went to the back of the line. And independent experts said that it would help grow our economy and shrink our deficits.

Had the House of Representatives allowed that kind of bill a simple yes-or-no vote, it would have passed with support from both parties, and today it would be the law. But for a year and a half now, Republican leaders in the House have refused to allow that simple vote.

Now, I continue to believe that the best way to solve this problem is by working together to pass that kind of common sense law. But until that happens, there are actions I have the legal authority to take as President—the same kinds of actions taken by Democratic and Republican presidents before me—that will help make our immigration system more fair and more just.

Tonight, I am announcing those actions.

First, we'll build on our progress at the border with additional resources for our law enforcement personnel so that they can stem the flow of illegal crossings, and speed the return of those who do cross over.

Second, I'll make it easier and faster for high-skilled immigrants, graduates, and entrepreneurs to stay and contribute to our economy, as so many business leaders have proposed.

Third, we'll take steps to deal responsibly with the millions of undocumented immigrants who already live in our country.

I want to say more about this third issue, because it generates the most passion and controversy. Even as we are a nation of immigrants, we're also a nation of laws. Undocumented workers broke our immigration laws, and I believe that they must be held accountable—especially those who may be dangerous. That's why, over the past six years, deportations of criminals are up 80 percent. And that's why we're going to keep focusing enforcement resources on actual threats to our security. Felons, not families. Criminals, not children. Gang members, not a mom who's working hard to provide for her kids. We'll prioritize, just like law enforcement does every day.

But even as we focus on deporting criminals, the fact is, millions of immigrants in every state, of every race and nationality still live here illegally. And let's be honest—tracking down, rounding up, and deporting millions of people isn't realistic. Anyone who suggests otherwise isn't being straight with you. It's also not who we are as Americans. After all, most of these immigrants have been here a long time. They work hard, often in tough, low-paying jobs. They support their families. They worship at our churches. Many of their kids are American-born or spent most of their lives here, and their hopes, dreams, and patriotism are just like ours. As my predecessor, President Bush, once put it: "They are a part of American life."

Now here's the thing: We expect people who live in this country to play by the rules. We expect that those who cut the line will not be unfairly rewarded. So we're going to offer the following deal: If you've been in America for more than five years; if you have children who are American citizens or legal residents; if you register, pass a criminal background check, and you're willing to pay your fair share of taxes—you'll be able to apply to stay in this country temporarily without fear of deportation. You can come out of the shadows and get right with the law. That's what this deal is.

Now, let's be clear about what it isn't. This deal does not apply to anyone who has come to this country recently. It does not apply to anyone who might come to America illegally in the future. It does not grant citizenship, or the right to stay here permanently, or offer the same benefits that citizens receive—only Congress can do that. All we're saying is we're not going to deport you.

I know some of the critics of this action call it amnesty. Well, it's not. Amnesty is the immigration system we have today—millions of people who live here without paying their taxes or playing by the rules while politicians use the issue to scare people and whip up votes at election time.

That's the real amnesty—leaving this broken system the way it is. Mass amnesty would be unfair. Mass deportation would be both impossible and contrary to our character. What I'm describing is accountability—a common-sense, middle-ground approach: If you meet the criteria, you can come out of the shadows and get right with the law. If you're a criminal, you'll be deported. If you plan to enter the U.S. illegally, your chances of getting caught and sent back just went up.

The actions I'm taking are not only lawful, they're the kinds of actions taken by every single Republican President and every single Democratic President for the past half century. And to those members of Congress who question my authority to make our immigration system work better, or question the wisdom of me acting where Congress has failed, I have one answer: Pass a bill.

I want to work with both parties to pass a more permanent legislative solution. And the day I sign that bill into law, the actions I take will no longer be necessary. Meanwhile, don't let a disagreement over a single issue be a dealbreaker on every issue. That's not how our democracy works, and Congress certainly shouldn't shut down our government again just because we disagree on this. Americans are tired of gridlock. What our country needs from us right now is a common purpose—a higher purpose.

Most Americans support the types of reforms I've talked about tonight. But I understand the disagreements held by many of you at home. Millions of us, myself included, go back generations in this country, with ancestors who put in the painstaking work to become citizens. So we don't like the notion that anyone might get a free pass to American citizenship.

I know some worry immigration will change the very fabric of who we are, or take our jobs, or stick it to middle-class families at a time when they already feel like they've gotten the raw deal for over a decade. I hear these concerns. But that's not what these steps would do. Our history and the facts show that immigrants are a net plus for our economy and our society. And I believe it's important that all of us have this debate without impugning each other's character.

Because for all the back and forth of Washington, we have to remember that this debate is about something bigger. It's about who we are as a country, and who we want to be for future generations.

Are we a nation that tolerates the hypocrisy of a system where workers who pick our fruit and make our beds never have a chance to get right with the law? Or are we a nation that gives them a chance to make amends, take responsibility, and give their kids a better future?

Are we a nation that accepts the cruelty of ripping children from their parents' arms? Or are we a nation that values families, and works together to keep them together?

Are we a nation that educates the world's best and brightest in our universities, only to send them home to create businesses in countries that compete against us? Or are we a nation that encourages them to stay and create jobs here, create businesses here, create industries right here in America?

That's what this debate is all about. We need more than politics as usual when it comes to immigration. We need reasoned, thoughtful, compassionate debate that focuses on our hopes, not our fears. I know the politics of this issue are tough. But let me tell you why I have come to feel so strongly about it.

Over the past few years, I have seen the determination of immigrant fathers who worked two or three jobs without taking a dime from the government, and at risk any moment of losing it all, just to build a better life for their kids. I've seen the heartbreak and anxiety of children whose mothers might be taken away from them just because they didn't have the right papers. I've seen the courage of students who, except for the circumstances of their birth, are as American as Malia or Sasha; students who bravely come out as undocumented in hopes they could make a difference in the country they love.

These people—our neighbors, our classmates, our friends—they did not come here in search of a free ride or an easy life. They came to work, and study, and serve in our military, and above all, contribute to America's success.

Tomorrow, I'll travel to Las Vegas and meet with some of these students, including a young woman named Astrid Silva. Astrid was brought to America when she was four years old. Her only possessions were a cross, her doll, and the frilly dress she had on. When she started school, she didn't speak any English. She caught up to other kids by reading newspapers and watching PBS, and she became a good student. Her father worked in landscaping. Her mom cleaned other people's homes. They wouldn't let Astrid apply to a technology magnet school, not because they didn't love her, but because they were afraid the paperwork would out her as an undocumented immigrant—so she applied behind their back and got in. Still, she mostly lived in the shadows—until her grandmother, who visited every year from Mexico, passed away, and she couldn't travel to the funeral without risk of being found out and deported. It was around that time she decided to begin advocating for herself and others like her, and today, Astrid Silva is a college student working on her third degree.

Are we a nation that kicks out a striving, hopeful immigrant like Astrid, or are we a nation that finds a way to welcome her in? Scripture tells us that we shall not oppress a stranger, for we know the heart of a stranger—we were strangers once, too.

My fellow Americans, we are and always will be a nation of immigrants. We were strangers once, too. And whether our forebears were strangers who crossed the Atlantic, or the Pacific, or the Rio Grande, we are here only because this country welcomed them in, and taught them that to be an American is about something more than what we look like, or what our last names are, or how we worship. What makes us Americans is our shared commitment to an ideal—that all of us are created equal, and all of us have the chance to make of our lives what we will.

That's the country our parents and grandparents and generations before them built for us. That's the tradition we must uphold. That's the legacy we must leave for those who are yet to come.

Thank you. God bless you. And God bless this country we love.

Critical Thinking

1. How is the present immigration system broken?
2. Is America still an immigrant nation that welcomes immigrants?
3. What should be done with undocumented immigrants?

Internet References

American Immigration Council
http://www.americanimmigrationcouncil.org/

New American Studies Web
https://blogs.commons.georgetown.edu/vkp/

Social Science Information Gateway
http://www.ariadne.ac.uk/issue2/sosig

Sociology—Study Sociology Online
http://edu.learnsoc.org/

Sociology Web Resources
http://www.mhhe.com/socscience/sociology/resources/index.htm

Sociosite
http://www.topsite.com/goto/sociosite.net

Socioweb
http://www.topsite.com/goto/socioweb.com

Obama, Barack. Remarks by the President in Address to the Nation on Immigration, November 20, 2014, delivered at the White House, Washington, D.C.

Unit 3

UNIT

Prepared by: Kurt Finsterbusch, *University of Maryland, College Park*

Problems of Poverty and Inequality

America is famous as the land of opportunity, and people from around the world have come to its shores in pursuit of the American dream. But how is America living up to this dream today? It is still a place for people to get rich, but it is also a place where people are trapped in poverty. This unit tells a number of stories of Americans dealing with advantages and disadvantages, opportunities and barriers, power, and powerlessness.

The first section of this unit deals with income inequality and the hardships of the poor. It documents that poverty is widespread in America. It explores the impacts of globalization on our economy detailing both the positive and the negative impacts. It examines the culture of poverty thesis and finds that it is a myth. The next section examines racial and ethnic issues. Racism continues to exist and one of the causes of the present strength of racism are the misperceptions embedded is a racist culture. Finally, the harmful attitudes toward Arab and Muslim Americans since 9/11 are appraised. The last section covers gender inequalities and issues. A major issue is whether women can have it all, meaning success both at work and raising children at home. This section also presents the facts on human sex trafficking in America, LGBT rights, and sexism against boys.

Article   Prepared by: Kurt Finsterbusch, *University of Maryland, College Park*

Overwhelming Evidence That Half of America Is In or Near Poverty

PAUL BUCHHEIT

Learning Outcomes

After reading this article, you will be able to:

- Have a good understanding of the definitions and extent of poverty in the United States.

- Understand which policies have reduced poverty.

- Know why so many people are poor.

The Charles Koch Foundation recently released a commercial that ranked a near poverty level $34,000 family among the Top one percent of poor people in the world. Bud Konheim, CEO and cofounder of fashion company Nicole Miller, concurred: "The guy that's making, oh my God, he's making $35,000 a year, why don't we try that out in India or some countries we can't even name. China, anyplace, the guy is wealthy."

Comments like these are condescending and self-righteous. They display an ignorance of the needs of lower-income and middle-income families in America. The costs of food and housing and education and health care and transportation and child care and taxes have been well defined by organizations such as the Economic Policy Institute, which calculated that a U.S. family of three would require an average of about $48,000 a year to meet basic needs; and by the Working Poor Families Project, which estimates the income required for basic needs for a family of four at about $45,000. The median household income is $51,000.

The following discussion pertains to the half of America that is in or near poverty, the people rarely seen by Congress.

1. The Official Poverty Threshold Should Be Much Higher

According to the Congressional Research Service (CRS), *"The poverty line reflects a measure of economic need based on living standards that prevailed in the mid-1950s . . . It is not adjusted to reflect changes in needs associated with improved standards of living that have occurred over the decades since the measure was first developed. If the same basic methodology developed in the early 1960s was applied today, the poverty thresholds would be over three times higher than the current thresholds."*

The original poverty measures were (and still are) based largely on the food costs of the 1950s. But while food costs have doubled since 1978, housing has more than *tripled,* medical expenses are *six times higher,* and college tuition is *eleven times higher.* The Bureau of Labor Statistics and the Census Bureau have calculated that food, housing, health care, child care, transportation, taxes, and other household expenditures consume nearly the *entire* median household income.

CRS provides some balance, noting that the threshold should also be impacted by safety net programs: *"For purposes of officially counting the poor, noncash benefits (such as the value of Medicare and Medicaid, public housing, or employer provided health care) and 'near cash' benefits (e.g., food stamps.) are not counted as income."*

But many American families near the median are not able to take advantage of safety net programs. Almost all, on the other hand, face the housing, health care, child care, and transportation expenses that point toward a higher threshold of poverty.

2. Almost Half of Americans Own, on Average, NOTHING

The bottom half of America own just 1.1 percent of the country's wealth, or about $793 billion, which is the same amount owned by the 30 richest Americans. ZERO wealth is owned by approximately the bottom 47 percent.

This nonexistent net worth is due in great part to the overwhelming burden of debt for Americans, which now includes college graduates entering the work force. The average student loan balance has risen 91 percent in the past 10 years.

3. Half of Americans are "Poor" or "Low-Income"

This is based on the Census Department's *Relative Poverty Measure* (Table 4), which is "most commonly used in developed countries to measure poverty." The Economic Policy Institute uses the term "economically vulnerable." With this standard, 18 percent of Americans are below the poverty threshold and 32 percent are below twice the threshold, putting them in the *low-income* category.

The official poverty rate increased by 25 percent between 2000 and 2011. Seniors and children feel the greatest impact, with 55 percent of the elderly and almost 60 percent of children classified as poor or low-income under the relative poverty measure. *Wider Opportunities for Women* reports that "sixty percent of women age 65 and older who live alone or live with a spouse have incomes insufficient to cover basic, daily expenses."

4. It's Much Worse for Black Families

Incredibly, while America's total wealth has risen from $12 trillion to $77 trillion in 25 years, the median net worth for black households has GONE DOWN over approximately the same time, from $7,150 to $6,446, adjusted for inflation. *State of Working America* reports that almost half of black children under the age of six are living in poverty.

5. Nearly Half of American Households Don't Have Enough to Hold Them for Three Months

That's according to the Corporation for Enterprise Development. Even more striking, a survey by Bankrate.com concluded that only *one in four* Americans has "six months' worth of expenses for use in emergency, the minimum recommended by many financial planning experts."

It Would Be Much Worse without the Safety Net

The Center on Budget and Policy Priorities estimates that without food stamps and other safety net initiatives, the poverty rate would be *double* the official rate. Economist Jared Bernstein quantifies the importance of Social Security, arguing that without retirement benefits the elderly poverty rate would be *five times* the current rate.

The Koch Foundation and Mr. Konheim need to look beyond their own circles of privilege before making insulting comments about the lower-income half of America.

Critical Thinking

1. What are the different views about the extent of poverty?
2. What evidence does Buchheit provide to show that almost half of Americans are poor?
3. How should poverty be addressed?

Create Central

www.mhhe.com/createcentral

Internet References

Joint Center for Poverty Research
   www.jcpr.org

New American Studies Web
   www.georgetown.edu/crossroads/asw

Social Science Information Gateway
   http://sosig.esrc.bris.ac.uk

Sociology—Study Sociology Online
   http://edu.learnsoc.org

Sociology Web Resources
   http://www.mhhe.com/socscience/sociology/resources/index.htm

Sociosite
   http://www.topsite.com/goto/sociosite.net

Socioweb
   http://www.topsite.com/goto/socioweb.com

PAUL BUCHHEIT is a college teacher, a writer for progressive publications, and the founder and developer of social justice and educational websites (UsAgainstGreed.org, PayUpNow.org, RappingHistory.org.

Slow Growth and Inequality Are Political Choices. We Can Choose Otherwise by Joseph E. Stiglitz

83

Article   Prepared by: Kurt Finsterbusch, *University of Maryland, College Park*

Slow Growth and Inequality Are Political Choices. We Can Choose Otherwise

JOSEPH E. STIGLITZ

Learning Outcomes

After reading this article, you will be able to:

- Describe the contradictions between historical American values of opportunity and justice and the current massive inequalities and injustices.

- Describe the inequalities that exist in the realms of education and health.

- Analyze the ways that political and economic institutions and structures serve the rich.

A rich country with millions of poor people. A country that prides itself on being the land of opportunity, but in which a child's prospects are more dependent on the income and education of his or her parents than in other advanced countries. A country that believes in fair play, but in which the richest often pay a smaller percentage of their income in taxes than those less well off. A country in which children every day pledge allegiance to the flag, asserting that there is "justice for all," but in which, increasingly, there is only justice for those who can afford it. These are the contradictions that the United States is gradually and painfully struggling to come to terms with as it begins to comprehend the enormity of the inequalities that mark its society—inequities that are greater than in any other advanced country.

Those who strive not to think about this issue suggest that this is just about the "politics of envy." Those who discuss the issue are accused of fomenting class warfare. But as we have come to grasp the causes and consequences of these inequities

we have come to understand that this is not about envy. The extreme to which inequality has grown in the United States and the manner in which these inequities arise undermine our economy. Too much of the wealth at the top of the ladder arises from exploitation—whether from the exercise of monopoly power, from taking advantage of deficiencies in corporate governance laws to divert large amounts of corporate revenues to pay CEOs' outsized bonuses unrelated to true performance, or from a financial sector devoted to market manipulation, predatory and discriminatory lending, and abusive credit card practices. Too much of the poverty at the bottom of the income spectrum is due to economic discrimination and the failure to provide adequate education and health care to the nearly one out of five children growing up poor.

The growing debate about inequality in America today is, above all, about the nature of our society, our vision of who we are, and others' vision of us. We used to think of ourselves as a middle-class society, where each generation was better off than the last. At the foundation of our democracy was the middle class—the modern-day version of the small, property-owning American farmer whom Thomas Jefferson saw as the backbone of the country. It was understood that the best way to grow was to build out from the middle—rather than trickle down from the top. This commonsense perspective has been verified by studies at the International Monetary Fund, which demonstrate that countries with greater equality perform better—higher growth, more stability. It was one of the main messages of my book *The Price of Inequality.* Because of our tolerance for inequality, even the quintessential American Dream has been shown to be a myth: America is less of a land of opportunity than even most countries of "old Europe."

The articles in this special edition of the *Washington Monthly* describe the way that America's inequality plays out at each stage of one's life, with several articles focusing in particular on education. We now know that there are huge disparities even as children enter kindergarten. These grow larger over time, as the children of the rich, living in rich enclaves, get a better education than the one received by those attending schools in poorer areas. Economic segregation has become the order of the day, so much so that even those well-off and well-intentioned selective colleges that instituted programs of economic affirmative action—explicitly trying to increase the fraction of their student body from lower socioeconomic groups—have struggled to do so. The children of the poor can afford neither the advanced degrees that are increasingly required for employment nor the unpaid internships that provide the alternative route to "good" jobs.

Similar stories could be told about each of the dimensions of America's outsized inequality. Take health care. America is unique among the advanced countries in not recognizing access to health care as a basic human right. And that means if you are a poor American, your prospects of getting adequate, let alone good, medical care are worse than in other advanced countries. Even after passage of the Affordable Care Act (ACA), almost two dozen states have rejected expanding vitally needed Medicaid, and more than forty million Americans still lacked health insurance at the beginning of 2014. The dismal statistics concerning America's health care system are well known: while we spend more—far more—on health care (both per capita and as a percentage of gross domestic product) than other countries, health outcomes are worse. In Australia, for instance, spending on health care per capita is just over two-thirds that in the United States, yet health outcomes are better—including a life expectancy that is a remarkable three years longer.

Two of the reasons for our dismal health statistics are related to inequalities at the top and the bottom of our society—monopoly profits reaped by drug companies, medical device makers, health insurers, and highly concentrated provider networks drive prices, and inequality, up while the lack of access to timely care for the poor, including preventive medicine, makes the population sicker and more costly to treat. The ACA is helping on both accounts. The health insurance exchanges are designed to promote competition. And the whole act is designed to increase access. The numbers suggest it's working. As for costs, the widespread predictions that Obamacare would cause massive health care inflation have proven false, as the rate of increase in health care prices has remained comparatively moderate over the last several years, showing once again that there is no necessary trade-off between fairness and efficiency. The first year of the ACA showed significant increases in coverage—far more significant in those states that implemented the Medicaid expansion than in those that refused to

do so. But the ACA was a compromise, leaving out dental and long-term extended care insurance.

Inequities in health care, then, are still with us, beginning even before birth. The poor are more likely to be exposed to environmental hazards, and mothers have less access to good prenatal care. The result is infant mortality rates that are comparable to some developing countries alongside a higher incidence of low birth weight (systemically correlated with poor lifetime prospects) than in other advanced countries. Lack of access to comprehensive health care for the 20 percent of American children growing up in poverty, combined with lack of access to adequate nutrition, makes success in school even less likely. With the cheapest form of food often being unhealthy carbohydrates, the poor are more likely to face problems of childhood diabetes and obesity. The inequities continue throughout life—culminating in dramatically different statistics on life expectancy.

All well and good, you might say: it would be nice if we could give free health care to all, free college education to all, but these are dreams that have to be tamed by the harsh realities of what we can afford. Already the country has a large deficit. Proposals to create a more equal society would make the large deficit even larger—so the argument goes. America is especially constrained because it has assumed the costly mission of ensuring peace and security for the world.

This is nonsense, on several counts.

The real strength of the United States is derived from its "soft power," not its military power. But growing inequality is sapping our standing in the world from within. Can an economic system that provides so little opportunity—where real median household income (half above, half below, after adjusting for inflation) is lower today than it was a quarter century ago—provide a role model that others seek to emulate, even if a few at the very top have done very well?

Moreover, what we can afford is as much a matter of priorities as anything else. Other countries, such as the nations of Scandinavia, have, for instance, managed to provide good health care to all, virtually free college education for all, and good public transportation, *and* have done just as well, or even better, on standard metrics of economic performance: incomes per head and growth are at least comparable. Even some countries that are far poorer than the United States (such as Mauritius, off the east cost of Africa) have managed to provide free college education and better access to health care. A nation must make choices, and these countries have made different ones: they may spend less on their military, they may spend less on prisons, they may tax more.

Besides, many of the distributional issues are related not to how much we spend but who we spend it on. If we include within our expenditures the "tax expenditures" buried in our tax system, we effectively spend a lot more on the housing of the rich than is generally recognized. Interest deductability on a mega-mansion could easily be worth $25,000 a year. And alone among advanced economies, the United States tends to invest more in schools with richer student bodies than in those with mostly poor students—an effect of U.S. school districts' dependence on local tax bases for funding. Interestingly, according to some calculations, the entire deficit can be attributed to our inefficient and inequitable health care system: if we had a better health care system—of the kind that provided more equality at lower cost, such as those in so many European countries—we arguably wouldn't even have a federal budget deficit today.

Or consider this: if we provided more opportunity to the poor, including better education and an economic system that ensured access to jobs with decent pay, then perhaps we would not spend so much on prisons—in some states spending on prisons has at times exceeded that on universities. The poor instead would be better able to seize new employment opportunities, in turn making our economy more productive. And if we had better public transportation systems that made it easier and more affordable for working-class people to commute to where jobs are available, then a higher percentage of our population would be working and paying taxes. If, like the Scandinavian countries, we provided better child care and had more active labor market policies that assisted workers in moving from one job to another, we would have a higher labor force participation rate—and the enhanced growth would yield more tax revenues. It pays to invest in people.

This brings me to the final point: we could impose a fair tax system, raising more revenue, improving equity, and boosting economic growth while reducing distortions in our economy and our society. (That was the central finding of my 2014 Roosevelt Institute white paper, "Reforming Taxation to Promote Growth and Equity.") For instance, if we just imposed the same taxes on the returns to capital that we impose on those who work for a living, we could raise some $2 trillion over ten years. "Loopholes" does not adequately describe the flaws in our tax system; "gaps" might be better. Closing them might end the specter of the very rich almost proudly disclosing that they pay a tax rate on their disclosed income at half the rate of those with less income, and that they keep their money in tax havens like the Cayman Islands. No one can claim that the inhabitants of these small islands know how to manage money better than the wizards of Wall Street; but it seems as though that money grows better in the sunshine of these beach resorts!

One of the few advantages of there being so much money at the top of the income ladder, with close to a quarter of all income going to the top 1 percent, is that slight increases in taxes at the top can now raise large amounts of money. And because so much of the money at the top comes from exploitation (or as economists prefer to call it, "rent seeking"—that is,

seizing a larger share of the national pie rather than increasing its size), higher taxes at the top do not seem to have much of an adverse effect on economic performance.

Then there's our corporate tax rate. If we actually made corporations pay what they are supposed to pay and eliminated loopholes we would raise hundreds of billions of dollars. With the right redesign, we could even get more employment and investment in the United States. True, U.S. corporations face one of the higher *official* corporate tax rates among the advanced countries; but the reality is otherwise—as a share of corporate income actually paid, our federal corporate taxes are just 13 percent of reported worldwide income. By most accounts, the amount of taxes actually paid (as a percentage of profits) is no higher than the average of other advanced countries. Apple Inc., Google Inc., and General Electric Co. have become the poster children of American ingenuity—making products that are the envy of the rest of the world. But they are using too much of that ingenuity to figure out how to avoid paying their fair share of taxes. Yet they and other U.S. corporations make full use of ideas and innovations produced with the support of the U.S. government, starting with the Internet itself. At the same time they rely on the talent produced by the country's first-rate universities, all of which receive extensive support from the federal government. They even turn to the U.S. government to demand better treatment from our trading partners.

Corporations argue that they would not engage in so much despicable tax avoidance if tax rates were lower. But there is a far better solution, and one that the individual U.S. states have discovered: have corporations pay taxes based on the economic activity they conduct in the United States, on the basis of a simple formula reflecting their sales, their production, and their research activities here, and tax corporations that invest in the United States at lower rates than those that don't. In this way we could increase investment and employment here at home—a far cry from the current system, in which we in effect encourage even U.S. corporations to produce elsewhere. (Even if U.S. taxes are no higher than the average, there are some tax havens—like Ireland—that are engaged in a race to the bottom, trying to recruit companies to make their country their tax home.) Such a reform would end the corporate stampede toward "inversions," changing a corporation's tax home to avoid taxes. Where they claim their home office is would make little difference; only where they actually do business would.

Other sources of revenue would benefit our economy and our society. Two basic principles of taxation are that it is better to tax bad things than good; and it is better to tax factors in what economists call "inelastic supply"—meaning that the amounts produced and sold won't change when taxes are imposed on them. Thus, if we taxed pollution in all of its forms—including carbon emissions—we could raise hundreds of billions of dollars every year, and have a better environment. Similarly, appropriately designed taxes on the financial sector would not only raise considerable amounts of money but also discourage banks from imposing costs on others—as when they polluted the global economy with toxic mortgages.

The $700 billion bank bailout pales in comparison to what the bankers' fecklessness has cost our economy and our society—trillions of dollars in lost GDP, millions of Americans thrown out of their homes and jobs. Yet few in the financial world have been held accountable.

If we required the banks to pay but a fraction of the costs they have imposed on others, we would then have further funds to undo some of the damage that they caused by their discriminatory and predatory lending practices, which moved money from the bottom of the economic pyramid to the top. And by imposing even slight taxes on Wall Street's speculative activities via a financial transactions tax, we would raise much-needed revenue, decrease speculation (thus increasing economic stability), and encourage more productive use of our scarce resources, including the most valuable one: talented young Americans.

Similarly, by taxing land, oil, and minerals more—and forcing those who extract resources from public land to pay the full values of these resources, which rightly belong to *all* the people, we could then spend those proceeds for public investments—for instance, in education, technology, and infrastructure—without resulting in less land, less oil, fewer minerals. (Even if they are taxed more, these resources won't go on strike; they won't leave the country!) The result: increased long-term investments in our economy would pay substantial future dividends in higher economic productivity and growth—and if the money was spent right, we could have more shared prosperity. The question is not whether we can afford to do more about our inequality; it is whether we can afford *not* to do more. The debate in America is not about eliminating inequality. It is simply about moderating it and restoring the American Dream.

Critical Thinking

1. What are the negative impacts of the massive inequality in America?

2. Do you agree with Stiglitz that a big part of the problem of inequality and its negative impacts is our priorities?

3. Is America inordinate in the extent that tax rules and other policies benefit the rich?

Internet References

New American Studies Web
   https://blogs.commons.georgetown.edu/vkp/
Social Science Information Gateway
   http://www.ariadne.ac.uk/issue2/sosig
Sociology—Study Sociology Online
   http://edu.learnsoc.org/
Sociology Web Resources
   http://www.mhhe.com/socscience/sociology/resources/index.htm
Sociosite
   http://www.topsite.com/goto/sociosite.net
Socioweb
   http://www.topsite.com/goto/socioweb.com

JOSEPH E. STIGLITZ, a Nobel Laureate in economics, is University Professor at Columbia University. His most recent book, coauthored with Bruce Greenwald, is *Creating a Learning Society: A New Approach to Growth, Development, and Social Progress.*

Stiglitz, Joseph E. "Conclusion: Slow Growth and Inequality Are Political Choices. We can Choose Otherwise," *Washington Monthly,* November 2014. Copyright © 2014 Washington Monthly Publishing, LLC Used with permission of Washington Monthly.

Article   Prepared by: Kurt Finsterbusch, *University of Maryland, College Park*

America's Misguided Approach to Social Welfare

How the Country Could Get More for Less

KIMBERLY J. MORGAN

Learning Outcomes

After reading this article, you will be able to:

- Explain how the U.S. welfare system compares with the European welfare systems.

- Discuss different ways of measuring the costs of welfare for comparative purposes.

- Identify the defective aspects of the American welfare system.

D ebates about the proper role and size of government dominated the 2012 U.S. presidential election. President Barack Obama; his Republican rival, Mitt Romney; and their surrogates relentlessly sparred over who should pay what taxes, who should get what benefits, and how Washington should manage major sectors of life, such as health care and education. What neither side made clear was how the United States stacks up against other developed countries. As other countries embraced big government and generous social policies in the middle of the twentieth century, the common wisdom goes, the United States sought a relatively small welfare state. And for partisans on both sides of the aisle, one of the key issues up for grabs on November 6 was whether such American exceptionalism would persist or fade away.

A closer look at U.S. social spending shows that it is indeed distinctive, but not in the ways that many believe. The United States does tax less and spend less on social programs than most of the rich democracies with which it is usually compared. But even so, the country has developed a large and complex system of social protection, one that involves a mix of government spending, tax-based subsidies, and private social spending.

In its own way, the U.S. welfare system delivers many of the same benefits as the systems in other developed countries, including health insurance, pensions, housing support, and child care. And when added together, the amount of resources the public and private sectors commit to all these forms of welfare is massive: as a percentage of GDP, for example, spending on the health and welfare of citizens is greater in the United States than in most advanced industrial economies. Yet the American way of distributing welfare is lopsided and incomplete. Even after the Obama administration's Affordable Care Act is fully implemented in 2014, for example, the share of the population without health insurance in the United States will remain higher than in any other advanced industrial country—even as the American public spends more on health care than publics anywhere else in the world. And the United States does not guarantee the basic rights of paid parental and sick leave—rights assured to most other workers across the industrial world. In essence, Washington's reliance on private social benefits and services—often provided by businesses to their employees rather than by the government to everybody—ensures good coverage for some but poor coverage for others. Those with well-paying jobs usually get the best benefits, and those with low-paying or no jobs get worse ones. As a result, the United States' system of social protection does less to reduce poverty and inequality than that of virtually any other rich democracy.

Despite what some think, patching the U.S. social safety net need not mean setting the country on a path to socialism. The United States is on the far end of the spectrum when it comes to private social provision and tax-based benefits, but many other countries rely on a diverse mix of public and private welfare and tax subsidies, often leading to more equality and efficiency. The difference is that their systems consciously strive for those goals and are deliberately designed to ensure broad public access to benefits. It is time for Washington to take those models seriously in figuring out how to fix its own.

Who Benefits?

By one common measure of social policy—direct public spending on social programs as a percentage of GDP—the United States ranks near the bottom of the list of rich democracies. Only a few such countries, including Mexico, South Korea, and Turkey, spend less. But that measure is somewhat misleading and does not fully capture the resources the United States devotes to social welfare. More comprehensive calculations, such as the one for "net social expenditure" developed by the Organization for Economic Cooperation and Development (OECD), which includes taxes, pensions, health care and insurance, parental leave, unemployment benefits, child care, and related expenses, paint a different picture. According to the OECD figure, the United States has the fifth-highest social spending in the world, just after Sweden.

Net social expenditure provides a better account of countries' welfare efforts because it adds together direct public spending, tax-based spending, and private spending and takes into consideration the taxes people pay. Countries not only deliver benefits to their populations but tax them as well, effectively reducing the real value of benefits. Netting out taxes can make some countries' welfare states appear significantly less lavish than they might initially. As Andrea Louise Campbell recently wrote in these pages, the United States taxes its population less than most advanced industrial countries—so when people in the United States do get benefits, they get to keep most of them.

The United States ranks first in one particular component of the OECD's measure of net social expenditure, "tax breaks for social purposes." It is important to consider these in any picture of the American welfare state, because, as the political scientist Christopher Howard has shown, subsidies often do the same work as direct spending programs. From the Child and Dependent Care Credit, a tax reimbursement for child care, to the tax exemption for employer contributions to health insurance, to tax deductions for home mortgages, the federal government often uses this method to subsidize the well-being of its citizenry.

The United States is not the only country to use exclusions, exemptions, and other tax reductions to achieve social goals. In France, for instance, the income tax that households pay depends on the number of children in them, costing the French state around $18 billion in 2009, according to the Conseil des Prélèvements Obligatoires, an advisory council on taxation. In the Netherlands, parents receive a tax subsidy to help cover the cost of child care. About half of the OECD countries allow

taxpayers to deduct the interest they pay on home mortgages. Many allow tax breaks for private pensions, and in Australia, Canada, Ireland, and the Netherlands, those breaks are higher than they are in the United States.

Net social expenditure also includes private spending, whether mandated by the government (such as requirements that employers pay for sick leave) or voluntary (such as employer-provided pensions in the United States). As the scholars Jacob Hacker and Jennifer Klein have shown, the United States' reliance on voluntary private welfare is unique. Most adults in the United States receive benefits through their workplaces that include health insurance, pensions, dependentcare tax exclusions, and the like. This kind of private spending makes up nearly 40 percent of all U.S. social spending, compared with under 20 percent in the United Kingdom and about eight percent in France and Sweden.

Some think employer-provided benefits should not be included in measures of a country's social policy effort, because they do not involve the government's relations with its citizens and are thus not truly part of the public sphere. But if one wants to understand the total resources that societies devote to social welfare purposes and how those resources are allocated, one has to take such spending into consideration. And from the standpoint of households, ignoring private social benefits and tax breaks means leaving out a major source of their income security and well-being.

The Welfare Queen

One of the biggest canards about the American welfare state is that its primary function is to take from the rich and give to the poor. In reality, the vast majority of Americans benefit from some kind of government social program—about 96 percent, according to the political scientist Suzanne Mettler. And while there are some countries that do focus their social policies on helping the disadvantaged, the United States is not one of them.

Scholars have long assumed that the United States' welfare system resembles that of its English-speaking cousins in the Commonwealth of Nations, which tend to have strong strains of market liberalism and thus favor private spending over public spending. Australia, Canada, and New Zealand, for example, all fall near the bottom of the scale of public spending on social welfare. But these countries, like the United Kingdom, devote a relatively high proportion of their spending to programs that are contingent on the recipients' having low incomes. In Australia, for instance, more than a third of direct public spending goes to means-tested programs, and in Canada and the United Kingdom, almost a quarter does.

In the United States, however, only about seven percent of direct public spending goes to means-tested benefit programs. To be fair, this figure understates U.S. expenditures on low-income people because it leaves out in-kind benefits—benefits, such as health care (including Medicaid and the Children's Health Insurance Program), that are provided free or at reduced cost, as opposed to direct cash transfers. Nevertheless, according to an analysis by the Center on Budget and Policy Priorities, in 2010, 20 percent of entitlement spending in the United States went to the top ten percent of households, 58 percent of entitlement spending went to middle-income households, and 32 percent went to the bottom 20 percent.

Indirect benefits in the United States flow disproportionately to those in the middle and at the top of the income ladder. Some of the major U.S. tax breaks, such as the home mortgage interest deduction and that for charitable contributions, especially benefit those rich enough to take out a large mortgage or give large amounts of money to charity. Moreover, most tax benefits in the United States are designed as deductions—which help only those with large liabilities—rather than as possible sources of actual refunds, which would help lower-income citizens. (The Earned Income Tax Credit and the Child Tax Credit are notable exceptions, which is why they are so important to low-income parents.) In many other OECD countries, low-income families receive a much more generous and comprehensive array of tax subsidies and benefits, including family allowances, tax breaks for children, and subsidized child care.

Private social benefits in the United States, finally, also tend to accrue to middle- and upper-income people, since better-paying jobs usually come with more extensive benefit packages. Figures from the U.S. Bureau of Labor Statistics' National Compensation Survey reveal that the higher the average wage at a firm, the more likely that firm is to offer health coverage, retirement accounts, and life insurance. Thus, 85 percent of private firms whose average wage is in the top 25th percentile make retirement benefits available to their employees, but only 38 percent of firms whose average wage is in the bottom 25th percentile do. And the same is true for other types of benefits: 84 percent of private firms with average wages in the top 25th percentile offer paid sick leave, whereas just 29 percent of those paying wages in the bottom 25th percentile do.

Since U.S. social welfare spending is not directed primarily at the poor, it does little to reduce the country's rate of poverty or inequality. The United States ranks fourth from the bottom among OECD countries in terms of its poverty rate, just below Turkey and above Israel, Mexico, and Chile. The United States also has one of the most unequal distributions of income of the advanced industrial democracies. Although many countries have experienced rising poverty and inequality in recent decades because of economic, demographic, and technological changes, what sets the United States apart is how weakly these trends have been counteracted by tax and spending policies. Comparing poverty rates across countries before taxes are levied and benefits are paid is one way to show this. According to

OECD data from the end of the last decade, whereas taxes and transfers brought down poverty rates by 20 percentage points in the United Kingdom and by 25 percentage points in France, they did so by only ten percentage points in the United States.

In sum, U.S. social welfare spending is comparatively high but only minimally redistributive. Unfortunately, Washington's track record is also mixed when it comes to assuring quality health care for all, sustaining livable incomes for senior citizens, and investing in the future productivity of the population at large.

The Money Pits

The large size of total social welfare spending in the United States has a lot to do with health care. In 2010, total health-care spending amounted to 17.6 percent of U.S. GDP, almost double the OECD average of 9.5 percent. The next-highest spender, the Netherlands, laid out 12 percent of its GDP on health care. The United States' unusually high spending on health care not only harms the fiscal balances of federal and state governments but also diverts economic resources away from other goals. Government has less to spend on other social or economic objectives, and households end up devoting significant chunks of their incomes to health-care costs. As a 2011 study by the health economists David Auerbach and Arthur Kellermann in the journal *Health Affairs* showed, between 1999 and 2009, median-income U.S. families of four saw their gross annual incomes rise, but the gain was offset by increased spending on health care.

Most other rich nations not only spend less than the United States does on health care; they also achieve better outcomes in both coverage and quality. All the other advanced industrial nations provide universal or near-universal health insurance, while in the United States, almost 16 percent of the population (or about 48 million people, including seven million children) currently lack health insurance. The Congressional Budget Office has estimated that even after the full implementation of the Affordable Care Act, about 30 million people will remain uninsured.

Claims that all this spending at least buys Americans excellent care are dubious. The United States does lead other nations in the availability of hightech treatments; it ranks second in per capita availability of MRI units, for example (with almost three times as many MRI machines as the OECD average) and third in per capita availability of CT scanners (with double the OECD average). But it is well below average in per capita availability of hospital beds, doctors, and doctor consultations.

Americans like to tell horror stories about waiting lists for medical procedures in other nations, and some of those stories are true, especially when it comes to elective procedures, such as hip replacements. But the United States falls short when it comes to access to basic care: according to a 2011 study by the Commonwealth Fund, a private foundation created to promote better health care, in 2008, only 43 percent of American adults could get a same- or next-day appointment to see a doctor about a medical condition, compared with 80 percent in the Netherlands, 62 percent in France, and 61 percent in the United Kingdom. Americans report experiencing medical mistakes more than people in similarly developed countries, too. Due in part to difficulties in gaining access to care, the Commonwealth report ranked the United States at the bottom of the 16 nations it studied in "preventable mortality"—deaths that could have been prevented if timely and effective care had been provided.

Retirement pensions are the other major U.S. outlay on social welfare. In this category, the country is in the upper third of OECD nations in direct public spending. And adding in other spending on pensions and survivors' benefits, the United States ranks well above many countries known for their largess, such as Canada, Denmark, and the Netherlands. Yet even this strongest part of the American safety net comes with some caveats. Social Security has been one of the most effective antipoverty programs in history, dramatically reducing the hardship of hundreds of millions of U.S. seniors over the decades. But it still only partially replaces retirees' incomes, and the remaining need is often inadequately filled by private retirement plans. According to calculations by the Center for Retirement Research at Boston College, at the current retirement age of 66, only 55 percent of households have enough savings, investments, and expected Social Security benefits combined to maintain their previous standards of living.

If expenditures on health care and Social Security are high, spending on families is low. Despite various tax subsidies aimed at this group, the United States ranks near the bottom of OECD countries when it comes to outlays on family welfare. In a study of 173 countries, Jody Heymann, founder and director of the Project on Global Working Families, and her colleagues found that the United States is one of only four in this group of countries that do not guarantee employees paid leave for childbirth. All European countries provide between 14 and 20 weeks of paid maternity leave, usually offering between 70 and 100 percent of wages, followed by a further period of paid or unpaid parental leave. By contrast, the United States mandates only that employers with 50 or more workers allow 12 weeks of unpaid family leave. And employers have not filled the gap on their own: a 2007 National Compensation Survey from the Bureau of Labor Statistics found that only about eight percent of employees in the private sector and 15 percent of those working for state or local government had access to paid family leave.

Direct and indirect public subsidies for child care are limited, moreover, and access to public or private early childhood education varies enormously by region and income group. In 2008, the percentage of American children between the ages of three and five who were enrolled in preschool was 56 percent. The percentages in Belgium, Denmark, France, Germany, Italy, New Zealand, Norway, Sweden, and the United Kingdom were between 90 and 100 percent. In other words, although the United States devotes considerable public and private resources to social welfare, it fails to effectively meet its public's needs.

The Socialism Canard

If American politicians ever acknowledge the shortcomings of U.S. social spending, they usually assume that the only alternative is European "socialism." In such a "government-centered society," in Romney's words, centralized state bureaucracies intrude on markets and the family; limit freedom by imposing taxes, mandates, and regulations; and force people into one-size-fits-all public services of poor quality. But such views of the social welfare policies of other nations are simplistic.

Several OECD countries have found ways to ensure widespread access to benefits and services without "socializing" the sectors in question. Australia, the Nordic countries, and most countries in southern Europe do all finance and provide health care through public agencies. However, in Canada, Japan, and much of continental Europe, although the government mostly pays for public health care, it is private actors and organizations that provide the health care itself. And in the continental European countries, private insurance either supplements a public insurance system (as in France and Germany) or is the dominant source of coverage (as in the Netherlands and Switzerland). In the Swiss system, for instance, all individuals have to buy insurance, insurers have to accept all who apply for coverage, and public subsidies ensure that coverage is affordable for all. (According to the Commonwealth Fund, about 30 percent of Swiss receive such subsidies.)

In terms of family welfare, in Germany, child care is mainly the responsibility of municipal governments, which funnel subsidies to nonprofit organizations that run daycare centers. In Australia, the Netherlands, and the United Kingdom, most child care is publicly subsidized and is provided by either nonprofit or for-profit entities. In France, publicly subsidized babysitters care for nearly one-third of children under three. Even in the Scandinavian countries, where publicly provided daycare is most common, the state offers considerable benefits to parents who care for their children at home.

The success of some public–private partnerships in Europe shows that generous, effective, and broadly accessible social welfare policies do not require large government bureaucracies staffed with armies of public servants. The government does not have to perform the work itself. But it does have to mandate its provision and monitor the agencies that perform it. Leaving social welfare up to private-sector employers without adequate public support or regulation ensures that many people will fall through the cracks. If Americans truly believe that basic social services are things that all citizens deserve, they should not be content with a social welfare system that often makes getting such services a matter of privilege or luck.

For example, rather than leaving it up to employers and individuals to take care of pension benefits, the government could mandate their provision, making them a required supplement on top of existing Social Security benefits. Washington might also consider requiring all employers to provide three months of paid family leave, with the benefits paid for by a combination of employer and employee contributions. A similar measure could mandate that employers offer paid sick days to all employees. Or the federal government could provide incentives for states to formulate such policies themselves, encouraging local experimentation while helping families across the country get what is considered an unquestioned right almost everywhere else. California and New Jersey have adopted paid family leave funded by employee contributions, and although the benefits are fairly low, all new parents—not just those with means or generous employers—can take paid time off from work.

Those interested in effective social policy could also look closely at the activities subsidized through the tax code. When budgets are tight and poverty is high, giving rich people thousands of dollars in tax breaks so they can buy expensive homes does not seem like a wise use of public resources. There is no reason why U.S. tax-based subsidies could not be adjusted according to income, with the deductions or credits getting phased out as citizens' incomes climb. Making more tax breaks refundable (instead of in the form of deductions), moreover, would guarantee that the benefits flowed to people who truly needed them, rather than to those higher up the income-distribution scale. Even after granting such subsidies, the government could continue to rely heavily on the private sector to deliver services, but it could do so at lower cost and to greater effect for a larger share of the population.

There is no easy political path to reforming a deeply entrenched status quo. Filling in the gaps of the American social welfare system to better help the less fortunate will involve limiting or eliminating some benefits enjoyed by others, generally those who are better off and far more politically powerful. These kinds of tough choices already loom, as the cost of health care continues to balloon and public finances are spread thin. But the lesson from peer countries is that the policy challenges themselves are not insurmountable: it is possible to provide better services to more people at a lower total cost than the United States does now, without massive government intervention, a dramatic loss of freedom, or any of the other supposed dangers lurking in the background.

Critical Thinking

1. What aspects of the American welfare system are relatively good and what aspects are relatively bad?
2. How would you improve the American welfare system?
3. To what extent does the government take from the rich and give to the poor?

Internet References

New American Studies Web
https://blogs.commons.georgetown.edu/vkp/

Social Science Information Gateway
http://www.ariadne.ac.uk/issue2/sosig

Sociology–Study Sociology Online
http://edu.learnsoc.org/

Sociology Web Resources
http://www.mhhe.com/socscience/sociology/resources/index.htm

Sociosite
http://www.topsite.com/goto/sociosite.net

Socioweb
http://www.topsite.com/goto/socioweb.com

KIMBERLY J. MORGAN is Associate Professor of Political Science and International Affairs at George Washington University.

Article   Prepared by: Kurt Finsterbusch, *University of Maryland, College Park*

Are You Racist?

Science is beginning to unmask the bigot inside your brain.

CHRIS MOONEY

Learning Outcomes

After reading this article, you will be able to:

- Explain how many consciously nonracist people are unconsciously racist.

- Explain how the deepest prejudice is a preference for one's own group.

- Describe the differences between conservatives and liberals and between races on their level of bias and prejudice.

"You're not, like, a total racist bastard," David Amodio tells me. He pauses. "Today."

I'm sitting in the soft-spoken cognitive neuroscientist's spotless office nestled within New York University's psychology department, but it feels like I'm at the doctor's, getting a dreaded diagnosis. On his giant monitor, Amodio shows me a big blob of data, a cluster of points depicting where people score on the Implicit Association Test. The test measures racial prejudices that we cannot consciously control. I've taken it three times now. This time around my uncontrolled prejudice, while clearly present, has come in significantly below the average for white people like me.

That certainly beats the first time I took the IAT online, on the website UnderstandingPrejudice.org. That time, my results showed a "strong automatic preference" for European Americans over African Americans. That was not a good thing to hear, but it's extremely common—51 percent of online test takers show moderate to strong bias.

Taking the IAT, one of the most popular tools among researchers trying to understand racism and prejudice, is both extremely simple and pretty traumatic. The test asks you to rapidly categorize images of faces as either "African American"

or "European American" while you also categorize words (like "evil," "happy," "awful," and "peace") as either "good" or "bad." Faces and words flash on the screen, and you tap a key, as fast as you can, to indicate which category is appropriate.

Sometimes you're asked to sort African American faces and "good" words to one side of the screen. Other times, black faces are to be sorted with "bad" words. As words and faces keep flashing by, you struggle not to make too many sorting mistakes.

And then suddenly, you have a horrible realization. When black faces and "bad" words are paired together, you feel yourself becoming faster in your categorizing—an indication that the two are more easily linked in your mind. "It's like you're on a bike going downhill," Amodio says, "and you feel yourself going faster. So you can say, 'I know this is not how I want to come off,' but there's no other response option."

You think of yourself as a person who strives to be unprejudiced, but you can't control these split-second reactions. As the milliseconds are being tallied up, you know the tale they'll tell: When negative words and black faces are paired together, you're a better, faster categorizer. Which suggests that racially biased messages from the culture around you have shaped the very wiring of your brain.

I went to NYU to learn what psychologists could tell me about racial prejudice in the wake of the shooting of a black teenager, Michael Brown, by a white police officer, Darren Wilson, in Ferguson, Missouri. We may never really know the exact sequence of events and assumptions that led to the moment when Brown, unarmed and, according to witnesses, with his hands in the air, was shot multiple times. But the incident is the latest embodiment of America's racial paradox: On the one hand, overt expressions of prejudice have grown markedly less common than they were in the Archie Bunker era. We elected, and reelected, a black president. In many parts of the country, hardly anyone bats an eye at interracial relationships. Most people do not consider racial hostility acceptable. That's why it was so shocking when Los Angeles Clippers owner Donald Sterling was caught telling his girlfriend not to bring black people to games—and why those comments led the NBA to ban Sterling for life. And yet, the killings of Michael Brown, Jordan Davis, Renisha McBride, Trayvon Martin, and so many others remind us that we are far from a prejudice-free society.

Science offers an explanation for this paradox—albeit a very uncomfortable one. An impressive body of psychological research suggests that the men who killed Brown and Martin need not have been conscious, overt racists to do what they did (though they may have been). The same goes for the crowds that flock to support the shooter each time these tragedies become public, or the birthers whose racially tinged conspiracy theories paint President Obama as a usurper. These people who voice mind-boggling opinions while swearing they're not racist at all—they make sense to science, because the paradigm for understanding prejudice has evolved. There "doesn't need to be intent, doesn't need to be desire; there could even be desire in the opposite direction," explains University of Virginia psychologist Brian Nosek, a prominent IAT researcher. "But biased results can still occur."

The IAT is the most famous demonstration of this reality, but it's just one of many similar tools. Through them, psychologists have chased prejudice back to its lair—the human brain.

We're not born with racial prejudices. We may never even have been "taught" them. Rather, explains Nosek, prejudice draws on "many of the same tools that help our minds figure out what's good and what's bad." In evolutionary terms, it's efficient to quickly classify a grizzly bear as "dangerous." The trouble comes when the brain uses similar processes to form negative views about groups of people.

But here's the good news: Research suggests that once we understand the psychological pathways that lead to prejudice, we just might be able to train our brains to go in the opposite direction.

Dog, cat. Hot, cold. Black, white. Male, female. We constantly categorize. We have to. Sorting anything from furniture to animals to concepts into different filing folders inside our brains is something that happens automatically, and it helps us function. In fact, categorization has an evolutionary purpose: Assuming that all mushrooms are poisonous, that all lions want to eat you, is a very effective way of coping with your surroundings. Forget being nuanced about nonpoisonous mushrooms and occasionally nonhungry lions—certitude keeps you safe.

But a particular way of categorizing can be inaccurate, and those false categories can lead to prejudice and stereotyping. Much psychological research into bias has focused on how people "essentialize" certain categories, which boils down to assuming that these categories have an underlying nature that is tied to inherent and immutable qualities. Like the broader sorting mechanism of categorization, an essentialist cognitive "style" emerges very early in our development and may to some extent be hardwired. Psychologist Susan Gelman of the University of Michigan explains it this way: The category of "things that are white" is not essentialized. It simply contains anything that happens to share the attribute of "white": cars, paint, paper, and so on. There's nothing deep that unites the members of this category.

But now consider white and black *people*. Like other human attributes (gender, age, and sexual orientation, for example), race tends to be strongly—and inaccurately—essentialized. This means that when you think of people in that category, you rapidly or even automatically come up with assumptions about their characteristics—characteristics that your brain perceives as unchanging and often rooted in biology. Common stereotypes with the category "African Americans," for example, include "loud," "good dancers," and "good at sports." (One recent study found that white people also tend to essentialize African Americans as magical—test subjects associated black faces with words like "paranormal" and "spirit.") Of course, these assumptions are false. Indeed, essentialism about any group of people is dubious—women are not innately gentle, old people are not inherently feebleminded—and when it comes to race, the idea of deep and fundamental differences has been roundly debunked by scientists.

Even people who know that essentializing race is wrong can't help absorbing the stereotypes that are pervasive in our culture. But essentialist thinking varies greatly between individuals. It's kind of like neurosis: We all have a little bit, but in some people, it's much more pronounced. In national polls, for example, fewer and fewer Americans admit openly to holding racist views. But when told to rate various groups with questions like, "Do people in these groups tend to be unintelligent or tend to be intelligent?" more than half of those asked exhibited strong bias against African Americans. Even the labels we use seem to affect our level of prejudice: Another study found that test subjects associated the term "black" with more negative attributes—such as low socioeconomic status—than "African American."

One of the earliest and most insightful researchers on these varying rates of bias was Else Frenkel-Brunswik, part of a pioneering generation of post-World War II psychologists who sought to understand why some people seem to find prejudiced and fascist ideas so appealing. Born in 1908 to a Jewish family in what is now Ukraine, Frenkel-Brunswik might never have managed to do her research at all had she not twice escaped the forces of prejudice herself. When she was young, a 1914 pogrom forced her family to flee to Vienna. When Germany annexed Austria in 1938, she sought refuge in the United States.

Frenkel-Brunswik's work came long before the days of high-tech tools like eye trackers and computer games that measure bias based on millisecond differences between reactions. Instead she used something far simpler: cards.

She studied young children, some of whom she had previously documented to be highly prejudiced and ethnocentric. In one of many experiments, Frenkel-Brunswik showed the children a sequence of cards . . . On the first card, the animal is clearly and distinctly a cat. On the last card, it is just as clearly and distinctly a dog. But in between, the cat slowly transforms into the dog.

At each of the stages, the children were asked to identify the animal on the card. Among the more prejudiced children, Frenkel-Brunswik noted something striking: As the image became increasingly ambiguous, "there was a greater reluctance to give up the original object about which one had felt relatively certain . . . a tendency not to see what did not harmonize with the first set as well as a shying away from transitional solutions." In other words, for these children, it was much harder to let go of the idea that a cat was a cat.

What Frenkel-Brunswik realized back in 1949, modern research reaffirms. The Implicit Association Test, after all, boils down to how your mind automatically links certain categories. "It's really how strongly you associate your category of 'black people' with the general category of 'good things' or 'bad things,'" David Amodio told me. "The capacity to discern 'us' from 'them' is fundamental in the human brain," he wrote in a 2014 paper. "Although this computation takes just a fraction of a second, it sets the stage for social categorization, stereotypes, prejudices, intergroup conflict and inequality, and, at the extremes, war and genocide." Call it the banality of prejudice.

The process of categorizing the world obviously includes identifying the group or groups to which you belong. And that's where the next psychological factor underpinning prejudice emerges. Much research has found that humans are tribal creatures, showing strong bias against those we perceive as different from us and favoritism toward those we perceive as similar.

In fact, we humans will divide ourselves into in-groups and out-groups even when the perceived differences between the specific groups are completely arbitrary. In one classic study, subjects are asked to rate how much they like a large series of paintings, some of which are described as belonging to the "Red" artistic school and others to the "Green" school. Then participants are sorted into two groups, red or green—not based on their favoring one school of painting, as they are made to think, but actually at random. In subsequent tasks, people consistently show favoritism toward the arbitrary color group to which they are assigned. When asked to allocate money to other participants, the majority of "reds" more generously fund other reds—despite the fact that they have never actually met them. The same goes for "greens."

The upshot of such "minimal group" experiments is that if you give people the slightest push toward behaving tribally,

they happily comply. So if race is the basis on which tribes are identified, expect serious problems.

As these experiments suggest, it is not that we are either prejudiced or unprejudiced, period. Rather, we are more and less prejudiced, based on our upbringings and experiences but also on a variety of temporary or situational prompts (like being told we're on the green team).

One simple, evolutionary explanation for our innate tendency toward tribalism is safety in numbers. You're more likely to survive an attack from a marauding tribe if you join forces with your buddies. And primal fear of those not in the in-group also seems closely tied to racial bias. Amodio's research suggests that one key area associated with prejudice is the amygdala, a small and evolutionarily ancient region in the middle of the brain that is responsible for triggering the notorious "fight or flight" response. In interracial situations, Amodio explains, amygdala firing can translate into anything from "less direct eye gaze and more social distance" to literal fear and vigilance toward those of other races.

We've seen how a variety of cognitive behaviors feed into prejudice. But you know what will really blow your mind? The way that prejudice (or rather, the cognitive styles that underlie it) can interfere with how our brains function—often for the worse.

Consider, for instance, research by Carmit Tadmor, a psychologist at the Recanati School of Business at Tel Aviv University. In one 2013 paper, Tadmor and her colleagues showed that racial prejudice can play a direct and causal role in making people less creative. We're not talking about artistic creativity here, but more like seeing beyond the constraints of traditional categories—"thinking outside the box."

Tadmor's team first uncovered a simple positive correlation between one's inclination to endorse an essentialist view of race (like associating racial differences with abilities and personality traits) and one's creativity. To measure the latter, the researchers used a simple open-ended test in which individuals are asked to list as many possible uses of a brick as they can think of. People who can think outside of traditional categories—realizing that a brick can be used for many things other than buildings (it can make a good paperweight, for starters)—score better. This study showed that people who essentialized racial categories tended to have fewer innovative ideas about a brick.

But that was just the beginning. Next, a new set of research subjects read essays that described race either as a fundamental difference between people (an essentialist position) or as a construct, not reflecting anything more than skin-deep differences (a nonessentialist position). After reading the essays, the subjects moved on to a difficult creativity test that requires you to identify the one key word that unites three seemingly unassociated words. Thus, for instance, if you are given the words "call," "pay," and "line," the correct answer is "phone."

Remarkably, subjects who'd read the nonessentialist essay about race fared considerably better on the creativity test. Their mean score was a full point—or 32 percent—higher than it was for those who read the essentialist essay.

It's not like the people in this study were selected because of their preexisting racial prejudices. They weren't. Instead, merely a temporary exposure to essentialist thinking seemed to hamper their cognitive flexibility. "Essentialism appears to exert its negative effects on creativity not through *what* people think but *how* they think," conclude Tadmor and her colleagues. That's because, they add, "stereotyping and creative stagnation are rooted in a similar tendency to overrely on existing category attributes." Those quick-judgment skills that allowed us to survive on the savanna? Not always helpful in modern life.

So, yes: Prejudice and essentialism are bad for your brain—if you value creative thinking, anyway. But they can also be downright dangerous.

At NYU, David Amodio sat me down to take another test called the Weapons Identification Task. I had no idea what I was in for.

In this test, like on the IAT, you have two buttons that you can push. Images flash rapidly on the screen, and your task is to push the left shift key if you see a tool (a wrench, or a power drill, say) and the right shift key if you see a gun. You have to go super fast—if you don't respond within half a second, the screen blares at you, in giant red letters, "TOO SLOW."

"It does that to keep you from thinking too much," Amodio would later explain.

But it's not just guns and tools flashing on the screen: Before each object you see a face, either white or black. The faces appear for a split second, the objects for a split second, and then you have to press a key. If you are faster and more accurate at identifying guns after you see a black face than after you see a white face, that would suggest your brain associates guns (and threat) more with the former. You might also be more inclined to wrongly think you see a gun, when it's actually just a tool, right after seeing a black face. (The weapons task was created by psychologist Keith Payne of the University of North Carolina-Chapel Hill in response to the tragic 1999 death of Amadou Diallo, a Guinean immigrant shot by New York City police after the officers mistook the wallet in his hand for a weapon.)

I'm sorry to ruin the suspense: I don't know what my score was on the Weapons Identification Task. The test ruffled me so much that I messed up badly. It is stressful to have to answer quickly to avoid being rebuked by the game. And it's even more upsetting to realize that you've just "seen" a gun that wasn't actually there, right after a black face flashed.

This happened to me several times, and then I suddenly found myself getting "TOO SLOW" messages whenever the object to be identified was a gun. This went on for many minutes and numerous trials. For a while, I thought the test was

broken. But it wasn't: I finally realized that rather than pressing the right shift key, I had somehow started pressing the enter key whenever I thought I saw a gun. It's almost like I'd subconsciously decided to stop making "gun" choices at all. (Psychoanalyze that.)

But don't take that as a cop-out: Before I (arguably) tried to dodge responsibility by pressing the wrong key, I clearly showed implicit bias. And it was horrifying.

The upshot of all of this research is that in order to rid the world of prejudice, we can't simply snuff out overt, conscious, full-throated racism. Nor can we fundamentally remake the human brain, with its rapid-fire associations and its categorizing, essentializing, and groupish tendencies. Instead, the key lies in shifting people's behavior, even as we also make them aware of how cultural assumptions merge with natural cognitive processes to create biases they may not know they have.

And that just might be possible. Take the Implicit Association Test: In a massive study, Brian Nosek of the University of Virginia and his colleagues tested 17 different proposed ways of reducing people's unconscious bias on the IAT. Many of these experimental interventions failed. But some succeeded, and there was an interesting pattern to those that did.

The single best intervention involved putting people into scenarios and mindsets in which a black person became their ally (or even saved their life) while white people were depicted as the bad guys. In this intervention, participants "read an evocative story told in second-person narrative in which a White man assaults the participant and a Black man rescues the participant." In other words, study subjects are induced to feel as if they have been personally helped or even saved by someone from a different race. Then they took the IAT—and showed 48 percent less bias than a control group. (Note: The groups in these various studies were roughly three-fourths white; no participants were black.)

Other variations on this idea were successful too: making nonblack people think about black role models, or imagine themselves playing on a dodgeball team with black teammates against a team of white people (who proceed to cheat). In other

---

Armed and Dangerous?

Denver police officers and community members were shown photos of black and white men—some holding guns, others holding harmless objects like wallets—and asked to press the "shoot" or "don't shoot" button for each image. The result: Cops were better than community members at determining whether a target was armed (and they fired faster), but they still showed bias against black targets.

words, it appears that our tribal instincts can actually be co-opted to decrease prejudice, if we are made to see those of other races as part of our team.

When it comes to weakening racial essentialism, Carmit Tadmor and her colleagues undertook a variety of experiments to try to produce what they called "epistemic unfreezing." Subjects were exposed to one of three 20-minute multimedia presentations: one exclusively about American culture, one exclusively about Chinese culture, and one comparing American and Chinese cultures (with different aspects of each culture, such as architecture or food, presented back to back). Only in the last scenario were subjects pushed to compare and contrast the two cultures, presumably leading to a more nuanced perspective on their similarities and differences.

This experimental manipulation has been found to increase creativity. But surprisingly, it also had a big effect on reducing anti-black prejudice. In one study, Tadmor et al. found that white research subjects who had heard the multicultural presentation (but not the American-only or Chinese-only presentation) were less likely than members of the other study groups to endorse stereotypes about African Americans. That was true even though the subjects had learned about Chinese and American cultures, not African American culture.

In a variation, the same 20-minute lecture also produced fewer discriminatory hiring decisions. After hearing one of the three kinds of lectures, white study subjects were shown a series of résumés for the position of "Sales Manager" at a company. The résumés were varied so that some applicants had white-sounding names, and some had black-sounding names. It's a research paradigm that has often been shown to produce discriminatory effects, which presumably occur through the manifestation of uncontrolled or implicit prejudices—but this time around, there was a glimmer of hope in the findings.

White subjects who had heard the lecture exclusively about American culture (with topics like Disney, Coca-Cola, and the White House) picked a white candidate over an equally qualified black candidate 81 percent of the time. Subjects who had heard a lecture exclusively about Chinese culture picked a white candidate a full 86 percent of the time. But subjects who had heard the culture-comparing lecture selected the white candidate only 56 percent of the time.

These studies clearly suggest that, at least for the relatively short time span of a psychology experiment, there are cognitive ways to make people less prejudiced. That's not the same as—nor can it be a substitute for—broader cultural or institutional change. After all, there is ample evidence that culture feeds directly into the mind's process of generating prejudices and adopting stereotypical beliefs.

Nonetheless, if prejudice has both a psychological side and a cultural side, we must address both of these aspects. A good start may simply be making people aware of just how

unconsciously biased they can be. That's particularly critical in law enforcement, where implicit biases can lead to tragic outcomes.

In fact, this phenomenon has been directly studied in the lab, particularly through first-person shooter tests, where subjects must rapidly decide whether to shoot individuals holding either guns or harmless objects like wallets and soda cans. Research suggests that police officers (those studied were mostly white) are much more accurate at the general task (not shooting unarmed people) than civilians, thanks to their training. But like civilians, police are considerably slower to press the "don't shoot" button for an unarmed black man than they are for an unarmed white man—and faster to shoot an armed black man than an armed white man. (Women weren't included—the extra variable of gender would have complicated the results.)

Such research has led to initiatives like the Fair and Impartial Policing program, which has trained officers across the United States on how implicit biases work and how to control them. Few officers look forward to these trainings, says program founder Lorie Fridell, a criminologist; they don't consider themselves to be racist. "Police are very defensive about this issue," she says. "That's because we have been dealing with this issue using outdated science. We treat them as if they have an explicit bias. They are offended by that."

So instead, Fridell's team focuses first on showing the officers the subtle ways in which implicit bias might influence their actions. For example: The trainers present a role-play where there are three people: a female victim of domestic violence, and a male and female comforting her. When the officers are asked to address the situation, says Fridell, most assume that the man is the perp. Then, the trainers reveal that it was actually the woman—and the officers learn that they do, in fact, act on bias. It's not because they are bad people; in fact, in their work, they may have experiences that reinforce stereotypes. Which is why it's important that police officers—who see the worst in people in their everyday duties—teach themselves not to *assume* the worst.

The program, which receives support from the US Department of Justice, has trained officers in more than 250 precincts and agencies, but it's hard to measure its success—there is no baseline comparison, since prejudiced policing isn't always rigorously documented. But the feedback is encouraging. "I have a new awareness of bias-based policing within my own agency," one participant wrote in an evaluation. "The presentation of scientific data provided me with a more convincing argument that supported the existence of unintentional, but widespread racial bias, which I was typically quick to dismiss."

Staff members at the University of California-Los Angeles-based Center for Policing Equity use implicit-bias research in a different way: They take unconscious prejudice as a given—and try to make changes within communities to ensure that it does as little damage as possible. A few years ago, Las Vegas was seeking to address police officers' use of force, especially against people of color. Most of the incidents occurred after pursuits of suspects on foot, the majority of which happened in nonwhite neighborhoods. Center president Phillip Atiba Goff explains that he knew how difficult it would be to change the pursuing officers' thinking. "You're an officer, you're pumping adrenaline, you don't have time to evaluate whether your implicit bias is driving your behavior," he says. So instead, the center worked with the department to make a small but meaningful tweak to the rules: In foot chases, the pursuing officer would no longer be allowed to touch the person being chased; if use of force was necessary, a partner who wasn't involved in the pursuit would step in. "We recognized implicit bias, and we took it out of the equation," Goff says. "We decoupled the prejudice from the behavior." Sure enough, use of force in foot chases—and, as a result, overall use of force against people of color—declined significantly shortly after the policy went into effect.

Unsettling though it is, the latest research on our brains could actually have some very positive outcomes—if we use it in the right way. The link between essentialism and creativity doesn't just tell us how we might reduce prejudice. It could also help us to become a more innovative country—by prioritizing diversity, and the cognitive complexity and boost in creativity it entails. The research on rapid-fire, implicit biases, meanwhile, should restart a debate over the role of media—the news segment that depicts immigrants as hostile job snatchers, the misogynistic lyrics in a song—in subtly imparting stereotypes that literally affect brain wiring. Indeed, you could argue that not only does the culture in which we live make us subtly prejudiced, but it does so against our will. That's a disturbing thought.

Especially when you consider how biases affect government policy. Consider this: In October 2012, researchers from the University of Southern California sent emails asking legislators in districts with large Latino populations what documentation was needed in order to vote. Half the emails came from people with Anglo-sounding names; the other half, Latino-sounding names. Republican politicians who had sponsored voter ID laws responded to 27 percent of emails from "Latino" constituents and 67 percent of emails from "white" constituents. For Republicans who'd voted against voter ID laws, the gap was far less dramatic—the response figures were 38 percent for Latino names and 54 percent for white names.

You can imagine how this kind of thing might create a vicious cycle: When biased legislators make it harder for certain communities to vote, they are also less likely to serve alongside lawmakers from those communities—thus making it less likely for a coalitional experience to change their biases.

So how do we break the cycle? We could require lawmakers to engage in exercises to recognize their own unconscious prejudice, like the Fair and Impartial Policing program does. Or we could even go a step further and anonymize emails they receive from constituents—thus taking implicit bias out of the equation.

Short of that, you can do something very simple to fight prejudice: Trick your brain. UNC-Chapel Hill's Payne suggests that by deliberately thinking a thought that is directly counter to widespread stereotypes, you can break normal patterns of association. What counts as counterstereotypical? Well, Payne's study found that when research subjects were instructed to think the word "safe" whenever they saw a black face—undermining the stereotypical association between black people and danger—they were 10 percent less likely than those in a control group to misidentify a gun in the Weapons Identification Task.

To be sure, it will take more than thought exercises to erase the deep tracks of prejudice America has carved through the generations. But consciousness and awareness are a start—and the psychological research is nothing if not a consciousness-raiser. Taking the IAT made me realize that we can't just draw some arbitrary line between prejudiced people and unprejudiced people, and declare ourselves to be on the side of the angels. Biases have slipped into all of our brains. And that means we all have a responsibility to recognize those biases—and work to change them.

Critical Thinking

1. Are you a racist? Explain.
2. How does evolutionary theory explain our unconscious racial biases?
3. What can we do about our unconscious biases?

Internet References

New American Studies Web
   https://blogs.commons.georgetown.edu/vkp/

Social Science Information Gateway
   http://www.ariadne.ac.uk/issue2/sosig

Sociology—Study Sociology Online
   http://edu.learnsoc.org/

Sociology Web Resources
   http://www.mhhe.com/socscience/sociology/resources/index.htm

Sociosite
   http://www.topsite.com/goto/sociosite.net

Socioweb
   http://www.topsite.com/goto/socioweb.com

Article   Prepared by: Kurt Finsterbusch, *University of Maryland, College Park*

Black Pathology and the Closing of the Progressive Mind

Ta-Nehisi Coates

Learning Outcomes

After reading this article, you will be able to:

- Understand the roles of both the culture of white supremacy and structural conditions in explaining the situation of blacks in the United States.

- Be able to evaluate the strength and weakness of the cultural explanation of the situation of blacks.

- Discuss the strengths of black culture.

Among opinion writers, Jonathan Chait is outranked in my esteem only by Hendrik Hertzberg. This lovely takedown of Robert Johnson is a classic of the genre, one I studied incessantly when I was sharpening my own sword. The sharpening never ends. With that in mind, it is a pleasure to engage Chait in the discussion over President Obama, racism, culture, and personal responsibility. It's good to debate a writer of such clarity—even when that clarity has failed him.

On y va.

Chait argues that I've conflated Paul Ryan's view of black poverty with Barack Obama's. He is correct. I should have spent more time disentangling these two notions, and illuminating their common roots—the notion that black culture is part of the problem. I have tried to do this disentangling in the past. I am sorry I did not do it in this instance and will attempt to do so now.

Need of moral instruction is an old and dubious tradition in America. There is a conservative and a liberal rendition of this tradition. The conservative version eliminates white supremacy as a factor and leaves the question of the culture's origin ominously unanswered. This version can never be regarded seriously. Life is short. Black life is shorter.

On y va.

The liberal version of the cultural argument points to "a tangle of pathologies" haunting black America born of oppression. This argument—which Barack Obama embraces—is more sincere, honest, and seductive. Chait helpfully summarizes:

The argument is that structural conditions shape culture, and culture, in turn, can take on a life of its own independent of the forces that created it. It would be bizarre to imagine that centuries of slavery, followed by systematic terrorism, segregation, discrimination, a legacy wealth gap, and so on did not leave a cultural residue that itself became an impediment to success.

The "structural conditions" Chait outlines above can be summed up under the phrase "white supremacy." I have spent the past two days searArguing that poor black people are not "holding up their end of the bargain," or that they are in ching for an era when black culture could be said to be "independent" of white supremacy. I have not found one. Certainly the antebellum period, when one third of all enslaved black people found themselves on the auction block, is not such an era. And surely we would not consider postbellum America, when freed people were regularly subjected to terrorism, to be such an era.

We certainly do not find such a period during the Roosevelt-Truman era, when this country erected a racist social safety net, leaving the NAACP to quip that the New Deal was "like a sieve with holes just big enough for the majority of Negroes to fall through." Nor do we find it during the 1940s, '50s and '60s, when African-Americans—as a matter of federal policy—were largely excluded from the legitimate housing market. Nor during the 1980s when we began the erection of a prison-industrial complex so vast that black males now comprise 8 percent of the world's entire incarcerated population.

And we do not find an era free of white supremacy in our times either, when the rising number of arrests for marijuana are mostly borne by African-Americans; when segregation drives a foreclosure crisis that helped expand the wealth gap; when big banks busy themselves baiting black people with "wealth-building seminars" and instead offering "ghetto loans" for "mud people"; when studies find that black low-wage applicants with no criminal record "fared no better than a white applicant just released from prison"; when, even after controlling for neighborhoods and crime rates, my son finds himself more likely to be stopped and frisked. Chait's theory of independent black cultural pathologies sounds reasonable. But it can't actually be demonstrated in the American record, and thus has no applicability.

What about the idea that white supremacy necessarily "bred a cultural residue that itself became an impediment to success"? Chait believes that it's "bizarre" to think otherwise. I think it's bizarre that he doesn't bother to see if his argument is actually true. Oppression might well produce a culture of failure. It might also produce a warrior spirit and a deep commitment to attaining the very things which had been so often withheld from you. There is no need for theorizing. The answers are knowable.

There certainly is no era more oppressive for black people than their 250 years of enslavement in this country. Slavery encompassed not just forced labor, but a ban on black literacy, the vending of black children, the regular rape of black women, and the lack of legal standing for black marriage. Like Chait, · 19th century Northern white reformers coming South after the Civil War expected to find "a cultural residue that itself became an impediment to success."

In his masterful history, *Reconstruction,* the historian Eric Foner recounts the experience of the progressives who came to the South as teachers in black schools. The reformers "had little previous contact with blacks" and their views were largely cribbed from *Uncle Tom's Cabin.* They thus believed blacks to be culturally degraded and lacking in family instincts, prone to lie and steal, and generally opposed to self-reliance:

Few Northerners involved in black education could rise above the conviction that slavery had produced a "degraded" people, in dire need of instruction in frugality, temperance, honesty, and the dignity of labor . . . In classrooms, alphabet drills and multiplication tables alternated with exhortations to piety, cleanliness, and punctuality.

In short, white progressives coming South expected to find a black community suffering the effects of not just oppression but its "cultural residue."

Here is what they actually found:

During the Civil War, John Eaton, **who, like many whites, believed that slavery had destroyed the sense of family obligation,** was astonished by the eagerness with which former slaves in contraband camps legalized their marriage bonds. The same pattern was repeated when the Freedmen's Bureau and state governments made it possible to register and solemnize slave unions. Many families, in addition, adopted the children of deceased relatives and friends, rather than see them apprenticed to white masters or placed in Freedmen's Bureau orphanages.

By 1870, a large majority of blacks lived in two-parent family households, a fact that can be gleaned from the manuscript census returns but also "quite incidentally" from the Congressional Ku Klux Klan hearings, which recorded countless instances of victims assaulted in their homes, "the husband and wife in bed, and . . . their little children beside them."

The point here is rich and repeated in American history—it was not "cultural residue" that threatened black marriages. It was white terrorism, white rapacity, and white violence. And the commitment among freed people to marriage mirrored a larger commitment to the reconstitution of family, itself necessary because of systemic white violence.

"In their eyes," wrote an official from the Freedmen's Bureau, in 1865. "The work of emancipation was incomplete until the families which had been dispersed by slavery were reunited."

White people at the time noted a sudden need in black people to travel far and wide. "The Negroes," reports one observer, "are literally crazy about traveling." Why were the Negroes "literally crazy about traveling?" Part of it was the sheer joy of mobility granted by emancipation. But there was something more: "Of all the motivations for black mobility," writes Foner, "none was more poignant than the effort to reunite families separated during slavery."

This effort continued as late the onset of the twentieth century, when you could still find newspapers running ads like this:

During the year 1849, Thomas Sample carried away from this city, as his slaves, our daughter, Polly, and son. . . . We will give $100 each for them to any person who will assist them . . . to get to Nashville, or get word to us of their whereabouts.

Nor had the centuries-long effort to destroy black curiosity and thirst for education yielded much effect:

Perhaps the most striking illustration of the freedmen's quest for self-improvement was their seemingly unquenchable thirst for education. . . . The desire for learning led parents to migrate to towns and cities in search of education for their children, and plantation workers to make the establishment of a school-house "an absolute condition" of signing labor contracts . . .

Contemporaries could not but note the contrast **between white families seemingly indifferent to education and blacks who "toil and strive, labour and endure in order that their children 'may have a schooling'."** As one Northern educator remarked: "Is it not significant that after the lapse of

144 years since the settlement [of Beaufort, North Carolina], the Freedmen are building the first public school-house ever erected here."

"All in all," Foner concludes, "the months following the end of the Civil War were a period of remarkable accomplishment for Southern blacks." This is not especially remarkable, if you consider the time. Education, for instance, was not merely a status marker. Literacy was protection against having your land stolen or being otherwise cheated. Perhaps more importantly, it gave access to the Bible. The cultural fruits of oppression are rarely predictable merely through theorycraft. Who would predicted that oppression would make black people hungrier for education than their white peers? Who could predict the blues?

And culture is not exclusive. African-American are Americans, and have been Americans longer than virtually any other group of white Americans. There is no reason to suppose that enslavement cut African-Americans off from a broader cultural values. More likely African-Americans contributed to the creation and maintenance of those values.

The African-Americans who endured enslavement were subject to two and half centuries of degradation and humiliation. Slavery lasted twice as long as Jim Crow and was more repressive. If you were going to see evidence of a "cultural residue" which impeded success you would see it there. Instead you find black people desperate to reconstitute their families, desperate to marry, and desperate to be educated. Progressives who advocate the nineteenth-century line must specifically name the "cultural residue" that afflicts black people, and then offer evidence of it. Favoring abstract thought experiments over research will not cut it.

Progressives who advocate the nineteenth-century line must name the "cultural residue" that afflicts black people, and then offer evidence of it. Abstract thought experiments will not cut it.

Nor will pretending that old debates are somehow new. For some reason there is an entrenched belief among many liberals and conservatives that discussions of American racism should begin somewhere between the Moynihan Report and the Detroit riots. Thus Chait dates our dispute to the fights in the '70s between liberals. In fact, we are carrying on an argument that is at least a century older.

The passage of time is important because it allows us to assess how those arguments have faired. I contend that my arguments have been borne out, and the arguments of progressives like Chait and the president of the United States have not. Either Booker T. Washington was correct when he urged black people to forgo politics in favor eliminating "the criminal and loafing element of our people" or he wasn't. Either W.E.B. Du Bois was correct when he claimed that correcting "the immorality, crime and laziness among the Negroes" should be the "first and primary" goal or he was not. The track record of progressive moral reform in the black community is knowable.

And it's not just knowable from Eric Foner. It can be gleaned from reading the entire Moynihan Report—not just the "tangle of pathologies" section—and then comparing it with Herb Gutman's *The Black Family in Slavery and Freedom*. It can be gleaned from Isabel Wilkerson's history of the Great Migration, *The Warmth of Other Suns*. One of the most important threads in this book is Wilkerson dismantling of the liberal theory of cultural degradation.

I want to conclude by examining one important element of Chait's argument—the role of the president of the United States who also happens to be a black man:

If I'm watching a basketball game in which the officials are systematically favoring one team over another (let's call them Team A and Team Duke) as an analyst, the officiating bias may be my central concern. But if I'm coaching Team A, I'd tell my players to ignore the biased officiating. Indeed, I'd be concerned the bias would either discourage them or make them lash out, and would urge them to overcome it. That's not the same as denying bias. It's a sensible practice of encouraging people to concentrate on the things they can control.

Obama's habit of speaking about this issue primarily to black audiences is Obama seizing upon his role as the most famous and admired African-American in the world to urge positive habits and behavior.

Chait's metaphor is incorrect. Barack Obama isn't the coach of "Team Negro," he is the commissioner of the league. Team Negro is very proud that someone who served on our staff has risen (for the first time in history!) to be commissioner. And Team Negro, which since the dawn of the league has endured biased officiating and whose every game is away, hopes that the commissioner's tenure among them has given him insight into the league's problems. But Team Negro is not—and should not be—confused about the commissioner's primary role.

"I'm not the president of black America," Barack Obama has said. "I'm the president of the United States of America."

Precisely.

And the president of the United States is not just an enactor of policy for today, he is the titular representative of his country's heritage and legacy. In regards to black people, America's heritage is kleptocracy—the stealing and selling of other people's children, the robbery of the fruits of black labor, the pillaging of black property, the taxing of black citizens for schools they can not attend, for pools in which they can not swim, for libraries that bar them, for universities that exclude them, for police who do not protect them, for the marking of whole communities as beyond the protection of the state and thus subject to the purview of outlaws and predators.

Obama-era progressives view white supremacy as something awful that happened in the past. I view it as one of the central organizing forces in American life.

The bearer of this unfortunate heritage feebly urging "positive habits and behavior" while his country imprisons some ungodly number of black men may well be greeted with applause in some quarters. It must never be so among those of us whose love of James Baldwin is true, whose love of Ida B. Wells is true, whose love of Harriet Tubman and our ancestors who fought for the right of family is true. In that fight America has rarely been our ally. Very often it has been our nemesis.

Obama-era progressives view white supremacy as something awful that happened in the past and the historical vestiges of which still afflict black people today. They believe we need policies—though not race-specific policies—that address the affliction. I view white supremacy as one of the central organizing forces in American life, whose vestiges and practices afflicted black people in the past, continue to afflict black people today, and will likely afflict black people until this country passes into the dust.

There is no evidence that black people are less responsible, less moral, or less upstanding in their dealings with America nor with themselves. But there is overwhelming evidence that America is irresponsible, immoral, and unconscionable in its dealings with black people and with itself. Urging African-Americans to become superhuman is great advice if you are concerned with creating extraordinary individuals. It is terrible advice if you are concerned with creating an equitable society. The black freedom struggle is not about raising a race of hyper-moral super-humans. It is about all people garnering the right to live like the normal humans they are.

Critical Thinking

1. How significant is the racism of white supremacy in holding back blacks today?
2. What is your view of the prospects for blacks today?
3. Why is racism still fairly strong?

Create Central

www.mhhe.com/createcentral

Internet References

ACLU Criminal Justice Home Page
www.aclu.org/crimjustice/index.html

Human Rights and Humanitarian Assistance
www.etown.edu/vl/humrts.html

New American Studies Web
www.georgetown.edu/crossroads/asw

Sociology—Study Sociology Online
http://edu.learnsoc.org

Sociology Web Resources
http://www.mhhe.com/socscience/sociology/resources/index.htm

Sociosite
http://www.topsite.com/goto/sociosite.net

Socioweb
http://www.topsite.com/goto/socioweb.com

Article   Prepared by: Kurt Finsterbusch, *University of Maryland, College Park*

When Slavery Won't Die: The Oppressive Biblical Mentality America Can't Shake

An interview with black theologian Kelly Brown Douglas on America's greatest sins.

VALERIE TARICO

Learning Outcomes

After reading this article, you will be able to:

- Explain the theory "that dominant men have a right or even responsibility to enforce social hierarchy. If women or slaves or children or ethnic and religious minorities or livestock step out of line, they must be punished to keep society in its proper order."

- Describe several areas in which iron age chattel culture plays a role.

- Describe how black young men have to behave in order not to become a victim of the oppressive mentality of people who could victimize them.

" *You rape our women and you're taking over our country. And you have to go.*" So said white supremacist Dylann Roof to black members of Emanuel AME Church in Charleston as he systematically executed nine, leaving one woman and a five-year-old child to bear witness to the slaughter.

The horror of the mass murder defies rational analysis. And yet, if we have any hope of a better future, we must analyze it—not just the circumstances or persons or events that led to this particular slaughter on this particular day, but the root attitudes and assumptions—the ancient strands of brutality and inequality that are woven into the fabric of our society.

In her article, "The Lethal Gentleman: The 'Benevolent Sexism' Behind Dylann Roof's Racism," sociologist Lisa Wade outlines how racism and sexism intersect in Roof's comments. The phrase "benevolent sexism" sounds jarring, but it is the term social scientists use when people attribute "positive traits to women that, nonetheless, justify their subordination to men:" *Women are beautiful and fragile; women are good with children; women are emotionally weak; God made woman as the perfect 'helpmeet' for man.* Roof's implication that white women need protecting from rape falls into this category.

One striking aspect of sexism and racism in Roof's statement is the sense of ownership it conveys: "Our women" in "our country" need to be protected from black men who either don't know their place or won't stay in it. White men can and should kill black men because they are having sex in our home territory with women who belong to us. We own America and we own the women who live here, and black men don't because if all was right in the world we would own them too.

The idea that women and minorities (along with children and members of other species) at some level *belong* to men of the dominant tribe can be traced all the way back to the culture and laws of the Iron Age and the concept of chattel. The term *chattel* is related to the term *cattle,* and human chattel, like cows, exist to serve their owners and must stay where they belong. In this view, dominant men have a right or even responsibility to enforce social hierarchy. If women or slaves or children or ethnic and religious minorities or livestock step out of line, they must be punished to keep society in its proper order.

I have written in the past about how Iron Age chattel culture underlies Religious Right priorities that might otherwise seem at odds: Why do the same people who oppose abortion also oppose protections and rights for children once they are born? What do opposition to marriage equality and opposition to contraception have in common? Why is the line between marriage and slavery so blurry in the Bible? How was American slavery influenced by the Iron Age worldview? Why does biblical literalism so often incline people to embrace sexual and racial inequality?

From within Christianity, Episcopal theologian and author Kelly Brown Douglas has written extensively about some of these same questions, with a particular focus on sexuality and the Black body. After the Trayvon Martin killing, she channeled her grief into a book, *Stand Your Ground: Black Bodies and the Justice of God.* In the interview that follows, Brown Douglas talks about the ancient concept of chattel, how it leads to the assumption that black bodies are "guilty, hypersexual, and dangerous," and how it underlies the slaughter, from Florida to New York to Charleston, that has left America reeling.

Tarico: You are the mother of a black son, so the horrendous epidemic of shootings we all have witnessed in recent years strikes very close to your heart.

Brown Douglas: I just couldn't shake the Trayvon Martin killing. At the time my son was 21 and I knew—as a 6' tall young man with locks that people would perceive him as a threat. My husband and I have tried to help our son understand how others perceive him as a black male. As his mother, I find myself continually reminding him that, while I will defend him to his death I don't want to defend him in his death. I have said, *If you are ever stopped by the police, even if they tell you to get on your knees, do it. A moment of humiliation could save your life.* When he's out there's not a moment that I don't fear for him, not because of anything he would do— he is a very responsible person—but because of how people might perceive him. So I am passionate about what is going on now, what is going on with our children. Somehow we have to change this world to make it safe for our children.

Tarico: In *Stand Your Ground,* you explore cultural values and beliefs that contribute to America's plague of racial violence including the sense of exceptionalism and manifest destiny— the idea that Anglo-Saxon European culture is fundamentally good, a light unto the world, something to be exported. When any of us has that kind of self-perception, it's hard to see ourselves as the bad guy, hard to see when we're doing harm.

Brown Douglas: To stop the harm, one of the first things that we have to understand is the complexity of violence.

We have to understand that this Anglo-Saxon exceptionalism is inherently violent because it is unjust particularly as it is unjust particularly as it suggests that certain people deserve the benefits of being treated with decency and dignity while others do not. Systems of injustice—racism, sexism, heterosexism—the ways that these systems manifest themselves systemically and structurally is violent. Anything that does harm to another is violent.

We seldom name the violence that is imbedded in the structures and systems of our society. We don't ask, where is the violence behind the violence? Yes, there are too many guns, and we should change that. But I'm speaking about the violence of injustice. Inasmuch as we don't begin to dismantle unjust discriminatory systems then we will consistently have violent eruptions that people respond to with more violence. Systemic and structural violence perpetuates a cycle of violence on all levels of society.

Tarico: Our handed-down cultural and religious traditions contain the concept of chattel, the idea that some people (and other species) exist for the benefit of others. Slavery is an extreme example of this. But even beyond overt slavery, you and I both write about how the residual of this concept continues to ripple down in our society.

Brown Douglas: When we talk about American slavery we have to talk about chattel slavery. Chattel doesn't mean simply that one person serves another, it means that one belongs to another. Black people were property. They were never meant to own their own labor or their own bodies. While I truly appreciate the way that female and black bodies intersect, the black body *came to this country as property.* When we talk about chattel in U.S. history, the only people who were considered nonhuman were those of African descent.

Tarico: Yes! Mercifully, by the time this country was founded, outright ownership of women was no longer the overt norm. In the Old Testament, women were literally governed by property law rather than personhood rights. A man, a father, essentially sold his daughter to another man to be a wife or slave. She was a valuable reproductive technology that produced economically valuable offspring that also belonged to the patriarch, who could beat or sell them or send them into war or even sacrifice them.

The notion of women as fully autonomous persons rather than property has taken centuries to emerge. During the American colonial era, single women could own real estate and other assets, but thanks to a legal concept called coverture, married women couldn't. "All men are created equal" really meant *men,* well, men who were white. A woman couldn't get a credit card on her own in the U.S. until 1974! When I was young, a woman couldn't obtain birth control without her husband's permission because her reproductive capacity belonged to him. Women in the South, including black women, have been of the last to get rights to control their own property and bodies. But that is a long way from literally being bought and sold in chains, as in the slave trade!

So this idea of people owning people is changing. But, damn, the process is slow. From your point of view, where do you see the residual of chattel culture in America today?

Brown Douglas: What we see is that some people have certain privileges because of who they are while other people are penalized because of who they are. Clearly the white male heterosexual body is the most privileged body and in as much as you lose one of those attributes you lose certain privileges. In your person you have less freedom, less right to the wages of freedom in your body. That is what we are struggling through in this country.

Tarico: The rape culture that we are struggling with on college campuses is rooted in the idea that men are entitled to women's bodies. Economic exploitation is rooted in the idea that might makes right, that powerful people have a right to exploit and consume the time, energy, productive capacity and reproductive capacity of the less powerful. The same could be said about environmental exploitation, that those who are most powerful have the right to exploit, consume, and take what they can; that other beings and their desires are secondary, if they matter at all.

As a theologian, you say that one way chattel culture gets justified is via "natural law" theology. What is that?

Brown Douglas: Natural law theology is a way of sanctifying this hierarchy of exploitation. It suggests that this wasn't just a human creation, but divine law. This was the way God designed things to be. For example, the whole idea was that God created black people as slaves not as full human beings. Slavery was legitimated specifically through Christianity.

Tarico: What are some echoes of natural law theology in the way that conservatives think today? How does it get translated into the modern language of the Religious Right?

Brown Douglas: We know that the discourse around women has been that God created women to serve men and to reproduce. Women have had to fight that battle for years, and continue to fight the battle that they were indeed not created to be subservient to men or to be reproductive machines. That is about natural law. The other way you see it is that marriage is supposed to be between a man and a woman—that's God's law according to various religious communities. Those are ways that we see "natural law" functioning in our culture today.

In racial relations, if one scanned some of the white supremacy rhetoric you see that too. Historically it is part of the rhetoric of the Klan. Today most people don't argue that in polite conversation, but we see it all the time when we place this religious canopy over discrimination. We sanctify discriminatory patterns. *If God wanted men and women to be equal, God would have created women to be different—not to be the bearers of children.* Or, *God created Adam and Eve not Adam and Steve.* Those are remnants of natural law. It functions in those places where people attempt to elevate social constructs and human laws so that they seem as if they are divine laws.

Tarico: I write mostly about women—about reproductive freedom and empowerment, and in our fight to create a new norm of chosen childbearing, this notion of women as chattel is hugely problematic. Specific verses from the Bible get cited to justify the GOP's assault on women. "Women will be saved through childbearing," for example. In the sphere of racial relations and justice, this notion of human chattel also gets tied in with sexuality—how black sexuality is seen, why blacks are seen as dangerous.

Brown Douglas: One thing that you'll notice is that marginalized oppressed people often are sexualized by the dominant narrative. You see that with LGBT people—the rhetoric is that they are indiscriminately promiscuous—as with black people and women. A couple of traditional cultural narratives come together here. In the conservative religious mindset, the only good sex is procreative sex. If you suggest that people are engaging in sexual activity for non-procreative reasons that's sinful and lustful—that's the Apostle Paul.

On top of that is this oppression narrative in which identity and sexuality get bound together. The late French philosopher Michel Foucault asked, Why is it that sexuality has become so significant in Western society that it becomes the source not just of reproduction but of truth? Why has it become the way people think of themselves and others? Foucault suggests that it is because sexuality is where the body and identity come together. If you can control the sexuality of a group of people, then you can control that.

Women are said to be driven by their passions and women's sexuality has to be controlled, and is only acceptable if it's procreative, which means men are controlling it. Sexualizing black people allowed black women to be used as breeders. It became a rationale for a black man to be lynched—because he was preying on white women. This is one way we have an overlap in how all women and black men are perceived as well as other marginalized groups. I wrote a book, *Sexuality and the Black Church,* in which I discuss this in more depth.

Tarico: How does this all play into a presumption of guilt? At the opening to your chapter on the Black body, you echo L. Z. Granderson's question, *Why are black murder victims put on trial?* Why *are* black murder victims put on trial?

Brown Douglas: Black people don't have the presumption of innocence. The concept of black people as chattel, that black people are not meant to occupy a free space and are dangerous when doing so, has been transformed into a notion of black people as criminal. If a black person has been accused of something then people assume that he or she is probably guilty, and our media representations of black people continue to reinforce this in the collective unconscious. There have been various studies which reveal that people have visceral automatic reactions to black bodies in which they see them as threatening. In one study police officers who were shown pictures of white and black men with and without guns were more likely to perceive that a black male had a gun even when he didn't and to miss a gun in the hands of a white male even when he had one. The stereotypes of the criminal black male and the angry black woman lead to the presumption of guilt.

Tarico: I write largely for an audience of non-theists and people who describe themselves as former Christians. Many of them look at the black community's response to an incident like the mass murder in Charleston and say, *I don't get it. How can so many Black people be Christian when Christianity has been such a tool of racial oppression against blacks? How can oppressed racial minorities embrace a sacred text that talks about chosen people and privileged blood lines?* What do you say to that?

Brown Douglas: That is the very question that compelled another book of mine called, *What's Faith Got to Do with It?* In the Black Christian tradition, the first time that Black people encountered God was not through their slaveholders. They knew God in freedom, as they encountered God through their African traditional religions. As black Christianity emerged during slavery, it emerged from an entirely different place than white Christianity. Black people understood that they were meant to be free, so God stood for freedom. Throughout history you see a black critique of White Christianity. The sum of the critique is this: If Christianity is used to oppress another that's not Christianity. What I ask is, How can one embrace a culture of oppression and claim to be Christian?

Tarico: What do you say to your own son about all of this?

Brown Douglas: I always told my son every morning as he was growing up, *There is no one greater than you but God and you are sacred.* I've always tried to teach him that he is not greater than anyone, that we are equal. God created us all, and the very breath we breathe comes from God—that is what makes us all sacred. Even when someone treats you as less than human, you must still affirm their humanity. I am working overtime these last two years to help him understand that, yes, this nation is racist and people do racist things but not all people are like that. And so, I try to teach him to respect people as he would respect himself, to affirm his humanity and to finds ways to affirm that of others. Most of all, I try to teach him not to get trapped in the cycle of hate because in the end, hate is self-destructive.

Critical Thinking

1. What are the root attitudes and assumptions that lie behind some of the violence directed at blacks who do nothing to provoke it?

2. What does "benevolent sexism" mean?

3. What are various other oppressive prejudices against Blacks?

Internet References

New American Studies Web
    https://blogs.commons.georgetown.edu/vkp/
Social Science Information Gateway
    http://www.ariadne.ac.uk/issue2/sosig
Sociology–Study Sociology Online
    http://edu.learnsoc.org/
Sociology Web Resources
    http://www.mhhe.com/socscience/sociology/resources/index.htm
Sociosite
    http://www.topsite.com/goto/sociosite.net
Socioweb
    http://www.topsite.com/goto/socioweb.com

VALERIE TARICO is a psychologist and writer in Seattle, Washington and the founder of Wisdom Commons. She is the author of "Trusting Doubt: A Former Evangelical Looks at Old Beliefs in a New Light" and "Deas and Other Imaginings." Her articles can be found at Awaypoint.Wordpress.com.

Article   Prepared by: Kurt Finsterbusch, *University of Maryland, College Park*

Back to the Real World

Why Feminism Should Focus Less on Culture

KATHA POLLITT

Learning Outcomes

After reading this article, you will be able to:

- Describe current feminist activities.

- Identify and discuss the key issues for women's economic advancement.

- Discuss the issues concerning enforcement and strengthening of the laws against sex discrimination.

Remember all those trend stories about the death of feminism? These days, feminism is everywhere: online, in the bookstore, on the small screen. Beyoncé is a feminist and so are Emma Watson and Taylor Swift, to say nothing of Tina Fey, Amy Poehler, Caitlin Moran, Lena Dunham, and Amy Schumer. Feminist issues make headlines: sexual assault on campus, domestic violence in the NFL, revenge porn, Gamergate, and, of course, the ongoing Republican war on women's reproductive rights.

Five years ago "rape culture" and "intersectionality" were barely comprehensible to anyone who hadn't majored in women's studies. Now they're familiar expressions.

For anyone who lived through the "I'm not a feminist but" decades when the typical op-ed by a woman was a plaintive sigh about picking up her husband's socks, today's out-spokenness comes as a huge relief. Full credit goes to the young activists who are taking up the torch, suing their universities for ignoring rape complaints, and founding new organizations. There are groups like Hollaback, which protests street harassment, and Vida, which monitors the number of women's bylines in magazines. There are a host of new abortion funds. Fund Texas Choice, which helps organize and pay for travel for Texans

whose near-by abortion clinics have been closed by stringent state laws, was founded by Lenzi Sheible, a twenty-year-old student.

Young women are bringing new creativity and vitality to old causes. To demystify abortion, Emily Letts videoed her own procedure and put it on YouTube; to encourage women to consider getting the most effective contraceptive method, Alison Turkos tweeted her IUD insertion.

Far be it from me to knock any woman—or man—who is trying to make life better for women in any way. The new feminism is great, and the issues it concentrates on are crucial. (Well, maybe we didn't need quite so many posts about Miley Cyrus fellating a giant hammer or Jaime's rape of Cersei in last season's *Game of Thrones*.) Issues of sexual self-determination—whether it's the right to decide when and if to have a child or the right to wear what you want—have always been central to feminism.

But there's a fundamental piece that gets a lot less attention than it deserves: economic issues. Of course, I immediately have to qualify that, because reproductive rights, which get plenty of attention, are an economic issue. Controlling the timing and frequency of child-bearing is basic to women's ability to get education and training, hold a job and advance at it, and raise their children well. Progressives who echo mainstream pundits by treating birth control and abortion as "cultural issues" have really not grasped what unplanned pregnancy does to the lives of girls and women. This late in the game, I wonder if they ever will.

But women need more than birth control and abortion access if they are to be full participants in economic and public life. Most women do eventually have kids, and many raise those kids on their own. Mothers or not, women need equal access to good jobs, equal pay, and an equal chance of promotion. A robust feminism has to tackle the many obstacles they face. Feminists have spilled barrels of ink over the limits of self-help manifestoes like Sheryl Sandberg's Lean In, with its emphasis on individual career strategizing in the corporate world. But where is the mass movement for the things these critics rightly argue are the real keys to women's advancement: paid parental leave, quality affordable childcare, universal public preschool, an end to job discrimination against pregnant women and mothers, and a renewed commitment to enforcing—and strengthening—laws against sex discrimination? Why slutwalk and not workerwalk or momwalk?

One reason is that activists tend to be young and childless. It's understandable: Those are the people who have the time and energy—and optimism—for political organizing. From their perspective, sex assaults on campus present a more immediate threat than lack of daycare on campus. (Nonetheless, millions of students are parents, especially in community colleges, and lack of affordable childcare seriously hampers their ability to stay in school.)

The trouble is, by the time a woman has a baby, it's too late to demand daycare. Besides, she's too busy and too tired. So she cobbles together the best solution she can for her immediate problem. Day-care, as a friend of mine noted when we were new mothers together, is something you really need for a few years, and then it's over and you move on.

Similarly, job discrimination isn't as obvious as it was back when young women went directly from the dean's list to the typing pool. Today, a woman can easily think she and her male classmates start their careers on an equal footing. But ten years later, she looks around and the men her age have somehow leaped ahead. What does she do then? In today's fluid and increasingly precarious work world, where unions are taking a royal beating, it can be hard to find solidarity.

But there's a deeper, more depressing reason why economic issues haven't caught fire. Childcare, afterschool, support for families—despite pockets of improvement, like Mayor Bill de Blasio's ambitious preschool-for-all plan for New York City, or paid parental leave in California, New Jersey, and Washington—these issues, for the most part, haven't budged in decades.

In some areas, like government assistance to poor families, they've gotten worse. With feminist issues, as with so many other aspects of American life, anything that involves spending public money, let alone setting up new "government bureaucracies," is going to be a heavy lift. Just look at the struggle around the Affordable Care Act.

Daycare may not be as controversial as it was ten or fifteen years ago. The recession made it clear that mothers' income was essential to keeping families afloat. But paying for it? Regulating it? Setting standards for teachers and providers? The last time publicly funded childcare was a real political possibility

was in 1971, when both houses of Congress passed the Comprehensive Child Care Bill, which President Nixon vetoed as "a communal approach to child-rearing" with "family-weakening implications."

Unlike campaigns against rape or street harassment or domestic violence, with their obvious villains—entitled men, misogynist cops, universities and athletic teams eager to avoid bad publicity—economic issues are rather dull and earnest. They don't generate many galvanizing headlines. They're more about dozens of obstacles and assumptions that taken together push women into second-class status at work, and into doing the bulk of domestic labor at home. Which is, of course, a socially approved role women have been raised to accept, even if they don't necessarily like it.

Fear of violence is engrained in women virtually from birth. But how many women really believe having a baby means they'll never have an interesting job again? Or that having a second baby might mean it's too difficult and too expensive to have a job at all? These are the realities young women suddenly confront in this country, because, despite the feminist transformation of our culture, we still have no system for making family life sustainable for women, unlike the rest of the developed world. By the time reality hits, it can be too late.

In the end, economic issues are crucial to the continued progress of women: They are what will either expand women's freedom, or limit it. Without paid parental leave, affordable childcare, and strong laws against job discrimination, women will always be held back at work, and their lesser earnings and opportunities will mean they have less bargaining power in their relationships with men. It is not an accident that women's labor-force participation has stagnated since around 1990, and so has the amount of time their male partners spend on household chores.

You can talk all you want about the importance of the unpaid caring labor women do in the home, and how unfair it is that society devalues this work. True gender equality is not going to happen as long as the workplace privileges men and lack of family supports push women out of their jobs and back into the kitchen.

Let's let Cersei take care of herself in her imaginary kingdom and make 2015 the year of the real world economic woman.

Critical Thinking

1. What type of feminist activity does Katha Pollitt most support and what type does she not think very promising?

2. Why does Pollitt say "The new feminism is great, and the issues it concentrates on are crucial?"

3. What economic issues does Pollitt push?

Internet References

New American Studies Web
https://blogs.commons.georgetown.edu/vkp/

Social Science Information Gateway
http://www.ariadne.ac.uk/issue2/sosig

Sociology–Study Sociology Online
http://edu.learnsoc.org/

Sociology Web Resources
http://www.mhhe.com/socscience/sociology/resources/index.htm

Sociosite
http://www.topsite.com/goto/sociosite.net

Socioweb
http://www.topsite.com/goto/socioweb.com

KATHA POLLITT *is a columnist for* The Nation *and the author of* PRO: Reclaiming Abortion Rights.

Article   Prepared by: Kurt Finsterbusch, *University of Maryland, College Park*

Sex Slaves on the Farm

Max Kutner

Learning Outcomes

After reading this article, you will be able to:

- Explain how many women are "trapped" in prostitution.
- Describe the methods used to get women into the sex industry and keep them there.
- Describe the sex servicing of farm workers.

From the passenger seat of the red Camaro convertible hurtling away from Southampton Road, Janet watched the scenery change from one-story houses to tobacco fields and apple orchards. She had come to Charlotte, North Carolina, to work on a farm, but she wasn't going to be picking—she and the three other women in the car were wearing high heels and see-through miniskirts, and they felt alone and afraid.

The thought of the violence to come terrified them. It was midday, and after about an hour on the road, the man behind the wheel, whom the women knew as Ricardo, a common fake name traffickers use, turned down a dirt path and stopped at a cluster of cheap cabins that had floors lined with mattresses. These beat-down shacks were home for more than 100 farm workers. In the main farm house nearby, the workers—mostly from Mexico, El Salvador, Honduras and Guatemala—were on their lunch break, eating chicken and rice.

The four women climbed out of the Camaro and went over to sheds near the cabins, where the workers kept their tools. The cement floors inside had crumbled through, exposing big dirt holes. While the women laid down rags, the men, filthy and reeking of sweat after spending all morning in the fields, quickly finished eating and formed lines outside the sheds, with as many as 50 men waiting for a woman. Ricardo stayed by the car, keeping lookout for police or anyone who might try to rob him and the women.

One by one, the men paid $30 to rape Janet and the other women. Most of them, having gone a long time without sex, lasted only a few minutes with Janet. Some were so violent she was sure they would have seriously hurt or even killed her if it weren't for Ricardo, watching over the operation. She remembers seeing that happen once, to a woman who came without a driver or a pimp; she says the farm workers threw the body in a dump.

At the end of the day, as the sun was setting, the women handed all the money they'd collected to Ricardo, and they made the drive back to Charlotte. In the car, all Janet wanted to do was rest, but she knew she had to call her pimp, hundreds of miles away, and report how many customers she had had and how much money she made. As soon as she arrived in Charlotte, Janet knew there would be johns waiting for her at the brothel. The next day would be the same routine, and that thought made her hate herself. She felt inhuman, like a machine.

Janet was forced into prostitution in Mexico by a boyfriend named Antonio in 1999; coyotes brought them across the border the following year, and they went to live with Antonio's family in the borough of Queens in New York City, where she was put to work in brothels. Every couple of weeks, a van would take her and other women and girls—some as young as 12—to Charlotte, where she would spend a week or more, forced to have sex with strangers at a brothel by night and at farm labor camps by day.

Sex trafficking flourishes in areas of male-dominated industries, such as fracking and oil boomtowns, military bases and, as a slew of recent court cases and victim accounts show, farm labor camps. The U.S. Department of State estimates that traffickers bring some 14,500 to 17,500 people into the United States each year.

"These organizations that victimize these women . . . transport them to where the business is," says James T. Hayes Jr., special agent in charge of Homeland Security Investigations in New York. Traffickers set up shop in metropolitan areas—they often choose Queens for its central location along the Eastern corridor to cities north and south, plus its big clientele base in New York City—and send women to farms near and far, ranging from Vermont to Florida. Officials don't know how many women are trapped in this city-to-farm sex pipeline, but experts say the number is growing every year. Keith V. Bletzer, an adjunct faculty member at Arizona State University who has studied prostitution in agricultural areas, says that until recent years, women went to farm labor camps on their own to sell sex out of financial necessity. Now, however, there is an organized crime element, with "other people recognizing that this might be a viable" source of income, he says. Rather than women selling sex to make a living, it's traffickers bringing them to farms as part of larger international operations.

In some cases, pimps posing as boyfriends lure victims and shuttle them from brothel to brothel. In other instances, coyotes smuggle women across the border and then force or coerce them into selling sex to pay off smuggling fees. The United Nations says criminals who once trafficked weapons and drugs have made women their latest commodity. "It's hugely profitable," says Lori Cohen, director of the anti-trafficking initiative at Sanctuary for Families. Smuggled drugs are quickly sold, but with a woman, "you bring her across the border once and you just keep using her body over and over again until she breaks down," she explains.

For Janet, who requested that *Newsweek* refer to her by the name she used most when she was a prostitute, that breakdown took more than a decade. "Your body is being sold," she says in Spanish through a Sanctuary for Families advocate. "It's almost like your body is no longer yours."

Her First Time

Widely considered the sex trafficking capital of the world, Tenancingo, Mexico, is two hours southeast of Mexico City. Many of the town's 10,000 residents are involved in prostitution; for young men, becoming a pimp means joining the family business. "It's a sex-trafficking city," says Human Trafficking Intervention Court Judge Toko Serita, "where generations of families and men are engaged in the business." Men there "recruit" women from elsewhere in Mexico, often by pretending to fall in love with them, and then bring them to Tenancingo, where the forced prostitution begins. From there, many pimps take their victims to work in Mexico City; some later go to the U.S., where there is more money to be made.

Janet grew up with her grandmother in Puebla, a half-hour drive from Tenancingo. "My childhood was very poor, but I have memories that make me laugh," she says. One day in 1998, when Janet was 23, she was walking home from her factory job when a car pulled up beside her. "Hi, my name is Ricardo," the man inside the car said. "Can I accompany you?"

"No," Janet said. "I don't know you."

The man persisted and asked if they could be friends. When they reached Janet's home, she finally said OK, they could be friends. Having recently split from the abusive father of her young daughter, Janet wasn't eager to bring someone new into her life. But the man from the car kept showing up. "He was very respectful of me. In Puebla, when a woman gets into a car with a man, the first thing the man does is he starts grabbing her. He wants to take you immediately to bed," she says. This man, however, "behaved very nicely."

In July 1999, after knowing Ricardo for a little more than year, Janet agreed to move in with his family in Tenancingo, leaving her daughter in the care of her grandmother. But when she arrived, she learned that his name was Antonio, not Ricardo, and that he was a pimp. His family lived in squalor, even worse than where Janet had grown up. Antonio's family slept in one room, and the animals they owned slept in another. Water poured in through the ceiling when it rained, and children ran around barefoot and played with soiled diapers. After six months, Janet decided to leave Antonio, but discovered she was pregnant and stayed.

That's when the abuse began. First, Antonio forced Janet to take pills so she would have a miscarriage. She did. Weeks later, he told her she had to become a prostitute. At first she protested, saying she had worked a good job in a factory and could find work like that again. But he insisted, and eventually she gave in. Her first time selling sex was on the streets of Mexico City. During that time, she recalls, "[the sex] was day and night and I felt terrible." After a year, Antonio told her that if they went to the U.S., family there could help them find legitimate work. Reluctantly, Janet agreed, and in June 2000 they made their way across the border and to Queens.

'Set Up to Be Invisible'

The vast majority of the country's estimated 3 million farmworkers were born outside the U.S. Like Janet, most of them came to America in search of opportunity and, also like Janet, are being steadily ground down by a system working against them. Few suburban supermarket shoppers know that federal labor laws exclude farmworkers from certain rights most Americans take for granted, such as overtime pay, days off, and collective bargaining. State by state, advocates have tried to change that, but Big Agriculture usually manages to thwart the efforts.

Seasonal crop farm laborers typically live in barracks for a few months at a time. At year-round livestock farms, workers live in cheap houses or trailers. "The average citizen wouldn't see them," Renan Salgado of the Worker Justice Center of New York says about where the workers live. "They are set up to be invisible." Because of their undocumented status, workers rarely leave the farms, relying instead on supervisors and middlemen to deliver everything from groceries to medical aid to women.

The scene is a volatile mix, ripe for violence. "People are just bored, and they're lonely," says Gonzalo Martinez de Vedia, also of the Worker Justice Center. "You have an entire population that is sitting at home for an entire season. Single men. There's a lot of drinking, substance abuse."

Workers tend to take out that frustration on female visitors. What happens on the farms, says Cohen, is rape. "I think there's a perception that when . . . you pay to have sex with someone, that means that you pay for the right to do whatever you want with that woman," she says. "The violence that our clients have experienced at the hands of their buyers is really shocking."

Hold the Children Hostage

Antonio had promised a better life for Janet north of the border, but their living conditions in Queens were horrific. "People were sleeping one on top of another, and all the women worked in prostitution," she says. Antonio's cousins were pimps, she learned, operating a family ring. Janet still had to sell sex, and a routine developed: Antonio would spend his days playing soccer and billiards, while Janet had to work at brothels in Queens and Boston. Once Antonio learned about the opportunity to sell sex to farmworkers, he began sending Janet to Charlotte. There, a white, one-story, three-bedroom house near the end of a winding road served as a brothel, offering johns a constant rotation of out-of-state women. Janet and the other victims would see men there from 7 at night to 3 in the morning, sleep until 11 A.M. and then be driven out to the farms.

"I felt like an animal," Janet says. "The men were very aggressive. They would grab me. They were pushing me. They would grab me by the neck. They would penetrate me really hard. So when they finished, it was like my salvation." Many men appeared to be on drugs; some refused to pay. She tried to make them wear condoms, but sometimes the condoms would break or the men would take them off. Janet says she had so many abortions—always done with Cytotec pills, widely used in the trafficking world—that she lost track of how many. She lived in constant fear. "I didn't even like to look at them," she says of her buyers.

Antonio still promised they would get married, and he told Janet he was sending the money she earned back to Mexico, where someone was building them a house. Antonio's cousins told their victims similar lies to keep them hoping and in line. "The traffickers are canny. They've figured out the sort of sweet spot that needs to be exploited," Cohen says. "It's almost like a script." The traffickers would also threaten that if a woman ran away or went to the police, they would harm her family back in Mexico. For one ring that serviced farmworkers, prosecutors learned the pimps went so far as to impregnate their victims just so they could hold the children hostage.

"The fear that the trafficking organizations place into their victims makes it sometimes difficult if not impossible to get a victim to actually admit that they're a victim," says James Hayes Jr. from Homeland Security Investigations. Sadly, some victims go to great lengths to protect their traffickers or return to their pimps, despite the help of law enforcement and advocates.

Around 2009, one of the pimps in Antonio's ring was arrested for domestic abuse, and Antonio fled to Mexico. However, he stayed in contact with Janet by phone and expected her to continue working and wiring him money. Meanwhile, Janet was in touch with her daughter, who was still in Mexico and had medical expenses stemming from an accident. To cover those expenses, Janet asked Antonio if she could use some of the money she made, but he refused. So she went to the Mexican Consulate in New York City for advice, and after she described her predicament, consulate staff contacted Sanctuary for Families.

That visit to the consulate set in motion an investigation by U.S. Immigration and Customs Enforcement, beginning in 2010. Investigators conducted surveillance and pored over phone, travel, and financial records, in order to identify and locate key members of the ring. With Janet's help, officials rescued 25 victims, arrested the pimps, and found Antonio hiding in Mexico. In 2012, officials extradited him, and he was sentenced in June 2014. He and three cousins all pleaded guilty and are now serving sentences ranging from 15 to 22 years.

The path that led Antonio to trafficking became clear in court materials. He was an orphan at the age of 6, after his mother abandoned him and his father died of alcoholism; an uncle in Tenancingo took him in but routinely beat him with a whip and starved him; he grew up without schooling, friends, or affection. Coming of age in Tenancingo, his lawyer wrote in a memorandum, Antonio saw "a culture that not only tolerated sex trafficking, but flaunted it with the showy extravagances of its participants." Antonio told his lawyer, "I wanted to be somebody."

The judge sentenced Antonio to 15 years behind bars, plus five years of supervised release. He must register as a sex offender and pay Janet $1.2 million in restitution, which will come from the money he made as a pimp and whatever he makes in prison job programs. While in prison, he will pay at least $20 per month, serving as a constant reminder of what he did.

On the day of the sentencing, appearing in a Brooklyn courtroom as Jane Doe No. 1, Janet finally confronted the man who had enslaved her for 11 years. "He did not treat me like a human being. He treated me like a sexual robot," she said in court. "For years I cried in silence. I carried the scars of Antonio's abuse every day, but I can no longer be silent. I am here today so Antonio and his family will no longer be able to force another woman into prostitution."

'The Fresh Meat Is Here'

The details from Janet's account are consistent with those another victim and multiple farmworkers provided to *Newsweek*. In New York, one former dairy farmworker in Lewis County says that once a week, a man would go to the farm with women and knock on workers' doors, saying, "*Llego la carne fresca*" ("The fresh meat is here") and "*Tu vas a pasar*" ("You are up"). Someone who provides services to farmworker camps in upstate New York says that his weekly farm visits coincide with those of the indentured women, and that the workers always tell him to hurry and serve them food before it's their "turn" for sex. Rates with the women range from $25 to $60.

"They're essentially prisoners, and they don't have free time, so it's easier for them when they're offered that opportunity, it's just right there," a former farmworker, Arturo Vasquez, who worked in upstate New York, said in Spanish through an advocate affiliated with the Robert F. Kennedy Center for Justice and Human Rights. He said he'd seen Latin American women on farms, as well as Chinese and Russian women.

A victim who asked that *Newsweek* refer to her as Katarin, the name she used as a prostitute, says she endured years of forced prostitution at farm labor camps. She was only 13 in 2010 when her future pimp approached the park bench where she was sitting in a village near Puebla after finishing her work shift at an ice cream shop. The boy, 16, introduced himself. She thought he was handsome, and after a week they were romantically involved. Three weeks after they met, she went to live with his family in Tenancingo. Five months later, they crossed the border by foot with smugglers into Arizona. Then they took a van to Queens, and three days later, he forced her into prostitution.

Katarin remembers drivers taking her to farms on Long Island, as well as in Delaware, New Jersey and Pennsylvania. She would see 30 to 40 men a day in bunks ridden with bedbugs; many of the men were violently drunk, and some would use knives or scissors to break open their condoms. "Sometimes they couldn't come because they were drinking so much, and they would get really mad because the time would be up and they hadn't finished," Katarin says in Spanish through Sanctuary for Families. By 2014, she had developed a vaginal infection that left her in unbearable pain, and when her pimp said she had to continue working, she decided to escape. She went to the police, who helped get her to a hospital and a safe house.

Her pimp ran away and remains at large.

Mr. All That

The man responsible for bringing down Antonio's ring is James Hayes Jr., who oversees the New York office for Homeland Security Investigations. Immigration work runs in Hayes's family; his grandfather was a customs inspector, and his father worked for the Immigration and Naturalization Service and U.S. Customs and Border Protection. In the mid-1990s, interested in a career in law enforcement, Hayes, now 41 and a Brooklyn native, chose border patrol over the New York Police Department. From there, he moved to Los Angeles to take down gangs, and he entered his current role in 2009. Since then, he says, his office has rescued more than 250 trafficking victims and made at least 150 trafficking-related arrests.

The case involving Janet's trafficker was one in a handful involving farmworker camps to go to court in recent years. In May 2014, following another bust by Hayes, a judge found two Mexican brothers guilty of running a ring that operated four brothels and trafficked women to farms in New Jersey. The brothers got life in prison, believed to be New York state's first life sentences for sex trafficking. Fifteen other members of the ring faced charges, including one man whose job was to sweep cars for tracking devices. "We saw with both [rings] very sophisticated levels of organization and very sophisticated delineations of responsibilities," Hayes says. Prosecutors believe the brothers' ring started as far back as 1999 and involved hundreds, and possibly thousands, of women.

In 2011, Hayes's Homeland Security Investigations counterpart down South, Brock Nicholson, helped bust the brothel in Charlotte where Janet had been shipped. In 2013, the Georgia attorney general announced an anti-trafficking campaign that singled out "rural communities where young girls are trucked in to be abused by farmworkers." And last February, Nicholson's five-year investigation into a Savannah-based ring, dubbed Operation Dark Night, concluded with the conviction of 23 defendants. At least two of the dozen victims Nicholson rescued had been forced to have sex with migrant laborers in sweet potato fields in Georgia and the Carolinas.

The problem exists in the Midwest too. In October, Michigan officials in Lenawee County, a rural area outside of Toledo, Ohio, accused a local man of trafficking two American women in their 20s to farmworkers there. "We've been investigating [sex trafficking to] migrant farms for years," says R. Burke Castleberry Jr., the county prosecuting attorney.

Two separate cases, prosecuted between 2011 and 2013, involved transporting women from Queens to farms in Vermont for sex. In one, which involved at least five women, the liaison between the pimp and farmworkers was a caseworker at the Vermont Department for Children and Families. He had taken advantage of the fact that workers depended on him for goods and services, and supplied them with not only clothing, for which he marked up the prices, but also women. His business cards said, "Don Chingon," which roughly translates to "Mr. All That." (There may be an added pun, since the verb *chingar* can mean "to have sex.") Prosecutors in both Vermont cases failed to prove that the women were trafficking victims, and so the men faced charges related only to interstate prostitution.

Hayes says his office is pursuing dozens of human trafficking cases. "Whether they're being taken to farms or nightclubs or apartments," he says, "we're focused on putting an end to it."

"I Wanted Love"

It's been several months since Janet confronted Antonio in court. She sits in a conference room on the 28th floor of a building in midtown Manhattan wearing a black jacket and purple shirt, her hair pushed back with a headband. There are panoramic views, but she focuses on the table in front of her, using a pencil to sketch her childhood home in Puebla. That was where she was happiest and felt safest, a time of blue *quinceanera* dresses and Christmas turkey dinners. Growing up there, she learned from her grandmother the importance of loving relationships. "I wanted to have a real marriage with love," she says. "It's something permanent."

Seeing Antonio locked up has brought some closure to Janet, now 38, though she continues to struggle with her past. "I lost the best moments of my life, when I could have been with my family," she said in court. Living in the U.S. on a special visa for trafficking victims, she has reunited with her daughter, now a teenager. These days, Janet attends counseling and has the support of a boyfriend, though she doesn't tell her friends her full story. She's escaped the clutches of slavery, but knows there are millions of people who are still in chains.

Critical Thinking

1. How does the illegal sex industry avoid law enforcement?
2. How does law enforcement work on sex trafficking cases?
3. Why are many of the pimps engaged in the sex trafficking also victims?

Internet References

New American Studies Web
https://blogs.commons.georgetown.edu/vkp/
Social Science Information Gateway
hhttp://www.ariadne.ac.uk/issue2/sosig
Sociology—Study Sociology Online
http://edu.learnsoc.org/
Sociology Web Resources
http://www.mhhe.com/socscience/sociology/resources/index.htm
Sociosite
http://www.topsite.com/goto/sociosite.net
Socioweb
http://www.topsite.com/goto/socioweb.com

Article   Prepared by: Kurt Finsterbusch, *University of Maryland, College Park*

Joe Biden Takes a Marriage Equality Victory Lap

On Thursday in Manhattan, the vice president looked back at the long battle—and what's next. But what really made this win inevitable was when love became the essence of marriage.

JAY MICHAELSON

Learning Outcomes

After reading this article, you will be able to:

- Present the main arguments against LGBT marriages.
- Present the main arguments in favor of LGBT marriages.
- Present the legal and social action history that led to the eventual legalization of LGBT marriages.

In a way, Jane Austen won the right to same-sex marriage.

Not Austen specifically, of course—though Mr. Darcy has been the object of much gay and straight adoration—but the centuries-long movement of which she is a part: the humanistic, romantic idea that love should conquer law.

Such was my impression at Thursday night's marriage equality victory lap at the swanky Cipriani New York, put on by the advocacy organization Freedom to Marry and its founder/guru, Evan Wolfson. He's the man who, more than any other individual, including Jane Austen, deserves the most credit for winning national marriage equality.

As Vice President Joe Biden, Wolfson, and others recognized, there were many, many factors that caused marriage equality to become the law of the land on June 26, 2015. But as Biden said, in a way, at the core of the movement has been a very straightforward proposition. Recalling a time when he and his father saw two men kissing, Biden said Thursday: "I looked at my Dad, and he said, 'they love each other—it's simple.'"

Of course, as Biden quickly added, the long march to marriage equality hasn't been that simple. Dozens of lawsuits have been filed, millions of philanthropic dollars spent, and a myriad of cultural moments marked, from *La Cage Aux Folles* to Ellen DeGeneres. "This is the civil rights issue of our generation," Biden told the cheering crowd. "And what you have accomplished didn't just take moral courage. It took physical courage."

That, too, is true. Recall ACT-UP activists demanding that an uncharacteristically speechless Ronald Reagan utter the word "AIDS." (It took him until September 1985, at which point 12,000 people had died.) Remember also the original transgender rioters at Stonewall and the first gay rights protest in front of the White House, in 1957, when 10 people risked their livelihoods to demand legal equality.

But what won the day, in the end, was neither constitutional legal theory nor radical societal change. It was clear at Cipriani that what won the day was—trigger alert, cynics—love.

Consider this version of the story. The arguments against same-sex marriage are many, but the majority of them insist it isn't really marriage at all but something lesser. This isn't love, it's lust, like bestiality or incest. ("Man on dog," in Rick Santorum's epitaph-worthy phrase.) Homosexuals were said to be perverts, psychological deviants, or sex fiends.

Only, gradually, it became clear that they aren't—at least, not in significantly greater number than heterosexuals.

In fact, as people got to know gays and lesbians, either personally or through the media, it turned out that most, though not all, were actually a little dull. They wanted love, equal rights, basic dignity. They wanted to live and let live.

(This outraged the non-dull gays, the radicals who wanted a movement of sexual liberation, but they turned out to be in the minority.)

Eventually, the arguments against gay marriage started to seem either mean, or abstract, or both. Sure, the Bible seems to say bad things about lascivious homosexual behavior, but that's not what Aunt Nancy and Aunt Lisa have, right?

And no one really took those abstractions about "gender complementarity" and procreation too seriously. They seemed like rationales for prejudice. How can you compare some philosophical argument with Jim Obergefell, flying his dying partner out of state so they could get married, only to have the marriage ignored by his home state of Ohio? Or with Edie Windsor?

Which is where Jane Austen comes in. If love really does conquer all—even if, in Austen, Shakespeare, and others, the lovers pay a serious price—then surely it conquers some abstract bloviating about the Bible. (Of course, it also didn't help that so many anti-gay pastors and politicians turned out to be closeted gays and so many priests turned out to be child molesters.)

And if marriage, again following Austen, is primarily about love, then how can it be denied to two consenting adults who are obviously, manifestly, in love?

I was personally involved in the marriage struggle—as a full-time activist, but playing a very bit part—from around 2008 to 2013. And I heard this firsthand from religious people, time and time again: "I used to believe it was wrong, but then my [daughter][friend][uncle] came out, and I had to think again."

I came to see victory as inexorable because there really was a truth of the matter, and it really was on our side. Our opponents were lying about our lives. If we just told the truth, we wouldn't win over everyone, but we'd win over enough.

Easy to say in 2015. But in 1983, when Evan Wolfson wrote his quixotic law review article arguing for a constitutional right to same-sex marriage, everyone thought he was crazy. As late as the 1990s, I myself thought marriage was the wrong battle to fight—too contentious, too soaked in the language of religion.

We were all wrong, and Wolfson was right.

Really, it was a two-pronged battle. The first prong was the set of cultural changes I've talked about already. The second was, indeed, a matter of law, and canny political strategy. Wolfson went state by state, winning some battles in the courts and a few in the legislature. He focused exclusively on marriage, building coalitions with willing conservatives—alienating many progressives in the process—and putting aside differences on other issues. He convinced several large LGBT organizations, each with their own interests, to coordinate their efforts.

And he made crucial legal arguments.

On Thursday in Biden's remarks, which seemed to be largely off the cuff, he pointed out that in the 1987 confirmation hearings of Robert Bork, he and the would-be Supreme Court justice had a passionate disagreement about the nature of constitutional rights. Bork, an originalist like Antonin Scalia, said the only rights guaranteed by the Constitution are those written in the Constitution. (Scalia said the same thing in his *Obergefell* dissent.)

Biden disagreed. Citing Wolfson's law review article, he said human rights are given by God and that the Constitution merely guarantees that they cannot be taken away. Exactly what those rights are—what "equal protection of the laws" means, for example—is subject to the evolution of moral and legal reasoning. Not judicial fiat, as the *Obergefell* dissenters charged, but argumentation, reason, and reflection on the ambit of human rights.

For decades after the Fourteenth Amendment was passed, Jim Crow laws oppressed those the amendment was specifically designed to protect. Were those laws really constitutional, simply because they weren't enumerated in the text of the Constitution or were present when it passed? Surely not. Surely, even if "equal protection" and "due process" meant one thing in 1868, they encompassed these later developments, as well.

Well, Biden won the battle, and Bork lost. And as the vice president pointed out, the man Reagan nominated in his place was Anthony Kennedy, the deciding vote in *Obergefell* and the author of all four major Supreme Court opinions on LGBT equality.

A cynic would say Biden just took even more credit for marriage equality—on top of the credit he already gets (and deserves) for beating his boss to the punch and saying in May 2012 that he believed that all couples, gay or straight, should be able to legally marry.

But Biden also noted that legal philosophy was never the driving force in the struggle. "The country has always been ahead of the court," he said. And he generously shared credit with the ballroom full of activists, donors, and ordinary citizens, many of whom had been fighting this battle for 30 years, well before it seemed inevitable to Johnny-Come-Latelys like me.

Biden insisted on looking forward to the next battle: anti-discrimination protection. "There are 32 states where you can get married in the morning and get fired in the afternoon," he said. "We must expose the darkness to justice."

At the same time, the reception was a kind of victory lap—combined with a retirement party for Freedom to Marry, which is admirably closing its doors, having accomplished its mission. The sponsor-provided vodka flowed freely, and Carly Rae Jepsen entertained the crowd.

I'm a pretty cynical guy, but I was honored to be among them.

Critical Thinking

1. Why do some people believe that gay marriages will threaten heterosexual marriages?

2. How are gays the same as heterosexuals and how are they different?

3. What were Biden's main arguments against the denial of marriage rights for LGBTs?

Internet References

New American Studies Web
https://blogs.commons.georgetown.edu/vkp/

Social Science Information Gateway
http://www.ariadne.ac.uk/issue2/sosig

Sociology—Study Sociology Online
http://edu.learnsoc.org/

Sociology Web Resources
http://www.mhhe.com/socscience/sociology/resources/index.htm

Sociosite
http://www.topsite.com/goto/sociosite.net

Socioweb
http://www.topsite.com/goto/socioweb.com

Article   Prepared by: Kurt Finsterbusch, *University of Maryland, College Park*

Do Boys Face More Sexism Than Girls?

CHRISTINA HOFF SOMMERS

Learning Outcomes

After reading this article, you will be able to:

- Discuss the ways boys and girls are treated differently in school.

- Critically consider the ways that schools function and the unintended consequences of these patterns.

W hen it comes to education, are boys the new girls? Are they facing more discrimination than their female peers, just because they are sexually different? According to recent studies, boys score as well as or better than girls on most standardized tests, yet they are far less likely to get good grades, take advanced classes or attend college. We asked prominent gender warriors, Michael Kimmel and Christina Hoff Sommers, to hash this one through in HuffPost's latest "Let's Talk" feature.

Michael: Christina, I was really impressed with your recent op-ed in the *Times*.

The first edition of your book, The War Against Boys: How Misguided Policies Are Harming Our Young Men, came out in 2000. Maybe I've optimistically misread, but it seemed to me that the change in your subtitle from "misguided feminism" (2000) to "misguided policies" indicates a real shift in your thinking? Does it? What's changed for boys in the ensuing decade? Have things gotten worse? Why revise it now? And what's changed for feminism that it's no longer their fault that boys are continuing to fall behind?

Christina: Thank you Michael. I am delighted you liked the op-ed. Boys need allies these days, especially in the academy. Yes, I regret the subtitle of the first edition was

"How Misguided Feminism is Harming Our Young Men." My emphasis was on *misguided*—I did not intend to indict the historical feminist movement, which I have always seen as one of the great triumphs of our democracy. But some readers took the book to be an attack on feminism itself, and my message was lost on them. Indeed, many dismissed the book as culture war propaganda. In the new edition (to be published this summer), I have changed the subtitle and sought to make a clear distinction between the humane and progressive feminist movement and a few hard-line women's lobbying groups who have sometimes thwarted efforts to help boys. I have also softened the tone: the problem of male underachievement is too serious to get lost in stale cultural debates of the 1990s.

Groups like the American Association of University Women and the National Women's Law Center continue to promote a girls-are-victims narrative and sometimes advocate policies harmful to boys. But it is now my view that boys have been harmed by many different social trends and there is plenty of blame to go round These trends include the decline of recess, punitive zero-tolerance policies, myths about armies of juvenile "super-predators" and a misguided campaign against single-sex schooling. As our schools become more feelings-centered, risk-averse, competition-free and sedentary, they have moved further and further from the characteristic sensibilities of boys.

What has changed since 2000? Back then almost no one was talking about the problem of male disengagement from school. Today the facts are well known and we are already witnessing the alarming social and economic consequences. (Have a look at a recent report from the Harvard Graduate School of Education—"Pathways to Prosperity"—about the bleak economic future of inadequately educated young

men.) The problem of school disengagement is most serious among boys of color and white boys from poor backgrounds—but even middle-class white boys have fallen
behind their sisters. My new book focuses on solutions.

The recent advances of girls and young women in school,
sports, and vocational opportunities are cause for deep satisfaction. But I am persuaded we can address the problems
of boys without undermining the progress of women. This is
not a zero-sum contest. Most women, including most feminist women, do not see the world as a Manichean struggle
between Venus and Mars. We are all in this together. The
current plight of boys and young men is, in fact, a women's
issue. Those boys are our sons; they are the people with
whom our daughters will build a future. If our boys are in
trouble, so are we all.

Now I have a question for you, Michael. In the past, you
seem to have sided with a group of gender scholars who
think we should address the boy problem by raising boys to
be more like girls. Maybe I am being overly optimistic, but
does your praise for my *New York Times* op-ed indicate a
shift in your own thinking?

Michael: Not at all. I'm not interested in raising boys to be
more like girls any more than I want girls to be raised more
like boys. The question itself assumes that there is a way to
raise boys that is different from the way we raise girls. To
me this is stereotypic thinking. I want to raise our children
to be themselves, and I think that one of the more wonderful
components of feminism was to critique that stereotype that
all girls are supposed to act and dress in one way and one
way only. Over the past several decades, girls have reduced
the amount of gender policing they do to each other: for
every "You are such a slut," a young woman is now equally
likely to hear "You go girl!" (Note: I am not saying one has
replaced the other; this is not some either/or, but a both/
and.) The reforms initiated in the 1970s for girls—Title IX,
STEM programs—have been an incontesible success. We
agree there, I think—and also that we need to pay attention
also to boys, because many are falling behind (though not
upper- and middle-class white boys as much, as you rightly
point out).

I think cultural definitions of masculinity are complex
and often offer boys contradictory messages. Just as there
are parts that may be unhealthy—never crying or showing your feelings, winning at all costs, etc.—there are also
values associated with manhood such as integrity, honor,
doing the right thing, speaking truth to power, that are not of
"redeemable" but important virtues. I wouldn't want to get
rid of them in some wholesale "Etch-a-Sketch" redefinition.

Our disagreement, I think, comes from what we see as
the source of that falling behind. My interviews with over

400 young men, aged 6–26, in *Guyland*, showed me that
young men and boys are constantly and relentlessly policed
by other guys, and pressured to conform to a very narrow
definition of masculinity by the constant spectre of being
called a fag or gay. So if we're going to really intervene
in schools to ensure that boys succeed, I believe that we
have to empower boys' resilience in the face of this gender
policing. What my interviews taught me is that many guys
believe that academic disengagement is a sign of their masculinity. Therefore, re-engaging boys in school requires that
we enable them to reconect educational engagement with
manhood.

My question to you: In your essay, you list a few reforms
to benefit boys that strike me as unproblematic, such as
recess, and some that seem entirely regressive, like single-
sex classes in public schools or single-sex public schools.
Is your educational vision of the future—a return to schools
with separate entrances for boys and girls—a return to the
past?

Christina: I hereby declare myself opposed to separate
entrances for boys and girls at school. And I agree that we
should raise children to be themselves. But that will often
mean respecting their gender. Increasingly, little boys are
shamed and punished for the crime of being who they are.
The typical, joyful play of young males is "rough and tum-
ble" play. There is no known society where little boys fail
to evince this behavior (girls do it too, but far less). In many
schools, this characteristic play of little boys is no longer
tolerated. Intrusive and intolerant adults are insisting "tug
of war" be changed to "tug of peace"; games such as tag
are being replaced with "circle of friends"—in which no
one is ever out. Just recently, a seven-year-old Colorado boy
named Alex Evans was suspended from school for throwing
an imaginary hand grenade at "bad guys" so he could "save
the world." Play is the basis of learning. And boys' super-
hero play is no exception. Researchers have found that by
allowing "bad guy" play, children's conversation and imagi-
native writing skills improved. Mary Ellin Logue (University of Maine) and Hattie Harvey (University of Denver) ask
an important question: "If boys, due to their choices of dramatic play themes, are discouraged from dramatic play, how
will this affect their early language and literacy development
and their engagement in school?"

You seem to think that single-sex education is "regressive." This tells me that you may not have been keeping up
with new developments. Take a close look at what is going
on at the Irma Rangel Young Women's Leadership School
and the Barack Obama Male Leadership Academy in Dallas.
There are hundreds of similar programs in public schools
around the country and they are working wonders with boys

and girls. Far from representing a "return to the past," these schools are cutting edge.

An important new study by three University of Pennsylvania researchers looked at single-sex education in Seoul, Korea. In Seoul, until 2009, students were randomly assigned to single-sex and coeducational schools; parents had little choice on which schools their children attended. After controlling for other variables such as teacher quality, student–teacher ratio, and the proportion of students receiving lunch support, the study found significant advantages in single-sex education. The students earned higher scores on their college entrance exams and were more likely to attend four-year colleges. The authors describe the positive effects as "substantial." With so many boys languishing in our schools, it would be reckless not to pay attention to the Dallas academies and the Korean school study. No one is suggesting these schools be the norm—but they may be an important part of the solution to male underachievement. For one thing, they seem to meet a challenge you identify: connecting male educational engagement with manhood.

Finally, a word about Title IX, which you call an "incontestable success." Tell that to all the young men who have watched their swimming, diving, wrestling, baseball and gymnastic teams eliminated. Title IX was a visionary and progressive law; but over the years it has devolved into a quota regime. If a college's student body is 60 percent female, then 60 percent of the athletes should be female— even if far fewer women than men are interested in playing sports at that college. Many athletic directors have been unable to attract the same proportions of women as men. To avoid government harassment, loss of funding, and lawsuits, they have simply eliminated men's teams.

Michael, I think you focus too much on vague and ponderous abstractions such as "cultural definitions of masculinity." Why not address the very real, concrete and harsh prejudice boys now face every day in our nation's schools? You speak of "empowering boys to resist gender policing." In my view, the most aggressive policing is being carried out by adults who seem to have ruled conventional masculinity out of order.

Michael: Well, my earlier optimism seems somewhat misplaced; it's clear that you changed the subtitle, and want to argue that it's not a zero sum game—these give me hope. But then you characterize Title IX exactly as the zero sum game you say you no longer believe in. I think some of the reforms you suggest—increased recess, for example—are good for both boys and girls. Others, like reading more science fiction, seem to touch the surface, and then only very lightly. Some others, like single-sex schools strike me as, to use your favorite word, misguided. (There is little empirical evidence that the sex of a teacher has a demonstrable

independent effect on educational outcomes.) It seems to me you mistake form for content.

I'd rather my son go to a really great co-ed school than a really crappy single-sex one. (It happens that single sex schools, whether at the secondary or tertiary level, are very resource-rich, with more teacher training and lower student–teacher ratios. Those things actually do matter.) It's not the form, Christina, but the content.

And the content we need is to continue the reforms initiated by feminist women, reforms that suggested *for the first time* that one size doesn't fit all. They didn't change the "one size," and impose it on boys; they expanded the sizes. Those reforms would have us pay attention to differences *among* boys and differences *among* girls, which, it turns out, are far larger than any modest mean difference that you might find between males and females. You'd teach to the stereotype— that rambunctious roll-in-the-mud "boys will be boys" boy of which you are so fond—and not the mean, that is some center of the distribution. Teaching to the stereotype flattens the differences among boys, which will crush those boys who do not conform to that stereotype: the artistic ones, the musical ones, the soft-spoken ones, the ones who aren't into sports.

If you'd actually talked to boys in your research, instead of criticizing Bill Pollack or Carol Gilligan, I think you'd see this. The incredible research by Niobe Way, for example, in her book *Deep Secrets,* shows that prior to adolescence, boys are emotionally expressive and connected in ways that will surprise you. Something happens to those exuberant, expressive, emotional boys in middle school or so, and what happens to them is masculinity, the ideology of gender, which is relentlessly policed by other guys.

In my more than 400 interviews with boys this was made utterly clear to me. I've done workshops with literally thousands of boys, and asked them about the meaning of manhood and where they get those ideas they have. The answer is overwhelming: it is other guys who police them, with the ubiquitous "that's so gay" and other comments.

I've said this above, so I'll use my last word to reiterate. Boys learn that academic disengagement is a sign of their masculinity. If we want to re-engage boys in education, no amount of classroom tinkering and recess and science fiction reading is going to address that. We will need to enable boys to decouple the cultural definition of masculinity from academic disengagement. We need to acknowledge the vast differences among boys; their beauty lies in their diversity. We need to stop trying to force them into a stereotypic paradigm of rambunctiousness and let them be the individuals they are. And the really good research that talks to boys, all sorts of boys, suggests to me that they are waiting for us to do just that.

Critical Thinking

1. Somers establishes that gender sexism goes both ways. In schools boys are disadvantaged. Outside schools girls are disadvantaged. Overall which gender do you think is disadvantaged?
2. How can the schools function more in step with the needs and psychology of boys without being less beneficial to girls?
3. Can some disadvantages in schools be compensated for?

Create Central

www.mhhe.com/createcentral

Internet References

New American Studies Web
www.georgetown.edu/crossroads/asw

Sociology—Study Sociology Online
http://edu.learnsoc.org/

Sociology Web Resources
http://www.mhhe.com/socscience/sociology/resources/index.htm

Sociosite
http://www.topsite.com/goto/sociosite.net

Socioweb
http://www.topsite.com/goto/socioweb.com

The Center for Education Reform
http://edreform.com/school_choice

Unit 4

Institutional Problems

UNIT

Prepared by: Kurt Finsterbusch, *University of Maryland, College Park*

Institutional Problems

This unit looks at the problems in four institutional areas: family, education, healthcare, and religion.

The family is the basic institution in society. Politicians and preachers are earnestly preaching this message today as though most people need to be convinced, but everyone already agrees. Nevertheless, families are having real problems, and sociologists should be as concerned as preachers. Unlike the preachers who blame couples who divorce for shallow commitment, sociologists point to additional causes such as the numerous changes in society that have had an impact on the family. For example, women have to work because many men do not make enough income to support a family adequately. So, women are working not only

to enjoy a career but also out of necessity. Working women are often less dependent on their husbands. As a result, divorce can be an option for neglected or badly treated wives.

The first section in this unit examines the connection between love and power in marriage and other important relationships and the changing nature of parent–children relationships. The following section deals with the costs of education: Can the United States improve first-through 12th-grade education without increasing costs, and are college costs worth it? The next section discusses the medical advances that can greatly extend life and how the Veterans Health Administration can be reformed. Finally, we look at religious persecution in the world today.

Article   Prepared by: Kurt Finsterbusch, *University of Maryland, College Park*

It's the Parents

Reihan Salam

Learning Outcomes

After reading this article, you will be able to:

- Describe how most parents work hard to help their children do well in the world.

- Show how Salam provides a good argument against actual equality of opportunity.

- Describe the role that neighborhoods play in the development and opportunities that young people have in America.

Almost all Americans agree that our society ought to strive for equality of opportunity—that no child's prospects should be limited by the circumstances of his or her birth. Yet achieving equality of opportunity in this sense is quite a bit harder than you might think. Throughout human history, parents have been motivated by a desire to better the lives of their children, and to this end parents routinely make sacrifices. It's often said that fatherhood is a force that restrains the worst impulses of men, and that motherhood fills women with a powerful urge to protect their children from the dangers of the wider world. Parents save, in the hope of building wealth that they can pass on to their offspring, when they'd prefer to spend. They withstand petty indignities rather than lash out violently at those who insult or otherwise undermine them, to avoid landing in jail or worse, all to help ensure that they can continue to meet their familial obligations. The parental desire to fulfill these obligations hasn't always been motivated by love or generosity of spirit alone: Fear of social disapproval has also played a role.

But what if parents were promised that, regardless of the choices they made, regardless of whether they planned carefully for the future or indulged in this or that vice, they could rest assured that it was the job of society to provide for their children? What if all parents came to believe that their own contributions to the well-being of their children were ultimately immaterial? According to this logic, one ought to expect the fortunes of children with absent fathers and those with attentive fathers to be essentially the same. Wouldn't you expect that the texture of society would start to change if people came to take this idea seriously, and that many parents would free themselves from the straitjacket of guilt, deferred gratification, and exhaustion that has long been at the heart of child-rearing? Could it be that the goal of equality of opportunity is fundamentally confused, as the prospects of children raised by nurturing parents will necessarily tend to be brighter than those of children raised by parents who for whatever reason can't or won't provide the same spiritual nourishment? Even children raised by loving parents can find themselves overwhelmed by material deprivation, which is one of the many compelling arguments for a social safety net. Yet one wonders whether we've led recent generations of parents astray by suggesting that the life chances of their children aren't ultimately in their hands.

To Robert Putnam, the renowned Harvard political scientist, the gap between the life chances of children raised in rich households and those raised in poor ones is a matter of grave concern. He is right. One can't read *Our Kids,* his latest book, without being deeply moved by the challenges facing the poor children he describes, in a series of vivid portraits drawn from across the country. Putnam's central observation is that because of rising inequality, the fates of rich and poor children in America are diverging. Though he acknowledges that it will take years before we have definitive proof that upward mobility for poor children is declining, and not just stagnant, he insists that we act now before it's too late.

In making his case, Putnam observes that while race is growing less powerful as an obstacle to upward mobility, class is growing more so. Neighborhoods are less likely to be racially segregated to day than in past decades, yet they are more likely to be segregated by income. Because children raised in poor neighborhoods tend to fare worse than children raised in non-poor neighborhoods, the rise of class segregation has profound consequences. Putnam draws on the work of Patrick Sharkey, a New York University sociologist and the author of *Stuck in Place,* a landmark study of neighborhood inequality. One of Sharkey's most striking findings is that children raised in non-poor neighborhoods by parents raised in poor neighborhoods fare roughly as well on cognitive tests as children raised in poor neighborhoods by parents raised in non-poor neighborhoods, and that both groups of children fare better than those raised in poor neighborhoods by parents raised in poor neighborhoods—and far worse than children raised in non-poor neighborhoods by parents raised in non-poor neighborhoods. That is, the negative consequences of growing up in a deprived community appear to be transmitted from one generation to the next, while the same is true of the positive consequences of growing up in a more prosperous and well-functioning community.

According to Putnam, these positive consequences flow from the fact that non-poor neighborhoods tend to be more cohesive than poor neighborhoods, and community members are more likely to cooperate with one another to advance their collective interests—a phenomenon sociologists have dubbed "collective efficacy." "Collective efficacy, reflected in trust in neighbors, is higher in richer, more educated neighborhoods, and that collective efficacy in turn helps all the young people in the neighborhood, regardless of family resources," writes Putnam. If growing up in communities defined by high levels of trust benefits all children, regardless of income, it seems vitally important that we do what we can to cultivate trust. So it seems worth noting that in 2007, Putnam famously, and reluctantly, concluded that more-diverse neighborhoods tend to be defined by lower levels of trust than less-diverse neighborhoods. Though Putnam expresses the hope that this distrust can be overcome, he's never offered a compelling roadmap as to how it can be.

Notably, Putnam generally defines "rich" parents as those who finished college and "poor" parents as those who did not, a definition that in a sense stacks the deck. Finishing college takes enormous self-discipline, particularly for those who weren't raised in stable families, or a great deal of support from family and friends. If finishing college is best understood as a proxy for the combined effect of self-discipline and strong social networks, one wishes that we could more rigorously study the lives of those who don't attend college, or who fail to finish, yet who are embedded in strong, supportive social networks.

Cultivating self-discipline and strengthening social networks have always been the work of families and communities. Now, however, as we see intensifying class segregation, and as fewer children are raised in neighborhoods with high levels of trust

and collective efficacy, government must act to ensure equality of opportunity, Putnam argues. He touts the virtues of wage subsidies, investment in early-childhood education, and community colleges, among other fairly modest ideas. All of these programs are expensive, and chances are that they'd be even more expensive if government were to make a serious effort to use them as a substitute for the social support that only strong families and communities can provide.

Yet it's not at all clear that even the most generously funded social programs will address the deeper problem, which is that our cultural turn away from harshly judging those parents who fail their children to averting our eyes from their short-sightedness and neglect has proven disastrous. Putnam himself is reluctant to blame parents, emphasizing instead that "to hold kids responsible for their parents' failings violates most Americans' moral sensibility." This strikes me as a dodge. We imprison violent criminals, despite the fact that their aggression can often be traced to chaotic childhoods. We don't do business with people who are dishonest and unreliable, though these traits may well have been survival mechanisms they developed as the children of neglectful parents. There is no way around holding kids responsible for their parents' failings, which is why it is so essential that we remind parents of that fact at every opportunity.

And finally, one wonders why Putnam never makes an obvious but important point: Given the large number of poor children already residing in the United States, should we at the very least consider limiting future immigration to families that can more than adequately provide for their children? Immigration contributes enormously to America's economic dynamism. Yet not all immigrants are the same: Some immigrants arrive in the U.S. with the skills and connections they need to enter the middle class, while others find that, while they're better off than they were in their countries of origin, they lack those same skills and connections, and their only hope of leading dignified American lives is to rely on substantial, ongoing public assistance. If we as a society are struggling to provide poor children with the resources they need to thrive, we should stop biting off more than we can chew.

Critical Thinking

1. Equality of opportunity is what America is supposed to stand for. How well does America live up to this standard today?

2. How do the generous actions of parents increase the inequality of opportunity in America?

3. What is the basis of increasing inequality of opportunity in America?

Internet References

New American Studies Web
https://blogs.commons.georgetown.edu/vkp/

Social Science Information Gateway
http://www.ariadne.ac.uk/issue2/sosig

Sociology—Study Sociology Online
http://edu.learnsoc.org/

Sociology Web Resources
http://www.mhhe.com/socscience/sociology/resources/index.htm

Sociosite
http://www.topsite.com/goto/sociosite.net

Socioweb
http://www.topsite.com/goto/socioweb.com

Article   Prepared by: Kurt Finsterbusch, *University of Maryland, College Park*

Modest Workplace Reforms Will Strengthen Families and the Economy

JUDITH WARNER

Learning Outcomes

After reading this article, you will be able to:

- Understand why "crunch time" is an appropriate title because families are being crunched by more dual earners, longer work hours, and longer hours of family responsibilities.

- Explain how some changes in the workplace could ameliorate some of the work–family stresses.

- Compare the differences in work–family relations between the lower class and the middle and upper classes.

Surveys consistently show that work–life conflict in the United States is epidemic. The problem is due not only to the presence of mothers in the workforce but also to the increase in conflicting demands placed on fathers. According to the Families and Work Institute, a New York–based research group, men now report more work–family conflict than women, and while the percentage of women reporting some or a lot of work–family conflict has remained more or less stable over the past few decades, the percentage of men with such conflicts rose from 35 percent in 1977 to 60 percent in 2008.

Work hours have risen, at least for those in the middle and upper-middle class. Between 1977 and 2002, dual-earner married couples with children saw their combined working hours shoot up by an average of ten hours a week, from eighty-one to ninety-one. By 2005, fully one-third of U.S. employees reported feeling chronically overworked. Today, adults employed full time in the United States work an average of forty-seven hours per week, with nearly 40 percent of full-time workers reporting that they work at least fifty hours a week.

Low-wage and hourly workers face a different set of time pressures. They routinely encounter highly unpredictable scheduling practices with last-minute work assignments, impromptu cancellations of work shifts without pay, or the chaos of being "on call," committed to working shifts for which they might or might not be needed.

All of this—combined with increasing pressures for more time-consuming and intensive parenting than was the norm for previous generations—contributes to an overwhelming sense of overload and lack of control. In November 2012, nearly three-quarters of respondents polled by the National Partnership for Women & Families said that they, their neighbors, and their friends experienced hardship in balancing high and often inflexible work demands with the equally high yet unpredictable responsibility of caring for family members at least somewhat often, and nearly 40 percent said they experienced such conflict "all the time" or "very often." University of Minnesota sociologist Erin L. Kelly and her co-authors found that approximately 70 percent of Americans now report "some interference between work and non-work."

The troublesome level of stress weighing on parents from work–family conflict is generally considered a private matter—a personal problem of the sort best addressed by yoga, relaxation exercises, or going out to coffee with friends. And yet a considerable body of research now indicates that, in fact, it should be considered a public health issue. Work–family conflict has been linked to mental and physical health problems, including the risk of heart disease, high blood pressure, poor sleep, depression, obesity, and addictive behaviors such as smoking and excessive alcohol consumption. It has also been associated with lower satisfaction with family, marriage, work, and life, generally.

The consequences for our economic growth and prosperity are alarming. Work–family conflict impairs worker productivity, commitment, and engagement, and increases turnover and absenteeism. Women in particular, who still disproportionately serve as the primary caregivers in their families even as they've increasingly become sole or co-breadwinners, are all too often pushed out of the workforce by the inflexible demands of their jobs or forced to consider less remunerative work that upends or destroys promising career tracks. If women can't work, earn, and spend to the full extent of their capabilities, then our national economic health suffers as a direct result of crimped or collapsing individual family budgets, lowered tax revenues, and lost productivity.

The health of our economy, then, as well as that of our families, will depend on finding ways to relieve destructive work–family conflict. But to do so we must directly confront the roots of this American epidemic, which are nestled in public policy decisions extending back over two generations. The face of the U.S. workforce and the shape of the American family have vastly changed over the past four decades, chiefly due to the movement of women into the paid workforce. In 1967, only roughly 28 percent of mothers were breadwinners or co-breadwinners, responsible for at least 25 percent of their family income. Today, 63 percent of all mothers make that essential contribution to their families' economic situation. And there's no going back. With income stagnant for all but the most wealthy over the past thirty years, and with incomes falling for low-income workers and many in the middle class, women's earnings are absolutely essential for most families to make ends meet.

Yet despite this massive alteration in the landscape of home and work, our policies and expectations for employees haven't much changed from the days of homemaker moms and sole-provider dads. The United States is the only industrialized nation that does not guarantee working mothers paid time off to care for a new child, and the only developed country that doesn't guarantee paid sick leave. What nationally mandated leave we have—provided by the Family and Medical Leave Act of 1993—is unpaid, with qualification restrictions so onerous that 40 percent of all American workers are excluded from coverage. Forty-three percent of all adult workers lack a single paid sick day. And 44 percent of working Americans are unable to arrange their work schedules to meet their responsibilities at home.

This lack of access to workplace flexibility and support, particularly among middle- and low-income earners, means that most parents are fully exposed to the stressors that make work–family conflict most toxic—"high demand and low control," as Rosalind B. King, program scientist for the Work, Family, Health, and Well-Being Initiative at the National Institute of Child Health and Human Development, puts it. "Changing working

conditions is the best prevention strategy for the dilemmas faced by working families," says King.

Recent studies seeking to measure the role of family-friendly workplace interventions in reducing work–family conflict and stress bear this out. In 2011, Erin Kelly, a sociologist at the University of Minnesota, and her colleagues published findings from a study of employees at Best Buy's corporate headquarters who were involved in a program to change their office culture so that they were rewarded for results rather than face time. These employees, Kelly found, reported getting more sleep and having more energy, a greater sense of control over their schedules, and less work–family stress. The human resource executives at the company who designed the program also reported large reductions in voluntary employee turnover and substantially increased productivity. Dozens of other companies have since adopted Best Buy's model.

Then there's research by Maureen Perry-Jenkins, a professor of psychology at the University of Massachusetts Amherst, who shows that having the ability to take time off for a doctor's appointment without fear of job or income loss led to less depression in mothers a year after their child's birth. Stable hours and consistent pay and benefits, Perry-Jenkins also finds, appeared to be protective of mothers' mental health, whereas the instability from ever-changing work schedules led to a lack of control, which was related to poorer mental health outcomes. Indeed, the mere perception of workplace support enhanced mothers' mental health, says Perry-Jenkins. The effects held for fathers, too. Perceptions of greater child care support were linked to less depression in fathers, and mothers' longer maternity leaves were linked to less anxiety in fathers over time.

Most of the published studies to date on the effects of workplace flexibility focus on voluntary employer-provided initiatives, which sadly are the only type of work–family policies available for most workers in the United States. The problem with relying upon such measures is, first, that they depend on the will and whims of chief executives—as Best Buy employees found, in early 2013, when a new CEO, Hubert Joly, did away with the popular practice—and, second, that they are least likely to be provided to the people who need them the most: low-income and hourly workers. More than 90 percent of high-wage employees report that their employers allow them to earn paid time off or to change their schedule if they have an urgent family issue. Less than half of private-sector workers in the bottom 25 percent of earners, however, can change their schedules under such circumstances, and only about half of middle-income workers have the right to these sorts of schedule changes.

The pattern holds steady for access to paid parental leave and paid sick days as well: 66 percent of high-wage workers have access to paid parental leave, compared with 11 percent of those who earn the lowest wages. Almost 80 percent of the highest-paid workers have access to earned sick time, but only 15 percent of the lowest-paid workers have the right to take paid time off if they or a family member get sick.

With implementation of family-friendly policies across the business landscape uneven, at best, the main way to truly alleviate toxic work–family stress for all working parents in the United States is through the universal protections of public policy, with provisions to ensure that employers cannot declare their workers "contract employees" who are exempt from workplace flexibility rules. Fortunately, the landscape for such measures has never been better.

Thirteen cities, among them Washington, D.C., New York City, Jersey City, Seattle, and, most recently, Patterson, New Jersey, now guarantee workers paid sick days, as do two states, Connecticut and California. In the past year, Rhode Island passed paid family leave legislation, joining California, New Jersey, and Washington State; advocates now have eyes on New York, Massachusetts, and Oregon to enact similar legislation. Vermont and San Francisco passed laws granting workers the right to request flexible work arrangements and predictable scheduling. In June, President Obama issued a memo that granted all federal employees the right to request flexible work arrangements.

National paid family leave—a policy idea that not so long ago was considered a pie-in-the-sky impossibility—is now poised to become a campaign issue in the 2016 presidential election. From an economic policy perspective, this public conversation could not be more timely. Between 1990 and 2010, our country fell from having the sixth-highest rate of female participation in the workforce among the twenty-two developed nation members of the Organisation for Economic Co-operation and Development to seventeenth on the list—a decline that economists Francine D. Blau and Lawrence M. Kahn at Cornell University suggest may be due to our lack of federal work–family policy.

To waste women's resources is foolhardy. The Congressional Budget Office predicted last year that the flattening-out of women's workforce participation will play a notable role in slowing down U.S. economic growth over the next decade. And the economists Heather Boushey, Eileen Appelbaum, and John Schmitt have calculated that, if women's employment *hadn't* risen the way it did from 1979 to 2012, our gross domestic product would have been roughly 11 percent lower at the end of that period.

For too many decades, children of professional working mothers were considered the victims of their mothers' ambitions. Now, with the overwhelming majority of families dependent on women's economic contributions—and our economy and future economic well-being on the line as well—it's time for policymakers to consider that the best interests of children, their parents, society, and the economy are fully aligned. We know now that families' mental, physical, and economic health depends not just on the presence but on the quality of parents' work as well—how much control they have, and how much stress they bring home at the end of the day. In addition, relieving stress at home results in more productive employees in the workplace. American parents are overloaded to a breaking point. That's a public health and economic risk we as a nation simply cannot afford.

Critical Thinking

1. Why do men now report more work–family conflict than women?
2. What are the various impacts of work–family stresses?
3. What can be done to improve this situation?

Internet References

New American Studies Web
https://blogs.commons.georgetown.edu/vkp/

Social Science Information Gateway
http://www.ariadne.ac.uk/issue2/sosig

Sociology–Study Sociology Online
http://edu.learnsoc.org/

Sociology Web Resources
http://www.mhhe.com/socscience/sociology/resources/index.htm

Sociosite
http://www.topsite.com/goto/sociosite.net

Socioweb
http://www.topsite.com/goto/socioweb.com

JUDITH WARNER is a senior fellow at the Center for American Progress and a contributing writer for the *New York Magazine*.

Article

Prepared by: Kurt Finsterbusch, *University of Maryland, College Park*

From Parent to Parenting
Children, Grandchildren, and Cultural Imperatives

JOSEPH EPSTEIN

Learning Outcomes

After reading this article, you will be able to:

- Explain the differences between how the author was raised and how he raised his children.

- Describe and explain the changes occurring because of the massive cultural shift that has occurred between the generations in this story.

As with lengths of skirts, lapels on men's suits, breastfeeding, and other more or less important customs, there are also fashions in fatherhood. The institution changes from generation to generation. As a man of *un age certain*—if numbers be wanted, mine is 78—my experience of fatherhood, both from the receiving and giving end, is likely to be different from those of younger contributors to this august volume.

I had the good fortune to have an excellent father. He was fair, utterly without neuroses, a model of probity, honorable in every way. Born in Canada, my father departed Montreal to make his fortune in Chicago at the age of 17, without bothering to finish high school. Until his forties, when he came to own his own business, he was a salesman, but without any of the slickness or slyness usually associated with the occupation. He made his sales by winning over customers through his amiability, his reliability, and the utter absence of con in his presentation. He was successful and became rich enough, in Henry James's phrase, "to meet the demands of his imagination," which weren't extravagant.

When, at the age of 18, it was time for me to go to college, my father told me that he would of course pay for my college education, but since I had shown so little interest in school, he wondered if I wouldn't do better to skip college. He thought

that I would make a terrific salesman. This, you have to understand, was intended as a serious compliment; one of two I remember his paying me. The other came years later and had to do with my taking care of a complicated errand for him. After I had accomplished what he wanted, he said, "You handled that in a very businesslike way."

If this sounds as if I am complaining, the grounds being emotional starvation from want of approval, be assured that I'm not. Approval wasn't an item high on the list of emotional expenditure in our family. (When in my early thirties I informed my mother that I, who have no advanced degrees, had been offered a job teaching at Northwestern University, she replied, "That's nice, a job in the neighborhood," and we went on talk of other things.) I cannot ever recall seeking my parents' approval; it was only their disapproval that I wished to avoid, and this because it might cut down on my freedom, which, from an early age, was generous and extensive.

The not-especially-painful truth is that my younger brother and I—and I believe this is true of many families of our generation—were never quite at the center of our parents' lives. Their own lives—rightly, I would say—came first. So many in my generation, I have noticed, were born five or six years apart from our next brother or sister. The reason for this is that parents of that day decided that raising two children born too close together was damned inconvenient. The standard plan was to wait until the first child was in school before having a second.

My parents were never other than generous to my brother and to me. They never knocked us in any way. We knew we could count on them. But we also knew they had lives of their own and that we weren't, as is now so often the case with contemporary parents, everything to them. My mother had her charities, her card games, her friends. My father had his work, where he was happiest and most alive.

My father's exalted status as a breadwinner was central to his position in our household. The breadwinning function of men in those days, when so few married women who worked, was crucial. Recall what a dim figure Pa Joad, in John Steinbeck's *Grapes of Wrath,* is; the reason is that he is out of work, without financial function, and so the leadership in the novel is ceded to Ma Joad, the mother and dominant figure in the family. Although my father was the least tyrannical of men, my mother felt that he was owed many small services. "Get your father's slippers," my mother would say. "Ask your father if he'd like a glass of water." We were instructed not to "rumple up the newspaper before your father comes home."

As a Canadian, my father had no interest in American sports, so he never took my brother and me to baseball or football games. (He did like boxing, and on a couple of occasions, he and I went to watch Golden Gloves matches together.) He certainly never came to watch me play any of the sports in which I participated. But then, in those days, no father did; his generation of fathers were at work—my father worked six days a week—and had no time to attend the games of boys. (I'm talking about pre-soccer days, and so girls in those days played no games.) Nor would it ever have occurred to me to want my father to watch me at play. One of the fathers among my friends did show up for lots of his son's games and was mocked behind his back for doing so; a Latinist among us referred to him as Omnipresent.

Although my father did not take me to sports or other events, or attend my own games, I nevertheless spent lots of time with him. From the age of 15 through 20, I drove with him to various midwestern state fairs, where he sold costume jewelry to concessionaires. I was, officially, his flunky, schlepping his sample case and doing most of the driving. We shared hotel rooms. What amazes me now that I think about those many hours we spent together is how little of that time was given to intimate conversation between us. I never told my father about my worries, doubts, or concerns, nor did he tell me his. We never spoke about members of our family, except, critically, of dopey cousins or older brothers of his who had gone astray. We talked a fair amount about his customers. He offered me advice about saving, the importance of being financially independent, about never being a show-off of any kind—all of it perfectly sound advice, if made more than a touch boring by repetition.

Neither of us, my father or I, craved intimacy with the other. I wouldn't have known how to respond to an invitation to intimacy from him. I would have been embarrassed if he had told me about any of his weaknesses or deep regrets. So far as I could surmise, he didn't have any of either. Since I was a small boy I recall his invocation, often repeated, "Be a man." A man, distinctly, did not reveal his fears, even to his father; what a man did with his fears was conquer them.

The generation of my father—men born in the first decade of the 20th century who came into their maturity during the Depression—was distinctly pre-psychological. In practice, this meant that such notions as insecurity, depression, or inadequacy of any sort did not signify as anything more than momentary lapses to be overcome by hitching up one's trousers and getting back to work. My father and I did not hug, we did not kiss, we did not say "I love you" to each other. This may seem strangely distant, even cold to a generation of huggers, sharers, and deep-dish carers. No deprivation was entailed here, please believe me. We didn't *have* to do any of these things, my father and I. The fact was, I loved my father, and I knew he loved me.

By the time I had children of my own, psychology had conquered with strong repercussions for child rearing. Benjamin Spock's book *Baby and Child Care* (1946), said in its day to be, after the Bible, the world's second-bestselling book, had swept the boards. Freudian theory was still in its ascendance. Under the new psychological dispensation, children were now viewed as highly fragile creatures, who if not carefully nurtured could skitter off the rails into a life of unhappiness and failure. As a young father, I was not a reader of Spock, nor was I ever a Freudian, yet so pervasive were the doctrines of Spock and Freud that their influence was unavoidable.

I was not a very good father; measured by current standards, I may have been a disastrous one. Having divorced from their mother when my sons were ten and eight years old, and having been given custody of them, I brought to my child rearing a modest but genuine load of guilt. I do not have any axiomatic truths about raising children except this one: Children were meant to be brought up by two parents. A single parent, man or woman, no matter how extraordinary, will always be insufficient.

Children, according to Dr. Spock and Dr. Freud, needed to be made to feel secure and loved. I couldn't do much about the first. But I proclaimed my love a lot to my sons, so often that they must have doubted that I really meant it. "You know I love you, goddamnit," I seem to recall saying too many times, especially after having blown my cool by yelling at them for some misdemeanor or other. Thank goodness I had boys; girls, I have discovered, cannot be yelled at, at least not with the same easy conscience.

Fortunately, my sons were fairly tough and independent characters. Neither of them as kids was interested in sports, so I didn't have to attend their Little League games. I took only a modest interest in their schooling. (My parents took none whatsoever in mine, which, given my wretched performance in school, was a break.) Nor did I trek out to Disneyland with them. My sons spent their Sundays with my parents, and my father, who turned out to be a fairly attentive grandfather, took them to the Museum of Science and Industry, the Adler Planetarium, the Shedd Aquarium, and other museums around Chicago. Raising children as a single parent, much of life during those years is now in my memory a blur—a blur of vast loads of laundry, lots of shopping, and less than first-class cookery (mine). "Dad, this steak tastes like fish," I remember one of my sons exclaiming, a reminder that I needed to do a better job of cleaning the broiler.

My oldest son, unlike his father, was good at school. When he was in high school, he took to playing rock at a high volume in his room. I asked him how he could study with such loud music blaring away. "I seem to be getting all A's, Dad," he said. "Are you sure you want me to turn the music down?" He went on to Stanford, my other son to the University of Massachusetts. I drove neither of them on what is now the middle-class parents' compulsory tour of campuses while their children are in their junior year of high school. Nor did I tell them to which schools they should apply. What I said is that I would pay all their bills, that I didn't need to look at their course selection or care about their major or grades, but only asked that they not make me pay for courses in science fiction or in which they watched movies. I visited each of them once while he was in college. I pasted no college decals on the back window of my car.

Some unknown genius for paradox said, "Married, single—neither is a solution." A similar formulation might be devised for the best time to have children: In one's twenties, thirties, forties, beyond—none seems ideal. In my generation, one married young—in my case, at 23—and had children soon thereafter. The idea behind this was to become an adult early and thereby assume the responsibilities of adulthood: wife, children, house, dogs, "the full catastrophe," as Zorba the Greek put it. Now nearly everyone marries later, and women often delay having children, whether married or not, until their late thirties, sometimes early forties.

In one's twenties, one has the energy, but usually neither the perspective nor the funds, to bring up children with calm and understanding. Later in life, when one is more likely to have the perspective and the funds, the energy has departed. In my own case, along with having children to take care of, I had my own ambition with which to contend. I worked at 40-hour-a-week jobs, wrote on weekends and early in the mornings before work, read in the evenings, picked up socks and underwear scattered around the apartment, took out garbage, and in between times tried to establish some mild simulacrum of order in the household.

Because of this hectic life, my sons got less attention but more freedom than those of their contemporaries who had both parents at home, and vastly more freedom than kids brought up during these past two decades when the now-still-regnant, child-centered culture has taken over in American life in a big way.

I have a suspicion that this cultural change began with the entrée into the language of the word *parenting*. I don't know the exact year that the word *parenting* came into vogue, but my guess is that it arrived around the same time as the new full-court press, boots-on-the-ground-with-heavy-air-support notion of being a parent. To be a parent is a role; parenting implies a job. It is one thing to be a parent, quite another to parent. "Parenting (or child rearing) is the process of promoting and supporting the physical, emotional, social, and intellectual development of a child from infancy to adulthood. Parenting refers to the aspects of raising a child aside from the biological relationship," according to the opening sentence of the Wikipedia entry on the subject. Read further down and you will find dreary paragraphs on "parenting styles," "parenting tools," "parenting across the lifespan," and more, alas, altogether too much more.

Under the regime of parenting, raising children became a top priority, an occupation before which all else must yield. The status of children inflated greatly. Much forethought went into giving children those pisselegant names still turning up everywhere: all those Brandys and Brandons and Bradys; Hunters, Taylors, and Tylers; Coopers, Porters, and Madisons; Britannys, Tiffanys, and Kimberlys; and the rest. Deep thought, long-term plans, and much energy goes into seeing to it that they get into the right colleges. ("Tufts somehow feels right for Ashley, Oberlin for Belmont.") What happens when they don't get into the right college, when they in effect fail to repay all the devout attention and care lavished upon them, is another, sadder story.

I began by talking about "fashions" in fatherhood, but I wonder if *fashions* is the right word. I wonder whether *cultural imperatives* doesn't cover the case more precisely. Since raising my sons in the hodgepodge way I did, I have become a grandfather, with two grandchildren living in Northern California and one, a granddaughter now in her twenties, living in Chicago. My second (and final) wife and I have had a fairly extensive hand in helping bring up our Chicago granddaughter, and I have to admit that, even though there is much about it with which I disagree, we have done so largely under the arrangements of the new parenting regime.

When this charming child entered the game, I had long since been working at home, with a loose enough schedule to allow me to bring up my granddaughter in a manner that violated just about everything I have mocked both in person and now in print about the way children are currently brought up. I drove her to school and lessons and usually picked her up afterward. I helped arrange private schools for her. I spent at least thrice the time with her that I did with my two sons combined. I heartily approved all her achievements. Yes—I report this with head bowed—when she was six years old, I took her to Disneyland. Worse news, I rather enjoyed it.

Not the "debbil," as the comedian Flip Wilson used to say, but the culture made me become nothing less than a hovering, endlessly bothering, in-her-face grandfather. (Pause for old Freudian joke: Why do grandparents and grandchildren get on so well? Answer: Because they have a common enemy.) The culture of his day condoned my father in his certainty that his business came before all else, allowing him to become an honorable if inattentive parent. The culture of my day allowed me to be a mildly muddled if ultimately responsible parent and still not entirely loathe myself. The culture of the current day dictated my bringing up my granddaughter, as I did with my wife's extensive help, as a nearly full-time job.

The culture of the current day calls for fathers to put in quite as much time with their children as mothers once did. In part this is owing to the fact that more and more women with children either need or want to work, and in part because, somehow, it only seems fair. Today if a father does not attend the games of his children, he is delinquent. If a father fails to take a strong hand in his children's education, he is deficient. If a father does not do all in his power to build up his children's self-esteem—"Good job, Ian"—he is damnable. If a father does not regularly hug and kiss his children and end all phone calls with "love ya," he is a monster. These are the dictates of the culture on—shall we call it?—"fathering" in our day, and it is not easy to go up against them; as an active grandparent, I, at least, did not find it easy.

Cultural shifts do not arrive without reason. Kids today, it is with some justice argued, cannot, owing to crime in all big cities, be left alone. They need to be more carefully protected than when I, or even my sons, were children. Getting into decent colleges and secondary and primary schools and, yes, even preschools is not the automatic business it once was. The competition for what is felt to be the best in this realm is furious; thought (and often serious sums of money) must go into it. Children are deemed more vulnerable than was once believed. How else to explain all those learning disabilities, attention deficits, and other confidence-shattering psychological conditions that seem to turn up with such regularity and in such abundance? The world generally has become a more frightening place, and any father with the least conscience will interpose himself between it and his children for as long as possible. One can no longer be merely a parent; one must be—up and at 'em—relentlessly parenting.

As a university teacher I have encountered students brought up under this new, full-time attention regimen. On occasion, I have been amused by the unearned confidence of some of these kids. Part of me—the part Flip Wilson's debbil controls—used to yearn to let the air out of their self-esteem. How many wretchedly executed student papers have I read, at the bottom of which I wished to write, "F. Too much love in the home."

Will all the attention now showered on the current generation of children make them smarter, more secure, finer, and nobler human beings? That remains, as the journalists used to say about the outcomes of Latin American revolutions, to be seen. Have the obligations of fathering made men's lives richer, or have they instead loaded men down with a feeling of hopeless inadequacy, for no man can hope to be the ideal father required in our day? How many men, one wonders, after a weekend of heavily programmed, rigidly regimented fun fathering with the kids, can't wait to return to the simpler but genuine pleasures of work? Only when the cultural imperative of parenting changes yet again are we likely to know.

"He that hath wife and children," wrote Francis Bacon, "hath given hostages to fortune, for they are impediments to great enterprises, either of virtue or mischief." Yet many centuries earlier, when Croesus, the richest man of his day, asked the wise Solon who was the most contented man in the world, thinking Solon would answer him—Croesus—Solon surprised him by naming an otherwise obscure Athenian named Tellus. The reason this was so, Solon explained, is that "he lived at a time when his city was particularly well, he had handsome, upstanding sons, and he ended up a grandfather, with all his grandchildren making it to adulthood."

Fathering children puts a man under heavy obligation and leaves him vulnerable to endless worry, not only about the fate of his children but of his children's children. This being so, the most sensible thing, one might think, is not to have children. But one would think wrong. Not to have children cuts a man off from any true sense of futurity and means that he has engaged life less than fully. Fatherhood, for all its modern-day complications, is ultimately manhood.

Critical Thinking

1. What are the advantages and disadvantages of the non-hugging family life of Epstein's childhood?

2. How did the massive cultural and behavioral changes come about?

3. Would you say that child rearing practices are better or worse today versus Epstein's childhood?

Internet References

New American Studies Web
https://blogs.commons.georgetown.edu/vkp/

Social Science Information Gateway
http://www.ariadne.ac.uk/issue2/sosig

Sociology—Study Sociology Online
http://edu.learnsoc.org/

Sociology Web Resources
http://www.mhhe.com/socscience/sociology/resources/index.htm

Sociosite
http://www.topsite.com/goto/sociosite.net

Socioweb
http://www.topsite.com/goto/socioweb.com

JOSEPH EPSTEIN, *who has written for* Commentary *for a half century, contributed "Who You Calling a Coward?" to last month's issue. This essay appears in* The Dadly Virtues, *a collection edited by Jonathan V. Last and published this month by Templeton Press.*

Article   Prepared by: Kurt Finsterbusch, *University of Maryland, College Park*

Myths and Reality About Student Debt and the Cost of Higher Education

RICHARD EKMAN

Learning Outcomes

After reading this article, you will be able to:

- Understand how colleges and universities are adapting to changing economic conditions in higher education.

- Learn some useful good advice about college from this article.

- Evaluate Ekman's defense of the costs of higher education as well as the criticism of these costs.

L adies and gentlemen, it's a pleasure to talk with you today about the future of American education, a subject much in the news as an object of criticism by policy makers and consumer groups. Several myths have grown up about American higher education—what works and what doesn't; what college does cost and what it should cost; who goes to college and who cannot. Today I want to address a handful of the most egregious myths. Here they are:

- A college education costs too much and is a bad long-term investment.
- A private college education costs more than a family can afford.
- Colleges have not reduced costs.
- Student debt is out of control.
- The students with the greatest financial need don't receive the greatest amount of financial aid.
- Only the children of wealthy families attend private colleges.
- Liberal arts majors don't get jobs.

The more these myths are repeated, the more people tend to believe them. I've become alarmed by the dangerously inaccurate picture that these caricatures of American higher education present.

If you look at the changing demographics of the 18-year-old population, you will see that today's college-goers are different from those of a generation earlier. They are drawn largely from low- and middle-income families; they are often the first members of their families to go to college; they are increasingly members of racial and ethnic minority groups; and they come increasingly from the southwestern and southeastern regions of the United States. This demographic shift has put enormous pressure on the colleges located in the Southeast and Southwest to increase capacity quickly. Meanwhile, many private and some public colleges in the northern half of the country face shortfalls in enrollment and have underutilized facilities. By the way, the fastest growing enrollments are in community colleges.

We've had 18 years lead time to watch these trends develop. But after the financial meltdown of 2008, the situation took yet another turn. State governments are less able to support public universities. Tuition charges are up in order to close the gap. Meanwhile, private colleges and universities, most with small endowments to begin with, have earned low rates of return on investments, which means that they have trouble supporting the lower-income students who wish to enroll but require financial aid. So here we are today—with nearly 14 million students enrolled in four-year colleges and universities—a remarkable achievement for our country—but facing very difficult circumstances in many of America's four-year colleges and universities. While colleges did not create the economic recession, they along with all Americans have been scrambling to cope with it.

Some people think that college costs too much and wonder whether we too easily dismiss the honorable path to adulthood of learning a trade that does not require a college degree. There are several problems with this perspective. First, over a lifetime a person who has a college degree likely will earn $700,000–$1 million more than a high school graduate. Second, the main reason why the differential in lifetime earnings potential is so huge is that the old economy's jobs that one could qualify for on the basis of a high school diploma simply do not exist any more. Even factory jobs today require training in mathematics and computers. In other words, today's earnings gap is less the result of salary increases for college graduates and more the result of the evaporation of the jobs that could support a middle-class lifestyle but did not require a college education.

Some people believe they can bypass college and still earn a good income—the Bill Gates effect, if you will. Too much has been made of the rare college drop-outs who make good. Bill Gates is a very successful entrepreneur and a socially responsible philanthropist. As a Harvard student, he rarely went to class and eventually dropped out. But it's also the case that he was able to use Harvard's computer facilities in the middle of the night and talk with faculty members he knew. People who knew him as a high school student in Seattle say that he also had friends who were students at the University of Washington and gave him "unofficial" access to computing facilities! Like the occasional star athlete who makes it big, Gates is not a model for most young people. For most people, college is a worthwhile long-term investment.

America's colleges and universities are first-rate. Our 100 research universities dominate every list of the institutions worldwide that are the recognized leaders in research and innovation. The United States, with only 5 percent of the world's population, wins 80–90 percent of the world's scientific prizes year after year, including Nobel Prizes. But there are additional reasons to take pride in the 1,800 other four-year colleges in the United States. Fifty years ago, America began to expand access to higher education from fewer than half of all high school graduates to more than two-thirds today. We can be proud of the sustained generosity of both state and federal governments and of private donors who, over many years, have made possible this expansion of access. The Obama White House and several leading foundations have set the goal of continuing to increase the number of Americans with college degrees.

Despite these achievements, our colleges are criticized for being expensive, for not preparing students for productive lives, and for not being accessible to low-income students. Even in the US Congress—a body that is unable to reach consensus about almost anything—one of the few topics of bipartisan agreement, unfortunately, seems to be that higher education is doing a bad job.

The solutions proposed by public officials to these alleged problems are sometimes bizarre. The governor of one state, observing that recent graduates in engineering have better employment prospects than graduates with humanities majors, proposed earlier this year that the tuition for the state university's engineering program be set at a lower level than the tuition for humanities majors. You would think that differential tuition levels—a flawed concept, in any event—should reflect the large investment in laboratory facilities needed for an engineering program and the tiny investment needed for, say, a philosophy program that requires only a 20-page text by Aristotle and perhaps a eucalyptus tree to sit under.

I recognize that most high school students and their parents dream of an Ivy League education, of a college that will open doors to both great personal success and ample opportunities to play an important role in society. But the Ivy League can accept only so many students. The looming public policy questions at a time when we do need to produce more college graduates to assure future American competitiveness are: what form of massive, large-scale higher education will serve us best? How can we pay for the larger scale of access? Where do students—especially the increasing numbers of low-income, first-generation, and minority college students—have the greatest chance of success?

Contrary to the myth, students in long underrepresented populations on campuses account for about the same percentages in both private and state universities. The graduation rates of these students, however, are significantly higher at private colleges than at state universities, and both of these kinds of traditional institutions have higher graduation rates—for all categories of students—than the for-profit education providers. The five-year graduation rate for students at private nonprofit four-year colleges is 62 percent. For public colleges it is 51 percent. For for-profit education providers, it is 40 percent.

All these rates may strike you as too low compared with graduation rates a generation ago when college students were a smaller percentage of the population, so let us focus for a minute on the sub-groups of particular interest. Only 27 percent of Hispanic students at public universities earn their bachelor's degrees in four years; at private colleges it is 46 percent. For low-income students at public colleges, the five-year graduation rate is only 47 percent; at private colleges, 59 percent. At the end of six years, the numbers for low-income students have risen to 68 percent at private and 61 percent at public institutions, respectively, which is good news, but the six-year graduation rate for low-income students at for-profit colleges is still a shockingly low 18 percent.

Think about the implications of these completion rates: a Latino student who has good but not superstar grades at an inner-city high school in Los Angeles, who comes from a family with little income, and whose parents have no college background has a better chance of graduating from a nonelite private college than he or she does from a branch campus of the state university near his home; and a much better chance of success at either of these traditional kinds of colleges than in a for-profit college.

Actually, quite a few colleges, committed to providing college access to those who truly deserve it, have recently made a specialty of educating these students. Here's an example. Southern Vermont College in Bennington admitted an African American student from a New York City high school a few years ago. He had a B minus average in high school. His family had no money. He was being raised by his grandmother. At Southern Vermont, this young man blossomed. The following year, two students from that high school went to Southern Vermont. The following year Southern Vermont decided to recruit students from several New York city public high schools. Today the college has active recruitment programs underway in high schools in New York, Philadelphia, Washington, Buffalo, and Cleveland.

How can these students afford to go to a private college? The answer to this question also runs counter to popular myths. State universities are heavily subsidized by state governments, so the publicly advertised "sticker" price of tuition can be pretty low. Sadly, many state governments have in recent years reduced appropriations to state universities, although a few states have finally seen the bottom of the effects of the 2008 financial crisis and are now beginning to increase support for state universities again. Happily, New York state is one of these.

Private colleges, of course, often have higher sticker prices, because on average 59 percent of their revenue comes from tuition and fees. But not so well understood is that few students at private college pay the sticker price. Private colleges raise tremendous amounts of money to be used for scholarships. The average student pays about half the sticker price—say, $25,000 rather than $50,000 per year. The result is that low-income students can and do enroll in private colleges in sizable numbers. In fact, nearly 40 percent of all private college students are from low-income backgrounds.

Here's another myth-busting fact: a larger proportion of lower-income students enroll at smaller private colleges than at public research universities. How can that be? The explanation has two parts: First, some of the flagship public universities—Berkeley, Michigan, and Indiana, for example—are excellent universities and some of the students with the strongest high school records will prefer to study there regardless of their ability to pay more elsewhere. But second, most private colleges are truly committed to enrolling all deserving students and these colleges treat fundraising for scholarship money as a top priority—higher priority than new buildings or new faculty positions. Indeed, the amount of private scholarship money awarded to students at private colleges is six times as much as the amount of federal aid that is distributed to private college students.

Still, $25,000 is a lot of money, and some students do need to take out loans. We've all heard about the rare student who

has, quite irresponsibly, taken on $150,000 in loans. But that student is the rare exception—thank goodness. Here are the facts. Fully 28 percent of graduates of private colleges have no debt whatsoever. Another 29 percent have debts of under $20,000. The average amount of debt for all students is $28,000, but the average debt for those who actually graduate is below $20,000. Is this a lot of debt or a little? It is not a large amount of money in relation to the lifetime earnings premium of being a college graduate—up to $1 million more in salary. We need a sense of proportion. $25,000 is not a lot of money in relation to the price of other things—about equal to the price of a modest automobile that depreciates the minute you drive it off the lot, whereas a college degree appreciates in value. Most reassuring is that students with the least amount of debt fall into two categories—those with the lowest family incomes and those who have persisted in their studies and graduated in timely fashion. In other words, colleges follow honorable principles when distributing financial aid. The result has been that 79 percent of all private college graduates finish in four years in comparison with only 50 percent of public college graduates.

Journalists, however, have become fascinated by one statistic: the US total amount of student debt, now more than $1 trillion, is more than the total of credit card debt. But this figure is not evidence that college costs too much; it is instead an indication that more people are going to college than ever before and they are drawn from families without a lot of wealth. This is a good thing, an accomplishment by our society over two generations of which we should be proud, a fulfillment of one aspect of Lyndon Johnson's Great Society vision.

Colleges have tried to reduce costs and have succeeded. Over the past five years, net tuition and fees, adjusted for inflation, has actually declined by 3.5 percent. Many colleges have frozen tuition. Additional scholarship money has been raised and awarded. Several colleges have slashed tuition charges— Converse College in South Carolina, Cabrini College in Pennsylvania, Sewanee in Tennessee, and Hartwick College here in New York State are recent examples. Their assumption is that the "high tuition/high financial aid" model wastes a lot of people's time in negotiations and everyone would be better off getting to the bottom line right away. These colleges also believe that some very bright low-income students don't even apply to college and never learn about the financial aid available because the publicly announced sticker price scares them away.

This fact has some bearing on the national goals for higher education. One major goal is that our country needs more scientists and engineers. In fields of study that are cumulative, such as mathematics, science, and foreign languages, the rate of degree completion is higher in small colleges than at large universities. In fact, small colleges account for a disproportionately large share of those individuals who become career scientists and engineers. Look at the field of physics. In the United States, we produce too few PhD physicists who are Americans. The foreign-born graduate students at US universities, meanwhile, increasingly choose to return home to pursue their careers. The National Academy of Sciences issued reports by blue-ribbon commissions in 2005 and 2010 that express alarm, and call on universities and the federal government to do better.

But there is a cost-effective solution at hand. Think about this comparison. In the past five years, 16 people who were undergraduate physics majors at one large university, Texas A&M, completed PhDs in physics. In the same period, 17 people who did their undergraduate work at Swarthmore College, a much smaller institution, completed PhDs in physics. The same pattern holds true in chemistry. Oberlin College has exactly one-tenth the number of students as the University of Wisconsin at Madison and one-tenth the number of undergraduate chemistry majors. The numbers of those undergraduate chemistry majors who ultimately earn PhDs in chemistry is very small—about two or three per year who were Wisconsin undergraduates and about the same number who were Oberlin undergraduates, not one-tenth the number. If the United States needs more scientists, small colleges are the most cost-effective way to produce them. The same amount of taxpayers' money spent to educate college students who plan to be scientists and engineers will produce many more physicists and chemists if the funds are used to support students at smaller private colleges.

What about the world of work more generally? It's certainly reasonable for students to expect college to give them both a solid general education and the skills to obtain a job in a chosen profession. Are colleges preparing students for jobs? The answer is yes, but there is a caveat because new college graduates in the past few years have found it difficult to obtain jobs. This is not the fault of the colleges, but of an overall weak economy. Even so, it is still the case that the unemployment rate for college graduates is half the unemployment rate of non-graduates—4.6 percent versus 9.4 percent. For college graduates, the unemployment rate even at the depths of the recession never rose above 6.3 percent. The rates of employment of new graduates do vary more by field than by institution, and always have. Right now, petroleum engineers are in great demand; social workers are not. These patterns are cyclical. Today, those who majored in the former boom field of business are struggling to find work—a big change from just few years ago. A new college graduate in social work earns about $30,000; five years later the average salary rises to $46,000. If that person gets an advanced degree, the average salary rises to $60,000. A new college graduate who becomes a chemical engineer earns $51,000; five years later the salary has increased to $94,000.

But a new graduate in computer science earns $50,000; in five years the median salary has increased only to $81,000. We also know from past oil booms that the petroleum engineers who received a broad-based education in the liberal arts are going to fare better when the employment cycle gets to a low point, as it inevitably will, than the engineers whose educational background were narrow and technical.

Employers say that the skills they want in their new employees are those of problem-solving, creativity, clear written and oral expression, and the ability to work in teams. These are precisely the skills that the liberal arts teach and are emphasized in the small classes of liberal arts colleges.

In closing, let me say I hope these comments will help you to recognize inaccurate statements about higher education when you encounter them. If I were to convert the handful of myths I listed at the outset to true statements about the cost of education, here's what I'd say:

- A college education is well worth the cost. Going to college is the best long-term investment one can make to increase earnings potential over a lifetime.
- A private college education is affordable for families across all income brackets. Large numbers of low- and middle-income students enroll in private colleges every year.
- Colleges have gone to great lengths to reduce costs and raise a great deal of private support to offset costs.
- Student debt is not out of control. Taking on some debt to earn a college degree is a wise financial decision.
- The students with the greatest financial need do in fact receive most of the financial aid they need to complete their degrees at private colleges.
- Liberal arts majors do get jobs because they possess the skills that employers say they want most.

I hope everyone here will help to set the record straight. The myths are doing damage. Students are not making well-informed choices. Colleges are distracted by the need to respond to problems that don't exist. And our country is jeopardizing its global leadership by a failure to appreciate how effectively the American approach to higher education has served the nation for a very long time, and continues to do so today.

Thank you.

Critical Thinking

1. Does college cost too much? Is higher education worth the costs?
2. How are the financial issues of higher education affecting community colleges?
3. How should higher education costs change? Can they?

Create Central

www.mhhe.com/createcentral

Internet References

New American Studies Web
www.georgetown.edu/crossroads/asw

Sociology—Study Sociology Online
http://edu.learnsoc.org

Sociology Web Resources
http://www.mhhe.com/socscience/sociology/resources/index.htm

Sociosite
http://www.topsite.com/goto/sociosite.net

Socioweb
http://www.topsite.com/goto/socioweb.com

The American Studies Web
www.lamp.georgetown.edu/asw

The Center for Education Reform
http://edreform.com/school_choice

Article Prepared by: Kurt Finsterbusch, *University of Maryland, College Park*

Fighting Back Through Resistance: Challenging the Defunding and Privatization of Public Education

CURRY MALOTT

Learning Outcomes

After reading this article, you will be able to:

- Identify some of the negative consequences of many charter schools.

- Explain how this article argues that investments in higher education produces rich economic returns.

- Explain the pros and cons of privatizing the public schools.

The following speech was written and presented by Dr. Curry Malott, Assistant Professor in the College of Education at West Chester University of Pennsylvania June 16th, 2015, as part of the "Rally in West Chester for a State Budget Chester County Kids Deserve, which is part of a state-wide tour organized under "The Alliance to Reclaim our Schools." The tour is traveling all over the state rallying at all of the 13 universities (Bloomsburg University, California University, Clarion University, East Stroudsburg University, Edinboro University, Indiana University, Kutztown University, Lock Haven University, Mannsfield University, Millersville University, Shipensburg University, Slippery Rock University, and West Chester University) in the state system (Pennsylvania's State System of Higher Education), as well as in major cities where public K-12 education has been hit particularly hard by punishing austerity measures.

The premise of the "Reclaiming the Promise of Pennsylvania's Public Education" campaign is that the old Republican Governor, Tom Corbett, recently left office after having followed the national trend of defunding public education. This tour is designed to put pressure on the new Democratic Governor, Tom Wolfe, to make an effort to deliver on one of his key campaign promises, that is, to restore the millions of dollars that Corbett cut from public education while Governor.

The Alliance is not only advocating for a more adequately funded system of public education, but it is campaigning for a system of public education, through initiatives such as "A Road Map for the Schools Our Children Deserve," that put more emphasis on critical thinking and creativity than on test scores, again, challenging the national trend of high stakes testing associated with No Child Left Behind (NCLB) and the back door it open[ed] for privatizing public education. That is, by setting a one hundred percent proficiency goal (i.e., every student has to pass the high stakes exams) in a context with growing poverty (knowing that the number one predictor of academic achievement is rate of poverty), then schools would be set up to fail. According to NCLB, schools who repeatedly do not improve their average scores would be subject to alternative management options (i.e., taken over by for-profit management companies). The aforementioned Alliance and its Road Map, aware of the connections between schooling and who the government intervenes on behalf of, argues, within their call to "fund our public schools fully and fairly," for a call for ending "corporate tax loopholes," taxing "gas drillers" and "halting any new prison construction." This analysis demonstrates why Dr. Malott, whose work focuses on a Marxist approach to the history of education, education policy, and educational practice or pedagogy, was the local West Chester professor/activist/leader invited to speak. Other local activist educators have been invited to speak at the other stops of the tour, which is shaping up to be an important step in building a united educational front agitating against the ravages of capital, and for Dr. Malott, a communist future.

Sixteen years ago, in 1999, on the eve of the No Child Left Behind Act, which would prove to be the mechanism that would lead to the ongoing process of privatization and the more complete corporate takeover of public education, and subsequent attack on teacher unions, Bob Peterson, public school teacher, union activist, and a Rethinking Schools editor and writer, argued that to "meet these challenges, our public schools and our teacher unions should set two key goals: survival and justice." In addition to survival and justice, I think we need to add resistance to the list because we resist through our unions, our organizations, and through alliances such as, "The Alliance to Reclaim our Schools." In addition to defending public K-12 education, we resist by demanding that (PASSHE's Pennsylvania State System of Higher Education) mission to provide an affordable, high quality higher education is realized by agitating, with joy and without apology, for preserving the requested $458 million State System appropriation. Funding for public higher education in Pennsylvania is at a 17 year low. That is unacceptable, and we must fight back.

But students, educators and working people in general, as you know, and as this gathering is further evidence, have been resisting the attacks on our schools, our unions, and our ability to earn a descent wage. And as resistance movements flair up across the country and across the world, we should do whatever we can to be a part of them, from opt out movements in Seattle, to efforts to stop school closures in Philadelphia, to the Alliance to save Pennsylvania's Public Schools, to rebellions sparked by police departments that murder, with near impunity, the same black and brown students the schools have always tended to treat as inherently low achieving and thus as disposable, low-wage, unskilled laborers.

Again, as this rally, alliance, and campaign remind us, the struggle for the education our children deserve is building momentum. And as the Road Map this alliance has created points out, the struggle for a quality and well-funded public education system, from kindergarten through university, is intimately connected to a state and federal government whose revenue has been redirected away from public service programs, such as education, and toward corporate welfare for gas drillers, etc., and for turning public service programs into for-profit investment ventures, rather than attempting, however half-heartedly, to serve the so-called common good.

Again, public education is not just being defunded, it is also being privatized, which is not the same thing as private schools like Harvard who pride themselves on quality, whether real or imagined. On-line education, the University of Phoenix, and Charter school models are the most obvious examples of privatized schools. It is nearly common knowledge now that programs like those offered by the University of Phoenix do not produce quality education, but mountains of student debt contributing to the looming, potentially disastrous, student debt bubble.

Unfortunately, this is precisely what capitalism does to things it turns into commodities. That is, the quest to make a profit off of education has tended to result in the destruction of its use value, or its useful effect, that is, the quality of education, hurting other capitalists who rely on a well-educated work force. While increasing state appropriations for public education is bad for the education capitalists who want to degrade education so they can swoop in and pretend to save the day and take it over, increasing state appropriations is good for the vast majority of capitalists in the state of Pennsylvania who, again, rely on a well-educated work force.

If the current state wants to do right by the working people of Pennsylvania, then it should start by fully funding public education. After all, the state system of higher education in general, and West Chester University in particular, have an economic impact on the region that is significant. Consider:

- West Chester University is the 14th largest employer in Chester County employing 1,635 people.
- 7,127 additional jobs across the Commonwealth are supported through West Chester University's existence.
- For every one state dollar invested in West Chester University, $9.93 is returned to the Commonwealth's economy.
- Preserving the requested $458 million State System appropriation makes economic sense.
- Tragically, Pennsylvania's State System universities have endured a $90 million cut over the last four years and currently receive a state appropriation that is less than 17 years ago. It is estimated that this cut has cost local economies over 2,000 jobs. Workers want jobs, and capitalists want to make profits, and must hire workers to do so. Fully funding public education should be a no brainer.

In addition to properly funding public education systems, all of the goals of the road map to the schools our children deserve are important. For example, the map calls for "More learning and less testing" to ensure Pennsylvania schools meet student and family needs. This is a position that James Scanlon, superintendent of the West Chester Area School District supports. Scanlon has argued that, "learning should be challenging, but also enjoyable and exciting. Teaching should be dynamic and creative. We're missing so much of that because of these tests . . . I hope you will join me in advocating for change." Scanlon, we hear you.

One last example, the current Dean of the College of Education at West Chester University, Dean Witmer, my Dean, has brought the many concerns of the American Association of Colleges for Teacher Education concerning Arne Duncan's proposed regulations for higher education to our College of Education as a whole. Analysts are calling it No Child Left Behind for higher education because it would tie the accreditation of teacher education programs to the test scores of student teachers' future K-12 students. This is highly troubling, to say the least.

We are hearing more and more such stories of administrator's, from Witmer to Scanlon, who are challenging policies because they know they do not represent what the American people actually want and what students deserve. The fact that administrators are resisting should give us confidence, strength, and energy to continue to expand our important movement. Brothers and sisters, seize the time!

Critical Thinking

1. Do you favor or oppose the privatization of public schools at the K to 12 grade level?

2. This article pushes a greater emphasis on critical thinking and creativity than on test scores, as in the high stakes testing associated with No Child Left Behind. Do you agree with its point of view?

3. Why is our nation constantly reforming the schools?

Internet References

New American Studies Web
https://blogs.commons.georgetown.edu/vkp/

Social Science Information Gateway
http://www.ariadne.ac.uk/issue2/sosig

Sociology–Study Sociology Online
http://edu.learnsoc.org/

Sociology Web Resources
http://www.mhhe.com/socscience/sociology/resources/index.htm

Sociosite
http://www.topsite.com/goto/sociosite.net

Socioweb
http://www.topsite.com/goto/socioweb.com

Article Prepared by: Kurt Finsterbusch, *University of Maryland, College Park*

A Thousand Years Young

AUBREY DE GREY

Learning Outcomes

After reading this article, you will be able to:

- Understand that Aubrey de Grey's approach to life extension is to constantly rejuvenate the body as it deteriorates.

- Assuming that de Grey is right, consider how people would change their lifestyles.

- Understand the many specific treatments that would together greatly extend life.

An "antiaging activist" identifies the medical and biochemical advances that could eventually eliminate all the wear and tear that our bodies and minds suffer as we grow old. Those who undergo continuous repair treatments could live for millennia, remain healthy throughout, and never fear dying of old age.

Let me first say very explicitly: I don't work on longevity. I work on health. People are going to live longer as a result of the therapies I will describe, but extended longevity is a side effect—a consequence of keeping people healthy. There is no way in hell that we are going to keep people alive for a long time in a frail state. People will live longer only if we succeed in keeping them healthy longer.

The problem of aging is unequivocally humanity's worst medical problem. Roughly 100,000 people worldwide die every day of it, and there's an awful lot of suffering that happens before you die. But I feel that the defeat of aging in the foreseeable future is a realistic proposition. We will have medicine that will get aging under control to the same level that we now have most infectious diseases under control.

This article will describe what aging is, what regenerative medicine is, and what the various alternative approaches are to combat aging and postpone the ill health of old age. I'll then go into the details of the approach that I feel we need to take and what my expectations are for the future.

Regenerative medicine is any medical intervention that seeks to restore some part of the body—or the whole body—to how it was before it suffered some kind of damage. It could be damage that happened as the result of an acute injury, such as spinal cord damage. But it could also be damage that accumulated as a chronic condition over a long period of time.

Aging is a side effect of being alive in the first place. *Metabolism* is the word that biologists use to encompass all the aspects of being alive—all the molecular and cellular and systemic processes that keep us going from one day to the next and from one year to the next.

Ongoing lifelong side effects of metabolism—i.e., *damages*—are created throughout life. For whatever reason, damage is not repaired when it occurs. So damage accumulates. For a long time, the amount of damage is tolerable, and the metabolism just carries on. But eventually, damage becomes sufficiently extensive that it gets in the way of metabolism. Then metabolism doesn't work so well, and *pathologies*—all the things that go wrong late in life, all the aspects of age-related ill health—emerge and progress.

Geriatrics Versus Gerontology

Traditionally, there have been two themes within the study of aging that aim to actually do something about this process. One is the *geriatrics* approach, which encompasses pretty much everything that we have today in terms of medical treatments for the elderly.

The geriatrics approach is all about the pathology. It focuses on old people in whom the pathologies are already emerging, and strives to slow down their progression so that it takes longer for those pathologies to reach a life-threatening stage.

The *gerontology* approach, on the other hand, says that prevention is better than cure. This approach assumes that it will be more effective to dive in at an earlier point in the chain of events and clean up metabolism so that it creates these various types of damage at a slower rate than it naturally would. The effect would be to postpone the age at which damage reaches the level of abundance that is pathogenic.

The two approaches both sound pretty promising, but they're really not. The problem with the geriatrics approach is that aging is awfully chaotic, miserable, and complicated. There are many things that go wrong with people as they get older, and they tend to happen at much the same time. These problems interact, exacerbating each other, and damage accumulates. Even later in life, as damage continues to accumulate, the pathologies of old age become progressively more and more difficult to combat.

The geriatric approach is thus intervening too late in the chain of events. It's better than nothing, but it's not much better than nothing.

So that leaves us with the gerontology approach. Unfortunately, the gerontology approach has its own problem: Metabolism is complicated. What we know about how metabolism works is completely dwarfed by the utterly astronomical amount that we *don't* know about how metabolism works. We have no prospect whatsoever of being able to interfere in this process in a way that does not simply do more harm than good.

A Maintenance Approach

There are some Volkswagen Bugs that are 50 years old or more and still running. And the reason is because those VW Bugs have been extraordinarily well maintained. If you maintain your car only as well as the law requires, then it will only last 15 years or so. But if you do a lot more, then you can do a lot better. Maintenance works.

Now what does that tell us about the human body? Well, quite a lot, because the human body is a machine. It's a really complicated machine, but it's still a machine. So there is a third way of combating aging by postponing age-related ill health. This is the *maintenance* approach. We go in and periodically repair the damage that metabolism creates, so as to prevent that damage from accumulating and reaching the level that causes the pathology of old age to emerge and to progress.

Maintenance is a much more promising approach than either geriatrics or gerontology. First, the maintenance approach is preemptive, so it doesn't have this problem of this downward spiral of the geriatrics approach.

Second, the maintenance approach avoids the problem of the gerontology approach because it does not attempt to intervene with metabolism; we merely fix up the consequences. In other words, we let metabolism create these various types of damage at the rate that it naturally does, and then repair the damages before they cause pathology. We can get away with not understanding very much at all about how metabolism creates damage. We just have to characterize the damage itself and figure out ways to repair it.

That's pretty good news, but it gets better. It also turns out that damage is simpler than its causes or its consequences. All the phenomena that qualify as damage can be classified into one of seven major categories:

- Junk inside cells.
- Junk outside cells.
- Too few cells.
- Too many cells.
- Chromosome mutations.
- Mitochondria mutations.
- Protein crosslinks.

By "junk inside cells," I am referring to the molecular byproducts of normal biologic processes that are created in the cell and that the cell, for whatever reason, does not have the machinery to break down or to excrete. Those byproducts simply accumulate, and eventually the cell doesn't work so well. That turns out to be the main cause of cardiovascular disease and of macular degeneration.

"Junk outside cells" means things like senile plaques in Alzheimer's disease. This creates the same molecular damage, but in this case it is in the spaces between cells.

"Too few cells" simply means cells are dying and not being automatically replaced by the division of other cells. This is the cause of Parkinson's disease, the particular part of the brain in which neurons happen to die more rapidly than in most parts of the brain and they're not replaced. When there are too few of them, that part of the brain doesn't work so well.

But here's the really good news. We actually have a pretty good idea how to fix all of these types of damage. Here is the same list of types of damage, and on the right is the set of approaches that I feel are very promising for fixing them:

Damage	Treatment
Junk inside cells	Transgenic microbial hydrolases
Junk outside cells	Phagocytosis by immune stimulation
Too few cells (cell loss)	Cell therapy
Too many cells (death-resistant cells)	Suicide genes and immune stimulation
Chromosome mutations	Telomerase/ALT gene deletion plus periodic stem-cell reseeding
Mitochondria mutations	Allotopic expression of 13 proteins
Protein crosslinks	AGE-breaking molecules and enzymes

Stem-cell therapy replaces those cells that the body cannot replace on its own. That includes joint degeneration and muscular-skeletal problems. For example, arthritis ultimately comes from the degeneration of the collagen and other extracellular material in the joints, which happens as a result of insufficient regeneration of that tissue.

For some other medical conditions, such as Alzheimer's, we need to restore the functions of those cells that are already there by getting rid of the garbage accumulating outside them. Toward that purpose, there are phase-three clinical trials for the elimination of senile plaques in the brains of Alzheimer's patients. This is a technology using vaccination that we at the SENS Foundation are extending to the elimination of other types of extracellular garbage.

In fact, we now have an enormous amount of detail about how we're going to reverse each of the seven categories of age-related damage, so that's why I feel that my estimates of how long it's going to take to get there are likely to be borne out accurately.

The SENS Foundation: Doing Something About Aging

I'm the chief officer of a 501 (c) 3 public charity based in California. The mission of the SENS Foundation is to develop, promote, and enable widespread access to regenerative medicine as solutions to the disabilities and diseases of aging.

Is there any competition in this work? Are other people trying other things? The short answer is, Not really. There are other people, of course, looking at ways to postpone aging and age-related ill health. But regenerative medicine is really the only game in town when we're talking about serious postponement of age-related ill health. And SENS Foundation really is the hub of that concept.

We are a charity, so if you are a billionaire, please see me! But of course it's not just money we need. We need people's time and expertise. If you're a biologist, work on relevant things. Write to us and ask us for advice about what to work on, because we need more manpower in this area. If you're a conference organizer, have me to speak. If you're a journalist, come and interview me. It's all about getting the word out.

—Aubrey de Grey

Details: The SENS Foundation, www.sens.org; e-mail foundation @sens.org.

Case in Point: Cleaning the Cellular Garbage

I'm going to talk about one example: the garbage that accumulates inside cells. I'm going to explain what *transgenic microbial hydrolases* are.

White blood cells, called macrophages, sweep along a healthy adult's artery walls to clean up miscellaneous detritus, typically lipo-protein particles that were transporting cholesterol around the body from one place to another and that got stuck in the artery wall. Macrophages are very good at coping with cholesterol, but they are not so good at coping with certain derivatives of cholesterol, such as oxysterols. These contaminants end up poisoning macrophages. The macrophages become unable even to cope with native cholesterol, and then they themselves break down, lodging in the artery walls. This is the beginning of an atherosclerotic plaque. The results are cardiovascular disease, heart attacks, or strokes. In the eye, this phenomenon causes macular degeneration.

To combat this problem, we might adapt bioremediation technology from environmental decontamination. The technology that is used to break down pollutants in the environment could be adapted for biomedical purposes, breaking down the body's contaminants.

If we could apply this bioremediation process to our own cells, we could combat the initial process that turns young people into old people in the first place. A very simple idea. The question is, does it work? Bioremediation for getting rid of pollutants works really well: It's a thriving commercial discipline.

There are a number of oxidized derivatives of cholesterol, but the nastiest in abundance and toxicity is 7-ketocholesterol—public enemy number one in atherosclerosis. We have tried "feeding" it to many different strains of bacteria. Most of them can't do anything with it, but we've found two strains of bacteria that gorge themselves on it. After only 10 days, the material is completely gone.

The next step is to figure out how these bacteria are able to do this from a genetic basis. From there, we could try to turn 7-ketocholesterol back into native cholesterol. But there are other steps that we can use—remember that I said we're looking to avoid the problem of things neither being broken down nor excreted. There are modifications that we can make to compounds that are toxic that simply promote their excretion rather than promoting their degradation.

So that's all pretty good news. But don't get me wrong. This is really hard. This is a very ambitious, long-term project. The processes we hope to develop must work in vivo. What we are seeking is a truly definitive, complete cure for cardiovascular disease and for other pathologies caused by the accumulation of molecular garbage inside cells.

Escape Velocity: From Longevity to Immortality?

I do not claim that any of the work I've just described is going to be a "cure" for aging. I claim, rather, that it's got a good chance of adding 30 years of extra healthy life to people's lives. I call that *robust human rejuvenation*. And 30 years is better than nothing, but it sure does not equate to defeating aging completely. So what's the rest of my story?

The rest of the story is that it's not something that's going to work just on people who haven't been conceived yet. It's stuff that is going to work on people who are already middle-aged or older when the therapies arrive.

This is fundamentally what it all comes down to. The maintenance approach is so cool because repairing damage buys time.

At age zero, people start off with not much damage. Time goes on, they age, damage accumulates, reserve is depleted, and eventually, they get down to a certain point—the frailty threshold—and that's when pathologies start to happen. Then they're not long for this world.

Now take someone who is in middle age. You have therapies that are pretty good, but not perfect, at fixing the damage. They can be rejuvenated, but not all the way. These therapies do not reduce the rate at which damage is created. Aging happens at the normal rate.

Then we reapply the same therapies again and again. But consider that the interval between the first and second applications of these therapies to some particular individual may be 15 to 20 years. That's a long time in biomedical technology, and it means that the person is going to get new and improved therapies that will not only fix the types of damage that they could fix 15 years previously, but also fix some types of damage that they could not fix 15 years previously.

So after the second rejuvenation, our hero is not only more thoroughly rejuvenated than he would be if he'd gotten the old therapies, but he's actually more rejuvenated than he was when he got the old therapies, even though at that point he was chronologically younger. Now we see this phenomenon where we don't hit diminishing returns on additional therapies. People over the long term will be getting progressively younger as they're getting chronologically older. They'll remain far away from reaching the frailty threshold, however long they live. They will only be subjected to the risks of death and ill health that affect young adults. They never become more susceptible to ill health simply as a result of having been born a long time ago.

There's some minimum rate at which we have to improve the comprehensiveness of these therapies in order for the general trend in increased life span to be upwards rather than downwards. And that minimum rate is what I call *longevity escape velocity*. It's the rate at which these rejuvenation therapies need to be improved in terms of comprehensiveness following that first step—the first-generation therapies that give robust human regeneration—in order to stay one step ahead of the problem and to outpace the accumulation of damage that they cannot yet repair.

So is it realistic? Are we likely actually to reach longevity escape velocity and to maintain it? We are. Consider powered flight as an illustrated example: There are very big differences between fundamental breakthroughs and incremental refinements of those breakthroughs. Fundamental breakthroughs are very hard to predict. Mostly people think they're not going to happen right up until they already have happened.

Incremental refinements, meanwhile, are very much more predictable. Leonardo da Vinci probably thought he was only a couple of decades away from getting off the ground. He was wrong. But once the Wright brothers got there, progress was ridiculously rapid. It only took 24 years for someone to fly solo across the Atlantic (that was Lindbergh), 22 more years until the first commercial jet liner, and 20 more years until the first supersonic airlines.

Can we actually give more direct evidence that we are likely to achieve longevity escape velocity? I believe that we can.

An Age-Busting Virtuous Cycle

A few years ago I worked with others on a computer simulation of the aging process to see what the impact would be of these interventions coming in at a realistic schedule. We started by imagining a population of adults who were all born in 1999. Everyone is alive at age zero and almost everyone survives until age 50 or 60, at which point they start dropping like flies; hardly anyone gets beyond 100.

Next, we imagined another population whose intrinsic risk of death at any given age is the same as for the first, but who are receiving these therapies. But they only start receiving them when they are already 80 years old. That population's survival rate will actually mostly coincide with the first population's survival rate, because obviously half the population or so is dead by age 80 and those who are still living are already in a reasonably bad way.

But what if population number two started getting these therapies 10 years earlier, when they're only 70? Initially, the same story is the case—there is not a lot of benefit. But gradually, the therapies get the upper hand. They start to impose genuine rejuvenation on these people so that they become biologically younger and less likely to die. Some of them reach 150, by which time they have very little chance of dying of *any* age-related cause. Eventually, there is exactly no such risk.

And if they're 60 years old when the therapies begin? Then almost half of them will get to that point. So we calculated, group by group.

Here's the real kicker: I was ludicrously over-pessimistic in the parameters that I chose for this simulation. I said that we would assume that the therapy would only be doubled in their efficacy every 42 years. Now, 42 years: That's the difference between Lindbergh's *Spirit of St. Louis* and the *Concorde!* But even then, we unambiguously see longevity escape velocity.

So it's inescapable. If and when we do succeed in developing these rejuvenation therapies that give us those first couple of decades more of health and the postponement of age-related ill health, then we will have done the hard part. The sky is the limit after that.

Here is what it means. At the moment, the world record for life span is 122. We won't be getting anyone who is 150 until such time as we do develop these technologies that give us robust human rejuvenation. But we will have done the hard part, so people not much younger than that will be able to escape aging indefinitely, living even to age 1,000.

A 1,000 is not pulled out of the air. It's simply the average age—plus or minus a factor of two—that people would live to if we already didn't have aging, if the only risks of death were the same risks that currently afflict young adults in the Western world today.

Should we be developing these therapies? We are ignorant about the circumstances within which humanity of the future will be deciding whether to use these technologies or not. It could actually be a no-brainer that they will want to use them. And if we have prevented them from using them by not developing them in time, then future generations won't be very happy. So it seems to me that we have a clear moral obligation to develop these technologies so as to give humanity of the future the choice. And the sooner, the better.

Critical Thinking

1. Would you like to live 1,000 years? Aubrey de Grey says that the technology will be developed to make that happen for you or your grandchildren.
2. What would be the impacts on social life and society if healthy life extended for hundreds of years?
3. Why is de Grey's message largely ignored by the media?

Create Central

www.mhhe.com/createcentral

Internet References

National Institutes of Health (NIH)
www.nih.gov

Sociology—Study Sociology Online
http://edu.learnsoc.org

Sociology Web Resources
http://www.mhhe.com/socscience/sociology/resources/index.htm

Sociosite
http://www.topsite.com/goto/sociosite.net

Socioweb
http://www.topsite.com/goto/socioweb.com

AUBREY DE GREY is a biomedical gerontologist and chief science officer of the SENS Foundation (www.sens.org). He is the author (with Michael Rae) of *Ending Aging* (St. Martin's Press, 2007) and editor-in-chief of the journal *Rejuvenation Research*. This article draws from his presentation at WorldFuture 2011 in Vancouver.

Article

Prepared by: Kurt Finsterbusch, *University of Maryland, College Park*

Why Is Health Care So Expensive?

Why It's So High, How It Affects Your Wallet—and Yes, What You Can Do about It

CONSUMER REPORTS

Learning Outcomes

After reading this article, you will be able to:

- Describe the per capita health care costs for the United States compared to European countries since 1980.

- Discuss some of the other adverse aspects of the U.S. health care system.

- Explain the statement of George Halvorson, former chairman of Kaiser Permanente, "Prices are made up depending on who the payer is."

Person for person, health care in the U.S. costs about twice as much as it does in the rest of the developed world. In fact, if our $3 trillion health care sector were its own country, it would be the world's fifth-largest economy.

If you have health insurance, you may think it doesn't matter because someone else is paying the bill. You'd be wrong. This country's exorbitant medical costs mean that we all pay too much for health insurance. Overpriced care also translates into fewer raises for American workers. And to top it off, we're not even getting the best care for our money.

First, be aware that even if you have insurance, it doesn't always fully protect you. Four years ago, Joclyn Krevat, a 32-year-old occupational therapist from New York City, collapsed with a rare heart condition and ended up needing an emergency heart transplant. She had it done at a hospital in her health plan's network, but no one bothered to tell her that her transplant surgeons didn't take her insurance. They billed her $70,000 and sent collection agencies and lawyers after her while she was still home recuperating. In studying the problem,

Consumer Reports has heard dozens of similar tales about surprise out-of-network bills. (If you have one, consider sharing it with us).

Second, higher health care costs mean higher health insurance premiums for everyone. It's Health Insurance 101: Insurance is about pooling risk. That's a good thing because it protects you against unexpected costs—but companies have to collect enough in premiums to pay for members' health expenses. The higher the expenses for the risk pool, the higher the premiums for everyone—even if you received little or none of that care.

And if you're wondering why you can't get ahead financially, blame it on the fact that health care is eating your raises. Since 2000, incomes have barely kept up with inflation and insurance premiums have more than doubled. The average employer family health plan that cost companies $6,438 per staffer in 2000 shot up to $16,351 by 2013. That's money that could have gone into your paycheck but didn't because your employer had to spend it on your health insurance instead.

The kicker: We don't get much for our money. In a 2013 Commonwealth Fund study of 11 developed countries' health care systems, the U.S. ranked fifth in quality and worst for infant mortality. We also did the worst job of preventing deaths from treatable conditions, such as strokes, diabetes, high blood pressure, and certain treatable cancers.

No wonder that when *Consumer Reports* surveyed a representative sample of 1,079 American adults, we found considerable distress about high costs. Twelve percent said they had spent more than $5,000 of their own money on medical bills (not counting prescriptions or insurance premiums) in the previous year, and 11 percent said they had medical bills they had trouble paying. Large majorities said they wanted better information about cost and quality of their health care.

Made-up Prices and a Yen for Brand-name Hospitals

All of which brings us to the big question: Why exactly is our health care so expensive?

Health care works nothing like other market transactions. As a consumer, you are a bystander to the real action, which takes place between providers—hospitals, doctors, labs, drug companies, and device manufacturers—and the private and governmental entities that pay them. Those same providers are also pushing Americans into newer and more expensive treatments, even when there's no evidence they're any better.

"There is no such thing as a legitimate price for anything in health care," says George Halvorson, former chairman of Kaiser Permanente, the giant health maintenance organization based in California. "Prices are made up depending on who the payer is."

When Medicare is paying the bills, prices tend to be lower. That agency is by far the largest single source of revenue for most health care providers, which gives it more leverage to set prices. Private insurance companies and providers, on the other hand, bargain head-to-head over prices, often savagely. (If you see headlines in your area about such-and-such hospital leaving an insurer network, that's what's going on).

In regions with many competing providers, insurers can play them against each other to hold down prices. But where there are few providers, not so much. Providers know that, and are busily consolidating into larger groups to get more bargaining power. In your own community, you may have noticed new outpatient medical clinics sprouting up emblazoned with the name of a local hospital; that is hospitals buying up private medical practices to get more clout with insurers.

But the providers with the most clout are the brand-name medical centers, which hold special cachet for patients and are thus "must have" hospitals for many insurers. "In some markets the prestigious medical institutions can name their price," says Andrea Caballero, program director for Catalyst for Payment Reform, a national nonprofit trying to get a grip on health costs on behalf of large employers. "They may have brand names of high prestige but not necessarily deliver higher-quality care."

There are small but hopeful signs that health costs aren't growing quite as fast as they used to. Medicare's costs are stabilizing, for instance. It's too soon to tell whether that is a permanent trend.

But the "medical industrial complex" continues going for as much gold as it can, as the following examples show all too clearly.

Outrage No. 1: Why Do Just One Test When You Can Bill for Three?

Americans usually pay for health care by the piece: so much for each office visit, X-ray, outpatient procedure, etc. That approach leads to one thing: waste. Up to 30 percent of the care provided in this country is unnecessary, according to the Congressional Budget Office. "If you have a treatment that requires three CT scans and re-engineer it to require only one, it won't happen because two CT scan places will lose a source of revenue," says George Halvorson of Kaiser Permanente. "Piecework also rewards bad outcomes. It pays a lot if you have a heart attack but very little for preventing it."

Some insurance companies are making headway against overtreatment—which is why *Consumer Reports* has prepared a list of them in collaboration with the National Committee for Quality Assurance (NCQA), a nonprofit quality measurement and accreditation organization. (Read more about health plans that help members avoid unnecessary medical care).

Outrage No. 2: The $1,000-per-pill Hepatitis Drug

Here's a prime example of big pharma's we-charge-what-we-want syndrome: A new pill for hepatitis C has hit the market that, if taken by everyone who should take it, would cost Americans more per year than all other brand-name drugs combined. No one—not individuals, not private insurers, not Medicare—can do a thing about it. That's because here in the U.S., as long as the drug, Sovaldi, remains under patent, its owner, Gilead Sciences, can charge whatever it wants. At the moment that's $1,000 per pill, or $84,000 to $150,000 for a course of treatment.

"Drug companies charge what the market will bear, and in the United States the market will bear a lot," says Matt Salo, executive director of the National Association of Medicaid Directors, a policy group based in Washington, D.C.

Hepatitis C affects 3.2 million mostly boomer-aged Americans who got it through tainted blood transfusions (no longer a serious risk, thanks to new screening tests) and intravenous drug use. Left untreated, it can lead to liver failure and is the leading reason for liver transplants in the U.S. Older treatments were uncomfortable, took forever, came with unpleasant side effects, and didn't always work. With Sovaldi, you take the pill for a few months; it has a cure rate of about 90 percent in clinical trials.

The industry defends the price on the grounds that it's cheaper than a $500,000 liver transplant. But most people with untreated Hepatitis C never need a transplant; even after 20 years, the savings from not having to treat the disease's worst effects would offset only about 75 percent of Sovaldi's up-front costs, research suggests. Meanwhile, it would add $600 per person to the annual cost of a group health plan.

Outrage No. 3: Pushing the New and Flashy

One way for hospitals and medical practices to make gobs of money is to push a new, trendy procedure—even if it's no better than an older one. Prime example: prostate cancer surgery. Medical science still has little idea which treatments work best for the disease, or even who really needs to be treated, because many patients have cancer so indolent that they will die of something else long before it kills them.

None of that has stopped medical marketers from persuading hospitals to spend ever larger sums of money on so-called cutting-edge prostate cancer treatments to lure patients away from competitors.

The poster child for the phenomenon is robotic surgery, which your local hospital has probably bragged about.

First introduced for prostate cancer surgery in 2001, the $2 million machine—a collection of laparoscopic instruments operated remotely—went from being used for 6 percent of prostatectomies in 2004 to 83 percent in 2014, despite little evidence that it is better than other types of surgery even though it comes with a higher price tag.

"There's marketing value in a very expensive piece of technology, such as a robot, even if it doesn't work better," says Jeffrey C. Lerner, president of the ECRI Institute, a nonprofit health technology evaluation organization. "Nobody's ever going to put up a billboard about having the best bandage."

Three Ways You Can Help Rein in Expenses
1. Find out the real cost of your treatment

More and more insurers are disclosing at least some negotiated prices to members who register with their websites. Take advantage of that feature if your health plan offers it, especially for things you can plan in advance, such as imaging tests. In a recent experiment, people scheduled for CT scans or MRIs were called and told about cheaper alternatives of equal quality; they ended up saving participating insurers an average of $220 per scan—and prompted more expensive providers to cut their prices.

2. If you want the celeb doctor, pay extra

"Reference pricing" is when an insurer analyzes its past claims to set a reasonable price for a good-quality routine test or procedure and tells its customers that if they want to go to a higher-cost in-network provider, they can—but will be responsible for the difference between the reference price and the provider's price.

CalPERS, which buys health insurance for 1.3 million California state employees and retirees, set a reference price of $30,000 for routine hip and knee replacements after discovering it was paying as much as $110,000 for those procedures. In the first year, savings averaged $7,000 per patient—and several high-cost hospitals suddenly discovered that they, too, could offer $30,000 joint replacements. One caveat: This fix needs to be done carefully to make sure that quality stays high and consumers aren't caught by surprise.

3. Seek out a smaller medical network

You can save about 20 percent on premiums by signing up with a plan that has fewer providers than customary. Providers give the insurer a price break in exchange for fewer competitors. But before signing on, make sure that the network includes the doctors, hospitals, labs, and other services you need within a reasonable distance from your home and that they accept new patients.

Critical Thinking

1. Why is health care so expensive in the United States?
2. What is your response to the following three facts: $37.50 for a single Tylenol in the hospital, doctor who orders an MRI because he owns the machine, $1,000 for a single pill that treats Hepatitis?
3. What is wrong with the billing system in U.S. health care?

Internet References

New American Studies Web
   https://blogs.commons.georgetown.edu/vkp/
Social Science Information Gateway
   http://www.ariadne.ac.uk/issue2/sosig
Sociology—Study Sociology Online
   http://edu.learnsoc.org/
Sociology Web Resources
   http://www.mhhe.com/socscience/sociology/resources/index.htm
Sociosite
   http://www.topsite.com/goto/sociosite.net
Socioweb
   http://www.topsite.com/goto/socioweb.com

Unit 5

UNIT

Prepared by: Kurt Finsterbusch, *University of Maryland, College Park*

Crime, Violence, and Law Enforcement

This unit deals with criminal behavior and its control by the law enforcement system. The first line of defense against crime is the socialization of the young to internalize norms against harmful and illegal behavior. Thus families, schools, religious institutions, and social pressure are the major crime fighters, but they do not do a perfect job, and the police and courts have to handle their failures. Over the last half-century crime has increased, signaling for some commentators a decline in morality. If the power of norms to control criminal behavior diminishes, the role of law enforcement must increase, and that is what has happened.

The societal response to crime has been threefold: Hire more police, build more prisons, and toughen penalties for crimes. These policies by themselves can have only limited success. For example, putting a drug dealer in prison just creates an opportunity for another person to become a drug dealer. Another approach is to give potential criminals alternatives to crime. The key factor in this approach is a healthy economy that provides many job opportunities for unemployed young men. To some extent, this has happened and has caused the crime rate to drop. Programs that work with inner-city youth might also help, but budget-tight cities are not funding many programs like this. Amid the policy debates there is one thing we can agree upon: Crime has declined significantly in the past two decades (with a slight increase recently) after rising substantially for a half century.

This unit looks at several aspects of crime, law enforcement, and terrorism. It describes many injustices in the criminal justice system such as the tendency for the poor go to jail and rich go free. Too many people are imprisoned and for too long. Many innocent people are convicted. Gun laws are often inappropriate. The Stand Your Ground law has justified murders. Many reforms are needed but are not likely to be enacted given the public mood and the government impasse.

Article   Prepared by: Kurt Finsterbusch, *University of Maryland, College Park*

The Criminality of Wall Street

WILLIAM K. TABB

Learning Outcomes

After reading this article, you will be able to:

- Explain the power and influence of financial capital.

- Explain how financial capital caused the great recession of 2007–2008.

- Explain why the American people should reject and change the current financial system.

The current stage of capitalism is characterized by the increased power of finance capital. How to understand the economics of this shift and its political implications is now central for both the left and the larger society. There can be little doubt that a signature development of our time is the growth of finance and monopoly power.[1]

In 1980 the nominal value of global financial assets almost equaled global GDP. In 2005 they were more than three times global GDP.[2] The nominal value of foreign exchange trading increased from eleven times the value of global trade in 1980 to seventy-three times in 2009.[3] Of course it is not certain what this increase means, since such nominal values can fluctuate widely, as we saw in the Great Financial Crisis. They cannot be compared directly and without all sorts of qualifications to the value added in the real economy. But they do give an impressionistic sense of the enormous magnitude by which finance grew and came to dominate the economy. Between 1980 and 2007, derivative contracts of all kinds expanded from $1 trillion globally to $600 trillion.[4] Hedge funds and private equity groups, special investment vehicles, and mega-bank holding companies changed the face of Western capitalism. They also brought on the collapse from which we still suffer. Ordinary people may not be acquainted with the numbers (and even those best informed are not sure of their significance), but people generally understand in different and often deep ways what

has been happening: namely, an ongoing process of financialization that has come to dwarf production.

What is particularly important is that despite the huge bubble created by this metastasizing growth of finance, the economy did not expand as rapidly as it had in the postwar years, before the goods producing industries lost ground in terms of employment to other sectors of the economy, and when government spending was used actively to promote growth. While the nature of much of the growth that occurred then is certainly open to criticism from all sorts of standpoints, at the time there was widespread understanding in policy circles that government spending was necessary to absorb the surplus which capitalism generated.

It nonetheless became harder and harder to generate growth by the combination of government spending and financial inflation, and an overaccumulation of capital that grew more unhealthy over time culminated with the Great Recession in 2007–2008. A temporary stimulus created by the profusion of "fictitious capital," in the form of debt claims that did not have a counterpart in the real value of assets, was not sustainable. Nor was the "growth" as substantial as might have been expected from such an enormous financial explosion. In considering why this was the case we may start by noting a partial acceptance by important mainstream economists of the Marxist expectation of secular stagnation which was developed by Paul Baran and Paul Sweezy in their 1966 book, *Monopoly Capital*.

In a November 8, 2013 speech at the International Monetary Fund Larry Summers suggested that the United States might be stuck in what he correctly called "secular stagnation," described by *Bloomberg Businessweek* as "a slump that is not the product of the business cycle but a more-or-less permanent condition."[5] Summers's conclusion was deeply pessimistic. "If he is right, the economy is incapable of producing full employment without financial bubbles or massive stimulus, both of which tend to end badly."[6] The speech got a lot of attention. Summers after all had been a U.S. Treasury Secretary and is noted as one of the smartest, if not the most politic, economists around. He has accepted many millions from major financial firms he has advised and is widely understood as a Wall Street-oriented policy maker. Therefore, important people take his analysis seriously. It is also a powerful indictment not simply of financial capital, but of capitalism itself that the logic of its development now takes the form it does.

There have always been financial crises; as Marx long ago explained, they are part of capitalism. The question now being raised is whether the expansion of the parasitic financial control currently being experienced is historically unprecedented. It is prompted by the inability of the system to reinvest in the production of the goods and services people need. In short, the problem is the system, and more and more people are seeing this. I shall try and explain how and why it is true that, although we could potentially create the jobs and economic security, the ecological sustainability, and the participatory democracy we desire, existing class forces prevent this from happening.

Let us look first at some of the problems that we face due to the financialization of the economy. As the power of transnational corporations and international finance has grown (with financialization came globalization)—and new possibilities have been offered by computers, the Internet, and robotics—there has been a loss of middle-class jobs in the United States, and a race to the bottom in jobs globally. The political power of the very rich in the United States has grown, manifested in the increasing extent to which their income escapes taxation—as does that of corporate capital, which parks significant quantities of money in offshore tax havens and moves the profits they received in such abundance to low tax jurisdictions. Between increased consumer lending and marketing new financial products to investors, the financial industry grew dramatically. In 1950 it was equal to 2.8 percent of GDP; in 1980, 4.9 percent; and 7.9 percent in 2007.[7] Money management fees from mutual funds, hedge funds, and private equity accounted for over a third (36 percent) of the industry's increased share of GDP.[8] The other major source of growth was consumer lending, especially mortgage lending. According to the International Monetary Fund, in the advanced economies during the five years preceding 2007, the ratio of household debt to income rose by an average of 39 percent, to 138 percent.[9] When such credit booms go bust, the ensuing downturn is long-lasting and painful.

Finance contributes to GDP through income created in the FIRE (Finance, Insurance, and Real Estate) sector and through the "wealth effect," i.e., the increase in consumption that is the result of the gains in asset value—almost all of this is luxury consumption. But it generates little in the way of use values and can be seen as appropriating value produced by working people elsewhere in the economy—thus Matt Taibbi's colorful description of Goldman Sachs as "a great vampire squid wrapped around the face of humanity, relentlessly jamming its blood funnel into anything that smells like money."[10]

Harvard finance professor Jeremy Stein suggests "banks' private incentives lead them to overdo it."[11] One indication of the "overdoing" by today's newer aristocracy of finance is that financial profits as a percent of total domestic profits for 1998–2007 averaged 33 percent, with a few years (2001, 2002, and 2003) over 40 percent.[12] Needless to say, after the collapse the losses have been ours and not the bankers.

The top executives at Lehman Brothers and Bear Stearns, two investment banks that failed spectacularly, did quite well. Over the 2000–2007 period, the top five executives at Bear received cash bonuses in excess of $300 million and at Lehman in excess of $150 million. These numbers exclude what they received in sale of company shares. Unloading their banks' stock netted the ten executives $2 billion.[13]

The impact of financial incentives was devastating to many U.S. companies and their employees; as a combination of extracting maximum shareholder value and the extraction going to top executives removed resources from other shareholders and undermined corporate America's future prospects. And while Dodd-Frank and other legislation was supposed to make the system safe, the too big to fail banks are much bigger than they were before the crisis, with the six largest banks possessing assets equal to more than 60 percent of U.S. GDP.[14]

All this has created a different economic reality in the United States. The CIA's ranking of countries by income inequality finds the United States to have a higher degree of inequality than Egypt or Tunisia; as noted earlier the 1 percent have more wealth in the United States than the bottom 90 percent.[15] The Congressional Budget Office reported in 2011 that the top 1 percent of earners had more than doubled their share of the nation's income over the previous three decades.[16] A lot of these people are in finance.

Politically the power of finance capital comes from its having become a major source of financing for politicians; for instance, Hillary Clinton has received generous Wall Street contributions, including large speaking fees from the likes of Goldman Sachs. That there is so much buzz around a possible challenge from Elizabeth Warren, and that Obama was not able to get liberal senators to go along with Larry Summers as head of the Fed, are indications that there is wide recognition that mainstream Democrats are in Wall Street's pocket. Summers has received millions from venture capital and asset management firms. He has consulted for Citibank and Nasdaq. Because of the power of Wall Street there is not the needed financial regulation. And there is little to no penalty for financial fraud. This is hardly surprising. As former Delaware Senator Edward E. Kaufman commented to the *New York Times* in response to the Justice Department's failure to pursue financial wrongdoers in connection with the bursting of the housing bubble: the report of the Financial Fraud Enforcement Task force "fits a pattern that is scary for a democracy, that there really are two levels of justice in this country, one for the people with power and money and one for everyone else."[17]

The right always blames workers, unions, and the poor (most of whom, of course, are also workers) for being greedy. One of our tasks is to get the basic facts across to people.

The focus must be on the 1 percent whose share of after-tax income has doubled in the last thirty years and nearly tripled between 1980 and 2006. The top 1 percent took 95 percent of the gains between 2009 and 2012.[18] Real median income earnings for full-time workers between twenty-five and sixty-four have stagnated since their peak in the late 1970s. This may explain why the most recent poll shows 75 percent of Americans rating the state of the economy as "negative" or "poor."[19]

From 2000 to 2007, Emmanuel Saez's research tells us, the richest .001 percent doubled the share of total income they received to 6 percent of the total of all Americans, and the top 1 percent captured half of all of the overall growth between 1993 and 2007.[20] Between 1993 and 2012 the top 1 percent captures just over two-thirds of income growth.[21] This was the group the Republicans protected with the threat of closing down the government. But it is also the fraction of capital that supports the Clintons and Obama.

The tax system has become a joke for leading corporations, who can legally avoid taxation. An estimated 30 percent of multinational corporate profits passing through tax havens costs the U.S. taxpayer $255 billion annually; this includes not only lost individual income taxes but also vastly more in lost corporate taxation (based on crude calculations from the Government Accounting Office in 2008 of the one hundred largest U.S. companies' subsidiaries abroad and especially in tax havens).[22] Citigroup alone had over 400 tax-haven subsidiaries, ninety-one in Luxembourg, and another ninety in the Cayman Islands.[23] Apple, one of the most profitable and highly valued corporations, moves its profits to low-tax countries. Apple is an innovator in the tax area. It pioneered the accounting trick known as the "Double Irish With a Dutch Sandwich." Now used widely, this strategy routes profits through Irish subsidiaries and the Netherlands, and then to the Caribbean.[24] iTunes, it turns out, has a letter box and a few employees in Luxembourg where downloads made in Africa, the Middle East, or other places are registered as having originated for tax purposes. Its overseas stores are part of a system that routes sales through Cork, Ireland. The company has reorganized its corporate chart so it needs to reveal less information about its business practices. Through such techniques Apple manages to pay less than 10 percent in corporate income taxes in this country. As far as state taxes go, although its actual headquarters are in Cupertino, California, it claims a small office in Reno, Nevada for tax purposes, thereby denying the state of California and twenty other states millions of dollars in taxes. (While California's corporate income tax rate is 8.84 percent, Nevada's is zero).

The company explains that all of this is perfectly legal. It probably is.[25]

Greater inequality makes restoring economic growth hard because working people have less money to spend and so demand does not go up. The rich get so much of the surplus that this feeds new speculative activity and threatens a new collapse. Much of the surplus appropriated by the 1 percent cannot be realized from the sale of expanded output and so stays within the sphere of financial speculation (including loans—student, credit card, mortgage lending—and the bundling of receipts receivable from these loans as collateralized debt obligations that are pyramided and so eventually collapse).

It is important to understand that the various asset bubbles of recent years arose in large part from the large amount of surplus funds that could not find profitable investment in the "real economy," where goods and non-financial services are sold to businesses, government, and households. From 1980 when working-class incomes began a three decade plus period of stagnation and all the gains from productivity growth went to capital, to the present, there has been an enormous increase in inequality. Ordinary Americans, feeling pinched by their inability to maintain living standards, were compelled to borrow in an attempt to maintain them; they became an enormous source of profit to banks and other financial institutions. Mortgage debt, credit card debt, and student loans grew in absolute terms and as a proportion of national income. The campaign to delegitimize taxation forced governments to borrow in lieu [of] raising revenue, and government debt increased as well (with the wars in the Iraq and Afghanistan adding significantly to this debt).

Much of the assistance given to the major Wall Street banks was extended to them by the New York Federal Reserve at the time it was headed by soon-to-be Secretary of the Treasury Timothy Geithner. Serving on the board of the New York Fed were people such as JP Morgan CEO Jamie Dimon, who was asked in senate hearings by Senator Bernie Sanders, "How do you sit on a board, which approves $390 billion of low-interest loans to yourself?" Dimon was hardly the only self-interested banker on the board. As another member of the committee, Senator Barbara Boxer, stated, "There is a clear conflict of interest . . . not a perceived conflict of interest, but a real conflict of interest when bank presidents and employees of banks sit on the very boards that regulate them and sometimes bail them out." Soon-to-be Senator Elizabeth Warren also called on Dimon to step down from the board of directors of the New York Fed.

The extent to which central banks prop up financial institutions has grown enormously. Between 2007 and the end of 2012, the central banks flooded the world with trillions of dollars in liquidity to support asset markets and keep banks solvent. This process continues with quantitative easing—essentially printing money—to avoid collapse, and holding interest rates to historic lows (a fraction of a percent above zero). Yet, despite these efforts, the global economy stagnates.

The goal of course is to lower borrowing costs and stimulate financial markets. This has been achieved, but the impacts desired—encouraging more spending and real investment outside of finance—have been disappointing. This is hardly a surprise. Central bankers are the first to say that expanding the money supply is not a substitute for better fiscal policy. In the absence of governments creating demand to replace the lack of private spending and addressing structural problems in the economy, central banks can have only limited positive impact. Households already burdened by large debt positions are not inclined to borrow more—indeed the fact that consumer debt is creeping up again, much of that as student debt, is more a sign of desperation on the part of households than anything else.

There are all sorts of reasons to worry about the impact of extended low interest rates which feed new asset bubbles. One might also be concerned about the quality of the tens of billions of mortgage-backed securities that the Fed has been buying each month.[26] The Bank of Japan is buying corporate debt and stock, an intervention in the market that, while it holds the economy up, also distorts allocation. Such emergency measures, if carried on too long, may come back to haunt central bankers and governments when they eventually try to unwind these positions.

Almost daily headlines tell of one bank or another being hit with a large suit by the Justice Department for some "brazen" fraud including "robo-signing" and preying on the unsophisticated. The names of those agreeing to settle with the government are a Who's Who of U.S. finance. From defective mortgage processes that hoodwinked homeowners, to dishonest debt collecting and foreclosures, to credit card lawsuits where the bank or collection agency cannot prove that the person owes the debt (the situation in 90 percent of the cases, according to a judge who presides over as many as a hundred such cases a day), the headlines never cease.[27] A 2012 audit by San Francisco county officials of hundreds of recent foreclosures determined that almost all involved either legal violations or suspicious documentation.[28] Violations ranged from the failure to notify borrowers when their loans fell into default (as required by law) to auctioning properties where banks and other assignees had no proof of ownership. Nationally the foreclosure system was found to be riddled with false documents, forged signatures, and all manner of other abuses.

The big banks lobby to influence mortgage rules so they can continue practices that make them money. Federal and state authorities allowed the banks to settle for their extensive illegal activities with a mere $26 billion worth of relief, a small part of the damage they had done in wrongful denials of loan motivations, wrongful foreclosures, and other documented abuses.[29] Certainly the settlement did not end bank abuses. People who paid off debts years before are harassed by collection agencies. People who have been cheated on their mortgages are cheated again in a new round of abuse coming with the loans that are supposed to help them stay in their homes—this by brokers selling new mortgages especially targeting the elderly. Foreign banks are charged with money laundering for assisting U.S. citizens to avoid taxes owed. Private investors who bought toxic collateralized debt obligations, believed to have been sold by banks knowing they would soon collapse, continue to pursue compensation in the courts.

Perhaps the most lasting impact of the Great Recession, holding back recovery, was the housing market collapse. Millions lost their homes while millions of other homeowners went underwater, owing more on their mortgages than their homes were worth. Many borrowed up to 90 percent of the selling price and then, having negative equity and facing foreclosure, were unable to sell because of the millions of other homes that stood empty, holding prices down.

The Obama administration has had to come up with plan after plan even where federal subsidies to banks are involved, with each and every one a failure from a homeowner's standpoint, largely because bank participation is voluntary. With housing values so drastically reduced, and vacant properties bringing whole neighborhoods down, local governments face declining property tax income which ravages local finances and adds to budget deficits. They thus have little choice but to make deeper cuts in public services and lay off teachers and police. We are all, the metaphorical 99%, paying to restore the banks' profitability while for the majority the economy is stuck in an extended secular stagnation with widespread, and from a socialist perspective unnecessary, suffering of working people.

This is at some level understood, especially by young people, half of whom when polled by the Pew Research Center for People & the Press favor socialism and reject capitalism.[30] They have lived through constantly deteriorating economic conditions coupled with increased corruption and cronyism; they expect, if nothing is done fundamentally to change things, that they will have to continue their struggle to live in an economy in which they incur insupportable student debt that, because of failing job prospects, promises a life of indentured servitude to the banks.

The shrillness of the hard right and the obtuseness of the mainstream media not withstanding, the system stands exposed to a substantial extent. More people of all ages see the Federal Reserve and Treasury Department efforts to support the banks at all cost as preventing changes they can believe in. The general attitude of solicitousness to the banks shown by the administration has been termed the Geithner Doctrine, to call attention to the clear policy choice to protect the banks from any threat to their post-bailout recovery. While most people may not understand all the details of corporate abuse and financial manipulations, the prominent movement slogans both capture the essence of Wall Street criminality and propose solutions. Indeed, those with ears to hear and eyes to see recognize the truth in now familiar placards: "America Is Not Broke," "Tax the Rich," "Money Is Not Speech," "Assure Everybody a Good Job," "Young, Educated, and Unemployed," "Corporations Are Not People," "Stop Foreclosures," "Speculation Never Creates Anything," "Wall Street: Where Crime Really Pays," "Economic Inequality Is the Enemy of Prosperity," "Stop the Wars," and "Trickle Down Is Baloney." The majority support for Occupy Wall Street and its project strongly suggests that ordinary people understand the demands of the movement.

These placards announce the unjust state of things. They are not really asking a corrupt political system to meet demands. They are not really asking the 1% for anything. They are saying "we need a society and we will create a society in which there is not a 1% and a 99% and these injustices will not exist." This is not to say that participants do not want Obama to change, that they do not have ideas for meaningful reforms. But it does say that the system itself is on trial as it has not been since the 1930s. Undergirding even the mildest reforms and the most idealistic hopes is an undercurrent of rejection of the system under which we live. There is discovery of the truth, in the words of Dorothy Day, a foremother of the movement, that "Our Problems Stem from Our Acceptance of this Filthy Rotten System." People increasingly do not accept it. The issue is not only to make this rejection manifest but to develop sustainable institutional forms of resistance and transformation.

Notes

1. The classic analysis of this problem on the left, describing the role of monopoly, stagnation, and financial expansion was provided by Harry Magdoff and Paul Sweezy. See, for example, their article "The Logic of Stagnation," *Monthly Review* 38, no. 5 (October 1986): 1–19.

2. Charles R. Morris, *Two Trillion Dollar Meltdown* (Philadelphia: Perseus, 2008), 140.

3. Charles Leadbetter, "The Right Kind of Innovation," *Financial World,* February 2011, https://fw.ifslearning.ac.uk.

4. See William K. Tabb, *The Restructuring of Capitalism in Our Time* (New York: Columbia University Press, 2012), 100.

5. "Larry Summers at IMF Economic Forum, Nov. 8," November 8, 2013, http://youtube.com; "Larry Summers has a Wintry Outlook on the Economy," *Bloomberg Business Week,* November 18, 2013, http://businessweek.com.

6. Ibid.

7. Robin Greenwood and David Scharfstein, "The Growth of Modern Finance," *Journal of Economic Perspectives,* 27, no.2 (2013): 3–28, http://pubs.aeaweb.org.

8. Ibid.

9. International Monetary Fund, *World Economic Outlook,* August 2012, chapter 3, http://imf.org.

10. Matt Taibbi, "The Great American Bubble Machine," *Rolling Stone,* July 9, 2009, http://rollingstone.com.

11. Jeremy C. Stein, "Central Banking and Financial Stability," October 2011, 31, www.bancaditalia.it.

12. *Economic Report of the President, 2014,* Table B-91, http://whitehouse.gov.

13. Tabb, *The Restructuring of Capitalism in Our Time.*

14. Simon Johnson, "Testimony Submitted to the Subcommittee on Financial Institutions and Consumer Protection, Senate Committee on Banking, Housing, and Urban Affairs, Hearing on 'Examining the GAO Study on Government Support for Bank Holding Companies,'" January 8, 2014, http://piie.com.

15. Central Intelligence Agency, *World Fact Book,* accessed March 2013, https://cia.gov.

16. Congressional Budget Office, "Trends in the Distribution of Income," October 25, 2011, http://cbo.gov.

17. "A Loan Fraud War That's Short on Combat," *New York Times,* March 15, 2014, http://nytimes.com.

18. Emmanuel Saez, "Striking it Richer: The Evolution of Top Incomes in the United States," September 3, 2013, http://elsa.berkeley.edu.

19. "October 2013 Post-ABC Poll-Obama, Republicans and Shutdown Fallout," *Washington Post,* October 25, 2013, http://washingtonpost.com.

20. Saez, "Striking it Richer."

21. Ibid.

22. "Revealed: Global Super-Rich Has At Least $21 Trillion Hidden in Secret Tax Havens," *Tax Justice Network,* July 22, 2012, http://taxjustice.net; United States Government Accountability Office, "International Taxation: Large US Corporations and Federal Contractors with Subsidiaries in Jurisdictions Listed as Tax Havens or Financial Privacy Jurisdictions," December 2008, http://media.washingtonpost.com/wp-srv; Kenneth Thomas, "Offshore Accounting on the Rise and Costing Taxpayers," *Fiscal Times,* July 29, 2012.

23. U.S. GAO, "International Taxation."

24. Charles Duhigg and David Kocieniewski, "How Apple Sidesteps Billions in Taxes," *New York Times,* April 28, 2012, http://nytimes.com.

25. Ibid; "Apple's Response on Its Tax Practices," *New York Times,* April 28, 2012, http://nytimes.com.

26. Schuyler Velasco, "Bernanke, Fed Say No Taper. Will Housing Bounce?," *Christian Science Monitor,* September 18, 2013, http://csmonitor.com.

27. Jessica Silver-Greenberg, "Problems Riddle Moves to Collect Credit Card Debt," *New York Times,* August 12, 2012, http://dealbook.nytimes.com.

28. Gretchen Morgenson, "Audit Uncovers Extensive Flaws In Foreclosures," *New York Times,* February 15, 2012, http://nytimes.com.

29. Mark Memmott, "Settlement Reached with Banks on Relief for Some Homeowners," *NPR, the Two-Way,* February 9, 2012, http://npr.org/blogs.

30. "Little Change in Public's Response to 'Capitalism,' 'Socialism'," *PewResearch Center for the People & the Press,* December 28, 2011, http://people-press.org.

Critical Thinking

1. How did financial capital acquire so much power?
2. What are the consequences of financial capital having so much power?
3. What is the future of financial capital?

Internet References

New American Studies Web
https://blogs.commons.georgetown.edu/vkp/

Social Science Information Gateway
http://www.ariadne.ac.uk/issue2/sosig

Sociology—Study Sociology Online
http://edu.learnsoc.org/

Sociology Web Resources
http://www.mhhe.com/socscience/sociology/resources/index.htm

Sociosite
http://www.topsite.com/goto/sociosite.net

Socioweb
http://www.topsite.com/goto/socioweb.com

WILLIAM K. TABB'S most recent book is *The Restructuring of Capitalism in Our Time* (Columbia University Press, 2012). This article is based on a talk given to the Left Labor Project in New York City November 25, 2013 in preparation for action fighting back against Wall Street.

Article

Prepared by: Kurt Finsterbusch, *University of Maryland, College Park*

This Man Was Sentenced to Die in Prison for Shoplifting a $159 Jacket: This Happens More Than You Think

ED PILKINGTON

Learning Outcomes

After reading this article, you will be able to:

- Understand the U.S. criminal justice system and how it works.

- Analyze the thesis that the U.S. criminal justice system is too punitive.

- Understand why crazy laws are not removed.

At about 12.40 P.M. on 2 January 1996, Timothy Jackson took a jacket from the Maison Blanche department store in New Orleans, draped it over his arm, and walked out of the store without paying for it. When he was accosted by a security guard, Jackson said: "I just needed another jacket, man."

A few months later Jackson was convicted of shoplifting and sent to Angola prison in Louisiana. That was 16 years ago. Today he is still incarcerated in Angola, and will stay there for the rest of his natural life having been condemned to die in jail. All for the theft of a jacket, worth $159.

Jackson, 53, is one of 3,281 prisoners in America serving life sentences with no chance of parole for nonviolent crimes. Some, like him, were given the most extreme punishment short of execution for shoplifting; one was condemned to die in prison for siphoning petrol from a truck; another for stealing tools from a tool shed and yet another for attempting to cash a stolen cheque.

"It has been very hard for me," Jackson wrote to the American Civil Liberties Union (ACLU) as part of its new report on life without parole for nonviolent offenders. "I know that for my crime I had to do some time, but a life sentence for a jacket value at $159. I have met people here whose crimes are a lot badder with way less time."

Senior officials at Angola prison refused to allow the *Guardian* to speak to Jackson, on grounds that it might upset his victims—even though his crime was victimless. But his sister Loretta Lumar did speak to the *Guardian*. She said that the last time she talked by phone with her brother he had expressed despair. "He told me, 'Sister, this has really broke my back. I'm ready to come out.'"

Lumar said that she found her brother's sentence incomprehensible. "This doesn't make sense to me. I know people who have killed people, and they get a lesser sentence. That doesn't make sense to me right there. You can take a life and get 15 or 16 years. He takes a jacket worth $159 and will stay in jail forever. He didn't kill the jacket!"

The ACLU's report, *A Living Death*, chronicles the thousands of lives ruined and families destroyed by the modern phenomenon of sentencing people to die behind bars for nonviolent offences. It notes that contrary to the expectation that such a harsh penalty would be meted out only to the most serious offenders, people have been caught in this brutal trap for sometimes the most petty causes.

Ronald Washington, 48, is also serving life without parole in Angola, in his case for shoplifting two Michael Jordan jerseys from a Foot Action sportswear store in Shreveport, Louisiana, in 2004. Washington insisted at trial that the jerseys were reduced in a sale to $45 each—which meant that their combined value was below the $100 needed to classify the theft as a felony; the prosecution disagreed, claiming they were on sale for $60 each, thus surpassing the $100 felony minimum and opening him up to a sentence of life without parole.

"I felt as though somebody had just taken the life out of my body," Washington wrote to the ACLU about the moment he learnt his fate. "I seriously felt rejected, neglected, stabbed right through my heart."

He added: "It's a very lonely world, seems that nobody cares. You're never ever returning back into society. And whatever you had or established, its now useless, because you're being buried alive at slow pace."

Louisiana, where both Washington and Jackson are held, is one of nine states where prisoners are serving life without parole sentences for nonviolent offences (other states with high numbers are Alabama, Florida, Mississippi, Oklahoma, and South Carolina). An overwhelming proportion of those sentences—as many as 98 percent in Louisiana—were mandatory: in other words judges had no discretion but to impose the swingeing penalties.

The warden of Angola prison, Burl Cain, has spoken out in forthright terms against a system that mandates punishment without any chance of rehabilitation. He told the ACLU: "It's ridiculous, because the name of our business is 'corrections'—to correct deviant behaviour. If I'm a successful warden and I do my job and we correct the deviant behaviour, then we should have a parole hearing. I need to keep predators in these big old prisons, not dying old men."

The toll is not confined to the state level: most of those nonviolent inmates held on life without parole sentences were given their punishments by the federal government. More than 2,000 of the 3,281 individuals tracked down on these sentences by the ACLU are being held in the federal system. Overall, the ACLU has calculated that taxpayers pay an additional $1.8 billion to keep the prisoners locked up for the rest of their lives.

"It Doesn't Have to Be This Way"

Until the early 1970s, life without parole sentences were virtually unknown. But they exploded as part of what the ACLU calls America's "late-twentieth-century obsession with mass incarceration and extreme, inhumane penalties."

The report's author Jennifer Turner states that today, the United States is "virtually alone in its willingness to sentence nonviolent offenders to die behind bars." Life without parole for non-violent sentences has been ruled a violation of human rights by the European Court of Human Rights. The UK is one

of only two countries in Europe that still metes out the penalty at all, and even then only in 49 cases of murder.

Even within America's starkly racially charged penal system, the disparities in nonviolent life without parole are stunning. About 65 percent of the prisoners identified nationwide by the ACLU are African American. In Louisiana, that proportion rises to 91 percent, including Jackson and Washington, who are both black.

The United States has the highest incarceration rate in the world, with 2.3 million people now in custody, with the war on drugs acting as the overriding push-factor. Of the prisoners serving life without parole for nonviolent offences nationwide, the ACLU estimates that almost 80 percent were for drug-related crimes.

Again, the offences involved can be startlingly petty. Drug cases itemised in the report include a man sentenced to die in prison for having been found in possession of a crack pipe; an offender with a bottle cap that contained a trace of heroin that was too small to measure; a prisoner arrested with a trace amount of cocaine in their pocket too tiny to see with the naked eye; a man who acted as a go-between in a sale to an undercover police officer of marijuana—street value $10.

Drugs are present in the background of Timothy Jackson's case too. He was high when he went to the Maison Blanche store, and he says that as a result he shoplifted "without thinking." Paradoxically, like many of the other prisoners on similar penalties, the first time he was offered drug treatment was after he had already been condemned to spend the rest of his life in jail.

The theft of the $159 jacket, taken in isolation, carries today a six-month jail term. It was combined at Jackson's sentencing hearing with his previous convictions—all for nonviolent crimes including a robbery in which he took $216—that brought him under Louisiana's brutal "four-strikes" law by which it became mandatory for him to be locked up and the key thrown away.

The ACLU concludes that it does not have to be this way—suitable alternatives are readily at hand, including shorter prison terms and the provision of drug treatment and mental health services. The organisation calls on Congress, the Obama administration and state legislatures to end the imposition of mandatory life without parole for nonviolent offenders and to require resentencing hearings for all those already caught in this judicial black hole.

A few months after Timothy Jackson was put away for life, a Louisiana appeals court reviewed the case and found it "excessive," "inappropriate," and "a prime example of an unjust result." Describing Jackson as a "petty thief," the court threw out the sentence.

The following year, in 1998, the state's supreme court gave a final ruling. "This sentence is constitutionally excessive in that it is grossly out of proportion to the seriousness of the offence," concluded Judge Bernette Johnson. However, she found that the state's four strikes law that mandates life without parole could only be overturned in rare instances, and as a result she reinstated the sentence—putting Jackson back inside his cell until the day he dies.

"I am much older and I have learned a lot about myself," Jackson wrote to the ACLU from that cell. "I am sorry for the crime that I did, and I am a changed man."

Jackson expressed a hope that he would be granted his freedom when he was still young enough to make something of his life and "help others." But, barring a reform of the law, the day of his release will never come.

Critical Thinking

1. Laws and law enforcement are supposed to establish justice. In reality it establishes both justice and injustice. Why?

2. It seems that the most poignant cases of the miscarriage of justice applies to poor people. Why?

3. Pilkington argues against overpunishment. Discuss cases of underpunishment and explain the differences.

Create Central

www.mhhe.com/createcentral

Internet References

ACLU Criminal Justice Home Page
www.aclu.org/crimjustice/index.html

Human Rights and Humanitarian Assistance
www.etown.edu/vl/humrts.html

New American Studies Web
www.georgetown.edu/crossroads/asw

Sociology—Study Sociology Online
http://edu.learnsoc.org

Sociology Web Resources
http://www.mhhe.com/socscience/sociology/resources/index.htm

Sociosite
http://www.topsite.com/goto/sociosite.net

Socioweb
http://www.topsite.com/goto/socioweb.com

Pilkington, Ed, "Over 3,000 US prisoners serving life without parole for non-violent crimes," theguardian.com, November 13, 2013. Copyright Guardian News & Media Ltd 2013.

Article   Prepared by: Kurt Finsterbusch, *University of Maryland, College Park*

South Carolina's Police State

KEVIN ALEXANDER GRAY

Learning Outcomes

After reading this article, you will be able to:

- Analyze the things that are taken for granted by the police in North Carolina.

- Discuss the impact of secrecy versus surveillance on police behavior.

- Discuss how racism factors into these stories.

W hen accused murderer and former North Charleston patrolman Michael Thomas Slager's lawyer said his client "felt threatened," he may have been telling the truth. But it wasn't Slager's life that was threatened. It was his sense of authority. Sometimes, that can spark a life-ending escalation.

Walter Lamer Scott, a fifty-year-old veteran and father of four, was running away when officer Slager shot him repeatedly in the back on April 4. Slager, thirty-three, fired his taser at Scott, hitting him at least once. When Scott kept running, Slager opened fire. Eight times. Four bullets hit Scott in the back and one hit him in the ear.

Then, after slapping on handcuffs, Slager placed the taser next to Scott's body. "Shots fired and the subject is down," he told the dispatcher. "He took my taser."

Unfortunately for Slager, a Dominican immigrant named Feidin Santana, on his way to work, captured the crime using the video-camera on his phone. The video proved what many blacks take as gospel: Police lie.

A Gallup review of polling data from 2011 to 2014 showed that 59 percent of whites had "a great deal" or "quite a lot" of confidence in police, compared with only 37 percent of black respondents. Also, blacks rated police officers lower for honesty and ethics than whites. In Gallup data from 2010 to 2013, "59 percent of whites say the honesty and ethics of police officers is very high or high, compared with 45 percent of blacks."

Slager's shooting of Scott, for which he is facing a murder charge, is not going to drive these numbers up.

I t's bad enough that he shot his victim in the back. When I was growing up watching cowboy movies, the "code of the West" held that shooting someone in the back was a cowardly thing to do. But handcuffing a dead or dying black man lying face down in the dirt to cover up your misdeed is as low-down as you can go.

Other racial imagery comes to mind watching Santana's unwitting "snuff film." An enslaved African unsuccessfully trying to escape his deadly overseer. Or a black sharecropper, or civil-rights worker trying to elude the Klansman's noose.

After the video became public, the reaction of local authorities was swift. "I was sickened by what I saw," said police chief Eddie Driggers. North Charleston Mayor Keith Summey announced that the city would be equipping all of its officers with body cameras.

Yet the nature of Slager's stop—a busted brake light—and the actions of the officers who arrived on the scene immediately after the killing reveal deeper problems. Just as in Ferguson, Missouri, the Department of Justice will probably substantiate unequal enforcement against blacks, possibly including excessive ticketing, fees, and fines.

North Charleston has a 47 percent black population, yet the town's police department is 80 percent white. But hiring more black officers isn't necessarily a cure-all for a police department with a pattern of discriminatory race relations. Black officers can and do adopt the practices of their white counterparts.

The first cop to arrive at the scene after Scott's killing was black. The first official police report said that the officers performed first aid. They did not. The black officer arrived to assist Slager, not the dying man.

Racists harbor the illusion that it's just black people getting killed and they deserve it. Just read the comment sections of the various news reports on such incidents. Some folks will always believe that black people are inherently criminal. So when police and media mention drugs, guns, gang-related activities, or prior arrests, it validates their beliefs. Worse are those who don't consider themselves racists, black and white, who hear the indicting buzzwords, turn a blind eye, and tune it out.

Some things are clear. Police shoot at blacks more often than they shoot at whites, and they disproportionately kill them. Between 2010 and 2014, police in South Carolina shot at least 209 suspects and killed 79 of them. Of the suspects, 101 were black and 67 were white, according to data gathered by *The State* newspaper in Columbia, S.C. Among those killed, 34 were black and 41 were white (in 4 cases the suspect's race is unclear). In only 3 of the 209 cases were officers investigated for misuse of force, and no one was convicted.

Nationally, 1,215 white people and 932 blacks died at police hands from 2003 to 2009, according to the Justice Department. Other analysts put the number of police homicides between 2003 and 2011 at 7,427, an average of 928 per year. Nobody really knows the exact figure because police organizations don't report them.

We do know that in just the first four months of this year, there have been almost 400 police killings, according to KilledByPolice.net. Not just blacks, not just men, but men and women, old, young, mentally ill, white and Latino.

There have long been allegations of poor race relations and abusive police in North Charleston. Same story in Ferguson and in Baltimore. It's the same story with small and large police departments that operate in

Ten Ways to End the Scourge of Police Violence

1. Mandate the use of body cameras. Many police organizations already use dash cams and have pretty much accepted body cameras as the coming thing. There must be penalties, including losing your job, for tampering with or disabling a body cam.

2. Promote community policing where police actually get out of their cars and interact with community residents. This includes ending the different manifestations of "stop and frisk," the proliferation of K-9 units reminiscent of Bull Connor policing and apart-heid South Africa, and rejecting the failed "broken windows" policing practice.

3. Revive grassroots organizing and mobilization across race and ethnic lines. It used to be that the local (NAACP National Association for the Advancement of Colored People) chapters, at least in South Carolina, were where people went to report police abuse. The NAACP and organizations like Black Lives Matter need to reclaim that role—looking out for the citizens and taking these reports so that we can know what is going on out there in the community and act on it.

4. Create independent citizen review boards with subpoena power and the ability to recommend charges against rogue cops to a grand jury. We can't allow police to police themselves. And prosecutors more often than not unquestioningly defend the actions of police. We need to set up grassroots citizens' tribunals to collect policing data.

5. Curtail, if not end, the practice of shoot to kill. In the last five years in South Carolina, only four police

officers were killed in the line of duty—compared to the seventy-nine people killed by police. There is no empirical data that would substantiate an epidemic of violence against police officers in this state or country.

6. Collect accurate and reliable statistics on shootings by police. The lack of reporting requirements undermines trust in law enforcement.

7. Re-evaluate the military-to-police pipeline. Many municipalities hire people out of the military because of their service or combat experience. Yet serving the people isn't combat. The citizens are not "enemy combatants." It's not "us versus them."

8. Roll back the militarization of police departments. Decrease the size and use of SWAT teams, limit noknock searches, return and reject surplus war-fighting equipment and weapons for police.

9. Use psychological testing to weed out cops who are racist, sadistic, or likely to respond badly to stress.

10. Establish a Department of Justice review of police jurisdictions and departments with questionable community relations, much like the review of the Ferguson Police Department, to assess the economic impact and fairness of fines, fees and other such charges levied against citizens as well as the employment practices of those departments.

—Kevin Alexander Gray

predominantly black and low-income neighborhoods all over the United States.

Black people endure police talking to them disrespectfully. They live with the reality that a traffic stop can often be a situation where your life is in danger by someone who is supposed to be protecting you. They know how police act when they think nobody is watching and they think whites simply don't care or, worse, support what they do.

If that video of Walter Scott hadn't come out, the police would have covered up this murder. Scott's family sees a measure of justice being served with the murder charge against the officer.

If you believe your eyes, Slager's conduct is inconsistent with *Tennessee v. Garner,* a 1985 Supreme Court ruling which held that officers can use deadly force against a fleeing suspect only when there is probable cause that the suspect "poses a significant threat of death or serious physical injury to the officer or others." I believe my eyes. Yet I still believe Slager is presumed innocent until proven guilty. That he deserves the due process that he didn't extend to Walter Scott. I don't wish to see him suffer the same fate as Scott. Some police believe that killing black people, and treating them as subhuman when they think no one is looking, makes their lives safer. It does not. Bad cops make good cops bad when they turn a blind eye to abuse.

Critical Thinking

1. Why are so many unarmed black men being shot in North Carolina and elsewhere?
2. What are the statistics on police shootings and killings?
3. Will the abundance of cameras on cell phones and body cameras reduce the episodes reported here?

Internet References

New American Studies Web
https://blogs.commons.georgetown.edu/vkp/

Social Science Information Gateway
http://www.ariadne.ac.uk/issue2/sosig

Sociology–Study Sociology Online
http://edu.learnsoc.org/

Sociology Web Resources
http://www.mhhe.com/socscience/sociology/resources/index.htm

Sociosite
http://www.topsite.com/goto/sociosite.net

Socioweb
http://www.topsite.com/goto/socioweb.com

Kevin Alexander Gray is a writer and activist living in South Carolina.

Article   Prepared by: Kurt Finsterbusch, *University of Maryland, College Park*

Public Safety, Public Justice

First, we must acknowledge previous failure; and then we must go on to change our criminal justice philosophy and the relevant laws to reflect common sense and current worldwide knowledge and experience.

DANIEL ROSE

Learning Outcomes

After reading this article, you will be able to:

- Describe the ideal law enforcement system and compare it to the American system.

- Compare American law enforcement to law enforcement in other developed nations.

- Explain why "The Punishment Imperative" is a social disaster for the lower class and the economy.

The term "crisis" is represented in written Chinese by the characters for "danger" and "opportunity." This accurately describes the state of tension between America's racial and ethnic minorities and the police, as well as between our criminal justice system and a growing portion of the American public. The "danger" from destructive action stimulated by irresponsible demagogues is clear; the "opportunity" for constructive and positive action on legitimate civilian grievances is also. Sadly, the latter gets polemic but little well-reasoned and constructive thought.

Healing social rifts, diminishing tensions and increasing confidence in those who legally control violence in our society are national priorities, and we must take the long view. Yes, we must respect our police and look to them for protection; and yes, police practices—lawful and constitutional—should merit respect. And we clearly need: A) more accountable and effective leadership in our courts, prisons and police departments and more accountability for the few "bad eggs" in uniform; B) more effective use of prisoners' time during incarceration, including basic education and vocational training; and C) much improvement in our scandalously over-crowded and decrepit prisons.

But 40 years of criminal justice abuses must also be faced.

When it comes to incarceration, America has an unenviable record, with just 5% of the world's population but nearly 25% of the world's prisoners. Our prisoner recidivism rates are multiples of those of all other developed nations, and our death penalties for adults and life imprisonment for juveniles are at rates unheard of in other advanced countries. Many knowledgeable observers regard the U.S. criminal justice system as a national disgrace crying out for reform.

In addition, African-American imprisonment rates are six times that of Caucasians, while former Black "stop and frisk" rates in New York were indefensibly high. The statistics on Black/police interactions are heartbreaking; these problems also can no longer be ignored.

America's surging mass incarceration rates and huge black/white imprisonment disparities began in the 1960's, when increased drug use and open disrespect for the police accompanied youthful political dissent and social upheaval.

In 1964, Presidential candidate Barry Goldwater announced, "The abuse of law and order in this country is going to be an issue; at least I am going to make it one." In 1971, President Nixon declared a "War on Drugs." The number of people behind bars for non-violent drug offenses increased from 50,000 in 1960 to over 400,000 in 1997. Nationwide, the prison population skyrocketed eightfold since 1970 to 2.4 million today.

"Doubling the conviction rate in this country will do more to cure crime in America than quadrupling the funds for Hubert Humphrey's war on poverty," declared President Nixon, inaugurating a national period of severe mandatory sentences, zero tolerance, longer and harsher prison sentences and curtailment of rehabilitation services for prisoners. The infamous Rockefeller drug laws were introduced in 1973.

"Getting tough on crime" was bi-partisan. Jimmy Carter (formerly Governor of Georgia, one of the most repressive states in the nation) was an advocate. Bill Clinton pushed the Violent Crime Control and Law Enforcement Act of 1994, which stimulated the largest all-time expansion of imprisonment.

With fervor similar to that which accompanied alcoholic Prohibition (1920–1933), to reduce crime, America embarked on what has been called "The Punishment Imperative," now widely acknowledged to be a social disaster for the poor and uneducated and an annual $50 billion economic fiasco for state and city governments.

Where do we go from here? First, we must acknowledge previous failure; and then we must go on to change our criminal justice philosophy and the relevant laws to reflect common sense and current worldwide knowledge and experience.

As have all other advanced countries, we must replace punishment and isolation with crime prevention and prisoner rehabilitation as our criminal justice goals for protecting our society, with incarceration a tool to be used appropriately. And we must understand the relationship to crime of illiteracy and lack of basic education, mental health problems and lack of employment, along with gun laws that make our public the world's most armed.

Thoughtful discussion by an engaged public and calls for action should focus on:

Youthful Offenders

Non-violent youthful first offenders should not be incarcerated in cells with hardened criminals, where they are raped or forced to join gangs for protection. Incarcerated in separate facilities and protected from sexual abuse by inmates and prison staff, they should be tested for their ability to read, write and count; if deficient, they should be kept in remedial class until they learn. Ideally, they should also be given vocational training so on release they can earn a living. The possibilities of earlier parole for "good performance" should be explored.

The Mentally Disabled

Over half of those in U.S. prisons and jails have mental health problems, many of them serious. An estimated 15% should be in mental hospitals, or when released, not permitted to carry guns (and assassinate New York policemen).

Former Prisoners

Those who are released after prison should be prepared and encouraged to return to normal civilian life, without the severe limitation, restrictions and handicaps that only America requires for former inmates. Today, former prisoners are denied

Pell grants for education, access to public housing, the right to vote, even the possibility of enlisting in the armed forces, and their prior records make future employment difficult. Unlike other countries, we unwittingly encourage them to return to a life of crime.

Hardened Criminals

Repeat career criminals who have demonstrated their inability to take part in normal society should be isolated in prison, for our benefit if not for theirs.

Supervision of Police and Prisons

Armed and violent criminals are a menace to our society and a life-threatening challenge to police who must deal with them. No one should underestimate the courage and heroism of those who, for our protection, put themselves in harm's way. But there are ground rules.

"The deep-seated culture of violence directed against adolescents" (reported by the U.S. Attorney about New York's Rikers Island), the vicious and unprovoked beatings of prisoners by gangs of guards in Los Angeles County jails, (F.B.I. reports describe the level of violence and brutality there as "astonishing"); New York's "stop and frisk" practices, which until recently stopped young Black and Hispanic men without provocation, demanded they empty their pockets and, if marijuana was found, charged them with the serious crime of "public display of narcotics"—all are examples of abusive police power that must be examined, reported, reconsidered and reformed.

Police and the Community

It is in everyone's best interests to have a comfortable working relationship between the police and the community—based on mutual understanding, trust and respect. Lack of public safety on inner city streets and in schools—and attention to the horrendously high rate of Black-on-Black homicide—must be addressed openly. (Martin Luther King, Jr. said that the highest form of maturity is the ability to be self-critical.) The problems are obvious, but free, open and continuing communication between the police and elected public officials, clergy, educators and local organization leaders is the place to start.

Public Defenders

More effective legal defense provisions and legal aid should be made available to help the poor in their self-defense battle against established authorities, perhaps by volunteer lawyers.

Special Narcotics Courts

Some observers believe that narcotics crime should be dealt with by special courts and procedures, and that distinctions should be maintained between marijuana (increasingly legalized) and hard drugs like heroin and cocaine. This merits investigation and public discussion.

Rethink State Grand Jury Systems

The Grand Jury System appears to work well on the Federal level but much less well on the State, where local prosecutors—working closely with the police and often over-protective of them—have undue influence. This April, Wisconsin passed the nation's first law requiring a team of at least two investigations from an outside agency to lead reviews of deaths due to police killings, and a public report must be made if criminal charges are not filed. Other states are following suit.

Conclusion:

i) Prevention of crime and ii) the successful rehabilitation of former prisoners are the goals of the criminal justice systems in all other advanced countries, where certainty of punishment rather than severity is advocated, and where long isolation is less for punishment than to protect the public from those likely to be violent. Their success is manifest in their lower crime rates and very much lower prisoner recidivism rates, fewer broken homes and fewer socially-devastated communities.

Not rocket science, but common sense is what we require on these difficult questions, where fairness and prudence are joint concerns.

Last year only four countries accounted for nearly all executions worldwide: China, Iran, Saudi Arabia and the United States. There are today more than 41,000 people serving life without parole in the U.S. compared to 59 in Australia, 41 in England and 37 in the Netherlands; and those countries are safer than we are. We must ask why.

The "public safety" and "public justice" all other advanced nations have achieved we can have as well—if we will it.

Critical Thinking

1. What changes in law enforcement would do the most to improve police-community relations?

2. Why did the prison population skyrocket eightfold since 1970 to 2.4 million today?

3. What are some of the major problems of the American prison system?

Internet References

New American Studies Web
   https://blogs.commons.georgetown.edu/vkp/
Social Science Information Gateway
   http://www.ariadne.ac.uk/issue2/sosig
Sociology—Study Sociology Online
   http://edu.learnsoc.org/
Sociology Web Resources
   http://www.mhhe.com/socscience/sociology/resources/index.htm
Sociosite
   http://www.topsite.com/goto/sociosite.net
Socioweb
   http://www.topsite.com/goto/socioweb.com

Article   Prepared by: Kurt Finsterbusch, *University of Maryland, College Park*

It's Not Just about Race, It's about Power

Rethinking Policing after the Deaths of Eric Garner and Michael Brown

MATT WELCH

Learning Outcomes

After reading this article, you will be able to:

- Explain how the prosecutor controls the grand jury and how this can pervert justice.

- Explain the many unreasonable rules and practices which lead to the horrific outcome of the Eric Garner case.

- Discuss the role of racism in police practices.

O n December 2, Attorney General Eric Holder, the top law enforcement official in the country, went to Atlanta's Ebenezer Baptist Church to announce that the Justice Department would soon "institute rigorous new standards—and robust safeguards—to help end racial profiling, once and for all."

Neither time nor place was accidental. Ebenezer was the home church of civil rights hero Rev. Martin Luther King. And December 2 was one week after a grand jury in Ferguson, Missouri, opted to not indict Officer Darren Wilson in the shooting death of Michael Brown. Two days after the speech, a Staten Island grand jury would also decline to indict Officer Daniel Pantaleo in the choking death of Eric Garner. In both cases, the cops were white, the victims black. Both decisions touched off nationwide protests that were largely about race, with demonstrators consistently making the basic point that "black lives matter."

So in one sense Holder, the country's first African-American attorney general, was simply responding to the Zeitgeist of the moment, much the same way President Barack Obama did a day earlier at a White House summit meeting announcing a new task force to improve the relationship between police and communities of color. "[We need] to begin a process in which we're able to surface honest conversations with law enforcement, community activists, academics, elected officials, the faith community, and try to determine what the problems are and, most importantly, try to come up with concrete solutions that can move the ball forward," the president said.

But by focusing on the role of race to the exclusion of other contributing factors in these cases, both the powerless in the streets and the powerful in the suites were letting an important culprit off the hook: power itself.

Start with the grand jury process that produced both non-indictments. "The system is under the complete control, under the thumb, of prosecutors," Cato Institute Criminal Justice Director Tim Lynch told CBS News in December. "If they want an indictment they are going to get an indictment. If they don't want an indictment it won't happen."

This is an exact perversion of the grand jury's initial intent, as enshrined in the Fifth Amendment to the Constitution. "No person shall be held to answer for a capital or otherwise infamous crime, unless on a presentment or indictment of a Grand Jury," the provision reads. Grand juries, composed as they are from local citizens outside the criminal justice system, were supposed to impose a civilian check on potential prosecutorial overreach. But a design flaw was soon baked into the process: This alleged check on prosecutorial power depends absolutely on the contributions of the prosecutor himself.

"As a practical matter, the prosecutor calls the shots and dominates the entire grand jury process," Lynch and two co-authors wrote in a 2003 Cato paper on the grand jury system. "The prosecutor decides what matters will be investigated, what subpoenas will issue, which witnesses will testify, which witnesses will receive 'immunity,' and what charges will be included in each indictment. Because defense counsel are barred from the grand jury room and because there is no judge overseeing the process, the grand jurors naturally defer to the prosecutor since he is the most knowledgeable official on the scene."

Ken White, a libertarian attorney who runs the caustic blog Popehat, presented several cases to grand juries during his stint as a federal prosecutor in Los Angeles. "That experience," White wrote in a February 2014 post, "did not inspire confidence in the process. Rather, it taught me that the adage that a grand jury will indict a ham sandwich is an understatement. A better description would be that the prosecution can show a grand jury a shit sandwich and they will indict it as ham without looking up from their newspapers."

White continues: "The notion that the Supreme Court relies upon—that the grand jury has a 'historical role of protecting individuals from unjust persecution'—is not a polite fiction. A polite fiction would have some grounding in reality. It's an offensive fiction."

In practice, the only class reliably protected by grand juries is people that the local prosecutors don't actually want to prosecute. Namely, cops. The conflicts of interest here are beyond blatant: Prosecutors absolutely depend on the work and testimony of police to send defendants to jail. Grand juries absolutely depend on prosecutors to present information and guidance on whether to indict. There is no impartial judge, no adversarial check on the power of law enforcement.

So when protesters focus on the racial composition of grand juries that deliver results they don't agree with, it's a bit like complaining about the way a Great White Shark looks at you before biting off your leg. We cannot measure or re-engineer what lies in human hearts, but we can identify the criminal justice system's broken structures, perverse incentives, and wholly disproportionate tools.

Eric Garner was stopped on the street by cops looking to enforce New York's insanely high cigarette taxes. The city's notorious "stop and frisk" program, ostensibly justified by the need to enforce gun laws, is actually a method by which police harass residents of crime-ridden neighborhoods—which tend to be more poor and nonwhite—using drug laws as the legal weapon of choice. Police departments everywhere, of all racial compositions, have financial incentives to rack up low-level arrests and keep the low-hanging fruit of petty street violators in the revolving door of court appearances, fines, and late fees.

When you add into the mix the noxious and federally driven practice of civil asset forfeiture, whereby cops are allowed to seize and pocket the property of people who aren't even charged with a crime, then you can begin to understand how the citizens that police are supposed to protect begin looking more like marks that they are empowered to shake down.

Which is why the words of Obama and Holder ring so hollow. "Racial profiling," with very rare exception, does not describe a deliberate police policy of directing extra law enforcement at people based on skin pigment—that's already plenty illegal, due to federal civil rights law and the 14th Amendment, and it's also contrary to the basic mores of a modern America racially enlightened enough to elect an unimpressive black president twice. Instead, the term has become a catchall to bemoan the disproportionate racial impact of policing. You could just as easily use "racial profiling" to describe the disparate impacts of eminent domain seizures or bad public education policies.

The president says he wants "to try to determine what the problems are," but we know what many of them are already: a drug war that criminalizes victimless behavior and creates a black market economy, a judicial system that gives prosecutors and police a near blanket level of immunity for wrongdoing, a forensics system riddled with conflicts of interest and pseudoscience, a federal criminal code that has grown so large that people don't even know when they're breaking some dumb law. These critiques are not obscure; many of them have emanated from within the government itself.

America will always be having a "conversation about race," and rightly so, given our poisoned history. But by overracializing the cases drawing most attention, we quickly arrive at a wearying impasse, with Al Sharpton shouting on one side and Rudy Giuliani barking on the other.

There's a perhaps simpler way of looking at things, one that gets you more quickly to actual solutions instead of cud-chewing task forces. And that is: When you give government a powerful tool, the powerless will feel it first. Absolute power will be felt absolutely. How do we roll that back? Let's have a conversation.

Critical Thinking

1. What are the many rules and practices which protect the police from appropriate consequences for illegal actions, including murder?

2. How can the police gain from arresting or searching citizens?

3. Is it likely that the criminal justice system will be appropriately reformed?

Internet References

New American Studies Web
https://blogs.commons.georgetown.edu/vkp/

Social Science Information Gateway
http://www.ariadne.ac.uk/issue2/sosig

Sociology—Study Sociology Online
http://edu.learnsoc.org/

Sociology Web Resources
http://www.mhhe.com/socscience/sociology/resources/index.htm

Sociosite
http://www.topsite.com/goto/sociosite.net

Socioweb
http://www.topsite.com/goto/socioweb.com

Editor in Chief **MATT WELCH** is the co-host of *The Independents* on Fox Business Network.

Article   Prepared by: Kurt Finsterbusch, *University of Maryland, College Park*

"Broken Windows," Broken Lives, and the Ruse of "Public Order" Policing

NANCY A. HEITZEG

Learning Outcomes

After reading this article, you will be able to:

- Evaluate the consequences of the "Broken Windows" approach to policing.

- Examine the "Broken Windows" theory and the research that supports it.

Authors note: As we approach the one year anniversary of Eric Garner's death, New York City reached a settlement with his family, agreeing to pay $5.9 million to resolve a wrongful-death claim. The settlement is the latest in a long series of civil pay-outs (over $1 billion) made by the city to victims of (New York City Police Department NYPD).

But that has largely been the only accounting. While still under investigation, the officers involved in Garner's death will likely face no legal consequences. A Grand Jury has already declined to indict them. In fact, those who filmed the police action that killed Garner—Ramsey Orta and Tanisha Allen—have singularly received more police scrutiny than the killers themselves.

The Mayor, elected on a progressive wave, has co-signed continued NYPD repression—budgeting for 1300 new officers and standing in support of both broken windows and the chokehold. This, despite growing protests over police killings in NYC and across the nation. As of this writing, that number approaches 600, a rate of more than 3 dead per day.

The death of Eric Garner, which preceded that of Mike Brown by a month, reinvigorated a national call to end police violence against Black Lives. It continues apace, perhaps has even accelerated. And so we demand again in the name of Eric Garner and so many more:

"It Stops Today."

The murder of Eric Garner at the hands of NYPD brings to light again the never-ending unanswered questions. Unchecked police killings of mostly Black Men—one every 28 hours. Rampant racial profiling, most recently high-lighted in *Floyd v City of New York*. Excessive use of force, even in the handling of non-violent crime. Deadly restraint tactics, such as the choke-hold that killed Michael Stewart, killed Anthony Baez, and was supposedly banned in NYC despite being the on-going subject of more than 1000 civilian complaints.

Lurking behind all these atrocities is the flawed theory and fatal practice that makes it all possible: "Broken Windows" and public order policing. Widely promoted but rarely publicly critiqued, in light of Eric Garner, let's take a closer look.

Broken Windows: Flawed Theory and Practice

Broken Windows theory and the subsequent proliferation of "public ordering/quality of life/order maintainence" policing emerges from the seminal 1982 article, "Broken Windows: The Police and Neighborhood Safety" (George L. Kelling and James Q. Wilson, *Atlantic Monthly*). The theory basically claims that "disorder" leads to community withdrawal, loss of informal social control, and then, to more serious crime. One unattended broken window leads to more "physical disorder," then to "social disorder" in the form of public drunkenness, panhandlers, the homeless, taggers, public urinators, squee-gee men, and more, and finally in "criminal invasions" of neighborhoods that seem abandoned, unkempt or out of control. Perhaps, most importantly, the theory posits too that policing can prevent this, that a rigorous/repressive approach—sometimes "zero tolerance"—to public order crimes is necessary in order to curtail serious violent and property crimes.

Broken Windows has always been theoretically problematic. (See "Assessing "Broken Windows": A Brief Critique" by Randall G. Shelden and "Street Stops and Broken Windows: Terry, Race and Disorder in New York City" by Jeffery Fagan and Garth Davies for excellent overviews). It emerges from the tradition of criminology which searches vainly for individual and environmental causes of crime while ignoring the vast array of well-documented structural contributors such as poverty, unemployment, lack of quality education, and racism. Further, broken windows relies heavily on long discredited classical deterrence theory and the notion that participation in crime represents an individualized "rational choice" that can be averted by the threat of punishment, or policing.

This certainly did not dampen the appeal of this theory for those who saw the opportunity it offered for expanded police patrol and resources. Nor did it prevent police departments—most notably NYPD under the former and now current again Police Commissioner William Bratton—from rushing to implementation of this "theory" that was supported by neither logic nor data. Teamed up with then Mayor Rudy Giuliani, Bratton claimed to have "re-captured" the subways from fare dodgers and the homeless, and then turned attention to the streets armed with both zero tolerance tactics to search for drugs and guns, and a new form of crime mapping called "Compstat," a computer system that provides data for each precinct on arrests, complaints and other information about crime. In tandem, the two claimed credit for the decrease in New York City crime, using dubious data, but plenty of PR.

It should be noted that despite the claims that public order policing tactics had a direct impact on crime rates in NYC and elsewhere; there is little to no evidence to support this. Beyond this, the flawed and continued fixation with the ostensible connections between police practices and the reality of crime is misguided—there isn't one. Crime rates operate independently of police and criminal justice system practices, rising and falling according to larger social conditions. Don't take it from me—two of the top researchers on the police, David Bayley and Lawrence Sherman state it simply: "The police do not prevent crime. This is one of the best kept secrets of modern life."

What is widely known, is this: the police have the power to destroy and disrupt community, to harass individuals and entire groups of people without legal cause, injure, maim, and kill with impunity and little fear of recourse. All in the name of law and order.

Broken Windows makes that even easier, and in NYC, the result was, not a police induced decrease in crime, but rather an increase in police killings of citizens and civilian lawsuits/complaints.

Broken Windows: Racial Profiling and Gentrification in an Era of "Color-Blindness"

The reality of public order policing in NYC and elsewhere has been "harassment" policing, which has targeted communities of color and the poor. The rise of Broken Windows theory and related police practices neatly coincides with the War on the Poor, extensive criminalization of poverty/homelessness, Black motherhood, appearance and the use of public space, the escalation of the War on Drugs and attendant mass incarceration. It too provides a convenient "color-blind" cover for warrantless pretextual stops of "suspicious" people (read Black), mass arrests for minor offenses, and sweeps of entire communities. "Disorder" became the new proxy for race, and public order policing maintains the literal and figurative boundaries of whiteness. This certainly became clear via stop/frisk data revealed in *Floyd v City of New York:* over 86 percent of the stops were of Black or Latino individuals. Still Bratton's successor, Ray Kelly, argued that Blacks were"'under-stopped," despite the fact that nearly 90 percent of the people stopped were released without the officer finding any basis for a summons or arrest.

Money matters here too, as it always does, and public order policing offers a major tool in reclaiming space for economic interests vested in gentrification. In the Giuliani-Bratton 1990s, public order policing was the central tactic in the so-called "clean-up" of Times Square, pushing out the "disorderly" regulars to the city margins to make the space "safe" for the Disneys, the well-to-do and white, and out of town tourists. This trend continues unabated in NYC and elsewhere. Bratton, of-course, took his tactics to Los Angeles, where the "Safer Cities Initiative" displaced thousands of low income people of color in service of the gentrification of Skid Row. Observers note:

> Longtime residents and community organizers see what is happening on Skid Row as an extreme example of what is happening in cities across the United States: as predominantly white middle- and upper-middle-class people find urban centers increasingly desirable places to live, gentrification displaces lower-income communities of color. Policing strategies such as "broken windows" are often used to facilitate gentrification, resulting not only in displacement but increased incarceration of poor people of color.

Expect more of the same. Less [than] 100 days after his return as Police Commissioner, Bratton was meeting with real estate elites and retired US Army General Stanley McChrystal, touting a slideshow comparing crime rates with local real estate values, and encouraging still more collusion between the police and the military in support of poor doors, in pursuit of panhandlers, jaywalkers, food vendors or teenagers dancing on a train for money.

Coming soon too to a town near you.

Whose "Quality of Life?"

Broken Windows theory and the public order police tactics that have sprung from it have proven to be disastrous for communities of color. Under the color-blind guise of "safety" and "quality of life," white well—off property owners are protected from "disorder," spared the horror of having to refuse a panhandler or step over a drunk on the street. Meanwhile those deemed to be indicative of "disorder" themselves are displaced, endlessly policed, surveilled, brutalized, arrested just for being alive.

Eric Garner is dead because of public order policing. Murdered for Standing While Black and Suspected—of what? Selling loose cigarettes for 50 cents each. Can the general public finally come out of the brain-washed fog of fear to see how absurd, how obscene this actually is?

From the Malcolm X Grassroots Movement Statement on the Murder of Eric Garner by the NYPD:

> The 'broken windows' philosophy of policing, which purports that focusing resources on the most minor violations will somehow prevent larger ones, has consistently resulted in our rights being violated. We demand the criminal indictment and termination of the officers who unnecessarily attacked and killed Eric Garner. We also demand that the NYPD end the era of broken windows and militarized policing which has brought tragedy and mistrust of the police to many of our communities. We send our deepest condolences to the family of Eric Garner and support their struggle for justice in this case.

Broken Windows theory and public order policing is built and perpetuated on nothing but a ruse and many lies—it is profiling and apartheid, called by another name. Let the last words of Eric Garner mean more than just his last breath:

"It Stops Today."

Critical Thinking

1. Why do the police almost always get away with or on little punishment for killing unarmed black men?

2. How can police killings of unarmed black men be stopped?

3. What is the proper role of the police?

Internet References

New American Studies Web
  https://blogs.commons.georgetown.edu/vkp/

Social Science Information Gateway
  http://www.ariadne.ac.uk/issue2/sosig

Sociology–Study Sociology Online
  http://edu.learnsoc.org/

Sociology Web Resources
  http://www.mhhe.com/socscience/sociology/resources/index.htm

Sociosite
  http://www.topsite.com/goto/sociosite.net

Socioweb
  http://www.topsite.com/goto/socioweb.com

NANCY A. HEITZEG, Ph.D is a professor of sociology and director of the critical studies of race/ethnicity program at St. Catherine University. She is the author of *The School to Prison Pipeline: Education, Discipline, and Double Standards* (Praeger, 2015), and has written/presented widely on issues of race, class, gender and social control with particular attention to color-blind racism, the prison-industrial complex and the school-to-prison pipeline. She is, with Kay Whitlock, co-founder and co-editor of the Criminal Injustice series on the Critical Mass Progress blog.

Article   Prepared by: Kurt Finsterbusch, *University of Maryland, College Park*

Wrongful Convictions

Radley Balko

Learning Outcomes

After reading this article, you will be able to:

- Describe specific cases of wrongful convictions and understand some of the inexcusable actions by authorities that lead to these wrongful convictions.

- Understand the very large gap between proven wrongful convictions and the actual number of wrongful convictions.

- Understand the main reasons for wrongful convictions.

How many innocent Americans are behind bars?

When Paul House was finally released from prison in 2008, he was a specter of the man who had been sentenced to death more than 22 years earlier. When I visit his home in Crossville, Tennessee, in March, House's mother Joyce, who has cared for him since his release, points to a photo of House taken the day he was finally allowed to come home. In that photo and others from his last days in prison, House is all of 150 pounds, ashen and drawn, his fragile frame nearly consumed by his wheelchair. In most of the images he looks days away from death, although in one he wears the broad smile of a man finally escaping a long confinement.

When House's aunt called to congratulate him on his first day back, his mother handed him her cell phone so he could chat. He inspected the phone, gave her a frustrated look, and asked her to find him one that worked. That kind of Rip Van Winkle moment is common among people freed after a long stint in prison. Dennis Fritz, one of the two wrongly convicted men profiled in John Grisham's 2006 book *The Innocent Man*, talks about nearly calling the police upon seeing someone use an electronic key card the first time he found himself in a hotel after his release. He thought he'd witnessed a burglar use a credit card to jimmy open a door.

"Paul's first meal when he got home was chili verde," Joyce House says. "It's his favorite. And I had been waiting a long time to make it for him." And apparently quite a few meals after that. House, now 49, has put on 75 pounds since his release. More important, he has been getting proper treatment for his advanced-stage multiple sclerosis, treatment the Tennessee prison system hadn't given him.

The years of inadequate care have taken a toll. House can't walk, and he needs help with such basic tasks as bathing, feeding himself, and maneuvering around in his wheelchair. His once distinctively deep voice (which had allegedly been heard by a witness at the crime scene) is now wispy and high-pitched. He spends his time playing computer games and watching game shows.

In the hour or so that I visit with House, his mental facilities fade in and out. Communicating with him can be like trying to listen to a baseball game broadcast by a distant radio station. He will give a slurred but lucid answer to one question, then answer the next one with silence, or with the answer to a previous question, or just with a random assortment of words. He frequently falls back on the resigned refrain, "Oh, well," delivered with a shrug. The gesture and phrasing are identical every time he uses them. It's what House says to kill the expectation that he will be able to deliver the words others in the room are waiting for. It's his signal to stop waiting for him and move on.

In 1986 House was convicted of murdering Carolyn Muncey in Union County, Tennessee, a rural part of the state that shoulders Appalachia. He was sentenced to death. His case is a textbook study in wrongful conviction. It includes mishandled evidence, prosecutorial misconduct, bad science, cops with tunnel vision, DNA testing, the near-execution of an innocent man, and an appellate court reluctant to reopen old cases even in the face of new evidence that strongly suggests the jury got it wrong.

House also embodies the tribulations and frustrations that the wrongly convicted encounter once they get out. According to the doctors treating him, his current condition is the direct result of the inadequate care he received in prison. If he is ever granted a formal exoneration—a process that can be as much political as it is judicial—he will be eligible for compensation for his years behind bars, but even then the money comes with vexing conditions and limitations.

Since 1989, DNA testing has freed 268 people who were convicted of crimes they did not commit. There are dozens of other cases, like House's, where DNA strongly suggests innocence but does not conclusively prove it. Convicting and imprisoning an innocent person is arguably the worst thing a government can do to one of its citizens, short of mistakenly executing him. (There's increasing evidence that this has happened too.) Just about everyone agrees that these are unfathomable tragedies. What is far less clear, and still hotly debated, is what these cases say about the way we administer justice in America, what we owe the wrongly convicted, and how the officials who send innocent people to prison should be held accountable.

How Many Are Innocent?

According to the Innocence Project, an advocacy group that provides legal aid to the wrongly convicted, the average DNA exoneree served 13 years in prison before he or she was freed. Seventeen had been sentenced to death. Remarkably, 67 percent of the exonerated were convicted after 2000, the year that marked the onset of modern DNA testing. Each new exoneration adds more urgency to the question that has hovered over these cases since the first convict was cleared by DNA in 1989: How many more innocent people are waiting to be freed?

Given the soundness of DNA testing, we can be nearly certain that the 268 cleared so far didn't commit the crimes for which they were convicted. There are hundreds of other cases where no DNA evidence exists to definitively establish guilt or innocence, but a prisoner has been freed due to lack of evidence, recantation of eyewitness testimony, or police or prosecutorial misconduct. Those convictions were overturned because there was insufficient evidence to overcome reasonable doubt; it does not necessarily mean the defendant didn't commit the crime. It's unclear whether and how those cases should be factored into any attempt to estimate the number of innocent people in prison.

In a country where there are 15,000 to 20,000 homicides each year, 268 exonerations over two decades may seem like an acceptable margin of error. But reform advocates point out that DNA testing is conclusive only in a small percentage of criminal cases. Testing is helpful only in solving crimes where exchange of DNA is common and significant, mostly rape

and murder. (And most murder exonerations have come about because the murder was preceded by a rape that produced testable DNA.) Even within this subset of cases, DNA evidence is not always preserved, nor is it always dispositive to the identity of the perpetrator.

Death penalty cases add urgency to this debate. In a 2007 study published in the *Journal of Criminal Law and Criminology,* the Seton Hall law professor Michael Risinger looked at cases of exoneration for capital murder-rapes between 1982 and 1989, compared them to the total number of murder-rape cases over that period for which DNA would be a factor, and estimated from that data that 3 percent to 5 percent of the people convicted of capital crimes probably are innocent. If Risinger is right, it's still unclear how to extrapolate figures for the larger prison population. Some criminologists argue that there is more pressure on prosecutors and jurors to convict someone, anyone, in high-profile murder cases. That would suggest a higher wrongful conviction rate in death penalty cases. But defendants also tend to have better representation in capital cases, and media interest can also mean more scrutiny for police and prosecutors. That could lead to fewer wrongful convictions.

In a study published in the *Journal of Criminal Law and Criminology* in 2005, a team led by University of Michigan law professor Samuel Gross looked at 328 exonerations of people who had been convicted of rape, murder, and other felonies between 1989 and 2003. They found that while those who have been condemned to die make up just 1 percent of the prison population, they account for 22 percent of the exonerated. But does that mean capital cases are more likely to bring a wrongful conviction? Or does it mean the attention and scrutiny that death penalty cases get after conviction—particularly as an execution date nears—make it more likely that wrongful convictions in capital cases will be discovered?

Many states have special public defender offices that take over death penalty cases after a defendant has exhausted his appeals. These offices tend to be well staffed, with enough funding to hire their own investigators and forensic specialists. That sometimes stands in stark contrast to the public defender offices that handled the same cases at trial. Perversely, this means that in some jurisdictions, a defendant wrongly convicted of murder may be better off with a death sentence than with life in prison.

Even if we were to drop below the floor set in the Risinger study and assume that 2 percent of the 2008 prison population was innocent, that would still mean about 46,000 people have been convicted and incarcerated for crimes they didn't commit. But some skeptics say even that figure is way too high.

Joshua Marquis, the district attorney for Clatsop County, Oregon, is an outspoken critic of the Innocence Project and of academics like Risinger and Gross. He is skeptical of the belief that wrongful convictions are common. "If I thought that 3 to 5 percent of people in prison right now were innocent, I'd quit my job," Marquis says. "I'd become a public defender or something. Maybe an activist. Look, nobody but a fool would say that wrongful convictions don't happen. As a prosecutor, my worst nightmare is not losing a case—I've lost cases; I'll lose cases in the future. My worst nightmare is convicting an innocent person, and I tell my staff that. But the question here is whether wrongful convictions are epidemic or episodic. And I just don't think it's possible that the number could be anywhere near 3 to 5 percent."

Marquis and Gross have been butting heads for several years. In a 2006 *New York Times* op-ed piece, Marquis took the 328 exonerations Gross and his colleagues found between 1989 and 2003, rounded it up to 340, then multiplied it by 10—a charitable act, he wrote, to "give the professor the benefit of the doubt." He then divided that number by 15 million, the total number of felony convictions during the same period, and came up with what he said was an error rate of just 0.027 percent. His column was later quoted in a concurring opinion by U.S. Supreme Court Justice Antonin Scalia in the 2006 case *Kansas v. Marsh,* the same opinion where Scalia made the notorious claim that nothing in the U.S. Constitution prevents the government from executing an innocent person.

Gross responded with a 2008 article in the *Annual Review of Law and Social Science,* pointing out that his original number was by no means comprehensive. Those were merely the cases in which a judicial or political process had exonerated someone. The figure suggested only that wrongful convictions happen. "By [Marquis'] logic we could estimate the proportion of baseball players who've used steroids by dividing the number of major league players who've been caught by the total of all baseball players at all levels: major league, minor league, semipro, college and Little League," Gross wrote, "and maybe throw in football and basketball players as well."

Whatever the total number of innocent convicts, there is good reason to believe that the 268 cases in which DNA evidence has proven innocence don't begin to scratch the surface. For one thing, the pace of these exonerations hasn't slowed down: There were 22 in 2009, making it the second busiest name-clearing year to date. Furthermore, exonerations are expensive in both time and resources. Merely discovering a possible case and requesting testing often isn't enough. With some commendable exceptions . . . prosecutors tend to fight requests for post-conviction DNA testing. (The U.S. Supreme Court held in 2009 that there is no constitutional right to such tests.) So for now, the pace of genetic exonerations appears to be limited primarily by the amount of money and staff that

legal advocacy groups have to uncover these cases and argue them in court, the amount of evidence available for testing, and the willingness of courts to allow the process to happen, not by a lack of cases in need of further investigation.

It's notable that one of the few places in America where a district attorney has specifically dedicated staff and resources to seeking out bad convictions—Dallas County, Texas—has produced more exonerations than all but a handful of states. That's partly because Dallas County District Attorney Craig Watkins is more interested in reopening old cases than his counterparts elsewhere, and partly because of a historical quirk: Since the early 1980s the county has been sending biological crime scene evidence to a private crime lab for testing, and that lab has kept the evidence well preserved. Few states require such evidence be preserved once a defendant has exhausted his appeals, and in some jurisdictions the evidence is routinely destroyed at that point.

"I don't think there was anything unique about the way Dallas was prosecuting crimes," Watkins told me in 2008. "It's unfortunate that other places didn't preserve evidence too. We're just in a unique position where I can look at a case, test DNA evidence from that period, and say without a doubt that a person is innocent. . . . But that doesn't mean other places don't have the same problems Dallas had."

If the rest of the country has an actual (but undetected) wrongful conviction rate as high as Dallas County's, the number of innocents in prison for felony crimes could be in the tens of thousands.

The Trial and Conviction of Paul House

As with many wrongful convictions, the case against Paul House once seemed watertight. House was an outsider, having only recently moved to Union County when Carolyn Muncey was murdered in 1985, and he was an ex-con, having served five years in a Utah prison for sexual assault. He got into scuffles with locals, although he considered Muncey and her husband, Hubert, friends. When Muncey turned up dead, House was a natural suspect.

House has claimed he was innocent of the Utah charge. His mother, Joyce, says it was a he said/she said case in which her son pleaded guilty on the advice of his attorney. "He could have been paroled earlier if he had shown some remorse," she says. "But he said, 'I pled guilty the one time, because that's what the lawyer told me I should do. I'm not going to say again that I did something I didn't do.' He said he'd rather serve more time than admit to the rape again." Joyce House and Mike Pemberton, Paul House's attorney, are hesitant to go into much detail about the Utah case, and public records aren't available due to the plea bargain. But while what happened in Utah certainly makes House less sympathetic, it has no bearing on whether House is the man who killed Carolyn Muncey.

House also didn't do himself any favors during the Muncey investigation. In initial questioning, he lied to the police about where he was the night of the murder, saying he was with his girlfriend all night. But he later admitted he had gone for a walk at one point and had come back without his shoes and with scratches on his arms. He initially lied to police about the scratches too, saying they were inflicted by his girlfriend's cats. House later said he'd been accosted by some locals while on his walk, scuffled with them, then fled through a field, where he lost his shoes. (House would learn years later that his shoes were found by police before his trial. There was no blood or other biological evidence on them, potentially exculpatory information that was never turned over to House's lawyers.)

"I think it was a situation where you're on parole, you're an outsider, and this woman has just been killed near where you live," says Pemberton, House's attorney. "It wasn't smart of him to lie to the police. But it was understandable."

Carolyn Muncey's husband, who House's attorneys would later suspect was her killer, also lied about where he was when she was killed. He would additionally claim, falsely, that he had never physically abused her. Still, House was clearly the early suspect.

The strongest evidence against House was semen found on Muncey's clothing, which an FBI agent testified at trial "could have" belonged to House. DNA testing didn't exist in 1986, but the agent said House was a secretor, meaning he produced blood type secretions in other body fluids, including semen, and that the type secreted in semen found on Muncey's nightgown was a match to House's type A blood. About 80 percent of people are secretors, and about 36 percent of Americans have type A blood. The agent also said the semen found on Muncey's panties included secretions that didn't match House's blood type, but added, inaccurately, that House's secretion could have "degraded" into a match. Muncey's husband was never tested.

The other strong evidence against House was some blood stains on his jeans that matched Muncey's blood type, but not his own. Those stains on House's jeans did turn out to have been Muncey's blood; the question is how they got there.

House was never charged with rape; there were no physical indications that Muncey had been sexually assaulted. But the semen was used to put him at the crime scene, and the state used the possibility of rape as an aggravating circumstance in arguing that House should receive the death penalty.

House was convicted in February 1986. The morning after his conviction, just hours before the sentencing portion of his

trial, House slashed his wrists with a disposable razor. He left behind a suicide note in which he professed his innocence. Jail officials rushed him to a hospital in Knoxville, where doctors saved his life and stitched up his wounds. He was then sent back to the courthouse, where a jury sentenced him to death.

It wasn't until more than a decade later, in 1999, that the case against House began to erode. New witnesses came forward with accusations against Hubert Muncey, Carolyn's husband. Several said he was an alcoholic who frequently beat her. At an ensuing evidentiary hearing, two other women said Hubert had drunkenly confessed to killing his wife several months after the murder. When one went to the police with the information the next day, she said at the hearing, the sheriff brushed her off. Another witness testified that Hubert Muncey had asked her to lie to back up his alibi.

But it was the forensic evidence presented at that 1999 hearing that really unraveled the state's case. When House's attorneys were finally able to get DNA testing for the semen found on Carolyn Muncey's clothes, it showed that the semen was a match to Muncey's husband, not House. The state responded that rape was never part of their case against House (though it is why he was initially a suspect, it was the only conceivable motive, and it was presented as evidence in the sentencing portion of his trial). Besides, prosecutors argued, there was still the blood on House's jeans.

Except there were problems with that too. Cleland Blake, an assistant chief medical examiner for the state of Tennessee, testified that while the blood did belong to Muncey, its chemical composition indicated it was blood that had been taken after she had been autopsied. Worse still, three-quarters of a test tube of the blood taken during Muncey's autopsy went missing between the time of the autopsy and the time House's jeans arrived at the FBI crime lab for testing. The test tubes with Muncey's blood and House's jeans were transported in the same Styrofoam box. The blood on House's jeans, his attorneys argued, must have either been planted or spilled because of sloppy handling of the evidence.

It is extraordinarily difficult to win a new trial in a felony case, even in light of new evidence, and House's case was no exception. A federal circuit court judge denied his request for post-conviction relief, and the U.S. Court of Appeals for the 6th Circuit affirmed that decision. Somewhat surprisingly, the U.S. Supreme Court agreed to hear House's case, and in 2006 issued a rare, bitterly divided 5-to-3 ruling granting House a new trial.

The Supreme Court has occasionally thrown out death penalty convictions because of procedural errors or constitutional violations, but it's rare for the Court to methodically review the evidence in a capital case. Writing for the majority, Justice Anthony Kennedy did exactly that, finding in the end that "although the issue is close, we conclude that this is the rare case where—had the jury heard all the conflicting testimony—it is more likely than not that no reasonable juror viewing the record as a whole would lack reasonable doubt."

It was a surprising and significant victory for House. But it would be another three years before he would be released from prison.

How Do Wrongful Convictions Happen?

The most significant consequence of the spate of DNA exonerations has been a much-needed reassessment of what we thought we knew about how justice is administered in America. Consider the chief causes of wrongful convictions:

Bad Forensic Evidence

DNA technology was developed by scientists, and it has been thoroughly peer-reviewed by other scientists. Most of the forensic science used in the courtroom, on the other hand, was either invented in police stations and crime labs or has been refined and revised there to fight crime and obtain convictions. Most forensic evidence isn't peer-reviewed, isn't subject to blind testing, and is susceptible to corrupting bias, both intentional and unintentional. The most careful analysts can fall victim to cognitive bias creeping into their work, particularly when their lab falls under the auspices of a law enforcement agency. Even fingerprint analysis isn't as sound as is commonly believed.

A congressionally commissioned 2009 report by the National Academy of Sciences found that many other forensic specialties that are often presented in court with the gloss of science—hair and carpet fiber analysis, blood spatter analysis, shoe print identification, and especially bite mark analysis—lack the standards, peer review, and testing procedures of genuinely scientific research and analysis. Some are not supported by any scientific literature at all. Moreover, the report found, even the forensic specialties with some scientific support are often portrayed in court in ways that play down error rates and cognitive bias.

According to an Innocence Project analysis of the first 225 DNA exonerations, flawed or fraudulent forensic evidence factored into about half of the faulty convictions.

Eyewitness Testimony

Social scientists have known about the inherent weakness of eyewitness testimony for decades. Yet it continues to be the leading cause of wrongful convictions in America; it was a factor in 77 percent of those first 225 cases. Simple steps, such as making sure police who administer lineups have no knowledge of the case (since they can give subtle clues to witnesses, even

unintentionally) and that witnesses are told that the actual perpetrator may not be among the photos included in a lineup, can go a long way toward improving accuracy. But such reforms also make it more difficult to win convictions, so many jurisdictions, under pressure from police and prosecutor groups, have been hesitant to embrace them.

False Confessions

Difficult as it may be to comprehend, people do confess to crimes they didn't commit. It happened in about one-quarter of the first 225 DNA exonerations. Confessions are more common among suspects who are minors or are mentally handicapped, but they can happen in other contexts as well, particularly after intense or abusive police interrogations.

In a candid 2008 op-ed piece for the *Los Angeles Times*, D.C. Police Detective Jim Trainum detailed how he unwittingly coaxed a false confession out of a 34-year-old woman he suspected of murder. She even revealed details about the crime that could only have been known to police investigators and the killer. But Trainum later discovered that the woman couldn't possibly have committed the crime. When he reviewed video of his interrogation, he realized that he had inadvertently provided the woman with those very specific details, which she then repeated back to him when she was ready to confess.

Trainum concluded that all police interrogations should be videotaped, a policy that would not just discourage abusive questioning but also provide an incontrovertible record of how a suspect's confession was obtained. Here too, however, there has been pushback from some police agencies, out of fear that jurors may be turned off even by legitimate forms of questioning.

Jailhouse Informants

If you were to take every jailhouse informant at his word, you'd find that a remarkably high percentage of the people accused of felonies boast about their crimes to the complete strangers they meet in jail and prison cells. Informants are particularly valuable in federal drug cases, where helping a prosecutor obtain more convictions is often the only way to get time cut from a mandatory minimum sentence. That gives them a pretty good incentive to lie.

There is some disagreement over a prosecutor's duty to verify the testimony he solicits from jailhouse informants. In the 2006, Church Point, Louisiana, case of Ann Colomb, for example, Brett Grayson, an assistant U.S. Attorney in Louisiana, put on a parade of jailhouse informants whose claims about buying drugs from Colomb and her sons were rather improbable, especially when the sum of their testimony was considered as a whole. According to defense attorneys I spoke with, when one attorney asked him if he actually believed what his informants were telling the jury, Grayson replied that it doesn't matter if he believes his witnesses; it only matters if the jury does. He expressed a similar sentiment in his closing argument.

After indicating that he isn't familiar with the Colomb case and isn't commenting on Grayson specifically, Josh Marquis says that sentiment is wrong. "A prosecutor absolutely has a duty to only put on evidence he believes is truthful," Marquis says. "And that includes the testimony you put on from informants."

In a 2005 study, the Center on Wrongful Convictions in Chicago found that false or misleading informant testimony was responsible for 38 wrongful convictions in death penalty cases.

The professional culture of the criminal justice system. In addition to the more specific causes of wrongful convictions listed above, there is a problem with the institutional culture among prosecutors, police officers, forensic analysts, and other officials. Misplaced incentives value high conviction rates more than a fair and equal administration of justice.

Prosecutors in particular enjoy absolute immunity from civil liability, even in cases where they manufacture evidence that leads to a wrongful conviction. The only time prosecutors can be sued is when they commit misconduct while acting as investigators—that is, while doing something police normally do. At that point they're subject to qualified immunity, which provides less protection than absolute immunity but still makes it difficult to recover damages.

Marquis says this isn't a problem. "Prosecutors are still subject to criminal liability," he says. "In fact, my predecessor here in Oregon was prosecuted for misconduct in criminal cases. State bars will also hold prosecutors accountable."

But criminal charges are few and far between, and prosecutors can make egregious mistakes that still don't rise to the level of criminal misconduct. Professional sanctions are also rare. A 2010 study by the Northern California Innocence Project found more than 700 examples between 1997 and 2009 in which a court had found misconduct on the part of a prosecutor in the state. Only six of those cases resulted in any disciplinary action by the state bar. A 2010 investigation of federal prosecutorial misconduct by *USA Today* produced similar results: Of 201 cases in which federal judges found that prosecutors had committed misconduct, just one resulted in discipline by a state bar association. Prosecutorial misconduct was a factor in about one-quarter of the first 225 DNA exonerations, but none of the prosecutors in those cases faced any significant discipline from the courts or the bar.

There is also a common misconception that appeals courts serve as a check on criminal justice abuse. It is actually rare for an appeals court to review the evidence in a criminal case. Appeals courts make sure trials abide by the state and federal constitutions and by state or federal rules of criminal procedure, but they almost never second-guess the conclusions of juries.

In a 2008 article published in the *Columbia Law Review*, the University of Virginia law professor Brandon L. Garrett looked at the procedural history of the first 200 cases of DNA exoneration. Of those, just 18 convictions were reversed by appellate courts. Another 67 defendants had their appeals denied with no written ruling at all. In 63 cases, the appellate court opinion described the defendant as guilty, and in 12 cases it referred to the "overwhelming" evidence of guilt. Keep in mind these were all cases in which DNA testing later proved actual innocence. In the remaining cases, the appeals courts either found the defendant's appeal without merit or found that the errors in the case were "harmless"—that is, there were problems with the case, but those problems were unlikely to have affected the jury's verdict due to the other overwhelming evidence of guilt.

"We've seen a lot of exoneration cases where, for example, the defendant raised a claim of ineffective assistance of counsel," says Peter Neufeld, co-founder of the Innocence Project of New York. "And in those cases, the appellate courts often found that the defense lawyer provided substandard representation. But they would then say that the poor lawyering didn't prejudice the case because the evidence of guilt was so overwhelming. Well, these people were later proven innocent! If you have a test that is frequently producing erroneous results, there's either something wrong with the test, or there's something wrong with the way it's being implemented."

Life on the Outside

Paul House was diagnosed with multiple sclerosis in 2000, a year after the evidentiary hearing that would eventually lead to his release. But while House was convicted of Carolyn Muncey's murder less than a year after it happened, it took a decade after his conviction was called into serious question for House to get back home to Crossville. During those 10 years, the state's case continued to fall apart. So did House's body.

After the U.S. Supreme Court overturned House's conviction in 2006, Paul Phillips, the district attorney for Tennessee's 8th Judicial District and the man who prosecuted House in 1986, pushed ahead with plans to retry him. In December 2007, after a series of delays, Harry S. Mattice Jr., a U.S. district court judge in Knoxville, finally ordered the state to try House within 180 days or set him free. Those 180 days then came and went without House being freed, thanks to an extension granted by the 6th Circuit.

In another hearing held in May 2008, Phillips argued that House—who by that point couldn't walk or move his wheelchair without assistance—presented a flight risk. Later, Tennessee Associate Deputy Attorney General Jennifer Smith attempted to show that House presented a danger to the public because he was still capable of feeding himself with a fork, which apparently meant he was also capable of stabbing someone with one. House's bail was set at $500,000, later reduced to $100,000. In July 2008, an anonymous donor paid the bail, allowing House to finally leave prison.

That same month, Phillips told the Associated Press that he would send two additional pieces of biological evidence off for DNA testing: a hair found at the crime scene, and blood found under Carolyn Muncey's fingernails. House's defense team had asked to conduct its own testing of any untested biological evidence for years, but had been told that either there was no such evidence or, if there was, the state didn't know where it was. Philips told the A.P. that if the new tests didn't implicate House, he would drop the murder charge and allow House to go home. In February 2009 the results came back. They didn't implicate House, and in fact pointed to a third, unidentified man. In May of that year, Phillips finally dropped the charge. But he still wouldn't clear House's name, telling Knoxville's local TV station WATE, "There is very adequate proof that Mr. House was involved in this crime. We just don't know the degree of culpability beyond a reasonable doubt." (Phillips' office did not respond to my requests for comment.)

By the time House was diagnosed with M.S. in 2000, his symptoms were already severe, although it took his mother, and not a prison doctor, to notice something was wrong. "I was visiting him, and I brought along some microwave popcorn," Joyce House recalls. "He asked me to heat it up, and I said, 'No, you heat it up.' When he got up, he had to prop himself up and drag along the wall to get to the microwave. He couldn't even stand up straight." According to Joyce House, her son's doctors today say that the Tennessee prison system's failure to diagnose House's M.S. earlier—then treat it properly after it was diagnosed—may have taken years off his life. (M.S. is also exacerbated by stress.) The disease has also significantly diminished the quality of the life House has left.

Under Tennessee's compensation law for the wrongly convicted, if House is formally exonerated—and that's still a big if—he will be eligible for $50,000 for each year he was in prison, up to $1 million. But there's a catch. The compensation is given in annual $50,000 installments over 20 years. If House dies before then, the payments stop.

Most of the 27 states with compensation laws similarly pay the money off in installments. Last October, A.P. ran a story about Victor Burnette, a 57-year-old Virginia man who served eight years for a 1979 rape before he was exonerated by DNA testing in 2006. Burnette actually turned down the $226,500 the state offered in compensation in 2010 because he was offended by the stipulation that it be paid out over 25 years. Even after the DNA test confirmed his innocence, it took another three years for Burnette to officially be pardoned, which finally

made him eligible for the money. The installment plans make it unlikely that many exonerees—especially long-timers, who are arguably the most deserving—will ever see full compensation for their years in prison.

Only about half the people exonerated by DNA testing so far have been compensated at all. Most compensation laws require official findings of actual innocence, which eliminates just about any case that doesn't involve DNA. Some states also exclude anyone who played some role in their own conviction, which would disqualify a defendant who falsely confessed, even if the confession was coerced or beaten out of them.

Paul House has yet another predicament ahead of him. Even if he does win an official exoneration, and even if he somehow lives long enough to receive all of his compensation, he'll have to lose his health insurance to accept it. House's medical care is currently covered by TennCare, Tennessee's Medicare program. If he accepts compensation for his conviction, he will be ineligible. His $50,000 per year in compensation for nearly a quarter century on death row will then be offset by a steep increase in what he'll have to pay for his medical care.

These odd, sometimes absurd predicaments aren't intentionally cruel. They just work out that way. Paul House's attorney Mike Pemberton points out that the prosecutors in these cases aren't necessarily evil, either. "Paul Phillips is an honorable man, and an outstanding trial attorney," Pemberton says. "But on this case he was wrong." Pemberton, who was once a prosecutor himself, says the job can lend itself to tunnel vision, especially once a prosecutor has won a conviction. It can be hard to let go. We have a system with misplaced incentives and very little accountability for state actors who make mistakes. That's a system ripe for bad outcomes.

When I ask Paul House why he thinks it has taken so long to clear his name, he starts to answer, then stammers, looks away, and retreats again to Oh well, his cue to move on because he has no answer.

That may be an understandable response from a guy with advanced M.S. who just spent two decades on death row. But for too long our national response to the increasing evidence that our justice system is flawed has been the same sort of resignation. DNA has only begun to show us where some of those flaws lie. It will take a strong public will to see that policymakers address them.

Critical Thinking

1. DNA has proven many convicted murderers innocent. Discuss estimates of the number of wrongful convictions and the reasons for them.

2. Wrongful convictions reveal some of the injustices in the justice system. How should it be reformed?

Create Central

www.mhhe.com/createcentral

Internet References

ACLU Criminal Justice Home Page
www.aclu.org/crimjustice/index.html

Crime Times
www.crime-times.org

Human Rights and Humanitarian Assistance
www.etown.edu/vl/humrts.html

Sociology—Study Sociology Online
http://edu.learnsoc.org

Sociology Web Resources
http://www.mhhe.com/socscience/sociology/resources/index.htm

Sociosite
http://www.topsite.com/goto/sociosite.net

Socioweb
http://www.topsite.com/goto/socioweb.com

RADLEY BALKO (rbalko@reason.com) is a senior editor at reason.

From *Reason Magazine*, July 2011, pp. 20–33. Copyright © 2011 by Reason Foundation, 3415 S. Sepulveda Blvd., Suite 400, Los Angeles, CA 90034. www.reason.com

Article   Prepared by: Kurt Finsterbusch, *University of Maryland, College Park*

Statement for the Record: Worldwide Threat Assessment of the US Intelligence Community

James R. Clapper

Learning Outcomes

After reading this article, you will be able to:

* Describe the trends in cyber attacks and the types and severity of likely attacks.

* Describe the report's analysis of current terrorism and its danger to America.

* Present its analysis of the threat of weapons of mass destruction to America.

Introduction

Chairman McCain, Ranking Member Reed, Members of the Committee, thank you for the invitation to offer the United States Intelligence Community's 2015 assessment of threats to US national security. My statement reflects the collective insights of the Intelligence Community's extraordinary men and women, whom I am privileged and honored to lead. We in the Intelligence Community are committed every day to provide the nuanced, multidisciplinary intelligence that policymakers, warfighters, and domestic law enforcement personnel need to protect American lives and America's interests anywhere in the world.

Information available as of February 13, 2015 was used in the preparation of this assessment.

Global Threats
Cyber
Strategic Assessment

Cyber threats to US national and economic security are increasing in frequency, scale, sophistication, and severity of impact.

The ranges of cyber threat actors, methods of attack, targeted systems, and victims are also expanding. Overall, the unclassified information and communication technology (ICT) networks that support US Government, military, commercial, and social activities remain vulnerable to espionage and/or disruption. However, the likelihood of a catastrophic attack from any particular actor is remote at this time. Rather than a "Cyber Armageddon" scenario that debilitates the entire US infrastructure, we envision something different. We foresee an ongoing series of low-to-moderate level cyber attacks from a variety of sources over time, which will impose cumulative costs on US economic competitiveness and national security.

* A growing number of computer forensic studies by industry experts strongly suggest that several nations—including Iran and North Korea—have undertaken offensive cyber operations against private sector targets to support their economic and foreign policy objectives, at times concurrent with political crises.

Risk. Despite ever-improving network defenses, the diverse possibilities for remote hacking intrusions, supply chain operations to insert compromised hardware or software, and malevolent activities by human insiders will hold nearly all ICT systems at risk for years to come. In short, the cyber threat cannot be eliminated; rather, cyber risk must be managed. Moreover, the risk calculus employed by some private sector entities does not adequately account for foreign cyber threats or the systemic interdependencies between different critical infrastructure sectors.

Costs. During 2014, we saw an increase in the scale and scope of reporting on malevolent cyber activity that can be measured by the amount of corporate data stolen or deleted, personally identifiable information (PII) compromised, or remediation costs incurred by US victims. For example:

- After the 2012–13 distributed denial of service (DDOS) attacks on the US financial sector, JPMorgan Chase (JPMorgan) announced plans for annual cyber security expenditures of $250 million by the end of 2014. After the company suffered a hacking intrusion in 2014, JPMorgan's CEO said he would probably double JPMorgan's annual computer security budget within the next five years.

- The 2014 data breach at Home Depot exposed information from 56 million credit/debit cards and 53 million customer email addresses. Home Depot estimated the cost of the breach to be $62 million.

- In 2014, unauthorized computer intrusions were detected on the networks of the Office of Personnel Management (OPM) as well as its contractors, US Investigations Services (USIS) and KeyPoint Government Solutions. The two contractors were involved in processing sensitive PII related to national security clearances for Federal Government employees.

- In August 2014, the US company, Community Health Systems, informed the Securities and Exchange Commission that it believed hackers "originating from China" had stolen PII on 4.5 million individuals.

Attribution. Although cyber operators can infiltrate or disrupt targeted ICT networks, most can no longer assume that neither their activities will remain undetected nor can they assume that if detected, they will be able to conceal their identities. Governmental and private sector security professionals have made significant advances in detecting and attributing cyber intrusions.

- In May 2014, the US Department of Justice indicted five officers from China's Peoples' Liberation Army on charges of hacking US companies.

- In December 2014, computer security experts reported that members of an Iranian organization were responsible for computer operations targeting US military, transportation, public utility, and other critical infrastructure networks.

Deterrence. Numerous actors remain undeterred from conducting economic cyber espionage or perpetrating cyber attacks. The absence of universally accepted and enforceable norms of behavior in cyberspace has contributed to this situation. The motivation to conduct cyber attacks and cyber espionage will probably remain strong because of the relative ease of these operations and the gains they bring to the perpetrators. The result is a cyber environment in which multiple actors continue to test their adversaries' technical capabilities, political

resolve, and thresholds. The muted response by most victims to cyber attacks has created a permissive environment in which low-level attacks can be used as a coercive tool short of war, with relatively low risk of retaliation. Additionally, even when a cyber attack can be attributed to a specific actor, the forensic attribution often requires a significant amount of time to complete. Long delays between the cyber attack and determination of attribution likewise reinforce a permissive environment.

Threat Actors

Politically motivated cyber attacks are now a growing reality, and foreign actors are reconnoitering and developing access to US critical infrastructure systems, which might be quickly exploited for disruption if an adversary's intent became hostile. In addition, those conducting cyber espionage are targeting US government, military, and commercial networks on a daily basis. These threats come from a range of actors, including: (1) nation states with highly sophisticated cyber programs (such as Russia or China), (2) nations with lesser technical capabilities but possibly more disruptive intent (such as Iran or North Korea), (3) profit-motivated criminals, and (4) ideologically motivated hackers or extremists. Distinguishing between state and non-state actors within the same country is often difficult—especially when those varied actors actively collaborate, tacitly cooperate, condone criminal activity that only harms foreign victims, or utilize similar cyber tools.

Russia. Russia's Ministry of Defense is establishing its own cyber command, which—according to senior Russian military officials—will be responsible for conducting offensive cyber activities, including propaganda operations and inserting malware into enemy command and control systems. Russia's armed forces are also establishing a specialized branch for computer network operations.

- Computer security studies assert that unspecified Russian cyber actors are developing means to access industrial control systems (ICS) remotely. These systems manage critical infrastructures such as electric power grids, urban mass-transit systems, air-traffic control, and oil and gas distribution networks. These unspecified Russian actors have successfully compromised the product supply chains of three ICS vendors so that customers download exploitative malware directly from the vendors' websites along with routine software updates, according to private sector cyber security experts.

China. Chinese economic espionage against US companies remains a significant issue. The "advanced persistent threat" activities continue despite detailed private sector reports, public indictments, and US demarches, according to a computer security study. China is an advanced cyber actor; however, Chinese hackers often use less sophisticated cyber tools to access targets. Improved cyber defenses would require hackers to use more sophisticated skills and make China's economic espionage more costly and difficult to conduct.

Iran. Iran very likely values its cyber program as one of many tools for carrying out asymmetric but proportional retaliation against political foes, as well as a sophisticated means of collecting intelligence. Iranian actors have been implicated in the 2012–13 DDOS attacks against US financial institutions and in the February 2014 cyber attack on the Las Vegas Sands casino company.

North Korea. North Korea is another state actor that uses its cyber capabilities for political objectives. The North Korean Government was responsible for the November 2014 cyber attack on Sony Pictures Entertainment (SPE), which stole corporate information and introduced hard drive erasing malware into the company's network infrastructure, according to the FBI. The attack coincided with the planned release of a SPE feature film satire that depicted the planned assassination of the North Korean president.

Terrorists. Terrorist groups will continue to experiment with hacking, which could serve as the foundation for developing more advanced capabilities. Terrorist sympathizers will probably conduct lowlevel cyber attacks on behalf of terrorist groups and attract attention of the media, which might exaggerate the capabilities and threat posed by these actors.

Integrity of Information

Most of the public discussion regarding cyber threats has focused on the confidentiality and availability of information; cyber espionage undermines confidentiality, whereas denial-of-service operations and datadeletion attacks undermine availability. In the future, however, we might also see more cyber operations that will change or manipulate electronic information in order to compromise its integrity (i.e., accuracy and reliability) instead of deleting it or disrupting access to it. Decisionmaking by senior government officials (civilian and military), corporate executives, investors, or others will be impaired if they cannot trust the information they are receiving.

- Successful cyber operations targeting the integrity of information would need to overcome any institutionalized checks and balances designed to prevent the manipulation of data, for example, market monitoring and clearing functions in the financial sector.

Counterintelligence

We assess that the leading state intelligence threats to US interests in 2015 will continue to be Russia and China, based on their capabilities, intent, and broad operational scopes. Other states

in South Asia, the Near East, and East Asia will pose increasingly sophisticated local and regional intelligence threats to US interests. For example, Iran's intelligence and security services continue to view the United States as a primary threat and have stated publicly that they monitor and counter US activities in the region.

Penetrating the US national decisionmaking apparatus and Intelligence Community will remain primary objectives for foreign intelligence entities. Additionally, the targeting of national security information and proprietary information from US companies and research institutions dealing with defense, energy, finance, dual-use technology, and other areas will be a persistent threat to US interests.

Non-state entities, including transnational organized criminals and terrorists, will continue to employ human, technical, and cyber intelligence capabilities that present a significant counterintelligence challenge. Like state intelligence services, these non-state entities recruit sources and perform physical and technical surveillance to facilitate their illegal activities and avoid detection and capture.

The internationalization of critical US supply chains and service infrastructure, including for the ICT, civil infrastructure, and national security sectors, increases the potential for subversion. This threat includes individuals, small groups of "hacktivists," commercial firms, and state intelligence services.

Trusted insiders who disclose sensitive US Government information without authorization will remain a significant threat in 2015. The technical sophistication and availability of information technology that can be used for nefarious purposes exacerbates this threat.

Terrorism

Sunni violent extremists are gaining momentum and the number of Sunni violent extremist groups, members, and safe havens is greater than at any other point in history. These groups challenge local and regional governance and threaten US allies, partners, and interests. The threat to key US allies and partners will probably increase, but the extent of the increase will depend on the level of success that Sunni violent extremists achieve in seizing and holding territory, whether or not attacks on local regimes and calls for retaliation against the West are accepted by their key audiences, and the durability of the US-led coalition in Iraq and Syria.

Sunni violent extremists have taken advantage of fragile or unstable Muslim-majority countries to make territorial advances, seen in Syria and Iraq, and will probably continue to do so. They also contribute to regime instability and internal conflict by engaging in high levels of violence. Most will be unable to seize and hold territory on a large scale, however, as long as local, regional, and international support and resources are available and dedicated to halting their progress. The increase in the number of Sunni violent extremist groups also will probably be balanced by a lack of cohesion and authoritative leadership. Although the January 2015 attacks against Charlie Hebdo in Paris is a reminder of the threat to the West, most groups place a higher priority on local concerns than on attacking the so-called far enemy—the United States and the West—as advocated by core al-Qa'ida.

Differences in ideology and tactics will foster competition among some of these groups, particularly if a unifying figure or group does not emerge. In some cases, groups—even if hostile to each other— will ally against common enemies. For example, some Sunni violent extremists will probably gain support from like-minded insurgent or anti-regime groups or within disaffected or disenfranchised communities because they share the goal of radical regime change.

Although most homegrown violent extremists (HVEs) will probably continue to aspire to travel overseas, particularly to Syria and Iraq, they will probably remain the most likely Sunni violent extremist threat to the US homeland because of their immediate and direct access. Some might have been inspired by calls by the Islamic State of Iraq and the Levant (ISIL) in late September for individual jihadists in the West to retaliate for US-led airstrikes on ISIL. Attacks by lone actors are among the most difficult to warn about because they offer few or no signatures.

If ISIL were to substantially increase the priority it places on attacking the West rather than fighting to maintain and expand territorial control, then the group's access to radicalized Westerners who have fought in Syria and Iraq would provide a pool of operatives who potentially have access to the United States and other Western countries. Since the conflict began in 2011, more than 20,000 foreign fighters—at least 3,400 of whom are Westerners—have gone to Syria from more than 90 countries.

Weapons of Mass Destruction and Proliferation

Nation-states' efforts to develop or acquire weapons of mass destruction (WMD), their delivery systems, or their underlying technologies constitute a major threat to the security of the United States, its deployed troops, and allies. Syrian regime use of chemical weapons against the opposition further demonstrates that the threat of WMD is real. The time when only a few states had access to the most dangerous technologies is past. Biological and chemical materials and technologies, almost always dual-use, move easily in the globalized economy, as do personnel with the scientific expertise to design and use them. The latest discoveries in the life sciences also diffuse rapidly around the globe.

Iran Preserving Nuclear Weapons Option

We continue to assess that Iran's overarching strategic goals of enhancing its security, prestige, and regional influence have led it to pursue capabilities to meet its civilian goals and give it the ability to build missile-deliverable nuclear weapons, if it chooses to do so. We do not know whether Iran will eventually decide to build nuclear weapons.

We also continue to assess that Iran does not face any insurmountable technical barriers to producing a nuclear weapon, making Iran's political will the central issue. However, Iranian implementation of the Joint Plan of Action (JPOA) has at least temporarily inhibited further progress in its uranium enrichment and plutonium production capabilities and effectively eliminated Iran's stockpile of 20 percent enriched uranium. The agreement has also enhanced the transparency of Iran's nuclear activities, mainly through improved International Atomic Energy Agency (IAEA) access and earlier warning of any effort to make material for nuclear weapons using its safeguarded facilities.

We judge that Tehran would choose ballistic missiles as its preferred method of delivering nuclear weapons, if it builds them. Iran's ballistic missiles are inherently capable of delivering WMD, and Tehran already has the largest inventory of ballistic missiles in the Middle East. Iran's progress on space launch vehicles—along with its desire to deter the United States and its allies—provides Tehran with the means and motivation to develop longer-range missiles, including intercontinental ballistic missiles (ICBMs).

North Korea Developing WMD-Applicable Capabilities

North Korea's nuclear weapons and missile programs pose a serious threat to the United States and to the security environment in East Asia. North Korea's export of ballistic missiles and associated materials to several countries, including Iran and Syria, and its assistance to Syria's construction of a nuclear reactor, destroyed in 2007, illustrate its willingness to proliferate dangerous technologies.

In 2013, following North Korea's third nuclear test, Pyongyang announced its intention to "refurbish and restart" its nuclear facilities, to include the uranium enrichment facility at Yongbyon, and to restart its graphite-moderated plutonium production reactor that was shut down in 2007. We assess that North Korea has followed through on its announcement by expanding its Yongbyon enrichment facility and restarting the reactor.

North Korea has also expanded the size and sophistication of its ballistic missile forces, ranging from close-range ballistic missiles to ICBMs, while continuing to conduct test launches.

In 2014, North Korea launched an unprecedented number of ballistic missiles.

Pyongyang is committed to developing a long-range, nuclear-armed missile that is capable of posing a direct threat to the United States and has publicly displayed its KN08 road-mobile ICBM twice. We assess that North Korea has already taken initial steps toward fielding this system, although the system has not been flight-tested.

Because of deficiencies in their conventional military forces, North Korean leaders are focused on developing missile and WMD capabilities, particularly building nuclear weapons. Although North Korean state media regularly carries official statements on North Korea's justification for building nuclear weapons and threatening to use them as a defensive or retaliatory measure, we do not know the details of Pyongyang's nuclear doctrine or employment concepts. We have long assessed that, in Pyongyang's view, its nuclear capabilities are intended for deterrence, international prestige, and coercive diplomacy.

China's Expanding Nuclear Forces

The People's Liberation Army's (PLA's) Second Artillery Force continues to modernize its nuclear missile force by adding more survivable road-mobile systems and enhancing its silo-based systems. This new generation of missiles is intended to ensure the viability of China's strategic deterrent by providing a second strike capability. In addition, the PLA Navy continues to develop the JL-2 submarine-launched ballistic missile (SLBM) and might produce additional JIN-class nuclear-powered ballistic missile submarines. The JIN-class submarines, armed with JL-2 SLBMs, will give the PLA Navy its first longrange, sea-based nuclear capability. We assess that the Navy will soon conduct its first nuclear deterrence patrols.

Russia's New Intermediate-Range Cruise Missile

Russia has developed a new cruise missile that the United States has declared to be in violation of the Intermediate-Range Nuclear Forces (INF) Treaty. In 2013, Sergei Ivanov, a senior Russian administration official, commented in an interview how the world had changed since the time the INF Treaty was signed 1987 and noted that Russia was "developing appropriate weapons systems" in light of the proliferation of intermediate- and shorter-range ballistic missile technologies around the world. Similarly, as far back as 2007, Ivanov publicly announced that Russia had tested a ground-launched cruise missile for its Iskander weapon system, whose range complied with the INF Treaty "for now." The development of a cruise missile that is inconsistent with INF, combined with these statements about INF, calls into question Russia's commitment to this treaty.

WMD Security in Syria

In June 2014, Syria's declared (CW) stockpile was removed for destruction by the international community. The most hazardous chemical agents were destroyed aboard the MV CAPE RAY as of August 2014. The United States and its allies continue to work closely with the Organization for the Prohibition of Chemical Weapons (OPCW) to verify the completeness and accuracy of Syria's Chemical Weapons Convention (CWC) declaration. We judge that Syria, despite signing the treaty, has used chemicals as a means of warfare since accession to the CWC in 2013. Furthermore, the OPCW continues to investigate allegations of chlorine use in Syria.

Space and Counterspace

Threats to US space systems and services will increase during 2015 and beyond as potential adversaries pursue disruptive and destructive counterspace capabilities. Chinese and Russian military leaders understand the unique information advantages afforded by space systems and services and are developing capabilities to deny access in a conflict. Chinese military writings highlight the need to interfere with, damage, and destroy reconnaissance, navigation, and communication satellites. China has satellite jamming capabilities and is pursuing antisatellite systems. In July 2014, China conducted a nondestructive antisatellite missile test. China conducted a previous destructive test of the system in 2007, which created long-lived space debris. Russia's 2010 Military Doctrine emphasizes space defense as a vital component of its national defense. Russian leaders openly assert that the Russian armed forces have antisatellite weapons and conduct antisatellite research. Russia has satellite jammers and is pursuing antisatellite systems.

Transnational Organized Crime

Transnational Organized Crime (TOC) is a global, persistent threat to our communities at home and our interests abroad. Savvy, profit-driven criminal networks traffic in drugs, persons, wildlife, and weapons; corrode security and governance; undermine legitimate economic activity and the rule of law; cost economies important revenue; and undercut U.S. development efforts.

Drug Trafficking

Drug trafficking will remain a major TOC threat to the United States. Mexico is the largest foreign producer of US-bound marijuana, methamphetamines, and heroin, and the conduit for the overwhelming majority of US-bound cocaine from South America. The drug trade also undermines US interests abroad, eroding stability in parts of Africa and Latin America; Afghanistan accounts for 80 percent of the world's opium production.

Weak Central American states will continue to be the primary transit area for the majority of US-bound cocaine. The Caribbean is becoming an increasingly important secondary transit area for US- and European-bound cocaine. In 2013, the world's capacity to produce heroin reached the second highest level in nearly 20 years, increasing the likelihood that the drug will remain accessible and inexpensive in consumer markets in the United States, where heroin-related deaths have surged since 2007. New psychoactive substances (NPS), including synthetic cannabinoids and synthetic cathinones, pose an emerging and rapidly growing global public health threat. Since 2009, US law enforcement officials have encountered more than 240 synthetic compounds. Worldwide, 348 new psychoactive substances had been identified, exceeding the number of 234 illicit substances under international controls.

Criminals Profiting from Global Instability

Transnational criminal organizations will continue to exploit opportunities in ongoing conflicts to destabilize societies, economies, and governance. Regional unrest, population displacements, endemic corruption, and political turmoil will provide openings that criminals will exploit for profit and to improve their standing relative to other power brokers.

Corruption

Corruption facilitates transnational organized crime and vice versa. Both phenomena exacerbate other threats to local, regional, and international security. Corruption exists at some level in all countries; however, the symbiotic relationship between government officials and TOC networks is particularly pernicious in some countries. One example is Russia, where the nexus among organized crime, state actors, and business blurs the distinction between state policy and private gain.

Human Trafficking

Human trafficking remains both a human rights concern and a challenge to international security. Trafficking in persons has become a lucrative source of revenue—estimated to produce tens of billions of dollars annually. Human traffickers leverage corrupt officials, porous borders, and lax enforcement to ply their illicit trade. This exploitation of human lives for profit continues to occur in every country in the world—undermining the rule of law and corroding legitimate institutions of government and commerce.

Wildlife Trafficking

Illicit trade in wildlife, timber, and marine resources endangers the environment, threatens rule of law and border security in fragile regions, and destabilizes communities that depend on wildlife for biodiversity and ecotourism. Increased demand for ivory and rhino horn in Asia has triggered unprecedented increases in poaching in Africa. Criminal elements, often in collusion with corrupt government officials or security forces, are involved in poaching and movement of ivory and rhino horn across Africa. Poaching presents significant security challenges for militaries and police forces in African nations, which often are outgunned by poachers and their allies. Illegal, unreported, and unregulated fishing threatens food security and the preservation of marine resources. It often occurs concurrently with forced labor in the fishing industry.

Theft of Cultural Properties, Artifacts, and Antiquities

Although the theft and trafficking of cultural heritage and art are traditions as old as the cultures they represent, transnational organized criminals are acquiring, transporting, and selling valuable cultural property and art more swiftly, easily, and stealthily. These criminals operate on a global scale without regard for laws, borders, nationalities, or the significance of the treasures they smuggle.

Economics and Natural Resources

The global economy continues to adjust to and recover from the global financial crisis that began in 2008; economic growth since that period is lagging behind that of the previous decade. Resumption of sustained growth has been elusive for many of the world's largest economies, particularly in European countries and Japan. The prospect of diminished or forestalled recoveries in these developed economies as well as disappointing growth in key developing countries has contributed to a readjustment of energy and commodity markets.

Energy and Commodities

Energy prices experienced sharp declines during the second half of 2014. Diminishing global growth prospects, OPEC's decision to maintain its output levels, rapid increases in unconventional oil production in Canada and the United States, and the partial resumption of some previously sidelined output in Libya and elsewhere helped drive down prices by more than half since July, the first substantial decline since 2008–2009. Lower-priced oil and gas will give a boost to the global economy, with benefits enjoyed by importers more than outweighing the costs to exporters.

Macroeconomic Stability

Extraordinary monetary policy or "quantitative easing" has helped revive growth in the United States since the global financial crisis. However, this recovery and the prospect of higher returns in the United States will probably continue to draw investment capital from the rest of the world, where weak growth has left interest rates depressed.

Global output improved slightly in 2014 but continued to lag the growth rates seen before 2008. Since 2008, the worldwide GDP growth rate has averaged about 3.2 percent, well below its 20-year, pre-GFC average of 3.9 percent. Looking ahead, prospects for slowing economic growth in Europe and China do not bode well for the global economic environment.

Economic growth has been inconsistent among developed and developing economies alike. Outside of the largest economies—the United States, the EU, and China—economic growth largely stagnated worldwide in 2014, slowing to 2.1 percent. As a result, the difference in growth rates of developing countries and developed countries continued to narrow—to 2.6 percentage points. This gap, smallest in more than a decade, underscores the continued weakness in emerging markets, whose previously much higher average growth rates helped drive global growth.

Human Security
Critical Trends Converging

Several trends are converging that will probably increase the frequency of shocks to human security in 2015. Emerging infectious diseases and deficiencies in international state preparedness to address them remain a threat, exemplified by the epidemic spread of the Ebola virus in West Africa. Extremes in weather combined with public policies that affect food and water supplies will probably exacerbate humanitarian crises. Many states and international institutions will look to the United States in 2015 for leadership to address human security issues, particularly environment and global health, as well as those caused by poor or abusive governance.

Global trends in governance are negative and portend growing instability. Poor and abusive governance threatens the security and rights of individuals and civil society in many countries throughout the world. The overall risk for mass atrocities—driven in part by increasing social mobilization, violent conflict, and a diminishing quality of governance—is growing. Incidents of religious persecution also are on the rise. Legal restrictions on NGOs and the press, particularly those that expose government shortcomings or lobby for reforms, will probably continue.

Infectious Disease Continues to Threaten Human Security Worldwide

Infectious diseases are among the foremost health security threats. A more crowded and interconnected world is increasing the opportunities for human and animal diseases to emerge and spread globally. This has been demonstrated by the emergence of Ebola in West Africa on an unprecedented scale. In addition, military conflicts and displacement of populations with loss of basic infrastructure can lead to spread of disease. Climate change can also lead to changes in the distribution of vectors for diseases.

- The Ebola outbreak, which began in late 2013 in a remote area of Guinea, quickly spread into neighboring Liberia and Sierra Leone and then into dense urban transportation hubs, where it began spreading out of control. Gaps in disease surveillance and reporting, limited health care resources, and other factors contributed to the outpacing of the international Community's response in West Africa. Isolated Ebola cases appeared outside of the most affected countries—notably in Spain and the United States—and the disease will almost certainly continue in 2015 to threaten regional economic stability, security, and governance.

- Antimicrobial drug resistance is increasingly threatening global health security. Seventy percent of known bacteria have acquired resistance to at least one antibiotic that is used to treat infections, threatening a return to the pre-antibiotic era. Multidrug-resistant tuberculosis has emerged in China, India, Russia, and elsewhere. During the next twenty years, antimicrobial drug-resistant pathogens will probably continue to increase in number and geographic scope, worsening health outcomes, straining public health budgets, and harming US interests throughout the world.

- MERS, a novel virus from the same family as SARS, emerged in 2012 in Saudi Arabia. Isolated cases migrated to Southeast Asia, Europe, and the United States. Cases of highly pathogenic influenza are also continuing to appear in different regions of the world. HIV/AIDS and malaria, although trending downward, remain global health priorities. In 2013, 2.1 million people were newly infected with HIV and 584,000 were killed by malaria, according to the World Health Organization. Diarrheal diseases like cholera continue to take the lives of 800,000 children annually.

- The world's population remains vulnerable to infectious diseases because anticipating which pathogen might spread from animals to humans or if a human virus will take a more virulent form is nearly impossible. For example, if a highly pathogenic avian influenza virus like H7N9 were to become easily transmissible among humans, the outcome could be far more disruptive than the great influenza pandemic of 1918. It could lead to global economic losses, the unseating of governments, and disturbance of geopolitical alliances.

Extreme Weather Exacerbating Risks to Global Food and Water Security

Extreme weather, climate change, and public policies that affect food and water supplies will probably create or exacerbate humanitarian crises and instability risks. Globally averaged surface temperature rose approximately 0.8 degrees Celsius (about 1.4 degrees Fahrenheit) from 1951 to 2014; 2014 was warmest on earth since recordkeeping began. This rise in temperature has probably caused an increase in the intensity and frequency of both heavy precipitation and prolonged heat waves and has changed the spread of certain diseases. This trend will probably continue. Demographic and development trends that concentrate people in cities—often along coasts—will compound and amplify the impact of extreme weather and climate change on populations. Countries whose key systems—food, water, energy, shelter, transportation, and medical—are resilient will be better able to avoid significant economic and human losses from extreme weather.

- Global food supplies will probably be adequate for 2015 but are becoming increasingly fragile in Africa, the Middle East, and South Asia. The risks of worsening food insecurity in regions of strategic importance to the United States will increase because of threats to local food availability, lower purchasing power, and counterproductive government policies. Price shocks will result if extreme weather or disease patterns significantly reduce food production in multiple areas of the world, especially in key exporting countries.

- Risks to freshwater supplies—due to shortages, poor quality, floods, and climate change—are growing. These problems hinder the ability of countries to produce food and generate energy, potentially undermining global food markets and hobbling economic growth. Combined with demographic and economic development pressures, such problems will particularly hinder the efforts of North Africa, the Middle East, and South Asia to cope with their water problems. Lack of adequate water might be a destabilizing factor in countries that lack the management mechanisms, financial resources, political will, or technical ability to solve their internal water problems.

- Some states are heavily dependent on river water controlled by upstream nations. When upstream water infrastructure development threatens downstream access to water, states might attempt to exert pressure on their neighbors to preserve their water interests. Such pressure might be applied in international forums and also includes pressing investors, nongovernmental organizations, and donor countries to support or halt water infrastructure projects. Some countries will almost certainly construct and support major water projects. Over the longer term, wealthier developing countries will also probably face increasing water-related social

disruptions. Developing countries, however, are almost certainly capable of addressing water problems without risk of state failure. Terrorist organizations might also increasingly seek to control or degrade water infrastructure to gain revenue or influence populations.

Increase in Global Instability Risk

Global political instability risks will remain high in 2015 and beyond. Mass atrocities, sectarian or religious violence, and curtailed NGO activities will all continue to increase these risks. Declining economic conditions are contributing to risk of instability or internal conflict.

- Roughly half of the world's countries not already experiencing or recovering from instability are in the "most risk" and "significant risk" categories for regime-threatening and violent instability through 2015.

- Overall international will and capability to prevent or mitigate mass atrocities will probably diminish in 2015 owing to reductions in government budgets and spending.

- In 2014, about two dozen countries increased restrictions on NGOs. Approximately another dozen also plan to do so in 2015, according to the International Center for Nonprofit Law.

Critical Thinking

1. What is the basic message of the 2015 Report of the U.S. Intelligence Community on its worldwide threat assessment?

2. What is being done and can yet be done about cyber attacks?

3. Does this report reassure you or increase your fears?

Internet References

New American Studies Web
   https://blogs.commons.georgetown.edu/vkp/
Social Science Information Gateway
   http://www.ariadne.ac.uk/issue2/sosig
Sociology—Study Sociology Online
   http://edu.learnsoc.org/
Sociology Web Resources
   http://www.mhhe.com/socscience/sociology/resources/index.htm
Sociosite
   http://www.topsite.com/goto/sociosite.net
Socioweb
   http://www.topsite.com/goto/socioweb.com

Clapper, James R. "Statement for the Record: Worldwide Threat Assessment of the US Intelligence Community," Office of the Director of National Intelligence, February 2015.

Article   Prepared by: Kurt Finsterbusch, *University of Maryland, College Park*

A Problem from Heaven
Why the United States Should Back Islam's Reformation

AYAAN HIRSI ALI

Learning Outcomes

After reading this article, you will be able to:

• Describe the nature of the threat of radical Islam.

• Present Ayaan Hirsi Ali's suggestions for dealing with Islamic terrorism.

• Make judgments about how the United States should deal with Islamic nations and the jihadists.

W e have a problem—not a problem from hell, but one that claims to come from heaven. That problem is sometimes called radical, or fundamentalist, Islam, and the self-styled Islamic State is just its latest iteration. But no one really understands it. In the summer of 2014, Major General Michael Nagata, the commander of U.S. special operations forces in the Middle East, admitted as much when talking about the Islamic State, or ISIS. "We do not understand the movement," he said. "And until we do, we are not going to defeat it." Although Nagata's words are striking for their candor, there is nothing new about the state of affairs they describe. For years, U.S. policymakers have failed to grasp the nature of the threat posed by militant Islam and have almost entirely failed to mount an effective counteroffensive against it on the battlefield that matters most: the battlefield of ideas.

In the war of ideas, words matter. Last September, U.S. President Barack Obama insisted that the Islamic State "is not Islamic," and later that month, he told the UN General Assembly that "Islam teaches peace." In November, Obama condemned the beheading of the American aid worker Peter Kassig as "evil" but refused to use the term "radical Islam" to describe the ideology of his killers. The phrase is no longer heard in White House press briefings. The approved term is "violent extremism."

The decision not to call violence committed in the name of Islam by its true name—jihad—is a strange one. It would be as if Western leaders during the Cold War had gone around calling communism an ideology of peace or condemning the Baader Meinhof Gang, a West German militant group, for not being true Marxists. It is time to drop the euphemisms and verbal contortions. A battle for the future of Islam is taking place between reformers and reactionaries, and its outcome matters. The United States needs to start helping the right side win.

Tongue-tied

How did the United States end up with a strategy based on Orwellian Newspeak? In the wake of 9/11, senior Bush administration officials sounded emphatic. "This is a battle for minds," declared the Pentagon's no. 2, Paul Wolfowitz, in 2002. But behind the scenes, there was a full-blown struggle going on about how to approach the subject of Islam. According to Joseph Bosco, who worked on strategic communications and Muslim outreach in the Office of the Secretary of Defense from 2002 to 2004, although some American officials defined Islam as inherently peaceful, others argued that, like Christianity, it had to go through a reformation. Eventually, an uneasy compromise was reached. "We bridged the divide by saying that most contemporary Muslims practice their faith peacefully and tolerantly, but a small, radical minority aspires to return to Islam's harsh seventh century origins," Bosco wrote in *The National Interest.*

Administration officials could not even agree on the target of their efforts. Was it global terrorism or Islamic extremism? Or was it the alleged root causes—poverty, Saudi funding, past errors of U.S. foreign policy, or something else altogether? There were "agonizing" meetings on the subject, one participant told *U.S. News & World Report*. "We couldn't clarify what path to take, so it was dropped."

It did not help that the issue cut across traditional bureaucratic demarcations. Officers from the U.S. Army Civil Affairs and Psychological Operations Command argued for the integration of public diplomacy, press relations, and covert operations. State Department officials saw this as yet another attempt by the Pentagon to annex their turf. Veterans of the campaign trail warned against going negative on a religion—any religion—ahead of the 2004 election. For all these reasons, by the middle of that year, the Bush administration had next to no strategy. Government Accountability Office investigators told Congress that those responsible for public diplomacy at the State Department had no guidance. "Everybody who knows how to do this has been screaming," one insider told *U.S. News*. But outside Foggy Bottom, no one could hear them scream.

Administration officials eventually settled on the "Muslim World Outreach" strategy, which relied partly on humanitarian projects carried out by the U.S. Agency for International Development and partly on Arabic-language media outlets funded by the U.S. government, such as Alhurra (a plain vanilla TV news channel) and Radio Sawa (a 24-hour pop music station that targets younger listeners). In effect, "Muslim World Outreach" meant not touching Islam at all. Karen Hughes, who was undersecretary of state for public diplomacy and public affairs from 2005 to 2007, has said that she "became convinced that our nation should avoid the language of religion in our discussion of terrorist acts."

Here, if in few other respects, there has been striking continuity from Bush to Obama. From 2009 to 2011, Judith McHale served in the same position that Hughes had. "This effort is not about a 'war of ideas,' or winning the hearts and minds of huge numbers of people," McHale said in 2012. "It's about using digital platforms to reach that small but dangerous group of people around the world who are considering turning to terrorism and persuading them to instead turn in a different direction." The whole concept of "violent extremism" implies that the United States is fine with people being extremists, so long as they do not resort to violence. Yet this line of reasoning fails to understand the crucial link between those who preach jihad and those who then carry it out. It also fails to understand that at a pivotal moment, the United States has opted out of a debate about Islam's future.

The Failure

American policymakers have made two main arguments for avoiding the subject of Islam, one strategic, the other domestic. The first holds that the United States must not jeopardize its interests in the Middle East and other majority-Muslim parts of the world by casting aspersions on Islam. The second contends that the country must not upset the delicate balance in Western democracies between Muslim minorities and non-Muslim majorities by offending Muslims or encouraging so-called Islamophobes. Yet it is becoming harder and harder to sustain these arguments, since U.S. interests in the Middle East are in increasing jeopardy and since the domestic threat of militant Islam is far greater than the threat of a much-exaggerated Islamophobia.

The United States cannot wish away the escalating violence by jihadist groups or the evidence that substantial proportions of many Muslim populations support at least some of their goals (such as the imposition of sharia and punishing apostates and those who insult Islam with death). The Middle East and North Africa grow more violent by the day. A substantial part of Syria and Iraq has fallen to the Islamic State. Yemen has collapsed into anarchy. Islamists have set up bases in Libya. The militant Islamist group Boko Haram is causing grave instability in northern Nigeria, as well as in neighboring Niger and Cameroon.

The nonstrategy, in short, has failed. Indeed, the official U.S. position collapses when the United States' own Middle Eastern allies begin openly referring to Islamic extremism as a "cancer" (in the words of the United Arab Emirates' ambassador to the United States) and calling for a "revolution" in mainstream Islamic religious thinking (as Egyptian President Abdel Fattah el-Sisi has). As for the home front, an estimated 3,400 Westerners, many of them young men and women with promising futures, have voluntarily chosen to leave behind the West's freedoms and prosperity in order to join the Islamic State. More British Muslims have volunteered for the Islamic State than for the British military. The United States is not in this dire state, but the direction of travel is troubling. Already, more than 50 young American Muslims have tried to join the Islamic State, and around half of them have succeeded. It is time to change course.

The Opportunity

The first step is to recognize that the Muslim world is in the early stages of a religious reformation. To understand its nature, it is important to distinguish between the three different groups of Muslims in the world today. The first consists of Muslims who see the forcible imposition of sharia as their religious duty. The second group—the clear majority throughout the Muslim world—consists of Muslims who are loyal to the core creed and worship devoutly but are not inclined to practice or preach violence.

The third group consists of Muslim dissidents. A few, including myself, have been forced by experience to conclude that we cannot continue to be believers, yet we remain deeply engaged in the debate about Islam's future. But the majority of dissidents are reformist believers, among them clerics who have come to realize that their religion must change if its followers are not to be condemned to an interminable cycle of political violence.

Yet there are two fundamental obstacles to a reform of Islam. The first is that those who advocate it, even in the mildest terms, are threatened with death as heretics or apostates. The second is that the majority of otherwise peaceful and law-abiding Muslims are unwilling to acknowledge, much less to repudiate, the theological warrants for intolerance and violence embedded in their own religious texts.

Take the case of Al-Azhar University in Cairo, the most prestigious mainstream institution of Sunni religious education in the world. One former Al-Azhar student, Sufyan al-Omari, told the Belgian newspaper *De Standaard* in March that the Islamic State "does not fall from the sky." He continued: "The texts to which IS appeals for support are exactly what we learned at Al-Azhar. The difference is that IS truly puts the texts into practice." Following this logic, he said that he intended to join the Islamic State. Mohamed Abdullah Nasr, another recent graduate of Al-Azhar, did not express a desire to do the same. But, he pointed out, "even if Al-Azhar students don't join IS, they still retain these ideas in their head. They spread the ideology in their communities."

Critical thinking like Nasr's is at the core of the Muslim Reformation. Admittedly, the historical analogy is very rough. There are fundamental differences between the teachings of Jesus and those of Muhammad, to say nothing of the radically different organizational structures of the two religions—one hierarchical and distinct from the state, the other decentralized yet aspiring to political power. Nevertheless, three factors at work in the Middle East today resemble the drivers of religious reform in sixteenth-century Europe. First, new information technology has created an unprecedented communications network across the Muslim world. Second, a constituency for a reformation has emerged in major cities, consisting of people disenchanted with Islamist rule (as in Cairo and Tehran) or attracted by Western norms (as in London and New York). Third, there is also a political constituency for religious reform emerging in key regional states, such as Egypt and the United Arab Emirates.

Already, a growing number of ordinary citizens in the Muslim world, as well as in the West, are calling for reform. The Muslim Reformation will likely be driven by such lay reformers, rather than by the clergy, but a number of clerics are still playing an important role. Among them is Hassen Chalghoumi, the imam of the Drancy mosque, near Paris, who predicted earlier this year that "Islam will also follow the same historical pattern as Christianity and Judaism," in terms of reforming its doctrine. "However," he warned, "this battle for reform will not

be concluded if the rest of the world treats it as a solely internal battle and sits as an idle observer, watching the catastrophe as it unfolds."

Such Islamic thinkers envision a version of their religion that no longer exalts holy war, martyrdom, and life in the hereafter. Abd al-Hamid al-Ansari, a former dean of Islamic law at Qatar University, has said that he "would like the religious scholars, through their religious discourse, to make our youth love life, and not death." He has recommended that liberal reformers be permitted to sue inflammatory Islamic preachers for any harm that befalls them from the preachers' sermons. The Iraqi Shiite cleric Ahmad al-Qabbanji, meanwhile, has argued that "the Koran was created by the Prophet Muhammad, but was driven by Allah," a clear break with orthodoxy, which holds that the Koran is the direct word of God. As a report from the Middle East Media Research Institute explains, he proposes "a modifiable religious ruling based on *fiqh al-maqasid,* or the jurisprudence of the meaning"—code for a more flexible interpretation of sharia. Another reformer, Ayad Jamal al-Din, a Shiite cleric in Iraq who has argued for the separation of mosque and state, has framed the choice this way: "We must make a decision whether to follow man-made civil law, legislated by the Iraqi parliament, or whether to follow the fatwas issued by Islamic jurisprudents. We must not embellish things and say that Islam is a religion of compassion, peace, and rose water, and that everything is fine."

Like Christians and Jews centuries ago, Muslims today must critically evaluate their sacred texts in order to reform their religion. That is not an unreasonable request, as history shows. Of course, history also shows that the path to religious reform can be bloody. By the mid-seventeenth century, Europe had been ravaged by a century of warfare between Roman Catholics and Protestants. But the result was to create the room for the genuine freedom of thought that ultimately made the Enlightenment possible.

One of the most important of these freethinkers was Baruch Spinoza, a brilliant Jewish Dutch philosopher. For Spinoza, the Bible was a collection of loosely assembled moral teachings, not God's literal word. Spinoza was excommunicated from the Jewish community, and a council of the Dutch Reformed Church called his *Theological-Political Treatise* "the vilest and most sacrilegious book the world has ever seen." One of Spinoza's contemporaries, Adriaan Beverland, was even jailed and then banished from the provinces of Holland and Zeeland for questioning the notion of original sin. Yet both men died in their beds. And it is their ideas that prevail in the Netherlands today.

Defend the Dissidents

American presidents and secretaries of state need not give lectures on the finer points of Islamic orthodoxy. But it is not too much to ask them to support Islamic religious reform and make the fate of Muslim dissidents and reformers part of their negotiations with allies (such as Saudi Arabia) and foes (such as Iran) alike. At the same time, U.S. officials need to stop publicly whitewashing unreformed Islam.

There is a precedent for this proposal. During the Cold War, the United States systematically encouraged and funded anticommunist intellectuals to counter the influence of Marxists and other fellow travelers of the left by speaking out against the evils of the Soviet system. In 1950, the CIA-funded Congress for Cultural Freedom, dedicated to defending the noncommunist left, opened in Berlin. Leading intellectuals such as Bertrand Russell, Karl Jaspers, and Jacques Maritain agreed to serve as honorary chairs. Many of the congress' members were former communists—notably, Arthur Koestler—who warned against the dangers of totalitarianism on the basis of personal experience. Thanks to U.S. funding, the group was able to publish such magazines as *Encounter* (in the United Kingdom), *Preuves* (in France), *Der Monat* (in Germany), and *Quadrant* (in Australia).

As détente took hold in the late 1960s and 1970s, the war of ideas died down. When U.S. President Ronald Reagan took office in 1981, Radio Free Europe and Radio Liberty—anticommunist stations funded by the U.S. government—were operating with 1940s vacuum tube technology and rusting transmitter towers. Under Reagan, however, funding for the war of ideas was stepped up, largely through the U.S. Information Agency.

The conventional wisdom today is that the Cold War was won on economics. But this is a misunderstanding of history. In fact, in the 1950s and again in the 1980s, the United States appealed to people living behind the Iron Curtain not only on the basis of Americans' higher standards of living but also— and perhaps more importantly—on the basis of individual freedom and the rule of law. Soviet dissidents such as Aleksandr Solzhenitsyn, Andrei Sakharov, and Vaclav Havel did not condemn the Soviet system because its consumer goods were shoddy and in short supply. They condemned it because it was lawless, lying, and corrupt.

Today, there are many dissidents who challenge Islam with as much courage as the dissidents who spoke out against the Soviet Union. Just as critics of communism during the Cold War came from a variety of backgrounds and disagreed on many issues, so do modern critics of unreformed Islam. Qabbanji, for example, has expressed strong criticism of U.S. and Israeli foreign policy, whereas other reformers, such as Ansari, are more pro-American. But such differences are less important than what the reformers have in common. They are all challenging an orthodoxy that contains within it the seeds of an escalating jihad. Yet the West either ignores them or dismisses them as unrepresentative.

The United States' mistake in this regard has been twofold. First, after the collapse of communism in Russia, political leaders assumed that the United States would never face another ideological challenge. In 1998, Congress disbanded the U.S. Information Agency. Its functions were absorbed by other agencies. Then, officials assumed that Islam should not be engaged as an ideology at all. They did so mostly because they were— and remain—terrified of taking on Islam.

As William McCants of the Brookings Institution told *The Atlantic,* the Obama administration "is determined not to frame this [conflict] or have it be interpreted as a religious war." Indeed, McCants explicitly argued against taking the side of Muslim reformers because any U.S. intervention in the debate on the reform of Islam "can discredit the people who reach the same conclusions we do." But supporting dissidents who are pressing for a reform of Islam is hardly the same thing as waging a religious war. Nor does fighting the war of ideas mean trumpeting the U.S. policy of the day. It means focusing squarely on encouraging those who, for example, oppose the literal application of sharia to apostates and women or who argue that calls to wage holy war have no place in the twenty-first century.

Imagine a platform for Muslim dissidents that communicated their message through YouTube, Twitter, Facebook, and Instagram. Imagine ten reformist magazines for every one issue of the Islamic State's *Dabiq* or al Qaeda's *Inspire.* Imagine the argument for Islamic reform being available on radio and television in Arabic, Dari, Farsi, Pashto, and Urdu. Imagine grants and prizes for leading religious reformers. Imagine support for schools that act as anti-madrasahs.

Such a strategy would also give the United States an opportunity to shift its alliances to those Muslim individuals and groups that actually share its values and practices: those who fight for a true Muslim reformation and who currently find themselves maligned, if not persecuted, by the very governments Washington props up.

Back into the Ideological Arena

The task of backing Islamic reform cannot be carried out by the government alone; civil society has a crucial role to play. Indeed, all the major U.S. charitable foundations committed to humanitarian work can help Islam reform. The Ford Foundation, the Andrew W. Mellon Foundation, and the MacArthur Foundation—all of which boast endowments in the billions of dollars—have done almost nothing in this area. There have been many grants for the study of Islam, but almost none to promote its reform. The same goes for the United States' leading universities, which are currently paralyzed by their fear of being accused of "cultural imperialism" or, worst of all, "Orientalism."

I am not an Orientalist. Nor am I a racist, although like most critics of Islam, I have been accused of that, too. I do not believe in the innate backwardness of Arabs or Africans. I do not believe that the Middle East and North Africa are somehow doomed to a perpetual cycle of violence. I am a universalist. I believe that each human being possesses the power of reason, as well as a conscience. That includes all Muslims. At present, some Muslims ignore both reason and conscience by joining groups such as Boko Haram or the Islamic State, citing textual prescriptions and religious dogma to justify murder and enslavement. But their crimes are already forcing a reexamination of Islamic Scripture, doctrine, and law. This process cannot be stopped, no matter how much violence is used against would-be reformers.

Yes, the main responsibility for the Muslim Reformation falls on Muslims themselves. But it must be the duty of the Western world, as well as being in its self-interest, to provide assistance and, where necessary, security to those reformers who are carrying out this formidable task, just as it once encouraged those dissidents who stood up to Soviet communism. In her final testimony before Congress in January 2013, Secretary of State Hillary Clinton got it right. "We're abdicating the ideological arena," she said, "and we need to get back into it." Either that, or the problem from heaven will send the entire Muslim world—if not the entire world—to hell.

Critical Thinking

1. What is Islam? Is it peaceful, violent, or both?
2. Why is America so confused about ISIS and other Islamic terrorists?
3. Do you think that Islam is going through a reformation?

Internet References

New American Studies Web
https://blogs.commons.georgetown.edu/vkp/

Social Science Information Gateway
http://www.ariadne.ac.uk/issue2/sosig

Sociology—Study Sociology Online
http://edu.learnsoc.org/

Sociology Web Resources
http://www.mhhe.com/socscience/sociology/resources/index.htm

Sociosite
http://www.topsite.com/goto/sociosite.net

Socioweb
http://www.topsite.com/goto/socioweb.com

Article   Prepared by: Kurt Finsterbusch, *University of Maryland, College Park*

Low-Tech Terrorism

BRUCE HOFFMAN

Learning Outcomes

After reading this article, you will be able to:

- Understand the dangers of cyberterrorism.
- Describe how the United States can combat cyberterrorism.

Among the more prescient analyses of the terrorist threats that the United States would face in the twenty-first century was a report published in September 1999 by the US Commission on National Security/21st century, better known as the Hart-Rudman commission. Named after its cochairs, former senators Gary Hart and Warren Rudman, and evocatively titled *New World Coming,* it correctly predicted that mass-casualty terrorism would emerge as one of America's preeminent security concerns in the next century. "Already," the report's first page lamented, "the traditional functions of law, police work, and military power have begun to blur before our eyes as new threats arise." It added, "Notable among these new threats is the prospect of an attack on US cities by independent or state-supported terrorists using weapons of mass destruction."

Although hijacked commercial aircraft deliberately flown into high-rise buildings were not the weapons of mass destruction that the commission had in mind, the catastrophic effects that this tactic achieved—obliterating New York City's World Trade Center, slicing through several of the Pentagon's concentric rings and killing nearly 3,000 people—indisputably captured the gist of that prophetic assertion.

The report was also remarkably accurate in anticipating the terrorist organizational structures that would come to dominate the first dozen or so years of the new century. "Future terrorists will probably be even less hierarchically organized, and yet better networked, than they are today. Their diffuse nature will make them more anonymous, yet their ability to coordinate mass effects on a global basis will increase," the commission argued. Its vision of the motivations that would animate and subsequently fuel this violence was similarly revelatory. "The growing resentment against Western culture and values in some parts of the world," along with "the fact that others often perceive the United States as exercising its power with arrogance and self-absorption," was already "breeding a backlash" that would both continue and likely evolve into new and more insidious forms, the report asserted.

Some of the commission's other visionary conclusions now read like a retrospective summary of the past decade. "The United States will be called upon frequently to intervene militarily in a time of uncertain alliances," says one, while another disconsolately warns that "even excellent intelligence will not prevent all surprises." Today's tragic events in Syria were also anticipated by one statement that addressed the growing likelihood of foreign crises "replete with atrocities and the deliberate terrorizing of civilian populations."

Fortunately, the report's most breathless prediction concerning the likelihood of terrorist use of weapons of mass destruction (WMD) has not come to pass. But this is not for want of terrorists trying to obtain such capabilities. Indeed, prior to the October 2001 US-led invasion of Afghanistan, Al Qaeda had embarked upon an ambitious quest to acquire and develop an array of such weapons that, had it been successful, would have altered to an unimaginable extent our most basic conceptions about national security and rendered moot debates over whether terrorism posed a potentially existential threat.

But just how effective have terrorist efforts to acquire and use weapons of mass destruction actually been? The September 11, 2001, attacks were widely noted for their reliance on relatively low-tech weaponry—the conversion, in effect, of airplanes into missiles by using raw physical muscle and box cutters to hijack them. Since then, efforts to gain access to WMD have been unceasing. But examining those efforts results in some surprising conclusions. While there is no cause for complacency, they do suggest that terrorists face some inherent constraints that will be difficult for them to overcome. It is easier to proclaim the threat of mass terror than to perpetrate it.

The terrorist attacks on September 11 completely recast global perceptions of threat and vulnerability. Long-standing assumptions that terrorists were more interested in publicity than in killing were dramatically swept aside in the rising crescendo of death and destruction. The butcher's bill that morning was without parallel in the annals of modern terrorism. Throughout the entirety of the twentieth century no more than 14 terrorist incidents had killed more than a 100 people, and until September 11 no terrorist operation had ever killed more than 500 people in a single attack. Viewed from another perspective, more than twice as many Americans perished within those excruciating 102 minutes than had been killed by terrorists since 1968—the year widely accepted as marking the advent of modern, international terrorism.

So massive and consequential a terrorist onslaught naturally gave rise to fears that a profound threshold in terrorist constraint and lethality had been crossed. Renewed fears and concerns were in turn generated that terrorists would now embrace an array of deadly nonconventional weapons in order to inflict even greater levels of death and destruction than had occurred that day. Attention focused specifically on terrorist use of WMD, and the so-called Cheney Doctrine emerged to shape America's national-security strategy. The doctrine derived from former vice president Dick Cheney's reported statement that "if there's a one percent chance that Pakistani scientists are helping Al Qaeda build or develop a nuclear weapon, we have to treat it as a certainty in terms of our response." What the "one percent doctrine" meant in practice, according to one observer, was that "even if there's just a one percent chance of the unimaginable coming due, act as if it's a certainty." Countering the threat of nonconventional-weapons proliferation—whether by rogue states arrayed in an "axis of evil" or by terrorists who might acquire such weapons from those same states or otherwise develop them on their own—thus became one of the central pillars of the Bush administration's time in office.

In the case of Al Qaeda, at least, these fears were more than amply justified. That group's interest in acquiring a nuclear weapon reportedly commenced as long ago as 1992—a mere four years after its creation. An attempt by an Al Qaeda agent to purchase uranium from South Africa was made either late the following year or early in 1994 without success. Osama bin Laden's efforts to obtain nuclear material nonetheless continued, as evidenced by the arrest in Germany in 1998 of a trusted senior aide named Mamdouh Mahmud Salim, who was attempting to purchase enriched uranium. And that same year, the Al Qaeda leader issued a proclamation in the name of the "International Islamic Front for Fighting the Jews and Crusaders." Titled "The Nuclear Bomb of Islam," the proclamation declared that "it is the duty of Muslims to prepare as much force as possible to terrorize the enemies of God." When asked several months later by a Pakistani journalist whether Al Qaeda was "in a position to develop chemical weapons and try to purchase nuclear material for weapons," bin Laden replied: "I would say that acquiring weapons for the defense of Muslims is a religious duty."

Bin Laden's continued interest in nuclear weaponry was also on display at the time of the September 11 attacks. Two Pakistani nuclear scientists named Sultan Bashiruddin Mahmood and Abdul Majeed spent three days that August at a secret Al Qaeda facility outside Kabul. Although their discussions with bin Laden, his deputy Ayman al-Zawahiri and other senior Al Qaeda officials also focused on the development and employment of chemical and biological weapons, Mahmood—the former director for nuclear power at Pakistan's Atomic Energy Commission—claimed that bin Laden's foremost interest was in developing a nuclear weapon.

The movement's efforts in the biological-warfare realm, however, were far more advanced and appear to have begun in earnest with a memo written by al-Zawahiri on April 15, 1999, to Muhammad Atef, then deputy commander of Al Qaeda's military committee. Citing articles published in *Science,* the *Journal of Immunology* and the *New England Journal of Medicine,* as well as information gleaned from authoritative books such as *Tomorrow's Weapons, Peace or Pestilence* and *Chemical Warfare,* al-Zawahiri outlined in detail his thoughts on the priority to be given to developing a biological-weapons capability.

One of the specialists recruited for this purpose was a US-trained Malaysian microbiologist named Yazid Sufaat. A former captain in the Malaysian army, Sufaat graduated from the California State University in 1987 with a degree in biological sciences. He later joined Al Gamaa al-Islamiyya (the "Islamic Group"), an Al Qaeda affiliate operating in Southeast Asia, and worked closely with its military operations chief, Riduan Isamuddin, better known as Hambali, and with Hambali's own Al Qaeda handler, Khalid Sheikh Mohammed—the infamous KSM, architect of the September 11 attacks.

In January 2000, Sufaat played host to two of the 9/11 hijackers, Khalid al-Midhar and Nawaf Alhazmi, who stayed in his Kuala Lumpur condominium. Later that year, Zacarias Moussaoui, the alleged "twentieth hijacker," who was sentenced in 2006 to life imprisonment by a federal district court in Alexandria, Virginia, also stayed with Sufaat. Under KSM's direction, Hambali and Sufaat set up shop at an Al Qaeda camp in Kandahar, Afghanistan, where their efforts focused on the weaponization of anthrax. Although the two made some progress, biowarfare experts believe that on the eve of September 11 Al Qaeda was still at least two to three years away from producing a sufficient quantity of anthrax to use as a weapon.

Meanwhile, a separate team of Al Qaeda operatives was engaged in a parallel research-and-development project to produce ricin and chemical-warfare agents at the movement's Derunta camp, near the eastern Afghan city of Jalalabad. As one senior US intelligence officer who prefers to remain anonymous explained, "Al Qaeda's WMD efforts weren't part of a single program but rather multiple compartmentalized projects involving multiple scientists in multiple locations."

The Derunta facility reportedly included laboratories and a school that trained handpicked terrorists in the use of chemical and biological weapons. Among this select group was Kamal Bourgass, an Algerian Al Qaeda operative who was convicted in British courts in 2004 and 2005 for the murder of a British police officer and of "conspiracy to commit a public nuisance by the use of poisons or explosives." The school's director was an Egyptian named Midhat Mursi—better known by his Al Qaeda nom de guerre, Abu Kebab—and among its instructors were a Pakistani microbiologist and Sufaat. When US military forces overran the camp in 2001, evidence of the progress achieved in developing chemical weapons as diverse as hydrogen cyanide, chlorine and phosgene was discovered. Mursi himself was killed in 2008 by a missile fired from a U.S. Predator drone.

Mursi's death dealt another significant blow to Al Qaeda's efforts to develop nonconventional weapons—but it did not end them. In fact, as the aforementioned senior US intelligence officer recently commented, "Al Qaeda's ongoing procurement efforts have been well established for awhile now . . . They haven't been highlighted in the U.S. media, but that isn't the same as it not happening." In 2010, for instance, credible intelligence surfaced that Al Qaeda in the Arabian Peninsula—widely considered the movement's most dangerous and capable affiliate—was deeply involved in the development of ricin, a bioweapon made from castor beans that the FBI has termed the third most toxic substance known, behind only plutonium and botulism.

Then, in May 2013, Turkish authorities seized two kilograms of sarin nerve gas—the same weapon used in the 1995 attack on the Tokyo subway system—and arrested 12 men linked to Al Qaeda's Syrian affiliate, Al Nusra Front. Days later, another set of sarin-related arrests was made in Iraq of Al Qaeda operatives based in that country who were separately overseeing the production of sarin and mustard blistering agents at two or more locations.

Finally, Israel admitted in November 2013 that for the past three years it had been holding a senior Al Qaeda operative whose expertise was in biological warfare. "The revelations over his alleged biological weapons links," one account noted of the operative's detention, "come amid concerns that Al Qaeda affiliates in Syria are attempting to procure bioweapons—and may already have done so."

Indeed, Syria's ongoing civil war and the prominent position of two key Al Qaeda affiliates—Al Nusra Front and the Islamic State of Iraq and the Levant—along with other sympathetic jihadi entities in that epic struggle, coupled with the potential access afforded to Bashar al-Assad's chemical-weapons stockpiles, suggest that we have likely not heard the last of Al Qaeda's ambitions to obtain nerve agents, poison gas and other harmful toxins for use as mass-casualty weapons.

Nonetheless, a fundamental paradox appears to exist so far as terrorist capabilities involving chemical, biological and nuclear weapons are concerned. As mesmerizingly attractive as these nonconventional weapons remain to Al Qaeda and other terrorist organizations, they have also mostly proven frustratingly disappointing to whoever has tried to use them. Despite the extensive use of poison gas during World War I, for instance, this weapon accounted for only 5 percent of all casualties in that conflict. Reportedly, it required some 60 pounds of mustard gas to produce even a single casualty. Even in more recent times, chemical weapons claimed the lives of less than 1 percent (500) of the 600,000 Iranians who died in the Iran-Iraq war. The Japanese cult Aum Shinrikyo succeeded in killing no more than 13 people in its attack on the Tokyo underground in 1995. And, five years earlier, no fatalities resulted from a Tamil Tigers assault on a Sri Lankan armed forces base in East Kiran that employed chlorine gas. In fact, the wind changed and blew the gas back into the Tigers' lines, thus aborting the attack.

Biological weapons have proven similarly difficult to deploy effectively. Before and during World War II, the Imperial Japanese Army carried out nearly a dozen attacks using a variety of germ agents—including cholera, dysentery, bubonic plague, anthrax and paratyphoid, disseminated through both air and water—against Chinese forces. Not once did these weapons decisively affect the outcome of a battle. And, in the 1942 assault on Chekiang, 10,000 Japanese soldiers themselves became ill, and nearly 2,000 died, from exposure to these agents. "The Japanese program's principal defect, a problem to all efforts so far," the American terrorism expert David Rapoport concluded, was "an ineffective delivery system."

The challenges inherent in using germs as weapons are borne out by the research conducted for more than a decade by Seth Carus, a researcher at the National Defense University.

Carus has assembled perhaps the most comprehensive database of the use of biological agents by a wide variety of adversaries, including terrorists, government operatives, ordinary criminals and the mentally unstable. His exhaustive research reveals that no more than a total of 10 people were killed and less than a 1,000 were made ill as a result of about 200 incidents of bioterrorism or biocrime. Most of which, moreover, entailed the individual poisoning of specific people rather than widespread, indiscriminate attacks.

The formidable challenges of obtaining the material needed to construct a nuclear bomb, along with the fabrication and dissemination difficulties involving the use of noxious gases and biological agents, perhaps account for the operational conservatism long observed in terrorist tactics and weaponry. As politically radical or religiously fanatical as terrorists may be, they nonetheless to date have overwhelmingly seemed to prefer the tactical assurance of the comparatively modest effects achieved by the conventional weapons with which they are familiar, as opposed to the risk of failure inherent in the use of more exotic means of death and destruction. Terrorists, as Brian Jenkins famously observed in 1985, thus continue to "appear to be more imitative than innovative." Accordingly, what innovation does occur tends to take place in the realm of the clever adaptation or modification of existing tactics—such as turning hijacked passenger airliners into cruise missiles—or in the means and methods used to fabricate and detonate explosive devices, rather than in the use of some new or dramatically novel weapon.

Terrorists have thus functioned mostly in a technological vacuum: either aloof or averse to the profound changes that have fundamentally altered the nature of modern warfare. Whereas technological progress has produced successively more complex, lethally effective, and destructively accurate weapons systems that are deployed from a variety of air, land, sea—and space—platforms, terrorists continue to rely, as they have for more than a century, on the same two basic "weapons systems": the gun and the bomb. Admittedly, the guns used by terrorists today have larger ammunition capacities and more rapid rates of fire than the simple revolver the Russian revolutionary Vera Zasulich used in 1878 to assassinate the governor-general of St. Petersburg. Similarly, bombs today require smaller amounts of explosives that are exponentially more powerful and more easily concealed than the sticks of TNT with which the Fenian dynamiters terrorized London more than a century ago. But the fact remains that the vast majority of terrorist incidents continue to utilize the same two attack modes.

Why is this? There are perhaps two obvious explanations: ease and cost. Indeed, as Leonardo da Vinci is said to have observed in a completely different era and context, "Simplicity is the ultimate sophistication." The same can be said about *most* terrorist—and insurgent—weapons and tactics today.

Improvised explosive devices (IED) and bombs constructed of commercially available, readily accessible homemade materials now account for the lion's share of terrorist—and insurgent—attacks. The use of two crude bombs packed in ordinary pressure cookers that killed three people and injured nearly 300 others at last April's Boston Marathon is among the more recent cases in point. Others include the succession of peroxide-based bombs that featured in the July 2005 suicide attacks on London transport, the 2006 plot to blow up seven American and Canadian airliners while in flight from Heathrow Airport to various destinations in North America, and the 2009 attempt to replicate the London transport bombings on the New York City subway system.

The account of the construction of the bombs intended for the New York City attack presented in the book *Enemies Within* vividly illustrates this point. Written by two Pulitzer Prize-winning journalists, Matt Apuzzo and Adam Goldman, the book describes how the would-be bomber, an Afghanistan-born, permanent U.S. resident named Najibullah Zazi, easily purchased the ingredients needed for the device's construction and then, following the instructions given to him by his Al Qaeda handlers in Pakistan, created a crude but potentially devastatingly lethal weapon:

> For weeks he'd been visiting beauty supply stores, filling his carts with hydrogen peroxide and nail polish remover. At the Beauty Supply Warehouse, among the rows of wigs, braids, and extensions, the manager knew him as Jerry. He said his girlfriend owned hair salons. There was no reason to doubt him.

> On pharmacy shelves, in the little brown plastic bottles, hydrogen peroxide is a disinfectant, a sting-free way to clean scrapes. Beauty salons use a more concentrated version to bleach hair or activate hair dyes. At even higher concentrations, it burns the skin. It is not flammable on its own, but when it reacts with other chemicals, it quickly releases oxygen, creating an environment ripe for explosions. . . . Even with a cheap stove, it's easy to simmer water out of hydrogen peroxide, leaving behind something more potent. It takes time, and he had plenty of that.

Preparing the explosive initiator was only slightly more complicated, but considerably more dangerous. Hence, Zazi had to be especially careful. "He added the muriatic acid and watched as the chemicals crystallized," the account continues:

> The crystals are known as triacetone triperoxide, or TATP. A spark, electrical current, even a bit of friction can set off an explosion. . . .

The white crystal compound had been popular among Palestinian terrorists. It was cheap and powerful, but its instability earned it the nickname "Mother of Satan"....

When he was done mixing, he rinsed the crystals with baking soda and water to make his creation more stable. He placed the finished product in a wide-rimmed glass jar about the size of a coffee tin and inspected his work. There would be enough for three detonators. Three detonators inside three backpacks filled with a flammable mixture and ball bearings—the same type of weapon that left 52 dead in London in 2005....

He was ready for New York.

These types of improvised weapons are not only devastatingly effective but also remarkably inexpensive, further accounting for their popularity. For example, the House of Commons Intelligence and Security Committee, which investigated the 2005 London transport attacks, concluded that the entire operation cost less than £8,000 to execute. This sum included the cost of a trip to Pakistan so that the cell leader and an accomplice could acquire the requisite bomb-making skills at a secret Al Qaeda training camp in that country's North-West Frontier Province; the purchase of all the needed equipment and ingredients once they were back in Britain; the rental of an apartment in Leeds that they turned into a bomb factory; car rentals and the purchase of cell phones; and other incidentals.

The cost-effectiveness of such homemade devices—and their appeal to terrorists—is of course not new. Decades ago, the Provisional Irish Republican Army (PIRA) demonstrated the disproportionate effects and enormous damage that crude, inexpensive homemade explosive devices could achieve. In what was described as "the most powerful explosion in London since World War II," a PIRA fertilizer bomb made with urea nitrate and diesel fuel exploded outside the Baltic Exchange in April 1992, killing three people, wounding 90 others, leaving a 12-foot-wide crater—and causing $1.25 billion in damage. Exactly a year later, a similar bomb devastated the nearby Bishops Gate, killing one person and injuring more than 40 others. Estimates put the damage of that blast at $1.5 billion.

Long a staple of PIRA operations, in the early 1990s fertilizer had cost the group on average 1 percent of a comparable amount of plastic explosive. Although after adulteration fertilizer is admittedly far less powerful than plastic explosives, it also tends to cause more damage than plastic explosives because the energy of the blast is more sustained and less controlled.

Similarly, the homemade bomb used in the first attack on New York's World Trade Center in 1993—consisting of urea nitrate derived from fertilizer but enhanced by three canisters of hydrogen gas to create a more powerful fuel-air explosion—produced a similarly impressive return on the terrorists' investment. The device cost less than $400 to construct. Yet, it not only killed six people, injured more than a 1,000 others and gouged a 180-foot-wide crater six stories deep, but also caused an estimated $550 million in damages and lost revenue to the businesses housed there. The seaborne suicide-bomb attack seven years later on the USS *Cole*, a U.S. Navy destroyer anchored in Aden, Yemen, reportedly cost Al Qaeda no more than $10,000 to execute. But, in addition to claiming the lives of 17 American sailors and wounding 39 others, it cost the U.S. Navy $250 million to repair the damage caused to the vessel.

This trend toward the increased use of IEDS has had its most consequential and pernicious effects in Iraq and Afghanistan during our prolonged deployments there. As Andrew Bacevich, a retired U.S. Army officer and current Boston University professor, has written, "No matter how badly battered and beaten, the 'terrorists'" on these and other recent battlefields were not "intimidated, remained unrepentant, and kept coming back for more, devising tactics against which forces optimized for conventional combat did not have a ready response." He adds, "The term invented for this was 'asymmetric conflict,' loosely translated as war against adversaries who won't fight the way we want them to."

In Iraq and Afghanistan, both terrorists and insurgents alike have waged low-risk wars of attrition against American, British, allied and host military forces using a variety of IEDS with triggering devices as simple as garage-door openers, cordless phones and car key fobs to confound, if not hobble, among the most technologically advanced militaries in the history of mankind. "The richest, most-trained army got beat by dudes in manjammies and A.K.'s," an American soldier observed to a *New York Times* reporter of one such bloody engagement in Afghanistan five years ago.

Indeed, terrorists and insurgents in both Afghanistan and Iraq have demonstrated the effectiveness of even poorly or modestly armed nonstate adversaries in confronting superior, conventional military forces and waging a deadly war of attrition designed in part to undermine popular support and resolve back home for these prolonged deployments. Equally worrisome, these battle environments have become spawning grounds for continued and future violence: real-life training camps for jihadis and hands-on laboratories for the research and development of new and ever more deadly terrorist and insurgent tactics and techniques. "How do you stop foes who kill with devices built for the price of a pizza?" was the question posed by a *Newsweek* cover story about IEDS in 2007. "Maybe the question is," it continued, "can you stop them?"

At one point, IEDS were responsible for nearly two-thirds of military fatalities caused by terrorists and insurgents in Iraq and a quarter of the military fatalities in Afghanistan. According to one authoritative account, there was an IED incident every 15 minutes in Iraq during 2006. And, after the number of IED attacks had doubled in Afghanistan during 2009, this tactic accounted for three-quarters of military casualties in some areas.

These explosive devices often were constructed using either scavenged artillery or mortar shells, with military or commercial ordnance, or from entirely homemade ingredients. They were then buried beneath roadways, concealed among roadside refuse, hidden in animal carcasses or telephone poles, camouflaged into curbsides or secreted along the guard rails on the shoulders of roadways, put in boxes, or disguised as rocks or bricks strewn by the side of the road. As military vehicle armor improved, the bomb makers adapted and adjusted to these new force-protection measures and began to design and place IEDS in elevated positions, attaching them to road signs or trees, in order to impact the vehicles' unarmored upper structure.

The method of detonation has also varied as United States, allied and host forces have adapted to insurgent tactics. Command-wire detonators were replaced by radio-signal triggering devices such as cell phones and garage-door openers. These devices were remote wired up to 100 meters from the IED detonator to obviate jamming measures. More recently, infrared lasers have been used as explosive initiators. One or more artillery shells rigged with blasting caps and improvised shrapnel (consisting of bits of concrete, nuts, bolts, screws, tacks, ball bearings, etc.) have been the most commonly used, but the makeshift devices have also gradually become larger as multinational forces added more armor to their vehicles, with evidence from insurgent propaganda videos of aviation bombs of 500 lb. being used as IEDS. In some cases, these improvised devices are detonated serially—in "daisy chain" explosions—designed to mow down quick-reaction forces converging on the scene following the initial blast and first wave of casualties.

By 2011, the U.S. Defense Department had spent nearly $20 billion on IED countermeasures—including new technologies, programs, and enhanced and constantly updated training. A "massive new military bureaucracy" had to be created to oversee this effort and itself was forced to create "unconventional processes for introducing new programs," as a 2010 New America Foundation report put it. Yet, as the British Army found in its war against Jewish terrorists in Palestine 70 years ago, there is no easy or lasting solution to this threat, IED attacks had in fact become so pervasive in Palestine that in December 1946 British Army headquarters in Jerusalem issued a meticulously detailed 35-page pamphlet, complete with photographs and diagrams, describing these weapons, their emplacement and their lethal effects. Even so, as military commanders and civilian authorities alike acknowledged at the time, IEDS were then as now virtually impossible to defend against completely.

Perhaps the most novel and innovative use of IEDS, however, has been when they have been paired with toxic chemicals. Much as the Iraq conflict has served as a proving ground for other terrorist weapons and tactics, it has also served this purpose with chemical weapons. Between 2007 and 2010, more than a dozen major truck-bomb attacks occurred in Iraq involving conventional explosions paired with chlorine gas.

The most serious incident, however, was one that was foiled by Jordanian authorities in April 2004. It involved the toxic release of chemicals into a crowded urban environment and was orchestrated by the late Abu Musab al-Zarqawi, the founder and leader of Al Qaeda in Iraq. The Amman plot entailed the use of some 20 tons of chemicals and explosives to target simultaneously the prime minister's office, the General Intelligence Department's headquarters and the U.S. embassy. Although the main purpose of the coordinated operations was to conduct forced-entry attacks by suicide bombers against these three heavily protected, high-value targets, an ancillary intention is believed to have been the infliction of mass casualties on the surrounding areas by the noxious chemical agents deliberately released in the blasts. An estimated 80,000 people, Jordanian authorities claim, would have been killed or seriously injured in the operation.

The above attacks in Iraq and the foiled incident in Amman all underscore the potential for terrorists to attack a domestic industrial chemical facility with a truck bomb or other large explosive device, with the purpose of triggering the release of toxic chemicals. In this respect, the effects of prior industrial accidents involving chemicals may exert a profound influence over terrorists. In 2005, for instance, a train crash and derailment in South Carolina released some 60 tons of liquefied chlorine into the air, killing nine people and injuring 250 others. Considerably more tragic, of course, was the 1984 disaster at a Union Carbide chemical facility in Bhopal, India. Some 40 tons of methyl isocyanate were accidentally released into the environment and killed nearly 4,000 people living around the plant. Methyl isocyanate is one of the more toxic chemicals used in industry, with a toxicity that is only a few percent less than that of sarin.

The war on terrorism today generates little interest and even less enthusiasm. A decade of prolonged military deployments to Iraq and Afghanistan has drained both the treasuries and willpower of the United States, Great Britain, and many other countries, as well as the ardor and commitment that attended the commencement of this global struggle over a dozen years ago. The killings of leading Al Qaeda figures such as bin Laden and Anwar al-Awlaki—along with some 40 other senior commanders and hundreds of the group's fighters—have sufficiently diminished the threat of terrorism to our war-weary, economically preoccupied nations.

But before we simply conclude that the threat from either Al Qaeda or terrorism has disappeared, it would be prudent to pause and reflect on the expansive dimensions of Al Qaeda's WMD research-and-development efforts—and also to consider the continuing developments on the opposite end of the technological spectrum that have likewise transformed the threat against conventionally superior militaries and even against superpowers. Like it or not, the war on terrorism continues, abetted by the technological advances of our adversaries and thus far mercifully countered by our own technological prowess—and all the more so by our unyielding vigilance.

Critical Thinking

1. What kind of damages can cyberterrorists cause?
2. How can the United States defend against cyberterrorists?
3. Could cyberterrorism cause society to literally break down?

Create Central

www.mhhe.com/createcentral

Internet References

ACLU Criminal Justice Home Page
www.aclu.org/crimjustice/index.html

Human Rights and Humanitarian Assistance
www.etown.edu/vl/humrts.html

New American Studies Web
www.georgetown.edu/crossroads/asw

Sociology—Study Sociology Online
http://edu.learnsoc.org

Sociology Web Resources
http://www.mhhe.com/socscience/sociology/resources/index.htm

Sociosite
http://www.topsite.com/goto/sociosite.net

Socioweb
http://www.topsite.com/goto/socioweb.com

Terrorism Research Center
www.terrorism.com

BRUCE HOFFMAN is a contributing editor to *The National Interest,* a senior fellow at the U.S. Military Academy's Combating Terrorism Center, and a professor and director of the Center for Security Studies at Georgetown University.

Unit 6

UNIT

Prepared by: Kurt Finsterbusch, *University of Maryland, College Park*

Problems of Population, Environment, Resources, and the Future

This unit focuses on problems of the future (mostly from a worldwide perspective) and covers topics such as present population and environmental trends, problems with new technologies, and prospects for the future.

Some scholars are very concerned about the worsening state of the environment, and others are confident that technological developments will solve most of these problems. Because the debate is about the future, neither view can be proved or disproved. Nevertheless, it is important to look at the factors that are causing environmental decline and increasing the demands on the environment. One factor is population growth, so future demographics and their implications must be assessed. Another required assessment is a survey of the many environmental problems that need to be addressed. Especially important are food production problems and the current and potential impacts of global warming.

A key issue in predicting the future is how future technology will change conditions and prospects. One author in this unit argues that technology and innovation will save the planet. Another celebrates the potential to genetically design babies to have all desirable attributes and no flaws. Many futurists, however, are not so optimistic. There have been many positive trends in the past century, and many of these are expected to continue, but there have been some negative trends, and they might increase. Especially worrisome are trends in economic and political power and in ideologies that may be creating a world that Americans fear.

Article   Prepared by: Kurt Finsterbusch, *University of Maryland, College Park*

Happy Planet

Robert Adler

Learning Outcomes

After reading this article, you will be able to:

- Understand the present state of the planet.
- Explain recent and probable future land use changes.
- Consider the arguments about the current and probable future effects of human induced global warming.

The system isn't working. Or, depending on your point of view, it's working too well.

Our current economic system has lifted billions of people and entire nations out of poverty, and provides most people in the developed world with a standard of living that royalty couldn't dream of a century or two ago. The problem is that its very success—the intensity with which it motivates and finances the exploitation of nature, the multitudes who consume the cornucopia of goods and services it pours out, and the system's built-in drive for continual growth—is sending us headlong past critical natural boundaries.

The list is long and familiar: too much carbon dioxide warming the atmosphere and acidifying the ocean; too much land being cleared, leading to deforestation and desertification; overfishing causing crashes in one stock after another; and habitat destruction reducing biodiversity so drastically that some consider a sixth mass extinction to be under way. If we don't change course quickly, we will soon face extraordinary risks.

What's the alternative? The answer is simple on the face of it. Live within the limits of what nature can provide and process. Leave the land, ocean, atmosphere and biosphere to the next generation as healthy as we found them.

If we accept such a sustainable future as an important, even urgent, goal, some big questions loom for us in the developed world. What would sustainable living be like? Would it be a drab, subsistence-level existence, or could we still have vibrant lives? Is a sustainable world economically viable, or even possible? And if is it, how can we get there from here?

Not surprisingly, there's a wide range of possible answers to these questions. Some look at the ever-rising greenhouse gases, climate change and species loss and see a stark choice looming between catastrophe and drastic economic cutbacks. The 2 billion of us who are accustomed to a high-consumption lifestyle, together with governments and industries intent on "business as usual", won't voluntarily steer a path towards sustainability, says Richard Heinberg, a senior fellow at the Post Carbon Institute in Santa Rosa, California. The upshot will be a series of crises that will cumulatively "knock civilisation back on its heels", he says. At best, life for most of us in the world's richest countries might resemble that in some of today's poorer countries.

Others, however, argue that with renewable energy, sustainable use, reuse and "upcycling" of resources, and the smart design of everything from candy wrappers to cities, we can have both sustainability and abundance. Although nobody knows for sure what life in such a world would be like, a number of people have tried to envisage it.

Eric Sanderson, a conservation ecologist at the Wildlife Conservation Society in New York, depicts how life in the US might play out in his book, *Terra Nova: The New World after Oil, Cars and Suburbs*. He believes that innovations in four key areas—economics, renewable energy, transportation and urban environments—can work together to bring about rapid change. The book culminates with Sanderson and his wife travelling from New York to San Francisco in 2028 across a transformed country.

Green Vision

They live in a densely populated urban community in which residents travel mostly on foot or by bicycle, supplemented by public transport and shared electric vehicles. They cross the continent not by aeroplane but on energy-efficient, high-speed trains. In place of today's sprawling, gas-guzzling suburbs, they see lots of open country, much of it returning to woodlands and streams. Millions of people have decided to leave the suburbs and instead live in compact, self-sufficient and sustainably designed new towns. Some of these are standalone while others are communities within cities.

As Sanderson crosses the Midwest, instead of today's endless monocultures of corn, wheat and soy, he sees smaller farms using smart, diversified systems to grow crops and animals for local consumption, employing more people while using far fewer fertilisers and pesticides that take a lot of energy to produce.

A radically different energy system is visible everywhere—wind farms, solar fields and geothermal plants feed energy into a continent-spanning smart grid. The problem of storing energy for use when the sky is cloudy or the wind isn't blowing has largely been solved by pumping water from lower to higher reservoirs, then releasing it through turbines to generate power as needed.

Open for Business

Although Sanderson's timescale looks optimistic, his vision is not a utopian one. Use of renewable energy—wind, solar, geothermal and hydro—is surging worldwide. Electric vehicles are increasingly competitive. Homes, public buildings and many industrial processes are becoming far more energy efficient and we are charging ahead in terms of storing energy, sucking CO_2 out of the atmosphere, and generating fuels biologically or from sunlight and CO_2. "The technology that's in the pipeline is astonishing," says British environmentalist and author Jonathon Porritt. "I think we can now speak confidently about delivering the future we need. It's there. It's absolutely there."

Although challenging, the technological part of a transition to sustainability promises to be the easiest. The hard part—and it will be hard—is convincing economists, politicians and ordinary people worldwide to change how they live. To say that such changes are highly charged would be a huge understatement.

To most economists, continual growth is a necessity and a slowly growing economy, or a "steady state" economy that puts the health of the planet first, means catastrophe. Like worried doctors scrutinising an electrocardiogram, they track gross domestic product (GDP)—the market value of goods and services—diagnosing recessions and depressions by its downturns. Many see endless growth as the only way to create jobs and reduce poverty.

Not everyone agrees. Peter Victor, an ecological economist at York University in Toronto, modelled the Canadian economy from 2005 to 2035 under three conditions: business as usual, zeroing out all sources of economic growth, and a managed transition to a steady state—the sustainable option.

Business as usual produced no major surprises. The economy grew, but so did greenhouse gas emissions. Slamming on the economic brakes produced the catastrophe mainstream economists dread—GDP fell while unemployment and poverty soared.

The third scenario, which phased in a carbon tax, boosted anti-poverty programmes and reduced working hours, yielded results that mainstream economists would never have dreamed of: GDP per person rose and stabilised at about 150 percent of current levels, while unemployment, poverty and greenhouse gas emissions all fell. "It is possible for people to live well in a society in which economic stability rather than economic growth is the norm, where all its members flourish and social justice is served," Victor concludes.

On the global scale, the Intergovernmental Panel on Climate Change released a summary in April of the best climate modelling to date. It found that early implementation of policies to reduce climate change, including a global carbon tax and deploying all relevant technologies, could keep CO_2 below 450 parts per million, which would hold global warming below the critical 2°C threshold. Remarkably, those changes reduce economic growth by a maximum of 0.14 percent per year. That's not a misprint—a fraction of 1 percent per year.

The implication is that a sustainable world is economically feasible. It would certainly seem much better than heading full steam ahead into climate disaster. "You can't do business on a dead planet," points out US-based sustainability consultant Hunter Lovins.

Still, that doesn't tell us how to get there from here. Again there's no shortage of ideas. Ecologists, economists and politicians have proposed many initiatives to foster sustainability. Most repurpose tools we are familiar with—international agreements, laws and regulations, taxes and subsidies, plus new technologies. Others are more radical, advocating structural changes to key institutions such as banking and finance, corporations, land and resource ownership, and government. Many individuals, grass-roots groups such as the Transition Network, businesses such as Unilever, universities, cities such as Vancouver, and a few nations, including Iceland and Bhutan, are putting these ideas into practice.

Of course, most of us are not green crusaders. Yet we are already changing our lives, our work patterns and what we consume in ways that suggest the drive for sustainability may be pushing at an open door. For a start, we are driving less. The annual distance travelled by UK car and van drivers fell by 7 percent between 1995 and 2012. Germany, Australia, Japan and even the US all report the same trend. Why is that? Cost is a factor: young people are learning to drive later, put off by the price. We are also driving less to see friends and making fewer trips to the shops and to work by car—the rise in urban living, social media, online shopping and digital homeworking are seeing to that.

Driving less, and walking and cycling more are seen as positive lifestyle choices these days and are increasingly a feature of city living. Dense urban populations make recycling and other resource use more efficient, too. That doesn't mean a return to slums. If building materials can be produced sustainably and houses can be designed to be carbon-neutral, people can still live in ample and comfortable homes, says Mary Ritter, head of the European Union's climate innovation centre Climate KIC.

Porritt believes that the biggest changes will come in response to large popular movements galvanised by droughts, floods, famines and other crises. "Suddenly there's a shock to the system, and re-evaluation kicks in big time," he says. Yet some changes just happen and we hardly notice, such as putting out the recycling or insulating our lofts.

One of the most important is that we are having fewer children. Today the average woman has 2.43 children, fewer than half as many as 40 years ago. There is big population growth still to come in some places, especially sub-Saharan Africa where there is less access to contraception. But after quadrupling in the twentieth century, the world's population, currently at 7 billion, is unlikely to rise by more than 50 percent before settling down. So we can think about how we do sustainability with a stable population, rather than one that is continually growing.

Population is only one part of the equation, of course. Paul Ehrlich, author of *The Population Bomb*, points out that the amount of stuff people use and the resources needed to produce that stuff are the other issues we need to worry about. In the developed world, at least, there is growing evidence that we have reached "peak stuff". Individuals and society have got richer, and the rate at which we use resources has levelled off. Homes and factories are becoming more energy and water efficient and much of our new technology is smaller and lighter, reducing the amount of materials required to make them. So in many ways, the developed world is already dematerialising. The challenge is breaking the historic link between prosperity and energy and resource use fast enough.

Some argue that feeding extra mouths will still trash the planet—but it needn't. We already produce enough food to feed at least 10 billion people. But an estimated 40 percent of it is wasted: in the developing world it rots in warehouses or gets eaten by pests. In the developed world we mostly throw it away uneaten. Our food problems are mainly about distribution and affordability—not overall production. Add in a shift away from industrial agriculture to more local and sustainable alternatives and that's good news for a world that needs lots of food. "We're learning that you can produce more calories per acre with smaller farms", says environmentalist Bill McKibben.

Healthier and Happier

The solutions certainly won't be one-size-fits-all. It's possible to have a sustainable London and a sustainable Amazonia, but they will function very differently. "A renewable world depends on what you have close to hand", says McKibben.

So living sustainably need not be a step backwards. Some things will change, though. Meat will become a luxury, as its cost is pushed up thanks to the huge amounts of energy and water needed to farm livestock. And while we'll still be able

to take holidays, those weekend jaunts on budget airlines are likely to be a thing of the past because there is currently no tax on aircraft fuel.

Porritt believes that doing away with such counterproductive subsidies and tax havens is essential. A global carbon tax and a tax on financial transactions would help to fund ecosystem restoration, public health, education and other crucial steps towards sustainability. "Tax is such a powerful instrument to promote sustainability", he says. "It's absolutely fundamental to the transformation we're talking about".

Porritt and Sanderson are buoyant about the quality of life in a more equitable and sustainable world, without denying the difficulties ahead. "One of the reasons why I think we have failed is that we haven't given a sense of just how good a world it would be", admits Porritt.

All of which adds up to a vision of a sustainable world that is significantly different from the one that critics envisage. It might mean a leaner and slower way of life for some, but also a healthier, happier and more peaceful world for us and future generations to enjoy. We have the tools. What we do with them remains to be seen.

Critical Thinking

1. What have been the many benefits of the current economic system?

2. What have been the negative impacts of the current economic system?

3. What do you think will happen over the next 25 years?

Create Central

www.mhhe.com/createcentral

Internet References

New American Studies Web
www.georgetown.edu/crossroads/asw

Sociology—Study Sociology Online
http://edu.learnsoc.org

Sociology Web Resources
http://www.mhhe.com/socscience/sociology/resources/index.htm

Sociosite
http://www.topsite.com/goto/sociosite.net

Socioweb
http://www.topsite.com/goto/socioweb.com

The Hunger Project
www.thp.org

ROBERT ADLER is a science writer based in northern California and Oaxaca, Mexico.

Article   Prepared by: Kurt Finsterbusch, *University of Maryland, College Park*

What Happens When We All Live to 100?

If life-expectancy trends continue, that future may be near, transforming society in surprising and far-reaching ways.

GREGG EASTERBROOK

Learning Outcomes

After reading this article, you will be able to:

- Describe the new science of aging and its potential for helping people live substantially longer.

- Discuss the past record of research on life extending technologies.

- Explain the likely causes of increasing life expectancy over the past two centuries.

For millennia, if not for eons—anthropology continuously pushes backward the time of human origin—life expectancy was short. The few people who grew old were assumed, because of their years, to have won the favor of the gods. The typical person was fortunate to reach 40.

Beginning in the 19th century, that slowly changed. Since 1840, life expectancy at birth has risen about three months with each passing year. In 1840, life expectancy at birth in Sweden, a much-studied nation owing to its record-keeping, was 45 years for women; today it's 83 years. The United States displays roughly the same trend. When the 20th century began, life expectancy at birth in America was 47 years; now newborns are expected to live 79 years. If about three months continue to be added with each passing year, by the middle of this century, American life expectancy at birth will be 88 years. By the end of the century, it will be 100 years.

Viewed globally, the lengthening of life spans seems independent of any single, specific event. It didn't accelerate much as antibiotics and vaccines became common. Nor did it retreat much during wars or disease outbreaks. A graph of global life expectancy over time looks like an escalator rising smoothly. The trend holds, in most years, in individual nations rich and poor; the whole world is riding the escalator.

Projections of ever-longer life spans assume no incredible medical discoveries—rather, that the escalator ride simply continues. If anti-aging drugs or genetic therapies are found, the climb could accelerate. Centenarians may become the norm, rather than rarities who generate a headline in the local newspaper.

Pie in the sky? On a verdant hillside in Marin County, California—home to hipsters and towering redwoods, the place to which the Golden Gate Bridge leads—sits the Buck Institute, the first private, independent research facility dedicated to extending the human life span. Since 1999, scientists and postdocs there have studied ways to make organisms live much longer, and with better health, than they naturally would. Already, the institute's researchers have quintupled the life span of laboratory worms. Most Americans have never heard of the Buck Institute, but someday this place may be very well known.

Buck is not alone in its pursuit. The University of Michigan, the University of Texas, and the University of California at San Francisco are studying ways to slow aging, as is the Mayo Clinic. Late in 2013, Google brought its trove of cash into the game, founding a spin-off called the California Life Company (known as Calico) to specialize in longevity research. Six months after Calico's charter was announced, Craig Venter, the biotech entrepreneur who in the 1990s conducted a dramatic race against government laboratories to sequence the human genome, also founded a start-up that seeks ways to slow aging.

Should research find a life-span breakthrough, the proportion of the U.S. population that is elderly—fated to rise anyway, considering declining fertility rates, the retirement of the Baby Boomers, and the continuing uplift of the escalator—may climb even more. Longer life has obvious appeal, but it entails societal risks. Politics may come to be dominated by the old, who might vote themselves ever more generous benefits for which the young must pay. Social Security and private pensions could be burdened well beyond what current actuarial tables suggest. If longer life expectancy simply leads to more years in which pensioners are disabled and demand expensive services, health-care costs may balloon as never before, while other social needs go unmet.

With each passing year, the newly born live about three months longer than those born the prior year.

But the story might have a happy ending. If medical interventions to slow aging result in added years of reasonable fitness, life might extend in a sanguine manner, with most men and women living longer in good vigor, and also working longer, keeping pension and health-care subsidies under control. Indeed, the most-exciting work being done in longevity science concerns making the later years vibrant, as opposed to simply adding time at the end.

Postwar medical research has focused on specific conditions: there are heart-disease laboratories, cancer institutes, and so on. Traditional research assumes the chronic later-life diseases that are among the nation's leading killers—cardiovascular blockage, stroke, Alzheimer's—arise individually and should be treated individually. What if, instead, aging is the root cause of many chronic diseases, and aging can be slowed? Not just life span but "health span" might increase.

Drugs that lengthen health span are becoming to medical researchers what vaccines and antibiotics were to previous generations in the lab: their grail. If health-span research is successful, pharmaceuticals as remarkable as those earlier generations of drugs may result. In the process, society might learn the answer to an ancient mystery: Given that every cell in a mammal's body contains the DNA blueprint of a healthy young version of itself, why do we age at all?

Counting Yeast

"Here in our freezers we have 100 or so compounds that extend life in invertebrates," says Gordon Lithgow, a geneticist at the Buck Institute. He walks with me through labs situated on a campus of modernistic buildings that command a dreamlike view of San Pablo Bay, and encourage dreamlike thoughts. The 100 compounds in the freezer? "What we don't know is if they work in people."

The Buck Institute bustles with young researchers. Jeans and San Francisco 49ers caps are common sights—this could be a Silicon Valley software start-up were not microscopes, cages, and biological-isolation chambers ubiquitous. The institute is named for Leonard and Beryl Buck, a Marin County couple who left oil stocks to a foundation charged with studying why people age, among other issues. When the institute opened, medical research aimed at slowing aging was viewed as quixotic—the sort of thing washed-up hippies talk about while sipping wine and watching the sunset. A mere 15 years into its existence, the Buck Institute is at the bow wave of biology.

In one lab, researchers laboriously tamper with yeast chromosomes. Yeast is expedient as a research subject because it lives out a lifetime before an analyst's eyes, and because a third of yeast genes are similar to human genes. Deleting some genes kills yeast; deleting others causes yeast to live longer. Why deleting some genes extends life isn't known—Buck researchers are trying to figure this out, in the hope that they might then carry the effect over to mammals. The work is painstaking, with four microscopes in use at least 50 hours a week.

Buck employs Lilliputian electrocardiogram machines and toy-size CT scanners to examine the internal organs of mice, since the goal is not just to make them live longer but to keep them healthy longer, with less cancer or heart disease. Researchers curious about aging mainly work with mice, worms, flies, and yeast, because they are small and easily housed, and because they don't live long, so improvements to life expectancy are quickly observable. "Twenty years ago it was a really big deal to extend the life span of worms. Now any postdoc can do that," says Simon Melov, a Buck geneticist. Experiments funded by the National Institute on Aging have shown that drugs can extend a mouse's life span by about a quarter, and Buck researchers have been able to reverse age-related heart dysfunction in the same animal. Think how the world would be upended if human longevity quickly jumped another 25 percent.

The rubber will meet the road with human trials. "We hope to find five to 10 small molecules that extend healthy life span in mice, then stage a human trial," says Brian Kennedy, the Buck Institute's CEO. A drug called rapamycin—being tested at the institute and elsewhere—seems closest to trial stage and has revolutionary potential. But in addition to being ethically fraught, human trials of a life-extension substance will be costly, and might take decades. The entry of Google's billions into the field makes human trials more likely. Calico is tight-lipped about its plans—the company agreed to let me visit, then backed out.

What Do Whales Know That We Don't?

Anti-aging research is not without antecedents, some of which offer notes of caution. A generation ago, Linus Pauling, a winner of the Nobel Prize in chemistry, proposed that megadoses of vitamin C would retard aging. It turned out that at megadoses, vitamins can become toxic. If you take vitamins, swallow the amounts recommended by the Food and Drug Administration.

A decade ago, a biotech start-up called Sirtris sought to devise drugs that mimic the supposed health-giving properties of red wine. GlaxoSmithKline bought Sirtris for $790 million in today's dollars, money the company may wish it had back: Sirtris experiments have yet to lead to any practical product.

About 15 years ago, Bruce Ames, an accomplished scientist at the University of California at Berkeley, proposed that acetylcarnitine, which regulates the mitochondria of cells, combined with an antioxidant, might retard aging while treating mild Alzheimer's. *Antioxidant* has become a buzzword of supplement marketing and Dr. Oz–style quackery. Too much antioxidant would be unhealthy, since oxidation is essential to the body's respiration. Ames thought he had found a compound that safely moderates the pace at which cells use themselves up. He began dosing himself with acetylcarnitine, and continues to work at Berkeley, at age 85; whether he would have enjoyed such longevity anyway is unknowable. Pharmaceutical companies have shown little interest in Ames's idea—because it occurs naturally, acetylcarnitine cannot be patented, and, worse from Big Pharma's standpoint, the substance is inexpensive.

Today, lab results show a clear relationship between a restricted-calorie diet and longevity in mice. That eating less extends the life spans of small mammals is the strongest finding of anti-aging research to this point. A restrictive diet seems to put mouse cells into a state vaguely similar to hibernation; whether caloric restriction would work in people isn't known. A campaign against calories might seem to possess broad practical appeal, since what's recommended—eating less—costs nothing. But if the mice are any indication, one would need to eat a *lot* less, dropping caloric intake to the level at which a person feels hunger pangs throughout the day. "Caloric restriction is a fad diet in Northern California," Melov told me. "We had a caloric-restriction group come in to visit the institute. They did not look at all healthy."

Most research assumes that chronic diseases arise and should be treated individually. What if, instead, aging is the root cause of many chronic diseases, and aging can be slowed?

Recently, separate teams at Harvard, Stanford, and UC San Francisco reported that transferring the blood of adolescent mice into old, declining mice had a rejuvenating effect on the latter. The thought of the old rich purchasing blood from the young poor is ghoulish on numerous levels. The research goal is to determine what chemical aspect of youthful blood benefits mature tissue. Perhaps compounds in adolescent blood excite dormant stem cells, and a drug could be developed that triggers the effect without transfusion.

The Buck Institute and other labs have been looking for health-span DNA that may exist in other mammals. Whales are a lot less likely than people are to get cancer. Polar bears consume an extremely high-fat diet yet don't develop arterial plaque. If the biological pathways for such qualities were understood, a drug might be designed to trigger the effect in people. Mimicking what nature has already developed seems more promising than trying to devise novel DNA.

In worms, genes called daf-2 and daf-16 can change in a way that causes the invertebrates to live twice as long as is natural, and in good vigor. A molecular biologist named Cynthia Kenyon, among the first hires at Calico, made that discovery more than two decades ago, when she was a researcher at UC San Francisco. By manipulating the same genes in mice, Kenyon has been able to cause them to live longer, with less cancer than mice in a control group: that is, with a better health span. The daf-16 gene is similar to a human gene called foxo3, a variant of which is linked to exceptional longevity. A drug that mimics this foxo3 variant is rumored to be among Calico's initial projects.

A long time has passed since Kenyon's eureka moment about worm genes, and she's still far from proving that this insight can help people. But the tempo of the kind of work she does is accelerating. Twenty years ago, genetic sequencing and similar forms of DNA research were excruciatingly time-consuming. New techniques and equipment have altered that: for instance, one Silicon Valley lab-services firm, Sequetech, advertises, "Go from [cell] colony to sequence" in a day. The accelerating pace of genetic-information gathering may come in handy for health-span research.

The Buck Institute became cautiously optimistic about rapamycin when its life-extension properties were noticed in yeast. Lab mice dosed with rapamycin are dying off more slowly than they would naturally, and many of the old mice appear energetic and youthful. Devised to prevent rejection of transplanted organs, rapamycin seems to alter some chemistry associated with cellular senescence. (More on that later.) If the drug turns out to delay aging in people, it would be the greatest off-label pharmaceutical use ever. But don't ask your doctor for a prescription—health-span therapy based on rapamycin is years away, if it ever happens. Kennedy, the Buck Institute CEO, does not dose himself with rapamycin, whose side effects are not understood.

Smoke, Eat Red Meat, Live to 100

Researchers at the Buck Institute are lean: society's obesity problems are not in evidence there. Everyone takes the stairs; elevators are viewed as strictly for visitors. If there is a candy machine on the 488-acre grounds, it is well hidden. I met some researchers for lunch in a glass-and-chrome conference room (Buck's buildings were designed by I. M. Pei and fairly shout "Give me an architecture award!"). Lunch was an ascetic affair: water and a small sandwich with greens; no sides, soda, or cookies. Kennedy says he seldom eats lunch, and runs up to 20 miles weekly. Yet, even doing everything right by the lights of current assumptions about how to stave off aging, at age 47, Kennedy has wrinkle lines around his eyes.

Except with regard to infectious diseases, medical cause and effect is notoriously hard to pin down. Coffee, salt, butter: good, bad, or neither? Studies are inconclusive. Why do some people develop heart disease while others with the same habits don't? The Framingham Heart Study, in its 66th year and following a third generation of subjects, still struggles with such questions. You should watch your weight, eat more greens and less sugar, exercise regularly, and get ample sleep. But you should do these things because they are common sense—not because there is any definitive proof that they will help you live longer.

The uncertainty inherent in the practice of medicine is amplified when the subject is longevity, because decades might pass before anyone knows whether a particular drug or lifestyle modification does any good. Scrutinizing the very old has not been the gold mine some researchers hoped it would be. "Lifestyle studies of centenarians can be really puzzling," Kennedy says. "They smoke more and drink less than we might guess. Few are vegetarians. Nothing jumps out as a definitive cause of their long lives."

Among the first wide-scale efforts to understand gerontology was the Baltimore Longitudinal Study of Aging, begun by federal researchers in 1958 and ongoing. Its current director, Luigi Ferrucci, says, "The study has determined that disabilities among the elderly often have warning signs that can be detected in youth, and this insight might lead to early-life interventions that decrease late-life chronic disease. But on some of the big questions, such as whether longevity is caused mainly by genes or mainly by lifestyle and environment, we just have no idea at all."

Studies of twins suggest that about 30 percent of longevity is inherited. This is one of the factors that make researchers optimistic—if 30 percent of longevity is inherited, perhaps laboratories can design a compound that causes anyone's blood chemistry to mimic what happens in the bodies of those who were born with the DNA for long life. "But when we sequence the genome, only 1 percent seems linked to longevity," Ferrucci told me. "The other 99 percent of the presumed genetic effect is unexplained."

At medical conferences, Ferrucci likes to show physicians and researchers an elaborate medical profile of an anonymous patient, then ask them to guess her age. "Guesses are off by as much as 20 years too high or low," he says. "This is because medically, we do not know what 'age' is. The sole means to determine age is by asking for date of birth. That's what a basic level this research still is at."

Except with regard to infectious diseases, medical cause and effect is notoriously hard to pin down. Coffee, salt, butter: good, bad, or neither?

Aging brings with it, of course, senescence. Cellular senescence, a subset of the overall phenomenon, is a subject of fascination in longevity research.

The tissues and organs that make up our bodies are prone to injury, and the cells are prone to malfunctions, cancer being the most prominent. When an injury must be healed, or cancerous tissue that is dividing must be stopped, nearby cells transmit chemical signals that trigger the repair of injured cells or the death of malignant ones. (Obviously this is a simplification). In the young, the system works pretty well. But as cells turn senescent, they begin to send out false positives. The body's healing ability falters as excess production of the repair signal leads to persistent inflammation, which is the foundation of heart disease, Alzheimer's, arthritis, and other chronic maladies associated with the passage of time. Cars wear out because they cannot repair themselves; our bodies wear out because they lose the ability to repair themselves. If the loss of our ability to self-repair were slowed down, health during our later years would improve: a longer warranty, in the auto analogy.

"If we can figure out how to eliminate senescent cells or switch off their secretions," says Judith Campisi, who runs the Buck Institute's research on this topic, "then we could prevent or lessen the impact of many chronic diseases of aging. It's not a coincidence that incidence of these chronic diseases increases sharply after the age of 50, a time when senescent cells also increase in number. If you believe, as many scientists do, that aging is a prime cause of many chronic diseases, it is essential that we understand the accumulation of senescent cells." Rapamycin excites longevity researchers because it seems to switch off the repair signal mistakenly sent by senescent cells. Mayo Clinic researchers are studying other substances that dampen the effects of cellular senescence; some have proved to keep mice fit longer than normal, extending their health span. Many elderly people decline into years of progressive disability, then become invalids. If instead most people enjoyed reasonable vigor right up to the end, that would be just as exciting for society as adding years to life expectancy.

Big medical efforts tend to be structured as assaults on specific conditions—the "war on cancer" and so on. One reason is psychological: a wealthy person who survived a heart attack, or lost a parent to one, endows a foundation to study the problem. Another reason is symbolic: we tend to view diseases as challenges thrown at us by nature, to be overcome one by one. If the passage of time itself turns out to be the challenge, interdisciplinary study of aging might overtake the disease-by-disease approach. As recently as a generation ago, it would have seemed totally crazy to suppose that aging could be "cured." Now curing aging seems, well, only somewhat crazy.

The Escalator Debate

The life-expectancy escalator has for nearly two centuries risen about three months a year, despite two world wars, the 1918 influenza pandemic, the AIDS epidemic, and the global population's growing sevenfold—the latter deceptively important, because crowded conditions are assumed to more readily communicate disease. Will life-span increases continue regardless of what may happen in biotech? The yea position is represented by James Vaupel, the founder of Germany's Max Planck Institute for Demographic Research; the nay by Jay Olshansky, a professor of public health at the University of Illinois at Chicago.

In 2002, Vaupel published an influential article in *Science* documenting the eerily linear rise in life expectancy since 1840. Controversially, Vaupel concluded that "reductions in mortality should not be seen as a disconnected sequence of unrepeatable revolutions but rather as a regular stream of continuing progress." No specific development or discovery has caused the rise: improvements in nutrition, public health, sanitation, and medical knowledge all have helped, but the operative impetus has been the "stream of continuing progress."

Vaupel called it a "reasonable scenario" that increases will continue at least until life expectancy at birth surpasses 100. His views haven't changed. "The data still support the conclusions of the 2002 paper. Linear rise in life expectancy has continued," Vaupel told me earlier this year. In a recent report, the Centers for Disease Control and Prevention found that the age-adjusted U.S. death rate declined to a record low in 2011. Today the first four causes of death in the United States are chronic, age-related conditions: heart disease, cancer, chronic lower-respiratory diseases, and stroke. As long as living standards continue to improve, Vaupel thinks, life expectancy will continue to increase.

On the opposite side of this coin, Olshansky told me the rise in life expectancy will "hit a wall soon, if it hasn't already." He

noted, "Most of the 20th-century gains in longevity came from reduced infant mortality, and those were onetime gains." Infant mortality in the United States trails some other nations', but has dropped so much—down to one in 170—that little room for improvement remains. "There's tremendous statistical impact on life expectancy when the young are saved," Olshansky says. "A reduction in infant mortality saves the entire span of a person's life. Avoiding mortality in a young person—say, by vaccine—saves most of the person's life. Changes in medicine or lifestyle that extend the lives of the old don't add much to the numbers." Olshansky calculates that if cancer were eliminated, American life expectancy would rise by only three years, because a host of other chronic fatal diseases are waiting to take its place. He thinks the 21st century will see the average life span extend "another 10 years or so," with a bonus of more health span. Then the increase will slow noticeably, or stop.

> **"Avoiding mortality in a young person—say, by vaccine—saves most of the person's life. Changes in medicine or lifestyle that extend the lives of the old don't add much to the numbers."**

Whether human age may have a biological limit does not factor into this debate. A French woman who lived from 1875 to 1997, Jeanne Calment, had the longest confirmed life span, at 122. She's obviously an outlier, and while outliers don't tell us much, they do hint at what's possible. Her age at death was well beyond the average life span that either Vaupel or Olshansky are contemplating in their analyses. And in any case, various experts, at various times across the past century, have argued that life span was nearing a ceiling, only to be proved wrong.

Diminishing smoking and drunk driving have obviously contributed to declining mortality. Homicide has fallen so much—shootings aren't necessarily down, but improved trauma response saves more victims—that murder is no longer among the top 15 causes of death in the United States. Other health indicators seem positive as well. All forms of harmful air and water emissions except greenhouse gases are in long-term decline. Less smog, acid rain, and airborne soot foster longevity—the old are sensitive to respiratory disease—while declining levels of industrial toxins may contribute to declining cancer rates. Life expectancy can be as much as 18 years shorter in low-income U.S. counties than in high-income counties, but Obamacare should correct some of that imbalance: Romneycare, enacted in 2006 and in many ways Obamacare's precursor, reduced mortality in low-income Massachusetts counties. These and many other elements of Vaupel's "stream of continuing progress" seem to favor longevity. So does climate change: people live longer in warm climates than cold, and the world is warming.

Popular attention tends to focus on whether what we gulp down determines how long we live: Should people take fish oil and shop for organic probiotic kefir? The way our homes, families, and friendships are organized may matter just as much. Thomas Perls, a professor at Boston Medical Center who analyzes the genomes of centenarians, notes that Seventh-Day Adventists enjoy about a decade more life expectancy than peers of their birth years: "They don't drink or smoke, most are vegetarians, they exercise regularly even when old, and take a true weekly day of rest." But what really strikes Perls about Seventh-Day Adventists is that they maintain large social groups. "Constant interaction with other people can be annoying, but overall seems to keep us engaged with life."

For years, the American social trend has been away from "constant interaction with other people"—fewer two-parent homes, fewer children per home, declining participation in religious and community activities, grandparents living on their own, electronic interaction replacing the face-to-face in everything from work to dating. Prosperity is associated with smaller households, yet the large multigeneration home may be best for long life. There are some indications that the Great Recession increased multigeneration living. This may turn out to boost longevity, at least for a time.

The single best yardstick for measuring a person's likely life span is education. John Rowe, a health-policy professor at Columbia University and a former CEO of Aetna, says, "If someone walked into my office and asked me to predict how long he would live, I would ask two things: What is your age, and how many years of education did you receive?"

Jay Olshansky's latest research suggests that American women with no high-school diploma have experienced relatively small life-span increases since the 1950s, while the life expectancy of highly educated women has soared since then. Today the best-educated Americans live 10 to 14 years longer than the least educated, on average. "Nothing pops out of the data like the link between education and life expectancy," Olshansky says. "The good news is that the share of the American population that is less educated is in gradual decline. The bad news is that lack of education seems even more lethal than it was in the past."

Education does not sync with life expectancy because reading Dostoyevsky lowers blood pressure; college is a proxy for other aspects of a person's life. Compared with the less educated, people with a bachelor's degree have a higher income, smoke less, are less likely to be overweight, and are more likely to follow doctors' instructions. College graduates are more likely to marry and stay married, and marriage is good for your health: the wedded suffer fewer heart attacks and strokes than the single or divorced.

Many of the social developments that improve longevity—better sanitation, less pollution, improved emergency rooms—are provided to all on an egalitarian basis. But today's public high schools are dreadful in many inner-city areas, and broadly across states including California. Legislatures are cutting support for public universities, while the cost of higher education rises faster than inflation. These issues are discussed in terms of fairness; perhaps health should be added as a concern in the debate. If education is the trump card of longevity, the top quintile may pull away from the rest.

Aging and Politics

Society is dominated by the old—old political leaders, old judges. With each passing year, as longevity increases, the intergenerational imbalance worsens. The old demand benefits for which the young must pay, while people in their 20s become disenchanted, feeling that the deck is stacked against them. National debt increases at an alarming rate. Innovation and fresh thinking disappear as energies are devoted to defending current pie-slicing arrangements.

This isn't a prediction about the future of the United States, but rather a description of Japan right now. The Land of the Rising Sun is the world's grayest nation. Already the median age is 45 (in the U.S., by comparison, it is 37), and it will jump to 55 by 2040. As Nicholas Eberstadt, a demographer at the American Enterprise Institute, has noted, median age in the retirement haven of Palm Springs, California, is currently 52 years. Japan is on its way to becoming an entire nation of Palm Springs residents.

The number of Americans 65 or older could reach 108 million in 2050. That's like adding three more Floridas, inhabited entirely by seniors.

Japan's grayness stems from a very low fertility rate—not enough babies to bring down the average age—and strict barriers against immigration. The United States remains a nation of immigrants, and because of the continual inflow of young people, the U.S. median age won't go haywire even as life expectancy rises: the United Nations' "World Population Prospects" estimates that the U.S. median age will rise to 41 by mid-century.

Nonetheless, that Japan is the first major nation to turn gray, and is also the deepest in debt, is not encouraging. Once, Japan was feared as the Godzilla of global trade, but as it grayed, its economy entered a long cycle of soft growth. In 2012 the centrist Democratic Party of Japan, then holding the Diet, backed a tax whose goal was not to pay down what the country owes but merely to slow the rate of borrowing. The party promptly got the heave-ho from voters. Last year Japan's public debt hit $10 trillion, twice the nation's GDP.

Sheila Smith, a Japan specialist at the Council on Foreign Relations, told me, "Young people in Japan have some of the world's worst voter-participation rates. They think the old have the system so rigged in their favor, there's no point in political activity. The young don't seem excited by the future." News accounts of young Japanese becoming so apathetic that they've lost interest in having sex sound hard to believe, but may bear some truth.

Young urban Japanese surely are aware that their elders are ringing up bills to be handed to them, but they're also aware that if funding for the retired is cut, Grandma may want to move into their very small apartment. As life expectancy rises, a Japanese person entering the happy-go-lucky phase of early adulthood may find that parents and grandparents both expect to be looked after. Because the only child is common in Japan's newest generation, a big cast of aging people may turn to one young person for financial support or caregiving or both. Acceding to public borrowing may have become, to young Japanese, a way to keep older generations out of the apartment—even if it means crushing national debt down the road.

That America may become more like Japan—steadily older, with rising debt and declining economic growth—is unsettling. From the second half of the George W. Bush administration until 2013, U.S. national debt more than doubled. The federal government borrowed like there was no tomorrow. The debt binge, for which leaders of both political parties bear blame, was a *prelude* to the retirement of the Baby Boomers. Tomorrow has a way of coming.

Suppose the escalator slows, and conservative assumptions about life expectancy prevail. In a 2009 study, Olshansky projected future demographics under the "hit a wall" scenario. The number of Americans 65 or older, 43 million today, could reach 108 million in 2050—that would be like adding three more Floridas, inhabited entirely by seniors. The "oldest old" cohort, those 85 and older, may increase at least fivefold, to more than 6 percent of the U.S. citizenry. Olshansky projected that by 2050, life expectancy will extend three to eight years past the age used by the Social Security Administration to assess the solvency of its system, while forecasting that by 2050, Medicare and Social Security will rack up between $3.2 trillion and $8.3 trillion in unfunded obligations. (State and local governments

have at least another $1 trillion in unfunded pension liabilities.) These disconcerting numbers flow from the leading analyst who thinks that the life-span increase is slowing down.

When President Obama took office, Social Security's trustees said the current benefits structure was funded until 2037. Now the Congressional Budget Office says the year of reckoning may come as soon as 2031. States may be "funding" their pension obligations using fuzzy math: New York issues promissory notes; Illinois and New Jersey sell debt instruments distressingly similar to junk bonds. Many private pension plans are underfunded, and the Pension Benefit Guaranty Corporation, which on paper appears to insure them, is an accident looking for a place to happen. Twice in the past three years, Congress has voted to allow corporations to delay contributions to pension plans. This causes them to pay more taxes in the present year, giving Congress more to spend, while amplifying problems down the road. Social Security's disability fund may fail as soon as late 2016. Medicare spending is rising faster than Social Security spending, and is harder to predict. Projections show the main component of Medicare, its hospital fund, failing by 2030.

If chronic ailments related to aging can be prevented or significantly delayed, big-ticket line items in Medicare might not go off the rails.

The Congressional Budget Office estimates that over the next decade, *all* federal spending growth will come from entitlements—mainly Social Security and Medicare—and from interest on the national debt. The nonpartisan think tank Third Way has calculated that at the beginning of the Kennedy presidency, the federal government spent $2.50 on public investments—infrastructure, education, and research—for every $1 it spent on entitlements. By 2022, Third Way predicts, the government will spend $5 on entitlements for every $1 on public investments. Infrastructure, education, and research lead to economic growth; entitlement subsidies merely allow the nation to tread water.

If health span can be improved, the costs of aging-related disability may be manageable. Not that long ago, vast sums were spent on iron lungs and sanitariums for treatment of polio: preventing the disease has proved much less expensive than treating it. If chronic ailments related to aging can be prevented or significantly delayed, big-ticket line items in Medicare might not go off the rails.

But if health span does not improve, longer life could make disability in aging an economic crisis. Today, Medicare and

Medicaid spend about $150 billion annually on Alzheimer's patients. Absent progress against aging, the number of people with Alzheimer's could treble by 2050, with society paying as much for Alzheimer's care as for the current defense budget.

Many disabilities associated with advanced years cannot be addressed with pharmaceuticals or high-tech procedures; caregivers are required. Providing personal care for an aged invalid is a task few wish to undertake. Already many lists of careers with the most job openings are headed by "caregiver" or "nurse's aide," professions in which turnover is high.

As longevity increases, so too does the number of living grandparents. Families that once might have had one "oldest old" relative find themselves with three or four, all expecting care or money. At the same time, traditional family trees are being replaced with diagrams that resemble maps of the London Underground. Will children of blended families feel the same obligation to care for aging stepparents as they feel for biological parents? Just the entry of the phrase *birth parent* into the national lexicon suggests the magnitude of the change.

With Japan at the leading edge of lengthening life expectancy, its interest in robotics can be eerie. Foxconn, the Asian electronics giant, is manufacturing for the Japanese market a creepy mechanized thing named Pepper that is intended to provide company for the elderly. More-sophisticated devices may be in store. A future in which large numbers of very old, incapacitated people stare into the distance as robot attendants click and hum would be a bad science-fiction movie if it didn't stand a serious chance of happening.

The Problem of Aging Leadership

As the population ages, so do the political powers that be—and they're aging in place. Computerized block-by-block voting analysis and shameless gerrymandering—Maryland's new sixth congressional district is such a strange shape, it would have embarrassed Elbridge Gerry—lock incumbents into power as never before. Campaign-finance laws appear to promote reform, but in fact have been rigged to discourage challengers. Between rising life expectancy and the mounting power of incumbency, both houses of Congress are the oldest they've ever been: the average senator is 62 years old; the average representative, 57.

A graying Congress would be expected to be concerned foremost with protection of the status quo. Government may grow sclerotic at the very time the aging of the populace demands new ideas. "There's already a tremendous advantage to incumbency," one experienced political operative told me. "As people live longer, incumbents will become more entrenched. Strom Thurmond might not be unusual anymore. Many from both

parties could cling to power too long, freezing out fresh thinking. It won't be good for democracy." The speaker was no starry-eyed radical: he was Karl Rove.

The nine justices on the first Supreme Court sat an average of nine years; the last nine to depart, an average of 27 years.

Now think of the Supreme Court as life expectancy increases. The nine justices on the first Court sat an average of nine years; the last nine to depart, an average of 27 years. John Paul Stevens, the most recent to retire, was a justice for 35 years. If Clarence Thomas lives to the actuarial life expectancy of a male his current age, he could be a Supreme Court justice for 40 years.

The Framers would be aghast at the idea of a small cadre of unelected potentates lording it over the body politic for decades. When the Constitution was written, no one could have anticipated how much life span would increase, nor how much power the Supreme Court would accrue. If democracy is to remain vibrant as society ages, campaign laws must change to help challengers stand a chance versus incumbents, and the Constitution must be amended to impose a term limit on the Supreme Court, so confirmation as a justice stops being a lifetime appointment to royalty.

A New View of Retirement

In 1940, the typical American who reached age 65 would ultimately spend about 17 percent of his or her life retired. Now the figure is 22 percent, and still rising. Yet Social Security remains structured as if longevity were stuck in a previous century. The early-retirement option, added by Congress in 1961—start drawing at age 62, though with lower benefits—is appealing if life is short, but backfires as life span extends. People who opt for early Social Security may reach their 80s having burned through savings, and face years of living on a small amount rather than the full benefit they might have received. Polls show that Americans consistently underestimate how long they will live—a convenient assumption that justifies retiring early and spending now, while causing dependency over the long run.

James Vaupel has warned that refusing to acknowledge longevity's steady march "distorts people's decisions about how much to save and when to retire" and gives "license to politicians to postpone painful adjustments to Social Security." Ronald Reagan was the last president to push through legislation to account for life-span changes. His administration increased the future eligible age of full Social Security benefits from

65 to 66 or 67, depending on one's birth year. Perhaps 99 percent of members of Congress would agree in private that retirement economics must change; none will touch this third rail. Generating more Social Security revenue by lifting the payroll-tax cap, currently $117,000, is the sole politically attractive option, because only the well-to-do would be impacted. But the Congressional Budget Office recently concluded that even this soak-the-rich option is insufficient to prevent insolvency for Social Security. At least one other change, such as later retirement or revised cost-of-living formulas, is required. A fair guess is that the government will do nothing about Social Security reform until a crisis strikes—and then make panicked, ill-considered moves that foresight might have avoided.

Americans may decry government gridlock, but they can't blame anyone else for their own decisions. People's retirement savings simply must increase, though this means financial self-discipline, which Americans are not known for. Beyond that, most individuals will likely need to take a new view of what retirement should be: not a toggle switch—no work at all, after years of full-time labor—but a continuum on which a person gradually downshifts to half-time, then to working now and then. Let's call it the "retirement track" rather than retirement: a phase of continuing to earn and save as full-time work winds down.

Widespread adoption of a retirement track would necessitate changes in public policy and in employers' attitudes. Banks don't think in terms of smallish loans to help a person in the second half of life start a home-based business, but such lending might be vital to a graying population. Many employers are required to continue offering health insurance to those who stay on the job past 65, even though they are eligible for Medicare. Employers' premiums for these workers are much higher than for young workers, which means employers may have a logical reason to want anyone past 65 off the payroll. Ending this requirement would make seniors more attractive to employers.

Many people may find continuing to work but under the lower-stress circumstances of part-time employment to be preferable to a gold watch, then idleness. Gradual downshifting could help ease aging people into volunteer service roles, where there's never any end of things to do. The retirement track could be more appealing than traditional retirement. A longer health span will be essential to making it possible.

Longer Life as Directed Evolution

Understanding the evolutionary biology of aging might help the quest for improved health span. Each cell of the body contains DNA code for a fresh, healthy cell, yet that blueprint is not called on as we grow old. Evolutionists including Alfred Russel Wallace have toyed with the idea of programmed death—the notion that natural selection "wants" old animals to die in order to free up resources for younger animals, which may carry evolved genetic structures. Current thinking tends to hold that rather than trying to make older animals die, natural selection simply has no mechanism to reward longevity.

Felipe Sierra, a researcher at the National Institute on Aging, says, "Evolution doesn't care about you past your reproductive age. It doesn't want you either to live longer or to die, it just doesn't care. From the standpoint of natural selection, an animal that has finished reproducing and performed the initial stage of raising young might as well be eaten by something, since any favorable genetic quality that expresses later in life cannot be passed along." Because a mutation that favors long life cannot make an animal more likely to succeed at reproducing, selection pressure works only on the young.

A generation ago, theorists suspected that menopause was an evolutionary adaptation exclusive to the *Homo* genus—women stop expending energy to bear children so they can care longer for those already born, as mothers and grandmothers. This, the theory goes, increases children's chances of survival, allowing them to pass along family genes. Yet recent research has shown that animals including lions and baboons also go through menopause, which increasingly looks more like a malfunction of aging cells than a quality brought about by selection pressure. As for the idea that grandparents help their grandchildren prosper, favoring longevity—the "grandmother effect"—this notion, too, has fared poorly in research.

"Evolution doesn't care about you past your reproductive age. It doesn't want you either to live longer or to die, it just doesn't care."

The key point is: if nothing that happens after a person reproduces bears on which genes flourish, then nature has never selected for qualities that extend longevity. Evolution favors strength, intelligence, reflexes, sexual appeal; it does not favor keeping an organism running a long time. For example, a growing body needs calcium, so nature selected for the ability to metabolize this element. In later life, calcium causes stiffening of the arteries, a problem that evolution has no mechanism to correct, since hardened arteries do not occur until it's too late for natural selection to side with any beneficial mutation. Testosterone is essential to a youthful man; in an aging man, it can be a factor in prostate cancer. Evolution never selected for a defense against that.

Similar examples abound; the most important may be senescent cells. Natural selection probably favors traits that reduce the risk of cancer, because cancer can strike the young before reproductive age is reached. Senescence doesn't occur until evolution is no longer in play, so natural selection has left all mammal bodies with a defect that leads to aging and death.

If senescence could be slowed, men and women hardly would become immortal. Violence, accidents, and contagious disease still would kill. Even if freed of chronic conditions, eventually our bodies would fail.

But it is not credulous futurism to suppose that drugs or even genetic therapy may alter the human body in ways that extend longevity. Brian Kennedy, of the Buck Institute, notes, "Because natural selection did not improve us for aging, there's a chance for rapid gains. The latest BMWs are close to perfect. How can an engineer improve on them? But the Model T would be easy to improve on now. When young, genetically we are BMWs. In aging, we become Model Ts. The evolutionary improvements haven't started yet."

A Grayer, Quieter, Better Future

In the wild, young animals outnumber the old; humanity is moving toward a society where the elderly outnumber the recently arrived. Such a world will differ from today's in many outward aspects. Warm-weather locations are likely to grow even more popular, though with climate change, warm-weather locations may come to include Buffalo, New York. Ratings for football, which is loud and aggressive, may wane, while baseball and theatergoing enjoy a renaissance. The shift back toward cities, initiated by the educated young, may give way to another car-centric suburban and exurban growth phase.

The university, a significant aspect of the contemporary economy, centuries ago was a place where the fresh-faced would be prepared for a short life; today the university is a place where adults watch children and grandchildren walk to *Pomp and Circumstance.* The university of the future may be one that serves all ages. Colleges will reposition themselves economically as offering just as much to the aging as to the adolescent: courses priced individually for later-life knowledge seekers; lots of campus events of interest to students, parents, and the community as a whole; a pleasant college-town atmosphere to retire near. In decades to come, college professors may address students ranging from age 18 to 80.

Products marketed to senior citizens are already a major presence on television, especially during newscasts and weathercasts. Advertising pitched to the elderly may come to dominate the airwaves, assuming there still is television. But consumerism might decline. Neurological studies of healthy aging people show that the parts of the brain associated with reward-seeking light up less as time goes on. Whether it's hot new fashions or hot-fudge sundaes, older people on the whole don't desire acquisitions as much as the young and middle-aged do. Denounced for generations by writers and clergy, wretched

excess has repelled all assaults. Longer life spans may at last be the counterweight to materialism.

If health span extends, the nuclear family might be seen as less central. Bearing and raising children would no longer be the all-consuming life event.

Deeper changes may be in store as well. People in their late teens to late 20s are far more likely to commit crimes than people of other ages; as society grays, the decline of crime should continue. Violence in all guises should continue downward, too. Horrible headlines from Afghanistan or Syria are exceptions to an overall trend toward less warfare and less low-intensity conflict. As Steven Pinker showed in the 2011 book *Better Angels of Our Nature,* total casualties of combat, including indirect casualties from the economic harm associated with fighting, have been declining, even as the global population has risen. In 1950, one person in 5,000 worldwide died owing to combat; by 2010, this measure was down to one person in 300,000. In recent years, far more people have been killed by car crashes than by battle. Simultaneously, per capita military expenditure has shrunk. My favorite statistic about the world: the Stockholm International Peace Research Institute reports that, adjusting to today's dollars, global per capita military spending has declined by one-third in the past quarter century.

The end of the Cold War, and the proxy conflicts it spawned, is an obvious influence on the subsiding of warfare, as is economic interconnectedness. But aging may also be a factor. Counterculture optics notwithstanding, polls showed that the young were more likely to support the Vietnam War than the old were; the young were more likely to support the 2003 invasion of Iraq, too. Research by John Mueller, a political scientist at Ohio State University, suggests that as people age, they become less enthusiastic about war. Perhaps this is because older people tend to be wiser than the young—and couldn't the world use more wisdom?

Older people also report, to pollsters and psychologists, a greater sense of well-being than the young and middle-aged do. By the latter phases of life, material and romantic desires have been attained or given up on; passions have cooled; and for most, a rich store of memories has been compiled. Among the core contentions of the well-being research of the Princeton University psychologist Daniel Kahneman is that "in the end, memories are all you keep"—what's in the mind matters more than what you own. Regardless of net worth, the old are well off in this sense.

Should large numbers of people enjoy longer lives in decent health, the overall well-being of the human family may rise substantially. In *As You Like It,* Jaques declares, "Man in his time plays many parts, his acts being seven ages." The first five embody promise and power—infant, schoolboy, lover, soldier, and success. The late phases are entirely negative—pantaloon, a period as the butt of jokes for looking old and becoming impotent; then second childishness, a descent into senile dependency. As life expectancy and health span increase, the seven ages may demand revision, with the late phases of life seen as a positive experience of culmination and contentment.

Further along may be a rethinking of life as better structured around friendship than around family, the basic unit of human society since the mists of prehistory. In the brief life of previous centuries, all a man or woman could hope to accomplish was to bear and raise children; enervation followed. Today, life is longer, but an education-based economy requires greater investments in children—contemporary parents are still assisting offspring well into a child's 20s. As before, when the child-rearing finally is done, decline commences.

But if health span extends, the nuclear family might be seen as less central. For most people, bearing and raising children would no longer be the all-consuming life event. After child-rearing, a phase of decades of friendships could await—potentially more fulfilling than the emotionally charged but fast-burning bonds of youth. A change such as this might have greater ramifications for society than changes in work schedules or health-care economics.

Regardless of where increasing life expectancy leads, the direction will be into the unknown—for society and for the natural world. Felipe Sierra, the researcher at the National Institute on Aging, puts it this way: "The human ethical belief that death should be postponed as long as possible does not exist in nature—from which we are now, in any case, diverging."

Critical Thinking

1. What will be the social impacts of developing technologies which slow down the aging process and enable most people to live to 100?

2. How will retirement and work life adjust to much longer and healthier lives?

3. How will an older population alter our culture?

Internet References

New American Studies Web
https://blogs.commons.georgetown.edu/vkp/

Social Science Information Gateway
http://www.ariadne.ac.uk/issue2/sosig

Sociology–Study Sociology Online
http://edu.learnsoc.org/

Sociology Web Resources
http://www.mhhe.com/socscience/sociology/resources/index.htm

Sociosite
http://www.topsite.com/goto/sociosite.net

Socioweb
http://www.topsite.com/goto/socioweb.com

GREGG EASTERBROOK is a contributing editor of *The Atlantic*. He is the author of *The Leading Indicators* and *The King of Sports: Football's Impact on America*.

Article   Prepared by: Kurt Finsterbusch, *University of Maryland, College Park*

GMO Scientists Could Save Us All from Hunger, If We Let Them

The World Is Getting Hungrier. Fortunately, We're Also Getting Smarter.

TOM PARRETT

Learning Outcomes

After reading this article, you will be able to:

- Explain why Tom Parrett believes that the world is about to have a second green revolution.

- Explain how the genetically modified organism (GMO) processes work.

- Describe and explain several successes and failures of genetic modification.

A Nebraska Cornhusker frets as he surveys his drought-stunted crop. A Nigerian yam farmer digs up shrunken tubers. A Costa Rican coffee baron lays off hundreds of workers because a fungus has spoiled his harvest. I planted cherry trees in upstate New York last spring. One summer morning, they were denuded by Japanese beetles.

Such disasters are increasingly common on a planet buffeted by climate change and worldwide commerce, where heat burns crops, soil has been ruined by over-farming and drought, and bugs ride across oceans to feast on defenseless plants. Agronomists have been working on these problems for years, but the rapid population growth of humans makes overcoming these challenges increasingly urgent. If we can't feed the world, it will eventually feed on us.

The United Nations and experts say global food production will have to double by 2050, at which point the world population is expected to have grown from 7 billion today to well beyond 9 billion. That's just 35 years away, and there will be no new arable land then. In fact, there probably will be less. For example, 73 million acres of arable land in the U.S. were lost between 2002 and 2012, according to the U.S. Department of Agriculture (USDA); more was certainly made fallow during the last several years of severe drought. Looking ahead, growing conditions will only get harsher.

The solution, though, appears to be on the way: In 2012, a new tool was invented that revolutionizes how scientists can examine—and manipulate—plant genetic processes. It's called CRISPR-Cas9, and unlike its predecessors in the world of genetic modification, it is highly specific, allowing scientists to zero in on a single gene and turn it on or off, remove it or exchange it for a different gene. Early signs suggest this tool will be an F-16 jet fighter compared with the Stone Age spear of grafting, the traditional, painstaking means of breeding a new plant hybrid. Biologists and geneticists are confident it can help them build a second Green Revolution—if we'll let them.

"We now have a very easy, very fast and very efficient technique for rewriting the genome," said one of its inventors, Jennifer Doudna of the University of California, Berkeley, when the Innovative Genomics Initiative was launched in 2014. "[It] allows us to do experiments that have been impossible before." The speed and simplicity of CRISPR have momentous implications for agriculture: The process could lead to plants that can withstand what an increasingly overheated nature has in store. It could also result in a more nutritious yield, from less plant. Researchers have glommed on to it—they've already published more than 150 related scientific papers, and the publication rate is accelerating. "It's tough to keep up with all the papers that are coming out," says Joyce Van Eck, who runs a lab focused on the study of genetics-based crop improvement at Cornell University's Boyce Thompson Institute. "The field is exploding."

Pull on DNA's Zipper

CRISPR stands for—brace yourself—Clustered Regularly Interspaced Short Palindromic Repeats. The name comes from a trick that bacteria use to protect themselves from lethal viruses and phages, little cellular saboteurs. The "palindromic repeats" (gene sequences that read the same from either end) are immune response elements, genetic code the bacteria copy and incorporate from invading viruses so that, if they return, they can be easily identified. It's a bit like posting an FBI wanted poster or splashing enemy soldiers with glow-in-the-dark paint.

The technique requires two accomplices: molecules called guide RNA and a protein from a class labeled Cas. The most effective one found so far is Cas9. RNA has long been known to be the vehicle DNA needs to convey its message. In a cell, Cas9 prepares the chemical environment around a DNA molecule for interaction, then spurs RNA to find the selected section of DNA. Once it does, the RNA will guide the Cas9 into the DNA, where the Cas9 unzips DNA's double helix and does one of three things, depending on the chemical instructions scientists provide: It blunts this section's ability to work, stimulates it to go to work or excises selected genes. Then the cell's repair crew zips the DNA back up.

The process can easily modify plant DNA without changing the plant's essence—except to make it tastier, more nutritious, quicker to market, easier to ship, machine-pickable, less needy of water and/or able to flourish in a heat wave. And we can do it for big companies and small, the world at large and isolated communities.

In the old days, relying on hit-or-miss natural processes to breed plants took many years. Norman Borlaug, father of the first Green Revolution—a hugely successful effort to improve food-crop productivity in poor countries that began in the 1940s and eventually doubled or even quadrupled what many plants could produce—needed almost two decades to create a better wheat variety. With CRISPR-Cas9, we can compress that development cycle to a few days or weeks.

This is partly because we can now process, store and compare vast quantities of genetic data quickly and cheaply. The upshot for scientists has been the rapid growth in knowledge of cell chemistry and genes, and most important, our ballooning database of many species' genomes.

Ideally, we would know everything about the genome of all our favorite produce staples, down to the placement of every single gene. And this cataloging is happening with astonishing speed. Researchers at Kansas State University have sequenced the first and toughest of wheat's 20 chromosomes—and that one chromosome is far more complex than the entire rice genome. They say they'll be able to do the next 19 in three years. The result will be complete knowledge of the genome of the world's third-most cultivated crop, the one with the most

protein and arguably the grain that is most versatile as a food and cooking source.

Then, the amazing flexibility of CRISPR-Cas9 can be brought to bear. The idea is to use the process to replace a segment of a plant's genetic sequence entirely, a bit like exchanging a chunk of Lego blocks, to improve specific plant behavior. Imagine a wheat strain that thrives at the edge of a salt marsh in tropical Ecuador. Compared with Iowa's amber waves of grain, it's a runt that produces small, bitter kernels. But by adding bits of the Ecuadorian genome to the American variety, scientists make a strain that is more salt-tolerant and still provides a big yield. Both dry, salty Ecuador and dry, salty America would gain a better plant.

It's critical to note this has nothing to do with creating a new species. CRISPR-Cas9 is a tool that helps us adapt plants to new environments by fine-tuning their own genetic traits, using their own genes from plants they'd naturally breed with, such as their wild versions. As the tool targets a tiny segment of a plant's DNA, the plant stays the same species—technically, even the same genotype. As scientists see it, the technology respects a plant species for its evolutionary capacity to thrive over eons, while helping it evolve more quickly to adjust to today's environment. We are only putting our foot to the accelerator of natural plant processes.

Beautiful Tomatoes

Caution and guidelines are certainly called for. The early results of CRISPR-Cas9 tests have not been completely predictable. A published number is up to an 80 percent success rate, high for experimental stuff but not high enough for commercial applications. What can happen is "off-target DNA interactions," where "you accidentally modify a very similar sequence elsewhere in the genome," says Cornell's Van Eck. This was also a big problem in earlier genetic engineering technologies, which basically flooded a plant's genome with compounds, trusting that some would stick. CRISPR-Cas9 is comparatively precise, but some scientists remain cautious. The technology could and probably will get better; different versions of CRISPR-Cas9 could be developed, or scientists could find a new enzyme that does what CRISPR-Cas9 does more precisely.

On the other hand, Van Eck and her colleagues have proved that what they already have works beautifully with the tomato, a plant that's become "a model species, like the white rat in animal studies," she says. Soon she and others in the field will be working to improve the tomato's hardiness and disease resistance, with results that will come with what she terms "drummer-like precision"—the exactitude of, say, Elvin Jones or Charlie Watts—"because we can go in and target exactly the areas we want." Other early advances include a new version of rice that is more adaptable and has the ability to photosynthesize faster and more efficiently. That portends a future where, thanks to CRISPR-Cas9, scientists are at the rice control console, able to consider the available inputs—water, soil nutrients, temperature—and make adjustments to better control the outputs: productivity, nutritional value, resilience. All that's needed is for consumers to buy in.

Suspicions Trump Science

Biotech crops are already well-established around the world. The U.S. has approved about 100 genetically modified plants for use in agriculture. Virtually all cotton in India, a vital economic staple for the country, is genetically modified (GM), as is 90 percent of cotton grown in China. Four out of every five harvested soybeans on earth are genetically modified. Corn worldwide is 35 percent genetically modified. Bangladesh is considering a GM eggplant that could double its harvest by protecting it from worms. Food writer Mark Bittman recently pointed out that we've been happily eating harmless genetically modified, virus-resistant papayas for years, and that's Mr. Natural talking.

But some countries are balking. Mexico, where maize was first domesticated, must now import it to meet local demand because activists there will not allow genetically modified organism hybrids. Mexico's maize growers get yields 38 percent lower than the world average and three times below the U.S., where 90 percent of the maize crop is an insect-resistant GMO hybrid. Mexico's fields are beset by such crop ravishers as the corn earworm, black cutworm, and fall armyworm, which cost the country up to half its crops and incite farmers to spray their land with thousands of tons of chemical insecticides.

The European Union has approved just one genetically modified crop, a type of maize used for animal feed. The reasons are political and bureaucratic: A majority of member countries must approve a biotech plant, and anti-GMO sentiment runs strong in places where phrases like *naturel* and *natürliche* are more about what's been done for centuries than what it actually means for something to exist in or be caused by nature.

This genetic work has not just found detractors but also aroused fierce partisans. Take Golden Rice, for example. It's basic rice, but modified to produce its own vitamin A, potentially saving up to 2.8 million children a year from blindness and a million of them from death. Yet it sits in labs, unused. The notion of GMOs has spooked environmental groups such as Greenpeace, which has resisted GMOs with violent action, including destroying an experimental Golden Rice field last year in the Philippines. This despite the fact that Golden Rice is being offered to the world by a nonprofit, with no commercial stipulations, and is likely to save many lives.

The scientific consensus for the safety of GMOs is overwhelming. A recent Pew poll found that 88 percent of U.S. scientists think GMO technology is harmless. By contrast, only 33 percent of civilians agreed. A recent 7-1 U.S. Supreme Court decision concurred that genetically modified alfalfa is safe. The USDA, after arduous review, has allowed genetically modified sugar beets. Several independent studies so far have tested the effects of varieties of genetically modified crops on animals. In 2012, a meta-analysis of 12 long-term studies and 12 multigenerational studies was published in *Food and Chemical Toxicology;* it concluded "that GM plants are nutritionally equivalent to their non-GM counterparts and can be safely used in food and feed." And according to the independent organization Biofortified, more than a hundred such studies have been performed, with no harmful results found.

Anti-GMO activists tend to cite two scientific studies, which both involve rats, GM corn and the pesticide Roundup. Both were undertaken by French scientist Gilles-Éric Séralini and found that the rats fed the GM corn were more likely to die prematurely than a control group. But the journal that originally accepted the studies, *Food and Chemical Toxicology,* withdrew them, and every major scientific and food-safety organization in Europe has condemned them. Among the problems with the studies was that the strain of rats used in the test are cancer-prone—80 percent routinely develop tumors. "All we are seeing in these results is due to random variation in a poorly controlled experiment," Ian Musgrave, of the University of Adelaide, in South Australia, told *Forbes* when the studies were retracted.

Chances are, you've heard of Roundup (active ingredient: glyphosate). That's because it's the second in the supposed double punch that agrochemical company Monsanto has allegedly been throwing for years to create a cycle of financial dependence among farmers worldwide. Monsanto produces Roundup. Since 1996, it has also produced Roundup Ready crops, including soy, corn, and alfalfa, all genetically modified to be resistant to the herbicide—which means it can be used on fields to get rid of encroaching plant life without harming the crops. That's great for farmers. But these Roundup Ready seeds have a dark side: farmers who buy them sign an agreement saying they will not buy save any seeds from the resulting crop. In other words, they have to buy new seeds every year from Monsanto. This has all been incredibly lucrative for the company; it currently has a third of the $40 billion global seed business. The Monsanto/Roundup controversy continues to inflame passions: Among the many concerns that have been raised is the possibility that genetically modified DNA from the Roundup Ready plants might be contaminating non-GMO food supplies. Then there's the fact that glyphosate might be a health hazard—the World Health Organization says it is a probable carcinogen.

Meanwhile, "No GMO" is now being embraced by consumer brands; the ascendant "fast-casual" chain Chipotle posts just such a sign in its restaurants. It makes sense: If over two-thirds of Americans think GMOs are unhealthy, declaring yourself GMO-free is a lucrative proposition. Local governments are also weighing in. Vermont now demands that all GMO foods sold there be labeled as such. Two rural counties in Oregon have banned GMO crops within their borders.

Yet despite the conventional wisdom, startup money for GMO development in the U.S. and elsewhere is flowing like it's coming out of a fire hose, first for biomedical applications, from venture capitalists as well as traditional pharmaceutical companies such as GlaxoSmithKline, Celgene, and Novartis. U.S. startups include Caribou Biosciences, Editas, Intellia Therapeutics, CRISPR Therapeutics and CRISPR-Plant.

In China, where rural populations react to GMOs with dread and anger, the only genetically modified crop currently grown is Bittman's papaya. But China's mighty science establishment has thrown its weight behind genetic work, with 400 labs and 30,000 researchers. Labs there have already sequenced the genes of 3,000 varieties of rice, in preparation for matching them against one another to find the best traits for nutrition, yield and resistance to environmental stressors. One result someday soon will be what researchers have dubbed "green super rice." Even if the Chinese government can't sell genetically modified crops to its own people, there's a good chance the poor populations of Southeast Asia, Africa, and India will welcome the nourishment. Gengyun Zhang, head of life sciences for BGI, China's giant state-sponsored genetic engineering center, recently said, "With today's technology, I have no doubt that we can feed the world."

Critical Thinking

1. What is the fight over GMOs all about?
2. How could GMO scientists double the world's food supply?
3. Where do you stand on the GMO debate?

Internet References

New American Studies Web
https://blogs.commons.georgetown.edu/vkp/

Social Science Information Gateway
http://www.ariadne.ac.uk/issue2/sosig

Sociology—Study Sociology Online
http://edu.learnsoc.org/

Sociology Web Resources
http://www.mhhe.com/socscience/sociology/resources/index.htm

Sociosite
http://www.topsite.com/goto/sociosite.net

Socioweb
http://www.topsite.com/goto/socioweb.com

Article   Prepared by: Kurt Finsterbusch, *University of Maryland, College Park*

Conservative Climate Panel Warns World Faces "Breakdown of Food Systems" and More Violent Conflict

Joe Romm

Learning Outcomes

After reading this article, you will be able to:

- Understand that although the IPCC is often attacked, it still is the most authoritative report on global warming and probably the most reliable general report. This article by Romm presents some of the most salient findings of the IPCC report, although he cherry picks the scariest. Know what the pessimists draw from this report.

- Know what risks may be brought on by global warming.

- Separate what are highly speculative and what are highly probable consequences of global warming.

Humanity's choice (via IPCC): Aggressive climate action ASAP minimizes future warming. Continued inaction results in catastrophic levels of warming, 9°F over much of U.S.

The U.N. Intergovernmental Panel on Climate Change (IPCC) has issued its second of four planned reports examining the state of climate science. This one summarizes what the scientific literature says about "Impacts, Adaptation, and Vulnerability". As with every recent IPCC report, it is super-cautious to a fault and yet still incredibly alarming.

It warns that we are doing a bad job of dealing with the climate change we've experienced to date: "Impacts from recent climate-related extremes, such as heat waves, droughts, floods, cyclones, and wildfires, reveal significant vulnerability and exposure of some ecosystems and many human systems to current climate variability."

It warns of the dreaded RFCs ("reasons for concern"—I'm not making this acronym up), such as "breakdown of food systems linked to warming, drought, flooding, and precipitation variability and extremes." You might call them RFAs ("reasons for alarm" or "reasons for action"). Indeed, in recent years, "several periods of rapid food and cereal price increases following climate extremes in key producing regions indicate a sensitivity of current markets to climate extremes among other factors." So warming-driven drought and extreme weather have *already* begun to reduce food security. Now imagine adding another 2 billion people to feed while we are experiencing five times as much warming this century as we did last century!

No surprise, then, that climate change will "prolong existing, and create new, poverty traps, the latter particularly in urban areas and emerging hotspots of hunger." And it will "increase risks of violent conflicts in the form of civil war and inter-group violence"—though for some reason that doesn't make the list of RFCs.

In short, "We're all sitting ducks," as IPCC author and Princeton Prof. Michael Oppenheimer put it to the AP.

An Overly Cautious Report

As grim as the Working Group 2 report on impacts is, it explicitly has very little to say about the catastrophic impacts and vulnerability in the business as usual case where the Earth warms 4–5°C [7–9°F]—and it has nothing to say about even higher warming, which the latest science suggests we are headed toward.

The report states:

- "Relatively few studies have considered impacts on cropping systems for scenarios where global mean temperatures increase by 4°C [7°F] or more.
- ". . . few quantitative estimates [of global annual economic losses] have been completed for additional warming around 3°C [5.4°F] or above."

D'oh! You may wonder why hundreds of the world leading climate experts spend years and years doing climate science and climate projections, but don't bother actually looking at the impacts of merely staying on our current carbon pollution emissions path—let alone looking at the plausible worst-case scenario (which is typically the basis for risk-reducing public policy, such as military spending).

Partly it's because, until recently, climate scientists had naively expected the world to act with a modicum of sanity and avoid at all costs catastrophic warming of 7°F let alone the unimaginable 10°F (or higher) warming we are headed toward. Partly it's because, as a recent paper explained, "climate scientists are biased toward overly cautious estimates, erring on the side of less rather than more alarming predictions."

On top of the overly cautious nature of most climate scientists, we have the overly cautious nature of the IPCC. As the New York Times explained when the IPCC released the Working Group 1 report last fall:

"The I.P.C.C. is far from alarmist—on the contrary, it is a highly conservative organization," said Stefan Rahmstorf of the Potsdam Institute for Climate Impact Research in Germany, whose papers on sea level were among those that got discarded. "That is not a problem as long as the users of the I.P.C.C. reports are well aware of this. The conservatism is built into its consensus structure, which tends to produce a lowest common denominator on which a large number of scientists can agree."

That's why the latest report is full of these sorts of bombshells couched in euphemism and buried deep in the text:

By 2100 for the high-emission scenario RCP8.5, the combination of high temperature and humidity in some areas for parts of the year is projected to compromise normal human activities, including growing food or working outdoors.

Yes, "compromise." A clearer word would be "obliterate." And the "high-emission scenario RCP8.5"—an atmospheric concentration of carbon dioxide of about 936 parts per million—is in fact where we are headed by 2100 or soon thereafter on our current do-little path.

Bottom line: We are at risk of making large parts of the planet's currently arable and populated land virtually uninhabitable for much of the year—and irreversibly so for hundreds of years.

The Risk of Creating More Failed States

Here are two important conclusions from the report that the IPCC strangely puts 13 pages apart from each other:

1. **Violent conflict increases vulnerability to climate change.** Large-scale violent conflict harms assets that facilitate adaptation, including infrastructure, institutions, natural resources, social capital, and livelihood opportunities.
2. **Climate change can indirectly increase risks of violent conflicts in the form of civil war and intergroup violence by amplifying well-documented drivers of these conflicts such as poverty and economic shocks.** Multiple lines of evidence relate climate variability to these forms of conflict.

Separately, they are both worrisome. But together, they are catastrophic. Climate change makes violent conflict more likely—and violent conflict makes a country more vulnerable to climate change. So climate change appears poised to help create many more of the most dangerous situations on Earth: failed states. Syria may be turning into an early example.

The High Cost of Inaction

The IPCC's discussion of economic costs is equally muddled:

". . . the incomplete estimates of global annual economic losses for additional temperature increases of ~2°C are between 0.2 percent and 2.0 percent of income. Losses are more likely than not to be greater, rather than smaller, than this range. . . . Losses accelerate with greater warming, but few quantitative estimates have been completed for additional warming around 3°C or above."

It would have been nice if the IPCC had mentioned at this point that keeping additional temperature increases to ~2°C requires very aggressive efforts to slash carbon pollution starting now. As it is, the deniers, confusionists, and easily confused can (incorrectly) assert that this first sentence means global economic losses from climate change will be low. Again, that's only if we act now.

As Climate Science Watch noted Saturday, "Other estimates suggest the high impacts on global GDP with warming of 4°C (For example the Stern Review found impacts of 5–20% of global GDP)."

The costs of even higher warming, which, again, would be nothing more than business as usual, rise exponentially. Indeed, we've known for years that traditional climate cost-benefit analyses are "unusually misleading"—as Harvard economist Martin Weitzman warned colleagues, "we may be deluding ourselves and others." Again, that's because the IPCC is basically a best case analysis—while it largely ignores the business-as-usual case and completely ignores the worst case.

Remember, earlier this month, during the press call for the vastly better written climate report from the American Association for the Advancement of Science, a leading expert on risk analysis explained, "You really do have to think about worst-case scenarios when you are thinking about risk management. When it's a risk management problem, thinking about worst-case scenarios is not alarmist—it's just part of the job. And those worst-case scenarios are part of what drives the price."

So where are we now? The first IPCC report last fall revealed we are as certain that humans are dramatically changing the planet's climate as we are that smoking causes cancer. It found the best estimate is that humans are responsible for *all* of the warming we have suffered since 1950. It warned that on the continued do-little path, we are facing total warming from pre-industrial levels by 2100 headed toward 4°C (7°F), with much more rapid sea level rise than previously reported, and the prospects of large-scale collapse of the permafrost, with resultant release of massive amounts of greenhouse gases.

Now, "the IPCC's new report should leave the world in no doubt about the scale and immediacy of the threat to human survival, health, and wellbeing," which in turn shows the need for "radical and transformative change" in our energy system, as the British Medical Journal editorialized.

Every few years, the world's leading climate scientists and governments identify the ever-worsening symptoms. They give us the same diagnosis, but with ever-growing certainty. And they lay out an ever-grimmer prognosis if we keep ignoring their straightforward and *relatively* inexpensive treatment. Will we act on the science in time?

Critical Thinking

1. Evaluate how important it is to act strongly now to minimize the effects of global warming.

2. Try to determine how to make policies when conditions are uncertain and changing.

3. Is risk adversive the best policy with respect to global warming?

Create Central

www.mhhe.com/createcentral

Internet References

National Center for Policy Analysis
   www.ncpa.org

New American Studies Web
   www.georgetown.edu/crossroads/asw

Sociology—Study Sociology Online
   http://edu.learnsoc.org

Sociology Web Resources
   http://www.mhhe.com/socscience/sociology/resources/index.htm

Sociosite
   http://www.topsite.com/goto/sociosite.net

Socioweb
   http://www.topsite.com/goto/socioweb.com

Romm, Joe, "Conservative Climate Panel Warns World Faces 'Breakdown of Food System' and More Violent Conflict," ThinkProgress.org, March 30, 2014.

Article   Prepared by: Kurt Finsterbusch, *University of Maryland, College Park*

The Moral Case for Designer Babies

RONALD BAILEY

Learning Outcomes

After reading this article, you will be able to:

- Develop your personal view about genetic engineering of embryos.

- Try to provide the basis on which policies about genetic engineering should be determined.

- Understand why religious and secular groups are likely to feel differently about genetic engineering of children.

Should parents be allowed to know if their fetus will get Alzheimer's?

Should prospective parents seek information about gene variants that increase the risk their children will develop diseases as adults? Should physicians provide that information?

Some bioethicists believe that such prebirth testing is wrong, arguing that the information could stigmatize kids or lead parents to terminate pregnancies of genetically at-risk fetuses. Children, they contend, have a right to an "open future" unburdened by the knowledge of their genetic predispositions for adult onset illnesses.

Consider the situation of Amanda and Bradley Kalinsky, as reported on the front page of *The New York* Times in February. Amanda Kalinsky tested positive for the gene that produces Gerstmann–Straussler–Scheinker (GSS) disease, a form of early onset dementia. Several family members, including her father, had already succumbed to the sickness. When she found out that she was a carrier, she initially vowed never to have children.

But then Amanda and her husband learned that they could use preimplantation genetic diagnosis of their embryos to avoid passing the GSS gene to their kids. Fertility clinic specialists induced her to produce several eggs that were removed and then fertilized with her husband's sperm. The resulting embryos were tested for the gene, and only those that did not have it were implanted in her womb.

The happy result is that the Kalinskys are the parents of three children—3-year-old twins, Ava and Cole, and 9-month-old Tatum—who have been spared the prospect of suffering the disease that is likely to kill their mother. The cost for the first round of in vitro and testing was about $20,000, which the Kalinskys paid out of pocket. "I would travel that road a million times over if I had to," Amanda told the *Times,* "because in the end I was given the privilege of being their mother."

In the *Times* article, the Yeshiva University bio-ethicist David Wasserman argued that discarding the GSS-gene embryos is akin to concluding that people like Amanda Kalinsky should have never been born. But decisions about who should be born ought not to be placed in the hands of ethicists or physicians; they should be left up to the people whose lives and values are actually on the line.

For Kalinsky, the prospect of passing on her GSS gene was frightening enough that she initially ruled out reproducing. Preimplantation genetic diagnosis enabled her and her husband to have children that they wouldn't have otherwise. In either scenario, the child with the GSS gene was not going to be born; this way, there are three new humans on the planet.

The Kalinskys were focusing on a single gene. But now a new, much more comprehensive whole-genome screening test is enabling physicians to identify disease risks that parents might not have any reason to suspect, such as genes increasing the possibility of breast cancer or Alzheimer's disease. The new test sequences a fetus's genome based on DNA it sheds into its mother's bloodstream. So researchers can now reveal genetic predispositions ranging from trivial characteristics like eye color and propensity to baldness to the risk of cancer.

Is it ethical for physicians to sequence a fetus's genome and then tell parents what the genetic screening test uncovers?

Yes, argues Ignatia B. Van den Veyver of Baylor College in the January 2014 issue of *Prenatal Diagnosis*. Among other arguments, Van den Veyver wonders "whether we infringe autonomy by shielding information that may allow parents and young adults to make decisions about their future that take into consideration all aspects of their current or future health," adding: "It is not well established that not providing this predictive information is the only direction to preserve the right to an open future."

Indeed not. Apparently, what some bioethicists mean by "open future" is one in which both parents and children are kept ignorant of the ways their complement of genes may expose them to medical risks.

Prenatal whole-genome sequencing will also provide parents with information about their prospective child's genetic susceptibility to illnesses like lung cancer, arteriosclerosis, and diabetes. Armed with such genomic knowledge, mothers and fathers could make sure that they don't smoke around their kid and later explain why it's a really bad idea for him or her to take up a tobacco habit. Warned in advance about their child's heightened risk of diabetes, parents could devise a diet and exercise regimen aimed at preventing its onset.

The American Medical Association (AMA) got it right when it offered ethical guidance to its members on prenatal genetic screening way back in 1994. "If prenatal diagnosis is performed, the principle of patient autonomy requires that all medically relevant information generated from fetal tests be passed along to the parent or parents," the AMA declared. "While the physician should generally discourage requests for information about benign genetic traits, the physician may not ethically refuse to pass along any requested information in his or her possession. The final decision as to what information is deemed appropriate for disclosure can only fall to the parents, informed by the facts and recommendations presented to them by their physician."

More recently, in the January 16 *New England Journal of Medicine*, Ilana Yurkiewicz of Harvard Medical School, Lisa Soleymani Lehmann of Brigham and Women's Hospital, and Bruce Korf of the University of Alabama at Birmingham argue that it is ethical to provide parents with prenatal whole-genome sequencing information, because it is "a basic right of reproductive choice and parental autonomy; people may choose when, with whom, and how to reproduce, and they have the right to data that may inform these decisions." The trio also notes that women in the United States do not have to provide a reason for obtaining an abortion, so it is "difficult to justify restricting abortion in the case of a well-defined reason, such as genetic disease."

The researchers reject the notion that genetic ignorance is somehow liberating. "Instead of limiting a child's potential future, knowledge of genetic risks can offer a greater opportunity to inform possibilities for a good life," they point out.

And that's the essential point. Whatever some bioethicists might believe, autonomy is never enhanced by ignorance.

Critical Thinking

1. Evaluate the degree that genetic modification of embryos should be left to parents and the extent that society should set rules about this.

2. How would you have been improved by genetic engineering?

3. Assuming that the technology will improve, how would you act as a parent with respect to genetic engineering?

Create Central

www.mhhe.com/createcentral

Internet References

National Council on Family Relations (NCFR)
www.ncfr.com

National Institutes of Health (NIH)
www.nih.gov

New American Studies Web
www.georgetown.edu/crossroads/asw

Parenting and Families
www.cyfc.umn.edu/features/index.html

Sociology—Study Sociology Online
http://edu.learnsoc.org

Sociology Web Resources
http://www.mhhe.com/socscience/sociology/resources/index.htm

Sociosite
http://www.topsite.com/goto/sociosite.net

Socioweb
http://www.topsite.com/goto/socioweb.com

Science Correspondent **RONALD BAILEY** is the author of Liberation Biology (Prometheus).

Article   Prepared by: Kurt Finsterbusch, *University of Maryland, College Park*

How Innovation Could Save the Planet

Ideas may be our greatest natural resource, says a computer scientist and futurist. He argues that the world's most critical challenges—including population growth, peak oil, climate change, and limits to growth—could be met by encouraging innovation.

RAMEZ NAAM

Learning Outcomes

After reading this article, you will be able to:

- Understand both the benefits and the costs of long-term economic progress.

- Evaluate Ramez Naam's thesis that "Innovation could save the planet."

- Notice the many specific ideas and innovations that could address the major problems.

The Best of Times: Unprecedented Prosperity

There are many ways in which we are living in the most wonderful age ever. We can imagine we are heading toward a sort of science-fiction Utopia, where we are incredibly rich and incredibly prosperous, and the planet is healthy. But there are other reasons to fear that we're headed toward a dystopia of sorts.

On the positive side, life expectancy has been rising for the last 150 years, and faster since the early part of the twentieth century in the developing world than it has in the rich world. Along with that has come a massive reduction in poverty. The most fundamental empowerer of humans—education—has also soared, not just in the rich world, but throughout the world.

Another great empowerer of humanity is connectivity: Access to information and access to communication both have soared. The number of mobile phones on the planet was effectively zero in the early 1990s, and now it's in excess of 4 billion. More than three-quarters of humanity, in the span of one generation, have gotten access to connectivity that, as my friend Peter Diamand is likes to say, is greater than any president before 1995 had. A reasonably well-off person in India or in Nigeria has better access to information than Ronald Reagan did during most of his career.

With increased connectivity has come an increase in democracy. As people have gotten richer, more educated, more able to access information, and more able to communicate, they have demanded more control over the places where they live. The fraction of nations that are functional democracies is at an all-time high in this world—more than double what it was in the 1970s, with the collapse of the Soviet Union.

Economically, the world is a more equal place than it has been in decades. In the West, and especially in the United States, we hear a lot about growing inequality, but on a global scale, the opposite is true. As billions are rising out of poverty around the world, the global middle classes are catching up with the global rich.

In many ways, this is the age of the greatest human prosperity, freedom, and potential that has ever been on the face of this planet. But in other ways, we are facing some of the largest risks ever.

The Worst of Times: The Greatest Risks

At its peak, the ancient Mayan city of Tikal was a metropolis, a city of 200,000 people inside of a civilization of about 20 million people. Now, if you walk around any Mayan city, you see mounds of dirt. That's because these structures were all abandoned by about the mid-900s A.D. We know now what happened: The Mayan civilization grew too large. It overpopulated.

To feed themselves, they had to convert forest into farmland. They chopped down all of the forest. That, in turn, led to soil erosion. It also worsened drought, because trees, among other things, trap moisture, and create a precipitation cycle.

When that happened, and was met by some normal (not human caused) climate change, the Mayans found they didn't have enough food. They exhausted their primary energy supply, which is food. That in turn led to more violence in their society and ultimately to a complete collapse.

The greatest energy source for human civilization today is fossil fuels. Among those, none is more important than oil. In 1956, M. King Hubbert looked at production in individual oil fields and predicted that the United States would see the peak of its oil production in 1970 or so, and then drop. His prediction largely came true: Oil production went up but did peak in the 1970s, then plummeted.

Oil production has recently gone up in the United States a little bit, but it's still just barely more than half of what it was in its peak in the 1970s.

Hubbert also predicted that the global oil market would peak in about 2000, and for a long time he looked very foolish. But it now has basically plateaued. Since 2004, oil production has increased by about 4 percent, whereas in the 1950s it rose by about 4 percent every three months.

We haven't hit a peak; oil production around the world is still rising a little bit. It's certainly not declining, but we do appear to be near a plateau; supply is definitely rising more slowly than demand. Though there's plenty of oil in the ground, the oil that remains is in smaller fields, further from shore, under lower pressure, and harder to pump out.

Water is another resource that is incredibly precious to us. The predominant way in which we use water is through the food that we eat: 70 percent of the freshwater that humanity uses goes into agriculture.

The Ogallala Aquifer, the giant body of freshwater under the surface of the Earth in the Great Plains of the United States, is fossil water left from the melting and the retreat of glaciers in the end of the last Ice Age, 12,000–14,000 years ago. Its refill time is somewhere between 5,000 and 10,000 years from normal rainfall. Since 1960, we've drained between a third and a half of the water in this body, depending on what estimate you look at. In some areas, the water table is dropping about three feet per year.

If this was a surface lake in the United States or Canada, and people saw that happening, they'd stop it. But because it's out of sight, it's just considered a resource that we can tap. And indeed, in the north Texas area, wells are starting to fail already, and farms are being abandoned in some cases, because they can't get to the water that they once did.

Perhaps the largest risk of all is climate change. We've increased the temperature of the planet by about 2°F in the last 130 years, and that rate is accelerating. This is primarily because of the carbon dioxide we've put into the atmosphere, along with methane and nitrous oxide. CO_2 levels, now at over 390 parts per million, are the highest they've been in about 15 million years. Ice cores go back at least a million years, and we know that they're the highest they've been in that time. Historically, when CO_2 levels are high, temperature is also high. But also, historically, in the lifetime of our species, we've actually never existed as human beings while CO_2 levels have been this high.

For example, glaciers such as the Bear and Pedersen in Alaska have disappeared just since 1920. As these glaciers melt, they produce water that goes into the seas and helps to raise sea levels. Over the next century, the seas are expected to rise about 3 to 6 feet. Most of that actually will not be melting glaciers; it's thermal expansion: As the ocean gets warmer, it gets a little bit bigger.

But 3 to 6 feet over a century doesn't sound like that big a deal to us, so we think of that as a distant problem. The reality is that there's a more severe problem with climate change: its impact on the weather and on agriculture.

In 2003, Europe went through its worst heat wave since 1540. Ukraine lost 75 percent of its wheat crop. In 2009, China had a once-in-a-century level drought; in 2010 they had another once-in-a-century level drought. That's twice. Wells that had given water continuously since the fifteenth century ran dry. When those rains returned, when the water that was soaked up by the atmosphere came back down, it came down on Pakistan, and half of Pakistan was under water in the floods of 2010. An area larger than Germany was under water.

Warmer air carries more water. Every degree Celsius that you increase the temperature value of air, it carries 7 percent more water. But it doesn't carry that water uniformly. It can suck water away from one place and then deliver it in a deluge in another place. So both the droughts are up and flooding is up simultaneously, as precipitation becomes more lumpy and more concentrated.

In Russia's 2010 heat wave, 55,000 people died, 11,000 of them in Moscow alone. In 2011, the United States had the driest 10-month period ever in the American South, and Texas saw its worst wildfires ever. And 2012 was the worst drought in the United States since the Dust Bowl—the corn crop shrank by 20 percent.

So that's the big risk the world faces: that radical weather will change how we grow food, which is still our most important energy source—even more important than fossil fuels.

A number of people in the environmentalist movement are saying that we have to just stop growing. For instance, in his book *Peak Everything: Waking Up to the Century of Declines,* Richard Heinberg of the Post-Carbon Institute says that the Earth is full. Get used to it, and get ready for a world where you live with less wealth, and where your children live with less wealth, than any before.

I don't think this idea of stopping growth is realistic, because there are a top billion people who live pretty well and there are another 6 billion who don't and are hungry for it. We see demand rising for everything—water, food, energy—and that demand is rising not in the United States or Europe or Canada or Australia. It's rising in the developing world. This is the area that will create all of the increased demand for physical resources.

Even if we could, by some chance, say That's enough, sorry, we're not going to let you use these resources, which is doubtful, it wouldn't be just, because the West got rich by using those natural resources. So we need to find a different way.

Ideas as a Resource Expander, Resource Preserver, and Waste Reducer

The best-selling environmental book of all time, *Limits to Growth,* was based on computer modeling. It was a simple model with only about eight variables of what would happen in the world. It showed that economic growth, more wealth, would inevitably lead to more pollution and more consumption of finite resources, which would in turn take us beyond the limits and lead ultimately to collapse.

While it's been widely reported recently that its predictions are coming true, that's actually not the case. If you look at the vast majority of the numbers that the researchers predict in this model, they're not coming true.

Why did they get these things wrong? The most important thing that the forecasters did was underestimate the power of new ideas to expand resources, or to expand wealth while using fewer resources. Ideas have done tremendous things for us. Let's start with food.

In *The Population Bomb* (1968), Paul Ehrlich predicted that food supply could not support the population, just as Malthus did. But what's happened is that we've doubled population since 1960, and we've nearly tripled the food supply in total. We've increased by 30–40 percent the food supply per person since the 1960s.

Let's look at this on a very long time scale. How many people can you feed with an acre of land? Before the advent of agriculture, an acre of land could feed less than a thousandth of a person. Today it's about three people, on average, who can be fed by one acre of land. Preagriculture, it took 3,000 acres for one person to stay alive through hunting and gathering. With agriculture, that footprint has shrunk from 3,000 acres to one-third of one acre. That's not because there's any more sunlight, which is ultimately what food is; it's because we've changed the productivity of the resource by innovation in farming—and then thousands of innovations on top of that to increase it even more.

In fact, the reason we have the forests that we have on the planet is because we were able to handle a doubling of the population since 1960 without increasing farmland by more than about 10 percent. If we had to have doubled our farmland, we would have chopped down all the remaining forests on the planet.

Ideas can reduce resource use. I can give you many other examples. In the United States, the amount of energy used on farms per calorie grown has actually dropped by about half since the 1970s. That's in part because we now only use about a tenth of the energy to create synthetic nitrogen fertilizer, which is an important input.

The amount of food that you can grow per drop of water has roughly doubled since the 1980s. In wheat, it's actually more than tripled since 1960. The amount of water that we use in the United States per person has dropped by about a third since the 1970s, after rising for decades. As agriculture has gotten more efficient, we're using less water per person. So, again, ideas can reduce resource use.

Ideas can also find substitutes for scarce resources. We're at risk of running out of many things, right? Well, let's think about some things that have happened in the past.

The sperm whale was almost hunted into extinction. Sperm whales were, in the mid-1800s, the best source of illumination. Sperm whale oil—spermaceti—was the premier source of lighting. It burned without smoke, giving a clear, steady light, and the demand for it led to huge hunting of the sperm whales. In a period of about 30 years, we killed off about a third of the sperm whales on the planet.

That led to a phenomenon of "peak sperm-whale oil": The number of sperm whales that the fleet could bring in dropped over time as the sperm whales became more scarce and more afraid of human hunters. Demand rose as supply dropped, and the prices skyrocketed. So it looked a little bit like the situation with oil now.

That was solved not by the discovery of more sperm whales, nor by giving up on this thing of lighting. Rather, Abraham Gesner, a Canadian, discovered this thing called kerosene. He found that, if he took coal, heated it up, captured the fumes, and distilled them, he could create this fluid that burned very clear. And he could create it in quantities thousands of times greater than the sperm whales ever could have given up.

We have no information suggesting that Gesner was an environmentalist or that he cared about sperm whales at all. He was motivated by scientific curiosity and by the huge business opportunity of going after this lighting market. What he did was dramatically lower the cost of lighting while saving the sperm whales from extinction.

One more thing that ideas can do is transform waste into value. In places like Germany and Japan, people are mining landfills. Japan estimates that its landfills alone contain 10-year supplies of gold and rare-earth minerals for the world market.

Alcoa estimates that the world's landfills contain a 15-year supply of aluminum. So there's tremendous value.

When we throw things away, they're not destroyed. If we "consume" things like aluminum, we're not really consuming it, we're rearranging it. We're changing where it's located. And in some cases, the concentration of these resources in our landfills is actually higher than it was in our mines. What it takes is energy and technology to get that resource back out and put it back into circulation.

Ideas for Stretching the Limits

So ideas can reduce resource use, can find substitutes for scarce resources, and can transform waste into value. In that context, what are the limits to growth?

Is there a population limit? Yes, there certainly is, but it doesn't look like we're going to hit that. Projections right now are that, by the middle of this century, world population will peak between 9 billion and 10 billion, and then start to decline. In fact, we'll be talking much more about the graying of civilization, and perhaps underpopulation—too-low birthrates on a current trend.

What about physical resources? Are there limits to physical resource use on this planet? Absolutely. It really is a finite planet. But where are those limits?

To illustrate, let's start with energy. This is the most important resource that we use, in many ways. But when we consider all the fossil fuels that humanity uses today—all the oil, coal, natural gas, and so on—it pales in comparison to a much larger resource, all around us, which is the amount of energy coming in from our Sun every day.

The amount of energy from sunlight that strikes the top of the atmosphere is about 10,000 times as much as the energy that we use from fossil fuels on a daily basis. Ten seconds of sunlight hitting the Earth is as much energy as humanity uses in an entire day; one hour of sunlight hitting the Earth provides as much energy to the planet as a whole as humanity uses from all sources combined in one year.

This is an incredibly abundant resource. It manifests in many ways. It heats the atmosphere differentially, creating winds that we can capture for wind power. It evaporates water, which leads to precipitation elsewhere, which turns into things like rivers and waterfalls, which we can capture as hydropower.

But by far the largest fraction of it—more than half—is photons hitting the surface of the Earth. Those are so abundant that, with one-third of 1 percent of the Earth's land area, using current technology of about 14 percent-efficient solar cells, we could capture enough electricity to power all of current human needs.

The problem is not the abundance of the energy; the problem is cost. Our technology is primitive. Our technology for building solar cells is similar to our technology for manufacturing computer chips. They're built on silicon wafers in clean rooms at high temperatures, and so they're very, very expensive.

But innovation has been dropping that cost tremendously. Over the last 30 years, we've gone from a watt of solar power costing $20 to about $1. That's a factor of 20. We roughly drop the cost of solar by one-half every decade, more or less. That means that, in the sunniest parts of the world today, solar is now basically at parity in cost, without subsidies, with coal and natural gas. Over the next 12–15 years, that will spread to most of the planet. That's incredibly good news for us.

Of course, we don't just use energy while the Sun is shining. We use energy at night to power our cities; we use energy in things like vehicles that have to move and that have high energy densities. Both of these need storage, and today's storage is actually a bigger challenge than capturing energy. But there's reason to believe that we can tackle the storage problem, as well.

For example, consider lithium ion batteries—the batteries that are in your laptop, your cell phone, and so on. The demand to have longer-lasting devices drove tremendous innovations in these batteries in the 1990s and the early part of the 2000s. Between 1991 and 2005, the cost of storage in lithium ion batteries dropped by about a factor of nine, and the density of storage—how much energy you can store in an ounce of battery—increased by a little over double in that time. If we do that again, we would be at the point where grid-scale storage is affordable and we can store that energy overnight. Our electric vehicles have ranges similar to the range you can get in a gasoline-powered vehicle.

This is a tall order. This represents perhaps tens of billions of dollars in R&D, but it is something that is possible and for which there is precedent.

Another approach being taken is turning energy into fuel. When you use a fuel such as gasoline, it's not really an energy source. It's an energy carrier, an energy storage system, if you will. You can store a lot of energy in a very small amount.

Today, two pioneers in genome sequencing—Craig Venter and George Church—both have founded companies to create next-generation biofuels. What they're both leveraging is that gene-sequencing cost is the fastest quantitative area of progress on the planet.

What they're trying to do is engineer microorganisms that consume CO_2, sunlight, and sugar and actually excrete fuel as a byproduct. If we could do this, maybe just 1 percent of the Earth's surface—or a 30th of what we use for agriculture—could provide all the liquid fuels that we need. We would conveniently grow algae on saltwater and waste water, so biofuel production wouldn't compete for freshwater. And the possible yields are vast if we can get there.

If we can crack energy, we can crack everything else:

* Water. Water is life. We live in a water world, but only about a tenth of a percent of the water in the world is freshwater that's accessible to us in some way. Ninety-seven percent of the world's water is in the oceans and is salty. It used to be that desalination meant boiling water and then catching the steam and letting it condense.

Between the times of the ancient Greeks and 1960, desalination technology didn't really change. But then, it did. People started to create membranes modeled on what cells do, which is allow some things through but not others. They used plastics to force water through and get only the fresh and not the salty. As a result, the amount of energy it takes to desalinate a liter of water has dropped by about a factor of nine in that time. Now, in the world's largest desalination plants, the price of desalinated water is about a tenth of a cent per gallon. The technology has gotten to the point where it is starting to become a realistic option as an alternative to using up scarce freshwater resources.

* Food. Can we grow enough food? Between now and 2050, we have to increase food yield by about 70 percent. Is that possible? I think it is. In industrialized nations, food yields are already twice what they are in the world as a whole. That's because we have irrigation, tractors, better pesticides, and so on. Given such energy and wealth, we already know that we can grow enough food to feed the planet.

Another option that's probably cheaper would be to leverage some things that nature's already produced. What most people don't know is that the yield of corn per acre and in calories is about 70 percent higher than the yield of wheat. Corn is a C 4 photosynthesis crop: It uses a different way of turning sunlight and CO_2 into sugars that evolved only 30 million years ago. Now, scientists around the world are working on taking these C 4 genes from crops like corn and transplanting them into wheat and rice, which could right away increase the yield of those staple grains by more than 50 percent.

Physical limits do exist, but they are extremely distant. We cannot grow exponentially in our physical resource use forever, but that point is still at least centuries in the future. It's something we have to address eventually, but it's not a problem that's pressing right now.

* Wealth. One thing that people don't appreciate very much is that wealth has been decoupling from physical resource use on this planet. Energy use per capita is going up, CO_2 emissions per capita have been going up a little bit, but they are both widely outstripped by the amount of wealth that we're creating. That's because we can be more efficient in everything—using less energy per unit of food grown, and so on.

This again might sound extremely counterintuitive, but let me give you one concrete example of how that happens. Compare the ENIAC—which in the 1940s was the first digital computer ever created—to an iPhone. An iPhone is billions of times smaller, uses billions of times less energy, and has billions of times more computing power than ENIAC. If you tried to create an iPhone using ENIAC technology, it would be a cube a mile on the side, and it would use more electricity than the state of California. And it wouldn't have access to the Internet, because you'd have to invent that, as well.

This is what I mean when I say ideas are the ultimate resource. The difference between an ENIAC and an iPhone is that the iPhone is embodied knowledge that allows you to do more with less resources. That phenomenon is not limited to high tech. It's everywhere around us.

So ideas are the ultimate resource. They're the only resource that accumulates over time. Our store of knowledge is actually larger than in the past, as opposed to all physical resources.

Challenges Ahead for Innovation

Today we are seeing a race between our rate of consumption and our rate of innovation, and there are multiple challenges. One challenge is the Darwinian process, survival of the fittest. In areas like green tech, there will be hundreds and even thousands of companies founded, and 99 percent of them will go under. That is how innovation happens.

The other problem is scale. Just as an example, one of the world's largest solar arrays is at Nellis Air Force Base in California, and we would need about 10 million of these in order to meet the world's electricity needs. We have the land, we have the solar energy coming in, but there's a lot of industrial production that has to happen before we get to that point.

Innovation is incredibly powerful, but the pace of innovation compared to the pace of consumption is very important. One thing we can do to increase the pace of innovation is to address the biggest challenge, which is market failure.

In 1967, you could stick your hand into the Cuyahoga River, in Ohio, and come up covered in muck and oil. At that time, the river was lined with businesses and factories, and for them the river was a free resource. It was cheaper to pump their waste into the river than it was to pay for disposal at some other sort of facility. The river was a commons that anybody could use or abuse, and the waste they were producing was an externality. To that business or factory, there was no cost to pumping waste into this river. But to the people who depended upon the river, there was a high cost overall.

That's what I mean by a market externality and a market failure, because this was an important resource to all of us. But no one owned it, no one bought or sold it, and so it was treated badly in a way that things with a price are not.

That ultimately culminated when, in June 1969, a railway car passing on a bridge threw a spark; the spark hit a slick of oil a mile long on the river, and the river burst into flames.

The story made the cover of *Time* magazine. In many ways, the environmental movement was born of this event as much as it was of Rachel Carson's *Silent Spring*. In the following three years, the United States created the Environmental Protection Agency and passed the Clean Water and Clean Air acts.

Almost every environmental problem on the planet is an issue of the commons, whether it's chopping down forests that no one owns, draining lakes that no one owns, using up fish in the ocean that no one owns, or polluting the atmosphere because no one owns it, or heating up the planet. They're all issues of the commons. They're all issues where there is no cost to an individual entity to deplete something and no cost to over-consume something, but there is a greater cost that's external-ized and pushed on everybody else who shares this.

Now let's come back again to what Limits to Growth said, which was that economic growth always led to more pollution and more consumption, put us beyond limits, and ends with col-lapse. So if that's the case, all those things we just talked about should be getting worse. But as the condition of the Cuyahoga River today illustrates, that is not the case.

GDP in the United States is three times what it was when the Cuyahoga River caught on fire, so shouldn't it be more pol-luted? It's not. Instead, it's the cleanest it's been in decades. That's not because we stopped growth. It's because we made intelligent choices about managing that commons.

Another example: In the 1970s, we discovered that the ozone layer was thinning to such an extent that it literally could drive the extinction of all land species on Earth. But it's actu-ally getting better. It's turned a corner, it's improving ahead of schedule, and it's on track to being the healthiest it's been in a century. That's because we've reduced the emissions of CFCs, which destroy ozone; we've dropped the amount of them that we emit into the atmosphere basically to zero. And yet indus-try has not ground to a halt because of this, either. Economic growth has not faltered.

And one last example: Acid rain—which is primarily produced by sulfur dioxide emitted by coal-burning power plants—is mostly gone as an issue. Emissions of sulfur dioxide are down by about a factor of two. That's in part because we created a strategy called cap and trade: It capped the amount of SO_2 that you could emit, then allowed you to swap and buy emission credits from others to find the optimal way to do that.

The cost, interestingly enough, has always been lower than projected. In each of these cases, industry has said, This will end things. Ronald Reagan's chief of staff said the economy would grind to a halt, and the EPA would come in with lower cost estimates. But the EPA has always been wrong: The EPA cost estimate has always been too high.

Analysis of all of these efforts in the past shows that reducing emissions is always cheaper than you expect, but cleaning up the mess afterwards is always more expensive than you'd guess.

Today, the biggest commons issue is that of climate change, with the CO_2 and other greenhouse gases that we're pumping into the atmosphere. A logical thing to do would be to put a price on these. If you pollute, if you're pumping CO_2 into the atmosphere and it's warming the planet, so you're causing harm to other people in a very diffuse way. Therefore, you should be paying in proportion to that harm you're doing to offset it.

But if we do that, won't that have a massive impact on the economy? This all relates to energy, which drives a huge frac-tion of the economy. Manufacturing depends on it. Transport depends on it. So wouldn't it be a huge problem if we were to actually put a price on these carbon emissions?

Well, there has been innovative thinking about that, as well. One thing that economists have always told us is that, if you're going to tax, tax the bad, not the good. Whatever it is that you tax, you will get less of it. So tax the bad, not the good.

The model that would be the ideal for putting a price on pollution is what we call a revenue-neutral model. Revenue-neutral carbon tax, revenue-neutral cap and trade. Let's model it as a tax: Today, a country makes a certain amount of revenue for its government in income tax, let's say. If you want to tax pollution, the way to do this without impacting the economy is to increase your pollution tax in the same manner that you decrease the income tax. The government then is capturing the same amount of money from the economy as a whole, so there's no economic slowdown as a result of this.

This has a positive effect on the environment because it tips the scales of price. Now, if you're shopping for energy, and you're looking at solar versus coal or natural gas, the carbon price has increased the price of coal and natural gas to you, but not the cost of solar. It shifts customer behavior from one to the other while having no net impact on the economy, and probably a net benefit on the economy in the long run as more investment in green energy drives the price down.

Toward a Wealthier, Cleaner Future

The number-one thing I want you to take away is that pollution and overconsumption are not inevitable outcomes of growth. While tripling the wealth of North America, for instance, we've gone from an ozone layer that was rapidly deteriorating to one that is bouncing back.

The fundamental issue is not one of limits to growth; it's one of the policy we choose, and it's one of how we structure our economy to value all the things we depend upon and not just those things that are owned privately.

What can we do, each of us? Four things:

First is to communicate. These issues are divisive, but we know that beliefs and attitudes on issues like this spread word of mouth. They spread person to person, from person you trust to person you trust. So talk about it. Many of us have friends or colleagues or family on the other side of these issues, but talk about it. You're better able to persuade them than anyone else is.

Second is to participate. By that I mean politically. Local governments, state and province governments, and national governments are responsive when they hear from their constituents about these issues. It changes their attitudes. Because so few constituents actually make a call to the office of their legislator, or write a letter, a few can make a very large impact.

Third is to innovate. These problems aren't solved yet. We don't have the technologies for these problems today. The trend lines look very good, but the next 10 years of those trend lines demand lots of bright people, lots of bright ideas, and lots of R&D. So if you're thinking about a career change, or if you know any young people trying to figure out what their career is now, these are careers that (A) will be very important to us in the future and (B) will probably be quite lucrative for them.

Last is to keep hope, because we have faced problems like this before and we have conquered them every time. The future isn't written in stone—it could go good or bad—but I'm very optimistic. I know we have the ability to do it, and I think we will. Ultimately, ideas are our most important natural resource.

Critical Thinking

1. Do the facts seem to support an optimistic future or a pessimistic future?
2. What is the potential of new ideas and new technologies?
3. Technologies have brought great benefits and considerable problems. Can technologies and new ideas now solve those problems?

Create Central

www.mhhe.com/createcentral

Internet References

National Center for Policy Analysis
www.ncpa.org
Social Science Information Gateway
http://sosig.esrc.bris.ac.uk
SocioSite
www.pscw.uva.nl/sociosite/TOPICS/Women.html
Sociology—Study Sociology Online
http://edu.learnsoc.org
Sociology Web Resources
http://www.mhhe.com/socscience/sociology/resources/index.htm
Sociosite
http://www.topsite.com/goto/sociosite.net
Socioweb
http://www.topsite.com/goto/socioweb.com
WWW Virtual Library: Demography & Population Studies
http://demography.anu.edu.au/VirtualLibrary

RAMEZ NAAM is a computer scientist and author. He is a former Microsoft executive and current fellow of the Institute for Ethics and Emerging Technologies. He lives in Seattle, Washington.

Article   Prepared by: Kurt Finsterbusch, *University of Maryland, College Park*

Annual Report Card on Our Future

RICK DOCKSAI

Learning Outcomes

After reading this article, you will be able to:

- Better understand the state of the planet.

- Evaluate the significance of massive efforts to assess the state of the planet such as this one.

- Connect these findings to potential new policies.

The Millennium Project assesses where the world is gaining or losing ground.

The world community is in better shape than it should be, states the Millennium Project's leadership team in its 2013–14 State of the Future report. This volume, the international think tank's acclaimed annual "report card on the future of the world," finds that human health and living standards are trending upward but are doing so despite deficient stewardship of the planet and widespread occurrences of poor governance, political corruption, crime, and violence.

"When you consider the many wrong decisions and good decisions not yet taken—day after day and year after year around the world—it is amazing that we are still making as much progress as we are," the authors write.

The Millennium Project has been producing annual State of the Future reports since 1996. Each report makes a full-scale assessment of where life on Earth is heading, based on constantly incoming data from an international network of more than 4,500 contributing researchers. Like its predecessors, this year's report integrates the data into a list of 15 Global Challenges that require collaborative action by the world's leaders, along with a State of the Future Index (SOFI) that marks areas of life in which we are "winning," "losing," or experiencing "unclear or little change."

This report's SOFI cites some encouraging firsts. For the first time, we are "winning" on renewable energy—worldwide renewable capacity has been growing and is on track for a much larger growth spurt this decade. We are also winning for the first time on Gross National Investment Per Capita, Foreign Direct Investment, and Health Expenditures Per Capita.

Also, some positive trends from earlier years are still running strong. The number of physicians per capita is growing worldwide, as it was in 2011. The world is likewise winning on energy efficiency, a winning streak that started in 2012.

Other trends are not good. For the first time, we are losing on forest area. Also, greenhouse-gas emissions and our overall ecological footprint, two areas that have been on the "losing" side of the ledger for the past few years, are still losing areas today. Glaciers are melting and coral reefs are dying at accelerating rates as climate change gathers steam.

"The global situation for humanity continues to improve in general, but at the expense of the environment," the authors write.

All is not trending well for human life, either. The SOFI notes little or no progress on nuclear nonproliferation and HIV prevalence—areas in which we were winning in 2011. Some trends from 2012 or earlier are continuing to worsen, too—namely, income inequality, terrorism, and political corruption.

This year's 15 Global Challenges list additionally notes that global material waste increased 10-fold last century and could double again by 2025. The authors also voice concern over shrinking supplies of potable water. They call for new agricultural approaches that would consume less water, such as new ways to synthesize meat without growing animals, genetic engineering for higher-yielding and more drought-resistant crops, and cultivating insects as animal feed.

On the upside, literacy and IQ scores keep rising, and the growth of online educational resources could accelerate intellectual growth even further. Also, the prospects for a more peaceful world are on the upswing, thanks to democracy, international trade, Internet use, and news media all gaining ground; prosperity rising and poverty declining; crosscultural dialogues flourishing; and NGOs and regional organizations fostering community-led social reforms and peace accords.

Efforts to affirm women's rights are also making crucial gains. New worldwide campaigns to stop violence against women are expanding, while new mobile-phone apps and Internet sites are making it easier to report and publicize incidences of violence. Overall, the report projects that "slow but massive shifts in gender stereotypes will occur in the next few decades."

The Global Challenges section breaks each problem area down to the regional levels, as well. Readers will see specific takes on the energy, governance, and human and environmental health situations of Africa, Europe, North America, Latin America, and Asia and Oceania.

Some new issues have surfaced since 2012, such as poor nutrition. The authors explain that, while hunger is down throughout the world, much of the world's daily caloric intake is "empty calories" that satisfy hunger pangs but do little for overall health and contribute to weight gain and diabetes risk.

"It is not clear that food nutrient density will keep pace with human needs," they write.

The report lists several dozen steps that could remedy the situation. Among them are taxing unhealthy foods more heavily to subsidize healthier ones, posting "low nutritional value" warning labels on food packaging, breaking up agribusiness and food market monopolies, increasing investment in developing countries' agricultural R&D, and organizing school-based campaigns to encourage healthier eating.

Another concern is major construction along the world's coasts, where there is vulnerability to numerous environmental hazards. The authors give several pages of recommendations for safer development, such as more interdisciplinary and participatory urban planning that involves NGOs, ecologists, and the urban poor; building green, floating cities with newer materials; imposing compensation fees and higher taxes on activities that pollute; and organizing youth environmental groups to carry out habitat restoration.

The world has the means to further improve human life while preserving the planet's natural systems and resources, but it must marshal global intelligence and activism across national borders to an entirely new degree, the authors conclude. They stress the value of better information-gathering systems as guides to the process.

"Some of the world's toughest problems affect everyone almost instantly and do not end at national borders. In the future, solutions as well as problems must also cross boundaries—ideological as well as geographic," they write.

The 2013–14 State of the Future is an authoritative compendium of what we know about the future of humanity and our planet. Policy makers and advocates will find it to be a vast yet very readable source of insight on where the world's thorniest problems begin and where they might end.

Critical Thinking

1. Critique the 15 measures selected to measure the State of the Future by the Millennial Project.

2. How authoritative do you consider this report card? Why?

3. No one should be surprised that affluence and health are improving worldwide or that the environment is worsening, but why are governance, crime, and violence worsening?

Create Central

www.mhhe.com/createcentral

Internet References

National Center for Policy Analysis
    www.ncpa.org

New American Studies Web
    www.georgetown.edu/crossroads/asw

Sociology—Study Sociology Online
    http://edu.learnsoc.org

Sociology Web Resources
    http://www.mhhe.com/socscience/sociology/resources/index.htm

SocioSite
    www.pscw.uva.nl/sociosite/TOPICS/Women.html

Sociosite
    http://www.topsite.com/goto/sociosite.net

Socioweb
    http://www.topsite.com/goto/socioweb.com

WWW Virtual Library: Demography & Population Studies
    http://demography.anu.edu.au/VirtualLibrary

RICK DOCKSAI is senior editor of THE **FUTURIST**.

Docksai, Rick, "Annual Report Card on Our Future," *The Futurist*, vol. 48, 4, July/August 2014. Copyright © 2014 by World Future Society. All rights reserved. Used with permission.

Article

Prepared by: Kurt Finsterbusch, *University of Maryland, College Park*

Is a Digitally Connected World a Better Place?

The plusses and minuses of this "Brave New World" represent the greatest change to the way people live and interact on this planet humankind has ever seen. We'll see more change in the next five years than we've seen in the last five. If we take some basic precautions, I believe the utility of the mobile Internet far outweighs the risks.

DAN HESSE

Learning Outcomes

After reading this article, you will be able to:

- Explain the economic benefits of the Internet and digital connections.

- Explain the explosion of available knowledge and its impacts that are produced by the digital revolution.

- Discuss the issue of cyber attacks.

We are living at a time when technology is changing the world at a pace never before experienced in human history. Of all technological advances, in my view, the one that is changing the life we share on this planet the most, whether one lives in a G8 country or in the developing world, is the mobile Internet.

These dramatic changes bring with them many plusses, but also some negatives and risks. F. Scott Fitzgerald's quote, "The test of a first-rate intelligence is the ability to hold two opposed ideas in mind at the same time and still retain the ability to function" is perhaps a good theme for this talk.

I'm not claiming to have a first rate mind, but I have learned a bit about telecommunications during a 37-year career in the industry. Will Rogers said it well, "Everybody is ignorant, only in different subjects," and perhaps this could apply here as this is one of the few subjects I don't feel ignorant about.

I feel fortunate to have been in this rapidly-changing industry. I had the opportunity to launch AT&T's Internet division in the mid-90's when I was jokingly referred to as "Rubber Ducky" in the Halls of headquarters, a reference to the popular song about a trucker with a Citizens Band radio, as some thought that the Internet would be a passing fad like the CB. The BMW ad on TV with Katie Couric and Bryant Gumble brings back memories of the 90's.

After launching AT&T's Internet service provider business, Worldnet, I was sent to Seattle to run a recent acquisition, McCaw Cellular, which became AT&T Wireless.

Both the Internet and wireless were growth businesses, but it took the merging of the two for each to explode. When Internet browsers were put into cell phones (the early "smartphones" like the first IPhone in 2007), it was like peanut butter meeting chocolate. Wireless had been useful in connecting people with people, but when wireless connected people with the information and utility of the Internet, growth of both wireless and the Internet accelerated rapidly.

Wireless went from zero to 6 billion users in 25 years, the most rapidly-adopted technology in history. There are roughly ten cell phones produced daily for every baby born in the world.

Wireless's next big growth period will not be driven by cell phones. Wireless chips are, or will be, put into almost every object imaginable: motor vehicles, health monitors, home appliances, wearables like fitness bracelets and watches, even into our bodies. Connecting not people, but things to the Internet, what has been referred to as "machine to machine" or the "Internet of things" will usher in the next big growth phase. Cisco estimates there will be 25 billion things connected to the Internet this year and 50 billion things connected by 2020.

Some would argue that this much change to the way we live our lives and communicate with one another is a scourge. Others see a blessing. I don't know the answer. Bertrand Russell said, "The trouble with the world is that the stupid are cocksure and the intelligent are full of doubt," so I guess it's OK not to be sure. In the time I have tonight, I'll try to give you both sides of the argument.

First, let's consider the impact on the global economy. One study indicates that for each 10 percentage points of cell phone penetration (the percentage of the population with a cell phone), a nation's GDP increases from a half to one-and-a-half points. Recon Analytics projects that wireless will contribute $1.5 trillion to US GDP over the next ten years. And, with the rare exception of countries like North Korea, there is not a large difference in penetration rates between developed and developing countries. Peter Diamandis, in his book *Abundance,* gives the example of the Masai warrior in Africa with a smartphone and Google having better access to information than the US President had 15 years ago. From a telecom infrastructure perspective, wireless has allowed the developing world to "leap-frog" the expensive landline access networks deployed by more developed countries.

Some gaps still exist, between countries, and within countries, what is referred to as the "Digital Divide".North America has less than 10% of the world's wireless subscribers, but 45% of the 4G LTE connections.

The greatest economic benefits may still be ahead of us with the productivity that will be driven by the "Internet of things." The information gathered by billions of "always on" devices, utilizing cloud and quantum computing, sophisticated analytics and algorithms, machine learning and artificial intelligence could have great economic potential. For example, UPS uses these technologies to track packages and vehicles, and each mile saved per day per driver adds $50 million per year to the bottom line. On the other hand, if a company is going to invest in embedding 3G wireless chips in thousands of vehicles with long productive lives, they may require their wireless carrier to maintain an outdated technology like 3G longer instead of investing in 5G.

I've been watching the History Channel program "The Men Who Built America", about how this country and our way of life was radically transformed in the late 19th and early 20th centuries by Vanderbilt's rail-roads, Rockefeller's oil, Carnegie's steel, JP Morgan's electricity, and Ford's automobiles, and the important interrelationship of these industries. We're seeing this same kind of new industry creation and interrelationship now in the digital domain.

The business model of every industry could be transformed in a world where every device and every person is connected all the time. This is an enormous opportunity for those who understand this power and harness it. On the other hand, seismic disruption like this could usher in great risk to incumbents.

There are two areas of expertise every board of directors and every "C-suite" should be steeped in: the mobile Internet and cybersecurity. For good reason, cybersecurity is rising to the top of the business risk list. There are two kinds of companies: those that know and those that don't know they've been hacked. Attacks can be harmful to current and to future operations. Examples include loss of trade secrets, customer and financial information, online advertising "pay by the click" scamming, and outright extortion threats to the company's website or systems if a ransom isn't paid. Perhaps the greatest risk is to a company's valuable brand. Sony, Target and Home Depot are examples.

Just as systems that use the Internet increase productivity, protecting these systems reduce productivity by requiring added investment. It's estimated cybersecurity costs the typical firm of 1000+ employees $9 million/year. US labor productivity has been stagnant in recent years, perhaps partly due to the unproductive investments required for cybersecurity and for Sarbanes-Oxley compliance. The cybersecurity industry is a new industry, which will create some jobs, but like any new growth industry, it will come with its share of marketing hype.

There are opportunities and new challenges in education as well. Advanced Placement and specialized courses have historically only been available at large or elite high schools, but the connected Internet is democratizing education in the US and around the world through resources like online high school equivalent and college degrees, and the excellent Kahn Academy (which also has helped this father brush up on high school algebra in order to be a more effective tutor). But all students still do not have access to tablets or smartphones, or to high speed Internet access at school or at home in the evening when home-work needs to be done.

These tools create new challenges. 35% of teens admit to using cell phones to cheat, and 65% say others cheat using cell phones. Some worry about the effect this technology will have on the quality of spoken and written language. One study found 13% of people pretend to be talking on their phone to avoid interacting with those around them. You've likely seen students texting each other across the lunchroom table instead of conversing. If we call our sons, it goes to voicemail. We need to text them to get an answer. Few would claim texting is the epitome of the "King's English." 64% of teens were found to use improper grammar while texting, something many of us are regularly guilty of.

School administrators and parents have another new worry—cyberbullying. One study found one in ten students were victims of, and one in five participated in, cyberbullying. "Sexting" is a new word in the vernacular. 20% of teens admit to posting nude photos online.

An Elon University study found that students with this digitally enhanced education possess something called "fast-twitch wiring". "Always on" students are nimble, quick-acting multi-taskers, but with a thirst for instant gratification, quick fixes, and with little patience and deep-thinking.

But, social networking can be a constructive form of human interaction. I've used social media to connect with many old friends I would have lost touch with. Smartphones also allow us to be productive by staying in touch with the office at home or on vacation, which is certainly a quality-of-life double-edged sword. Some argue that the information and entertainment of the Internet improves the quality of life by reducing boredom.

The news is a form of education. Does the Internet improve the quality of news we get? From personal experience, and admitted to by reporters, the 24 hour online news cycle and the need to break a story first means verifying the accuracy of information or getting a second source often goes by the way-side. Reporters don't have the time that the next morning's paper edition gave them.

It also seems that "real" news curated by professionals is being replaced with the trivial from new news sources like Facebook, Twitter and Buzzfeed, with national or world events replaced by the exploits of Kim Kardashian, videos of water-skiing squirrels, or debates about the color of a dress.

On the other hand, the amount and depth of news available has never been greater. If you grew up in a "one paper town", far less news was available to you from around the globe vs. what you can access now at a reasonable cost.

Maybe talking to computers will replace some human interaction. I watched my son's fingers fly as he typed feverishly on his PC, and looking over his shoulder, I saw indecipherable characters—computer code. He was creating a new video game, for fun. On the one hand, this is encouraging to see, but on the other hand, will this essential new language create another wave of untrained "have-nots?" For example, appliance or engine repair is moving away from screwdrivers to software programming and analysis. And the new machines: self-driving cars, trucks, trains, robots, and self-diagnosing and self-repairing machines, may replace many jobs. 3D printer programming skills will replace craftsmanship in some industries. The same son owns two 3D printers he is very skilled with. If manufacturing done via 3D printer largely eliminates the need for assembly, what will happen to the economies of countries which depend on low-cost labor as their primary export? But, manufacturing and product design intellectual property is now much easier to steal or compromise.

To increase our safety, cell phones allow us to call 911, locate our children, provide alerts and information helpful with natural disasters and aid first-responders. Cell phone fundraising campaigns have raised millions for relief efforts.

But digital connectivity can reduce safety by distracting drivers. Texting while driving has led to fatalities, which is why you've seen wireless carriers join together with distracted driving campaigns.

Vehicles come connected with wireless digital monitoring capabilities for engines or tires and with GPS tracking and "On-Star"-like emergency buttons. These add to safety, but the reverse could be true if the connected vehicle is hacked.

In terms of environmental impact, computers use an enormous amount of energy to run and cool them. In addition, the US produces 2.5 million tons of e-waste annually, enough to fill a line of dump trucks from Washington DC to Disney World.

On the other hand, GPS saves fuel and miles driven as does teleconferencing and telecommuting, all enabled by mobile technology. Cell phones built to the new UL-E standard are more energy efficient, are designed for reuse and recycling, and contain fewer harmful chemicals. The mobile industry is also driving "dematerialization." The smartphone, akin to a Swiss Army Knife, can replace a PC, watch, alarm clock, camera, hand-held GPS, flashlight, transistor radio, portable music player, TV, even plastic credit cards, keeping a lot of material out of landfills.

Because early cell phones had small storage and processing capabilities, and networks were slow, even though these devices made music more portable, the cell phone industry contributed to what many consider the "Dark Age" of music fidelity.

Recorded music was "sampled" to create MP3 files and compressed streaming services, played through small tinny speakers or "throw away" low-fi earbuds included in the phone's box. But, new smartphones, like HTC's Harman/Kardon edition, not only come with high-quality earphones, but can play high-resolution audio files from sources like HDTracks, with approximately 60 times the musical information of an MP3 or streaming service, providing better fidelity than a compact disc. So, after helping to create the "Dark Age" of fidelity, the mobile Internet is helping to usher in a new "Golden Age" of sound.

Perhaps no industry will be transformed more by the mobile Internet than healthcare. Imagine taking a pill with a small wireless chip inside that sends a voltage to a patch you wear on your skin, which in turn communicates with your smartphone to tell your doctor how your medicine is interacting with your body's chemistry. No need to wait for blood work to return from the lab. This is in use today.

In much of the developing world, knowing whether water is safe to drink is a big issue. Photospectrometers to test the water for viruses, bacteria and toxins traditionally cost about $50,000. A capability has been developed to use a smartphone's camera and processor, plus about $200 in parts, to provide similar functionality.

Telemedicine has the potential to save billions and keep sick people at home, where they want to be and should be, to keep them from infecting others. Wearables like fitness bracelets, chips in pacemakers, and digital medical records are improvements, but also add risk if this information could be compromised or hacked. To take advantage of medical innovations, we may need to rethink our approval processes as well. When I ask entrepreneurs with health care innovations what their biggest challenge is, they don't say funding, they say the FDA.

If we live longer, couldn't the aging population become even more out-of-touch with current technology given the greater number of years out of the workforce? The elderly represent America's largest "minority" group. My personal view is that this group will benefit the most from the mobile Internet. Smartphone speech-to-text and text-to-speech capabilities can improve the quality of life for the hearing or visually impaired. Mobile health monitoring will help people live in their own homes longer, as will connected smart appliances, self-driving cars and connected robotic personal assistants.

Social media will help the elderly stay connected with family, friends and with those who share common interests. Crowdsourcing techniques will provide a way to tap into the collective expertise and wisdom of a graying society while stimulating this generation with renewed purpose.

So far, I've been discussing the tradeoffs this digital, connected world brings to education, the news, the environment, economies, health care, music, safety, and aging, but perhaps the greatest challenge will be balancing the tradeoff between the tremendous utility potential of the wireless Internet with threats to our privacy and security.

In terms of national security, despotic regimes are legitimately concerned with the access to information and communication capabilities of mobile devices and social networking. We likely would not have seen the "Arab Spring" regime changes in Egypt or Tunisia if citizens did not have the mobilizing power of cell phones. These countries had mobile penetration of roughly 90%. North Korea, on the other hand, keeps penetration low, at roughly 5%. And, we've read of countries censoring the Internet as a way of mitigating internal threats to their security.

Social networking, plus access to Google, Google maps, and emerging digital currencies can be a threat to democracies too in the hands of even small groups of terrorists, and we've read of how easy it is to learn how to make a bomb, or print an undetectable plastic gun using a 3D printer on the Internet.

The Internet was created based on trust to facilitate sharing information. 90% of the Internet is privately owned, not under government control. The Internet is basically an architecture and protocol that links multiple private networks, where the word "inter-net"came from. The challenge is balancing sharing with protecting information. Just as personal privacy and security is inversely related to utility, network security is also inversely related to utility. Network utility increases with network size, but larger networks have more points of vulnerability.

Woody Allen said, "There are two kinds of people in this world, good and bad. The good sleep better, but the bad seem to enjoy the waking hours more." One can't pick up the newspaper without reading about a computer attack, whether it be attributed to a state-sponsored or criminal APT (Advanced Persistent Threat), attempting to steal information from government, business, or individuals.

It seems like a Cold War is re-emerging, filled with suspicion. The good news is that the alleged cyber-attacks between nations haven't been as lethal as conventional war, but in conventional war, who the enemy is can be more apparent, as cyberattacks can take place from machines distributed across the globe. I've read that 25% of the machines used in the famous cyberattack against Estonia were US-based. And governments can support, yet hide behind, "patriotic hackers" to carry out attacks, giving a government plausible deniability. This complicates diplomacy. Responses are more complex when the effects are asymmetrical, when one side has much and the other very little to lose from a digital attack, like the US vs North Korea.

I can speak from personal experience that this new arena is difficult for Internet companies to navigate. Which CEO is more patriotic, the one who provides all of the information the government requests to help catch a criminal or prevent a terrorist attack, or the CEO whose company creates tools that make it difficult for law enforcement or the government to acquire a customer's information, believing protecting civil liberties is a higher calling. I don't have an answer, but there is perhaps no more important area for public/private dialogue and cooperation than this.

The most effective cyberattacks on companies have internal complicity, either by a mole or through an untrained employee. Well-trained employees don't plug in USB drives they don't know the origin of, don't click on links they're not sure about, don't connect to free Wi-Fi networks they don't know, recognize when social engineering or "phishing" attempts are being made, password protect all devices, and don't put company logos on themselves or their computers when traveling.

In conclusion, we all share a responsibility to protect the Internet. Please pattern or password protect your devices. A study showed that if your phone is lost or stolen, there is a 90% chance your data will be breached, and a 50% chance you'll never see your phone again. You can buy security apps like Lookout from your carrier to protect against malware and also remotely lock or wipe information from your phone.

There are a lot of free aps out there. Be careful. If it seems like they're asking for more personal information than the utility of the app requires, like access to your contacts and to your location, they probably are. It's free because you're paying by providing personal information. Be selective.

Laws may need to change to make the Internet safer. The U.S. President has made it easier for competitors in the same industries to share information to protect against attacks, what would have been an antitrust concern not long ago.

It can be argued that the meteoric growth in the Internet is because it has been unregulated. America's Internet looks like it may be regulated soon like a utility of centuries past. On a global level, Russia and China have urged the ITU (International Telecommunications Union) to govern the Internet, citing cybersecurity issues, a move resisted by the US and Europe who are concerned this will be a tool to limit freedom. Once again, there are two sides to this coin.

The plusses and minuses of this "Brave New World" represent the greatest change to the way people live and interact on this planet humankind has ever seen. We'll see more change in the next five years than we've seen in the last five. There are no absolutes, only shades of gray and two sides to practically every argument. If we take some basic precautions, I believe the utility of the mobile Internet far outweighs the risks.

I feel privileged to be able to hear what Admiral Rogers will have to say tonight. Continued dialogue and cooperation will be needed between governments, businesses and the citizens of the world to achieve a "Gold-ilocks" solution, a.k.a. getting it "just right."

Thank you.

Critical Thinking

1. Is a digitally connected world a better place?
2. What are the risks of the world wide Internet?
3. What are the changes that the Internet is likely to cause in the near future?

Internet References

New American Studies Web
https://blogs.commons.georgetown.edu/vkp/

Social Science Information Gateway
http://www.ariadne.ac.uk/issue2/sosig

Sociology–Study Sociology Online
http://edu.learnsoc.org/

Sociology Web Resources
http://www.mhhe.com/socscience/sociology/resources/index.htm

Sociosite
http://www.topsite.com/goto/sociosite.net

Socioweb
http://www.topsite.com/goto/socioweb.com

Article   Prepared by: Kurt Finsterbusch, *University of Maryland, College Park*

Globalization Is Good for You!

New research demonstrates the amazing power of open markets and open borders.

RONALD BAILEY

Learning Outcomes

After reading this article, you will be able to:

- Describe Bailey's view of globalization.

- Critically analyze the considerable evidence that Bailey provides that globalization has increased the equality of women, improved job opportunities, and expanded other benefits.

- Analyze the opposing ideas that theoretically freer trade should make most people better off but some countries could lose jobs with globalization.

How important is the open exchange of goods to the spreading of prosperity? This important: Since 1950, world trade in goods has expanded from $600 billion (in 2015 dollars) to $18.9 trillion in 2013. That's a more than 30-fold increase, during a period in which global population grew less than three-fold.

This massive increase in trade was kicked off in 1948 by the General Agreement on Tariffs and Trade, which began the liberalization process of lowering tariff and non-tariff barriers. As a result, autarkic national economies became more integrated and intertwined with one another. The World Bank reports that openness to trade—the ratio of a country's trade (exports plus imports) to its gross domestic product (GDP)—has more than doubled on average since 1950.

Immigration has also contributed significantly to economic growth and higher wages. Today some 200 million people, about 3 percent of the world's population, live outside their countries of birth. According to the Partnership for a New American Economy, 28 percent of all U.S. companies started in 2011 had immigrant founders—despite immigrants comprising

roughly 13 percent of the population. In addition, some 40 percent of Fortune 500 firms were founded by immigrants or their children.

All of this open movement of people and stuff across borders pays off in many measurable ways, some obvious, some more surprising.

Longer, Healthier Lives

A 2010 study in World Development, titled "Good For Living? On the Relationship between Globalization and Life Expectancy," looked at data from 92 countries and found that economic globalization significantly boosts life expectancy, especially in developing countries. The two Swedish economists behind the study, Andreas Bergh and Therese Nilsson, noted that as Uganda's economic globalization index rose from 22 to 46 points (almost two standard deviations) over the 1970–2005 period, average life expectancy increased by two to three years.

Similarly, a 2014 conference paper titled "The long-run relationship between trade and population health: evidence from five decades," by Helmut Schmidt University economist Dierk Herzer, concluded, after examining the relationship between economic openness and population health for 74 countries between 1960 and 2010, that "international trade in general has a robust positive long-run effect on health, as measured by life expectancy and infant mortality."

Women's Liberation

A 2012 working paper by University of Konstantz economist Heinrich Ursprung and University of Munich economist Niklas Potrafke analyzed how women fare by comparing globalization trends with changes in the Social Institutions and Gender Index (SIGI), which was developed by the

Organisation for Economic Co-operation and Development (OECD). SIGI takes several aspects of gender relations into account, including family law codes, civil liberties, physical integrity, son preference, and ownership rights. It's an index of deprivation that captures causes of gender inequality rather than measuring outcomes.

"Observing the progress of globalization for almost one hundred developing countries at ten year intervals starting in 1970," Ursprung and Potrafke concluded, "we find that economic and social globalization exert a decidedly positive influence on the social institutions that reduce female subjugation and promote gender equality." They further noted that since globalization tends to liberate women from traditional social and political orders, "social globalization is demonized, by the established local ruling class, and by western apologists who, for reasons of ideological objections to markets, join in opposing globalization."

Less Child Labor

A 2005 World Development study, "Trade Openness, Foreign Direct Investment and Child Labor," by Eric Neumayer of the London School of Economics and Indra de Soysa of the Norwegian University of Science and Technology, looked at the effects of trade openness and globalization on child labor in poor countries. Their analysis refuted the claims made by anti-globalization proponents that free trade induces a "race to the bottom," encouraging the exploitation of children as cheap laborers. Instead the researchers found that the more open a country is to international trade and foreign investment, the lower the incidence of exploitation. "Globalization is associated with less, not more, child labor," they concluded.

Faster Economic Growth

A 2008 World Bank study, "Trade Liberalization and Growth: New Evidence," by the Stanford University economists Romain Wacziarg and Karen Horn Welch, found that trade openness and liberalization significantly boost a country's rate of economic growth.

The authors noted that in 1960, just 22 percent of countries representing 21 percent of the global population had open trade policies. This rose to 73 percent of countries representing 46 percent of world population by the year 2000. The study compared growth rates of countries before and after trade liberalization, finding that "over the 1950–1998 period, countries that liberalized their trade regimes experienced average annual growth rates that were about 1.5 percentage points higher than before liberalization" and that "investment rates rose by 1.5–2.0 percentage points."

Higher Incomes

Trade openness boosts economic growth, but how does it affect per-capita incomes? A 2009 Rutgers University-Newark working paper, "Trade Openness and Income—a Re-examination," by economists Vlad Manóle and Mariana Spatareanu, calculated the trade restrictiveness indices for 131 developed and developing countries between 1990 and 2004. Its conclusion: A "lower level of trade protection is associated with higher per-capita income."

Less Poverty

A 2011 Research Institute of Industrial Economics working paper—"Globalization and Absolute Poverty—A Panel Data Study," by the Swedish economists Bergh and Nilsson—analyzed the effects of globalization and trade openness on levels of absolute poverty (defined as incomes of less than $1 per day) in 100 developing countries. The authors found "a robust negative correlation between globalization and poverty."

Interestingly, most of the reduction in absolute poverty results from better information flows—for example, access to cellphones—that improve the functioning of markets and lead to the liberalization of trade. For example, the globalization index score for Bangladesh increased from 8 points in 1980 to 30 points in 2000, which yielded a reduction in absolute poverty of 12 percentage points.

More Trees

A number of studies have found that trade openness tends to improve environmental quality in rich countries while increasing pollution and deforestation in poor countries. For example, a 2009 *Journal of Environmental Economics and Management* study by three Japanese researchers, titled "Does Trade Openness Improve Environmental Quality?," found that air and water pollution decline among rich-country members of the OECD, whereas it increases in poor countries as they liberalize and embark on the process of economic development.

But as poor countries become rich, they flip from getting dirtier to becoming cleaner. A 2012 *Canadian Journal of Agricultural Economics* study, "Deforestation and the Environmental Kuznets Curve in Developing Countries: A Panel Smooth Transition Regression Approach," explored the relationship between deforestation and real income for 52 developing countries during the 1972–2003 period. The study found that deforestation reverses when average incomes reach a bit more than $3,000 per year.

These studies basically confirm the Environmental Kuznets Curve hypothesis, in which various indicators of environmental degradation tend to get worse during the early stages of economic growth, but when average income reaches a certain point, subsequent economic growth leads to environmental improvement. Since trade openness and globalization boost economic growth and incomes, this suggests that opposing them slows down eventual environmental improvement in poor countries.

Peace

In 1943, Otto T. Mallery wrote, "If soldiers are not to cross international boundaries, goods must do so. Unless the shackles can be dropped from trade, bombs will be dropped from the sky." This insight was bolstered by a 2011 working paper, "Does Trade Integration Contribute to Peace?," by the University of California, Davis researcher Ju Hyun Pyun and the Korea University researcher Jong-Wha Lee. The two evaluated the effects of bilateral trade and global openness on the probability of conflict between countries from 1950 to 2000, and concluded that "an increase in bilateral trade interdependence significantly promotes peace." They added, "More importantly, we find that not only bilateral trade but global trade openness also significantly promotes peace."

More Productive Workers

The economic gains from unfettered immigration are vastly more enormous than those that would result from the elimination of remaining trade restrictions. Total factor productivity (TFP) is the portion of output not explained by the amount of inputs used in production. Its level is determined by how efficiently and intensely the inputs are utilized in production. In other words, it is all those factors-technology, honest government, a stable currency, etc.—that enable people to work "smarter" and not just harder.

A 2012 working paper titled "Open Borders," by the University of Wisconsin economist John Kennan, found that if all workers moved immediately to places with higher total factor productivity, it would produce the equivalent of doubling the world's supply of laborers. Using U.S. TFP as a benchmark, the world's workers right now are the equivalent of 750 million Americans, but allowing migration to high TFP regions would boost that to the equivalent of 1.5 billion American workers.

Think of it this way: A worker in Somalia can produce only one-tenth the economic value of a worker in the United States. But as soon as she trades the hellhole of Mogadishu for the comparative paradise of Minneapolis, she can immediately take advantage of the higher American TFP to produce vastly more.

Multiply that by the hundreds of millions still stuck in low-productivity countries.

Assuming everybody moved immediately, Kennan calculated that it would temporarily depress the average wages of the host countries' natives by 20 percent. If emigration were more gradual, there would be essentially no effects on native-born wages.

In a 2011 working paper for the Center for Global Development, "Economics and Emigration: Trillion Dollar Bills on the Sidewalk?," Michael Clemens reviewed the literature on the relationship between economic growth and migration. He concluded that removing mobility barriers could plausibly produce overall gains of 20–60 percent of global GDP. Since world GDP is about $78 trillion now, that suggests that opening borders alone could boost global GDP to between $94 and $125 trillion.

Better Job Prospects

A 2013 University of Munich working paper on immigration and economic growth by the University of Auvergne economist Ekrame Boubtane and her colleagues analyzed data from 22 OECD countries between 1987 and 2009. It found that "migration inflows contribute to host country economic prosperity (positive impact on GDP per capita and total unemployment rate)." The authors concluded that "immigration flows do not harm the employment prospects of residents, native- or foreign-born. Hence, OECD countries may adjust immigration policies to labour market needs, and can receive more migrants, without worrying about a potential negative impact on growth and employment."

In a 2009 National Bureau of Economic Research study, "The Effect of Immigration on Productivity: Evidence from U.S. States," the University of California, Davis economist Giovanni Peri looked at the effects of differential rates of immigration to various American states in the 1990s and 2000s. Peri found that "an increase in employment in a U.S. state of 1% due to immigrants produced an increase in income per worker of 0.5% in that state." In other words, more immigrants meant higher average wages for all workers.

Critical Thinking

1. What are some of the wonderful benefits that Bailey thinks will result from globalization?

2. What evidence does Bailey provide to show that globalization makes for longer and healthier lives?

3. With all the benefits of globalization why do so many people oppose it?

Internet References

New American Studies Web
https://blogs.commons.georgetown.edu/vkp/

Social Science Information Gateway
http://www.ariadne.ac.uk/issue2/sosig

Sociology—Study Sociology Online
http://edu.learnsoc.org/

Sociology Web Resources
http://www.mhhe.com/socscience/sociology/resources/index.htm

Sociosite
http://www.topsite.com/goto/sociosite.net

Socioweb
http://www.topsite.com/goto/socioweb.com

Science Correspondent **RONALD BAILEY** is the author of the forthcoming *The End of Doom: Environmental Renewal in the 21st Century* (St. Martin's).